Presented by
ASAYA MIYANAGA

2

Nicola
Traveling
Around
The Demons'
World

contents

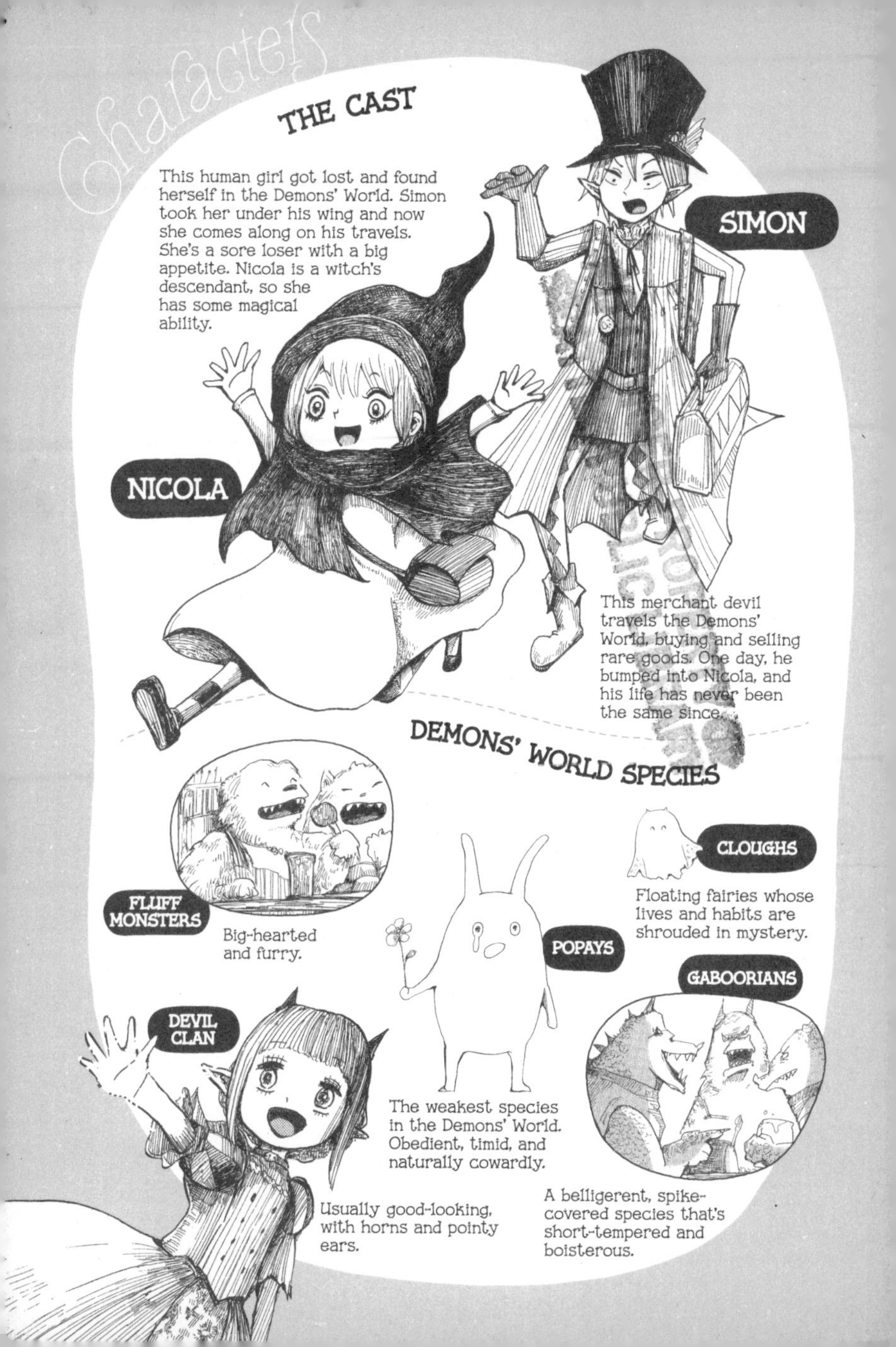
Characters
THE CAST
This human girl got lost and found herself in the Demons' World. Simon took her under his wing and now she comes along on his travels. She's a sore loser with a big appetite. Nicola is a witch's descendant, so she has some magical ability.
SIMON
NICOLA
This merchant devil travels the Demons' World, buying and selling rare goods. One day, he bumped into Nicola, and his life has never been the same since.
DEMONS' WORLD SPECIES
CLOUGHS
Floating fairies whose lives and habits are shrouded in mystery.
FLUFF MONSTERS
Big-hearted and furry.
POPAYS
The weakest species in the Demons' World. Obedient, timid, and naturally cowardly.
GABOORIANS
A belligerent, spike-covered species that's short-tempered and boisterous.
DEVIL CLAN
Usually good-looking, with horns and pointy ears.

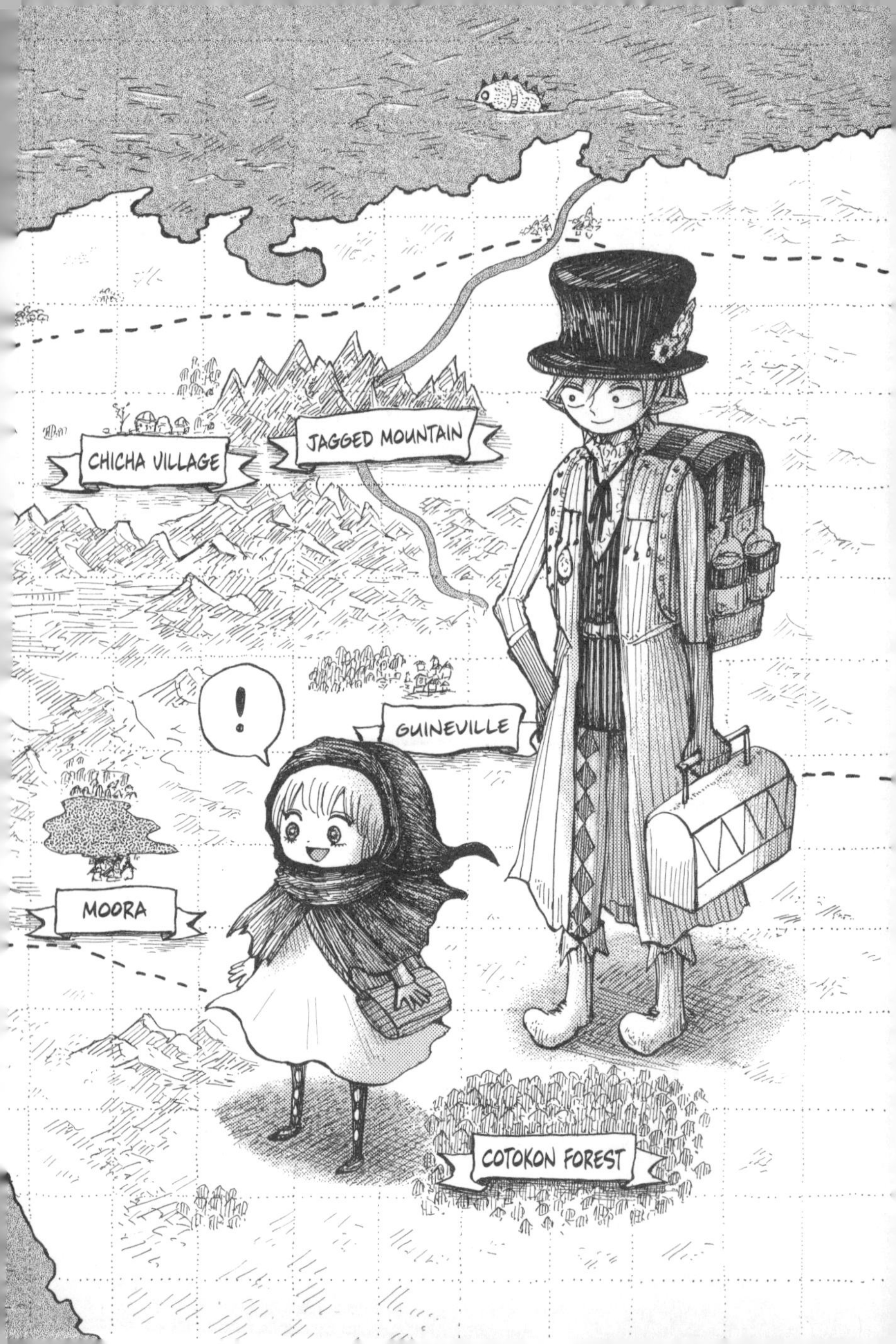
JAGGED MOUNTAIN
CHICHA VILLAGE
!
GUINEVILLE
MOORA
COTOKON FOREST

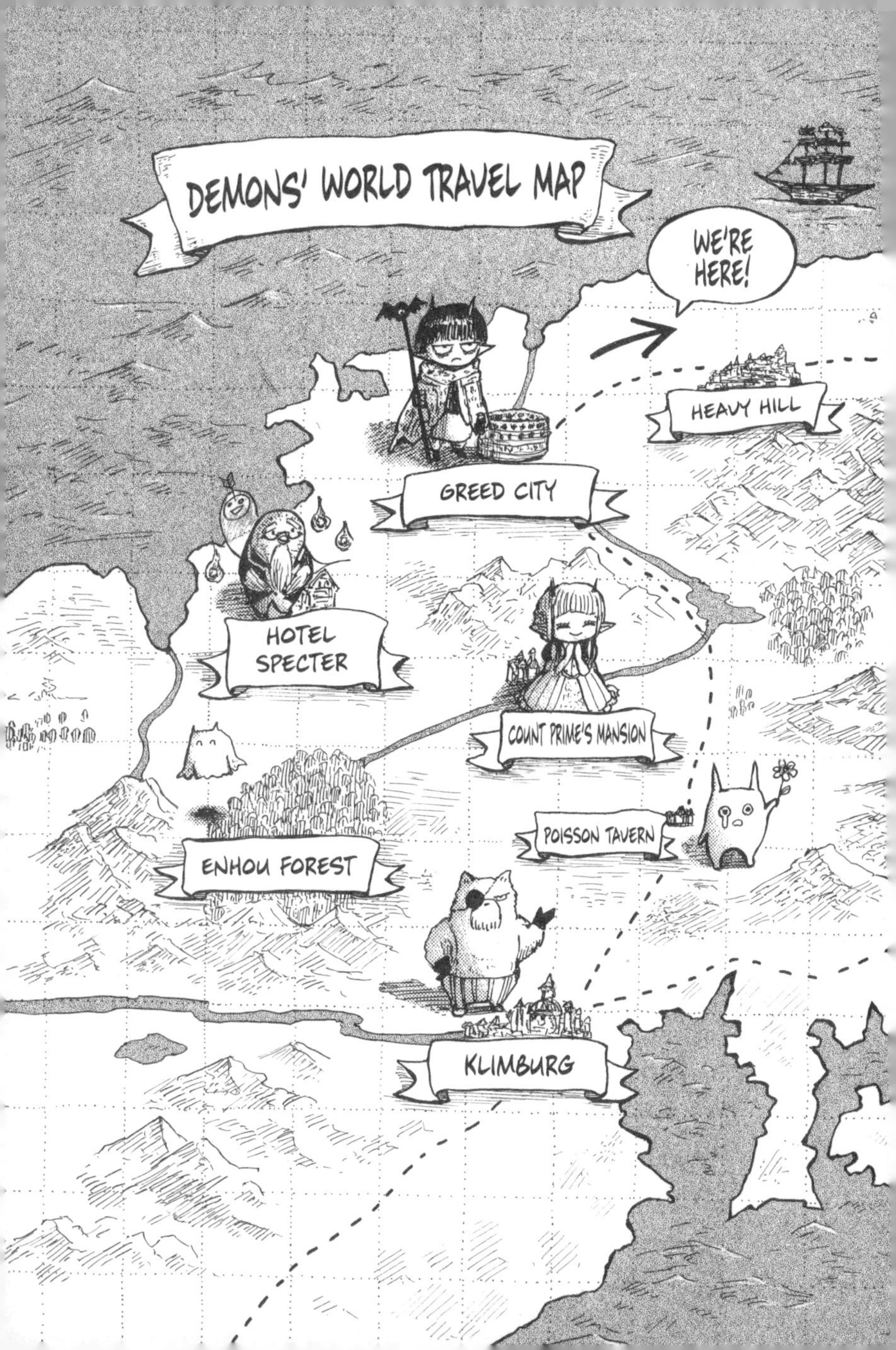
DEMONS' WORLD TRAVEL MAP
WE'RE HERE!
HEAVY HILL
GREED CITY
HOTEL SPECTER
COUNT PRIME'S MANSION
POISSON TAVERN
ENHOU FOREST
KLIMBURG

Nicola Traveling Around The Demons' World.

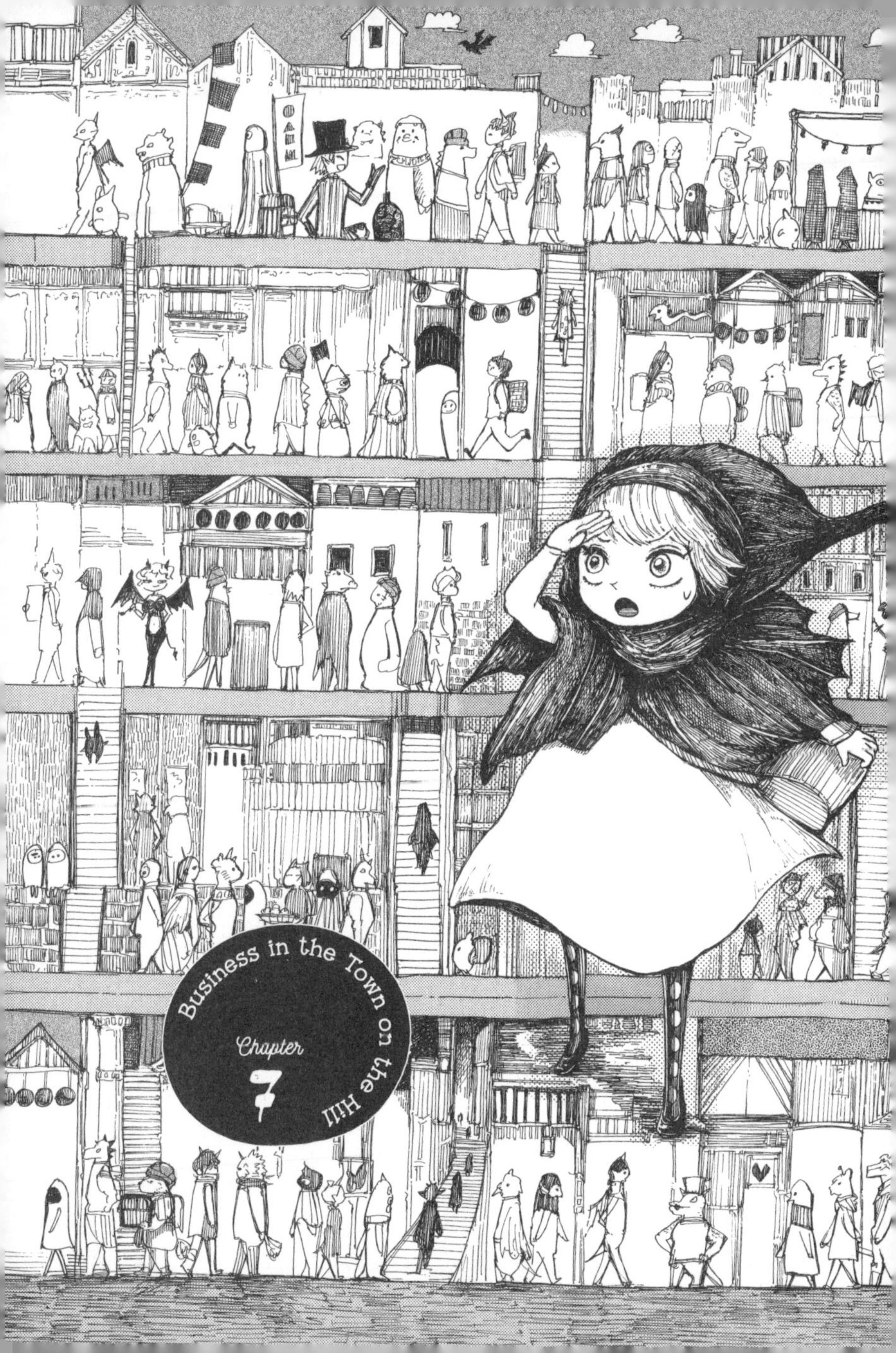
Business in the Town on the Hill
Chapter
7

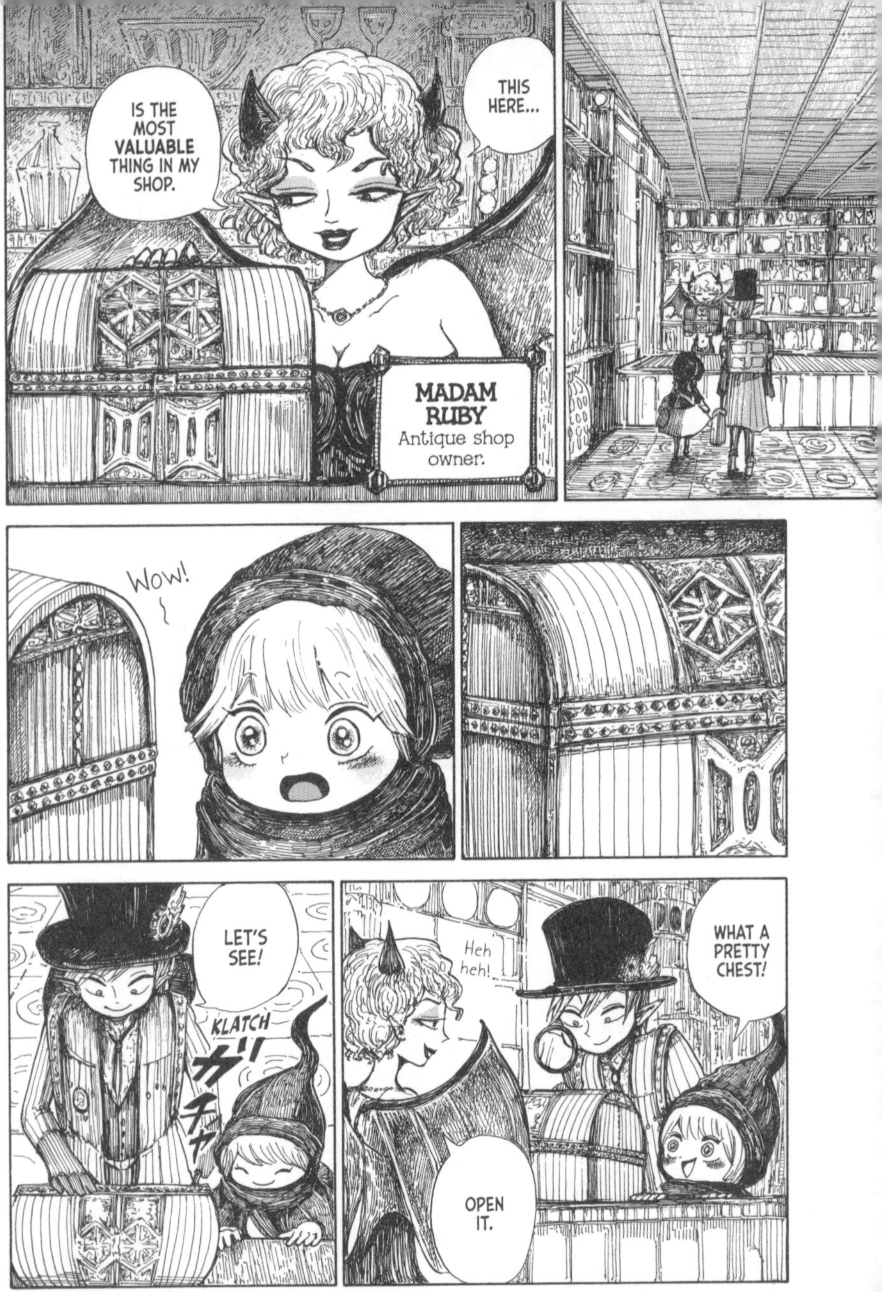
THIS HERE...
IS THE MOST VALUABLE THING IN MY SHOP.
MADAM RUBY
Antique shop owner.
Wow!
WHAT A PRETTY CHEST!
Heh heh!
OPEN IT.
LET'S SEE!
KLATCH
ガチャ

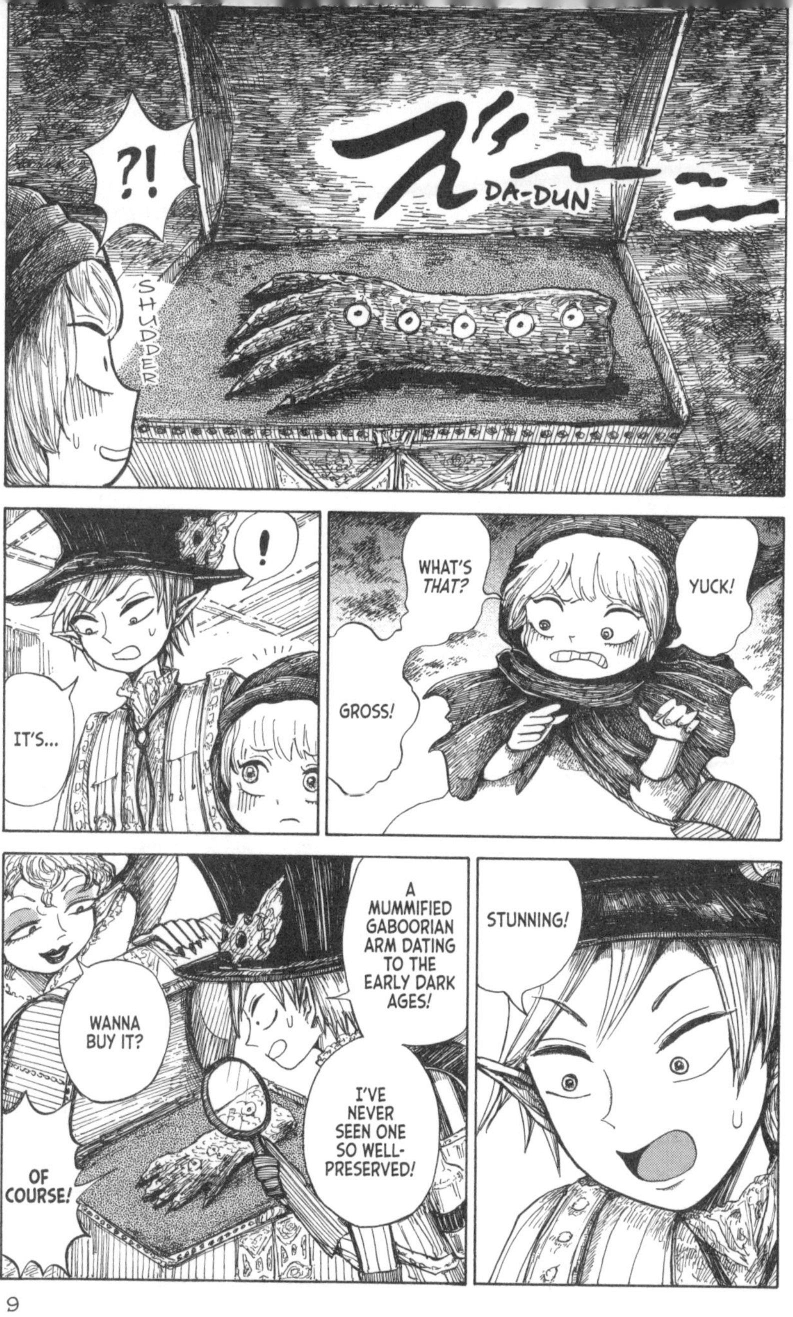
DA-DUN
?!
SHUDDER
YUCK!
WHAT'S *THAT*?
GROSS!
!
IT'S...
STUNNING!
A MUMMIFIED GABOORIAN ARM DATING TO THE EARLY DARK AGES!
I'VE NEVER SEEN ONE SO WELL-PRESERVED!
WANNA BUY IT?
OF COURSE!

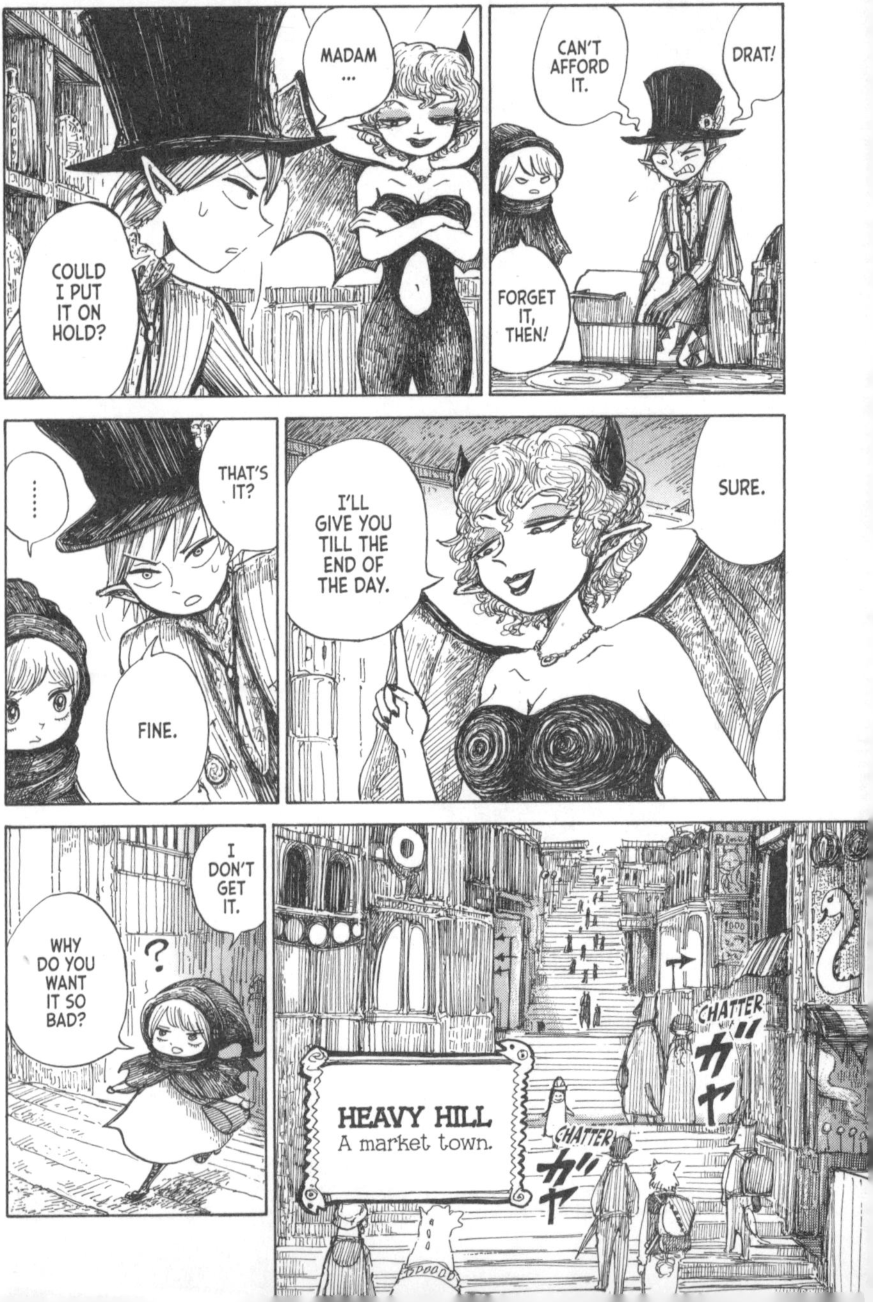
DRAT!
CAN'T AFFORD IT.
FORGET IT, THEN!
MADAM ...
COULD I PUT IT ON HOLD?
SURE.
I'LL GIVE YOU TILL THE END OF THE DAY.
THAT'S IT?
......
FINE.
HEAVY HILL
A market town.
CHATTER
ガヤ
CHATTER
ガヤ
I DON'T GET IT.
?
WHY DO YOU WANT IT SO BAD?

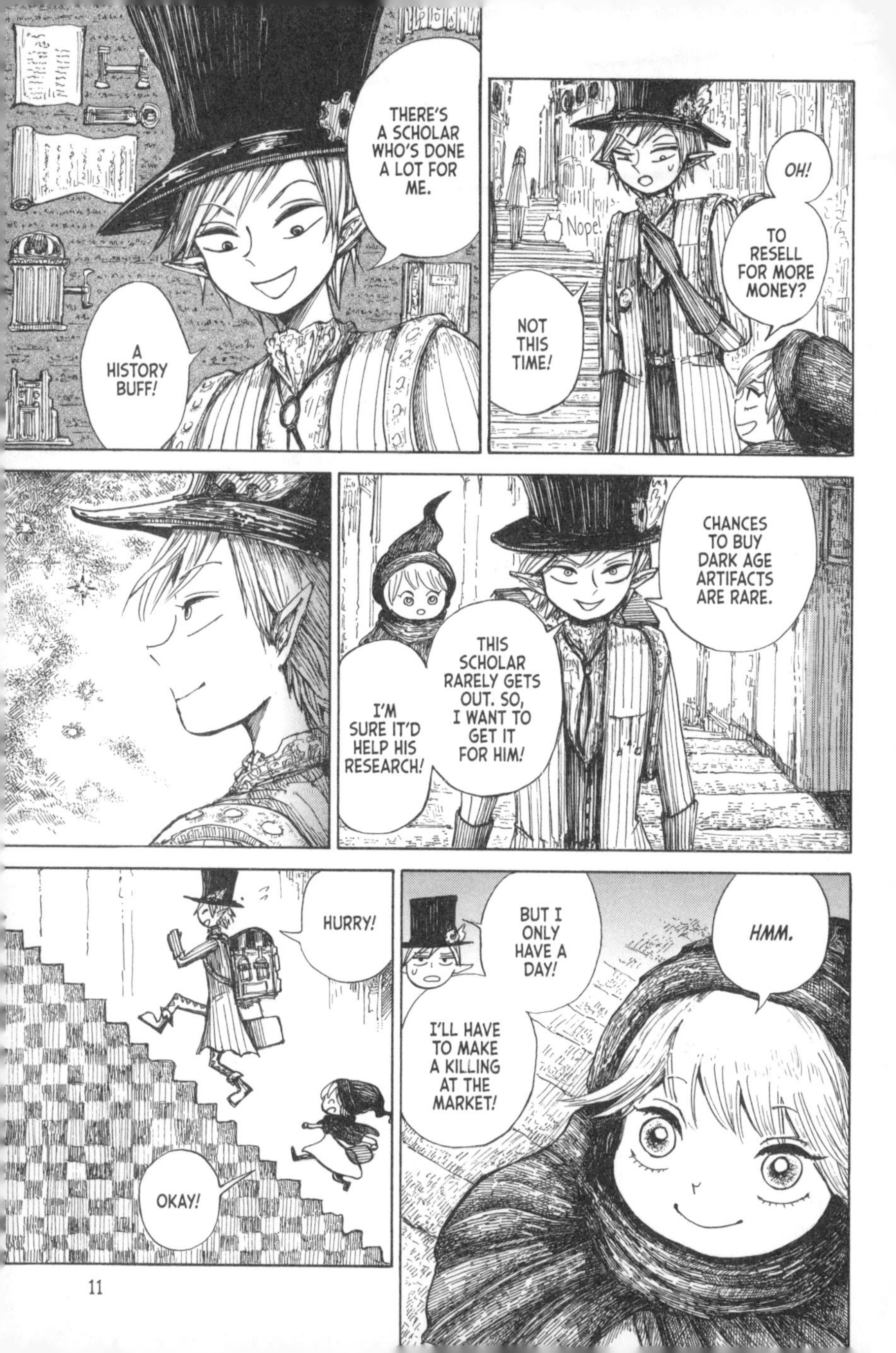
OH!
TO RESELL FOR MORE MONEY?
Nope!
NOT THIS TIME!
THERE'S A SCHOLAR WHO'S DONE A LOT FOR ME.
A HISTORY BUFF!
CHANCES TO BUY DARK AGE ARTIFACTS ARE RARE.
THIS SCHOLAR RARELY GETS OUT. SO, I WANT TO GET IT FOR HIM!
I'M SURE IT'D HELP HIS RESEARCH!
HMM.
BUT I ONLY HAVE A DAY!
I'LL HAVE TO MAKE A KILLING AT THE MARKET!
HURRY!
OKAY!

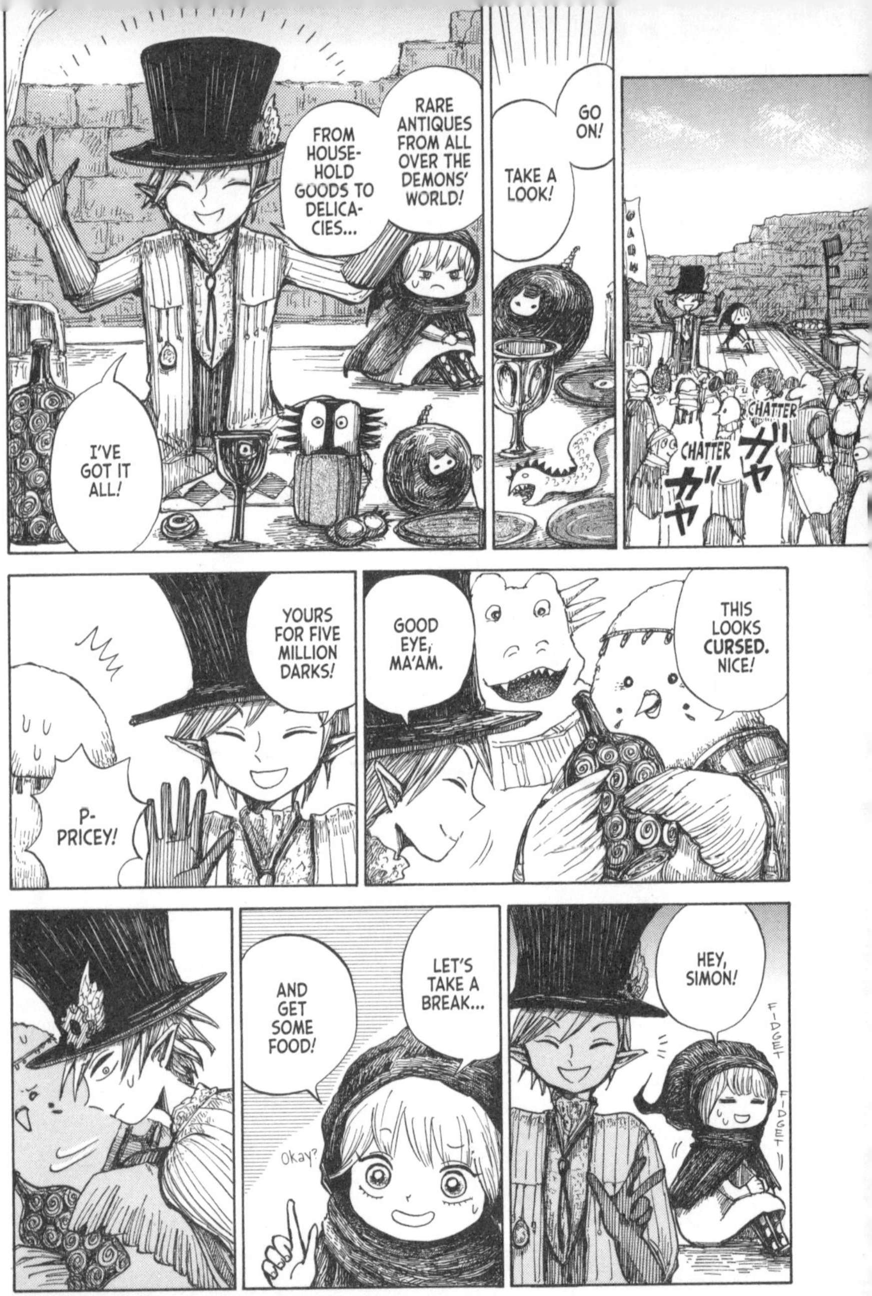
CHATTER
ガヤ
CHATTER
ガヤ
GO ON!
TAKE A LOOK!
RARE ANTIQUES FROM ALL OVER THE DEMONS' WORLD!
FROM HOUSE-HOLD GOODS TO DELICA-CIES...
I'VE GOT IT ALL!
THIS LOOKS CURSED. NICE!
GOOD EYE, MA'AM.
YOURS FOR FIVE MILLION DARKS!
P-PRICEY!
HEY, SIMON!
FIDGET
FIDGET
LET'S TAKE A BREAK...
AND GET SOME FOOD!
Okay?

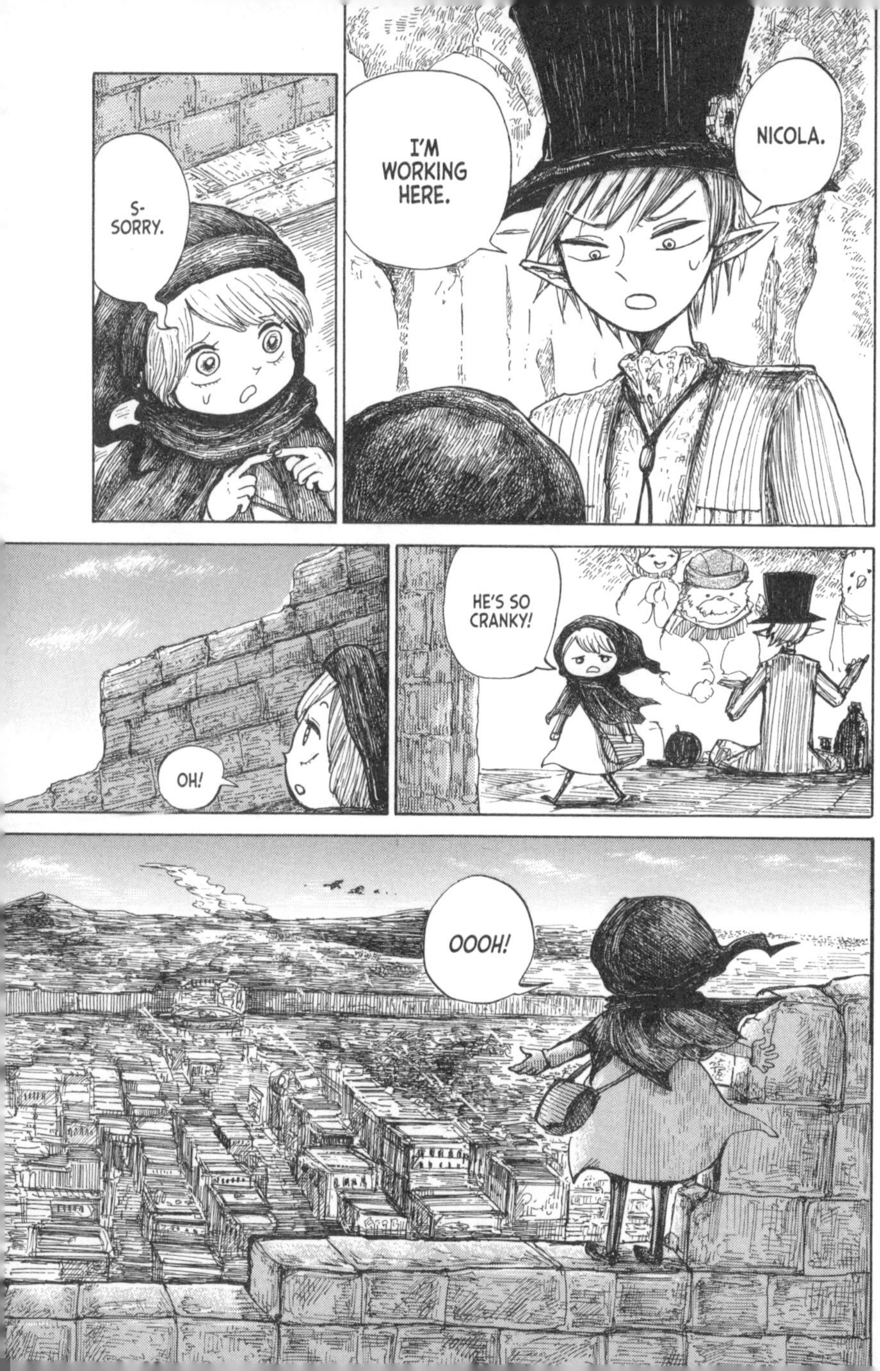
NICOLA.
I'M WORKING HERE.
S-SORRY.
HE'S SO CRANKY!
OH!
OOOH!

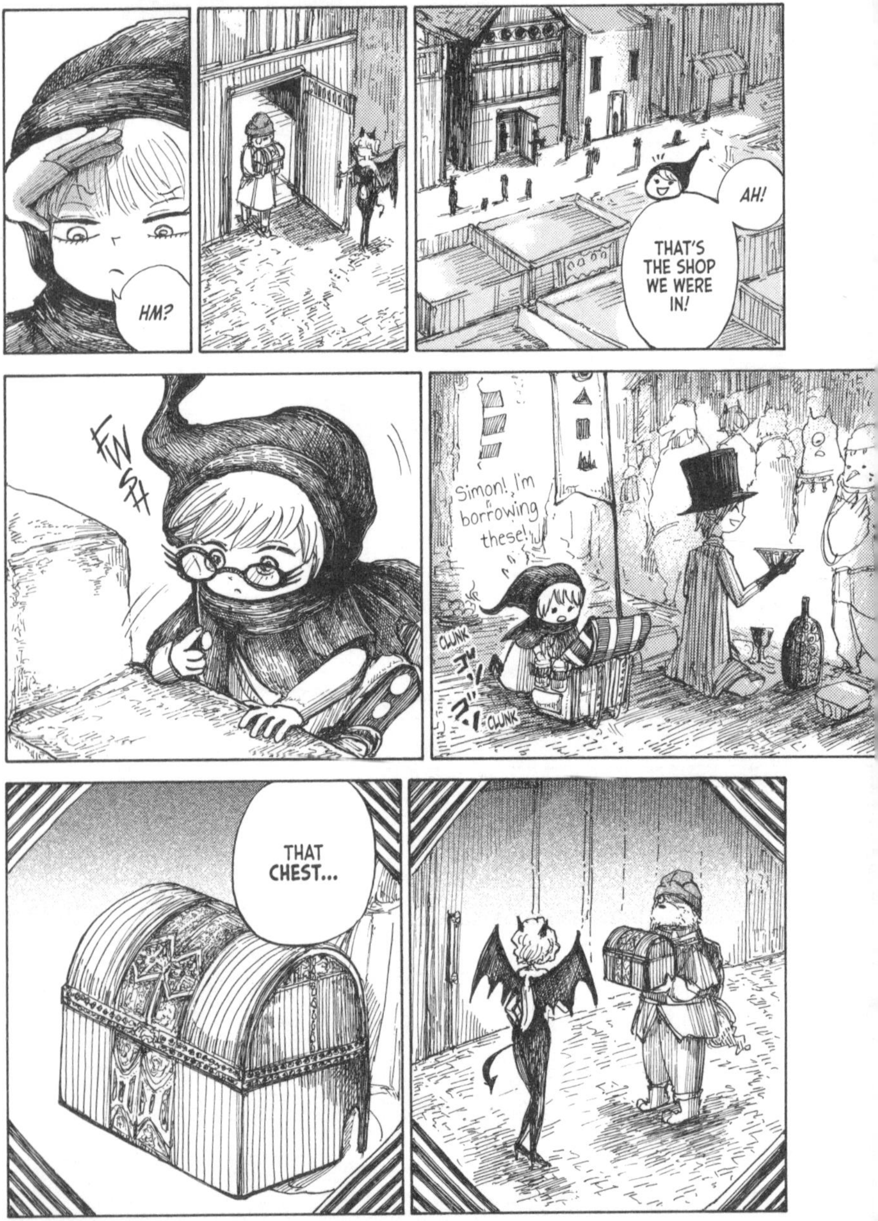
AH!
THAT'S THE SHOP WE WERE IN!
HM?
Simon! I'm borrowing these!
CLUNK
CLUNK
FWSH
THAT CHEST...

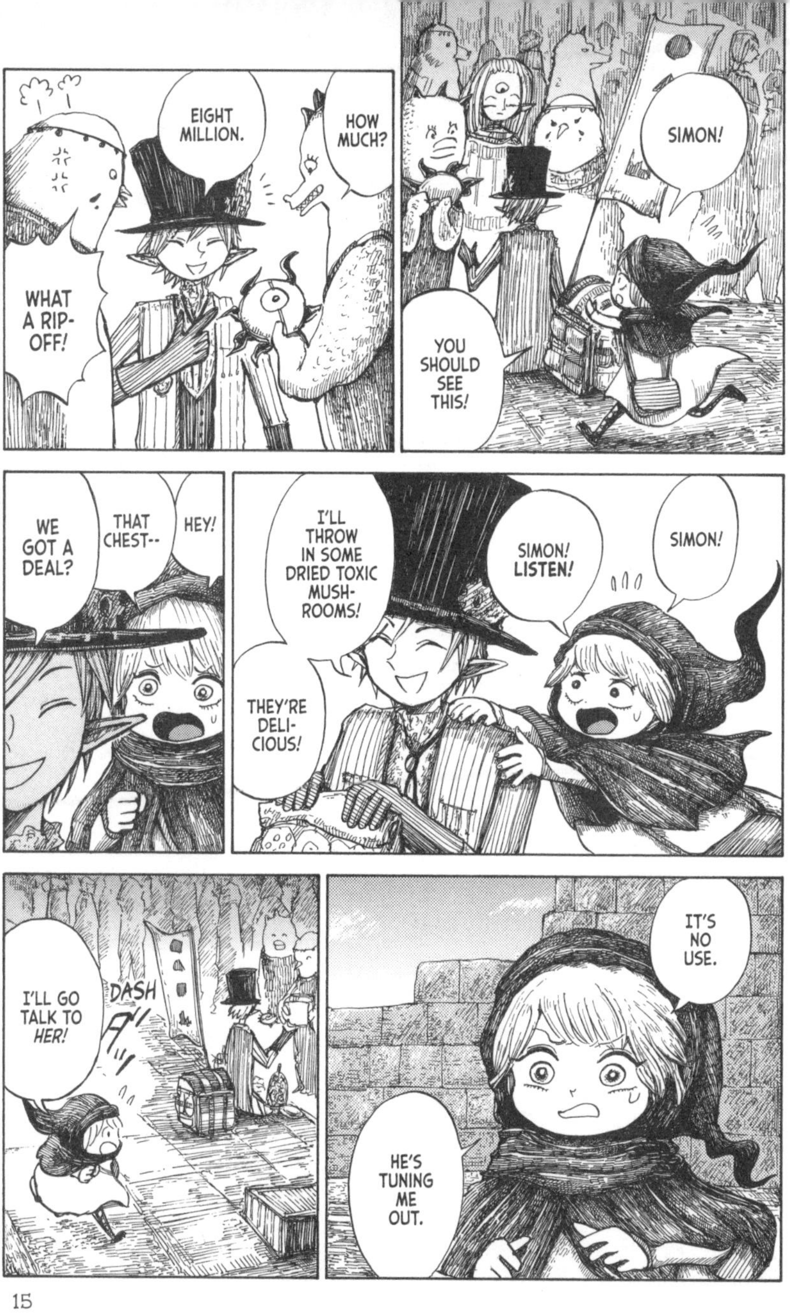
SIMON!
YOU SHOULD SEE THIS!
HOW MUCH?
EIGHT MILLION.
WHAT A RIP-OFF!
SIMON!
SIMON! **LISTEN!**
I'LL THROW IN SOME DRIED TOXIC MUSHROOMS!
THEY'RE DELICIOUS!
HEY!
THAT CHEST--
WE GOT A DEAL?
IT'S NO USE.
HE'S TUNING ME OUT.
DASH
I'LL GO TALK TO *HER!*

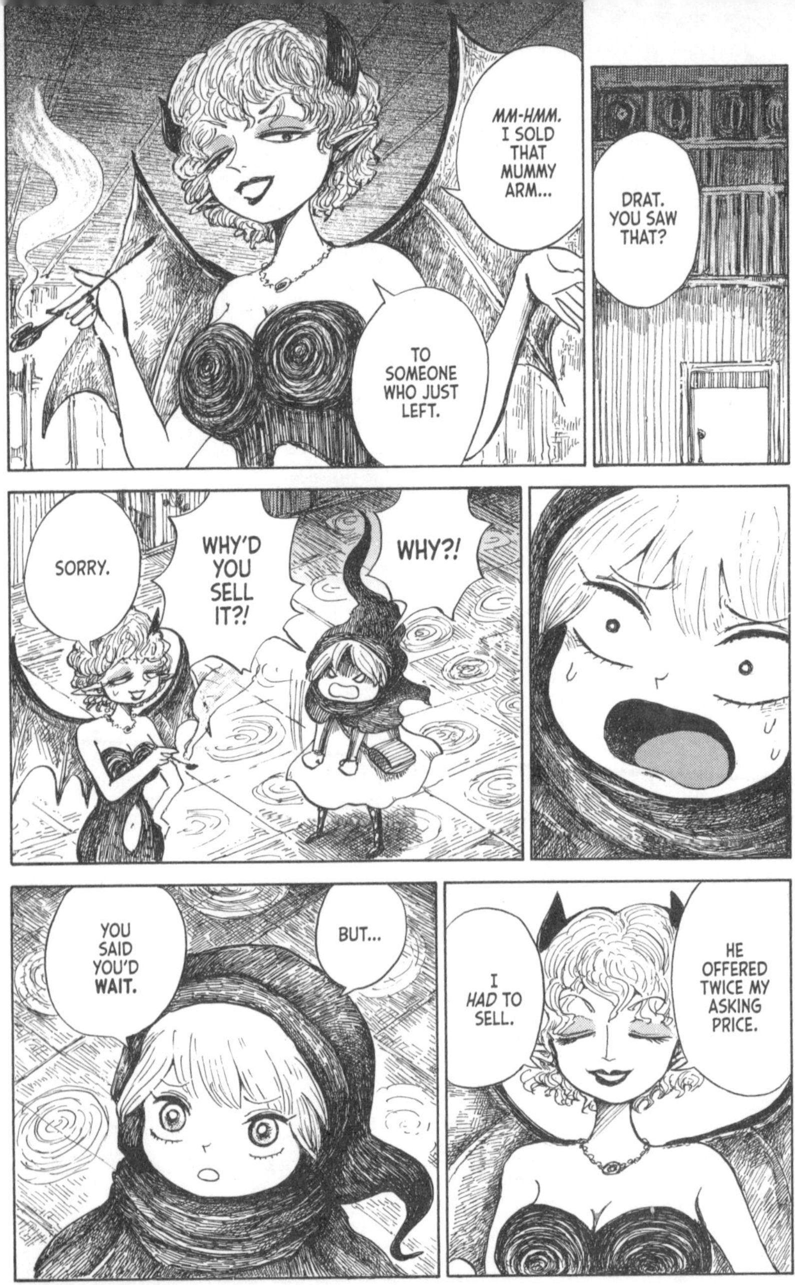
DRAT. YOU SAW THAT?
MM-HMM. I SOLD THAT MUMMY ARM...
TO SOMEONE WHO JUST LEFT.
WHY?!
WHY'D YOU SELL IT?!
SORRY.
HE OFFERED TWICE MY ASKING PRICE.
I *HAD* TO SELL.
BUT...
YOU SAID YOU'D WAIT.

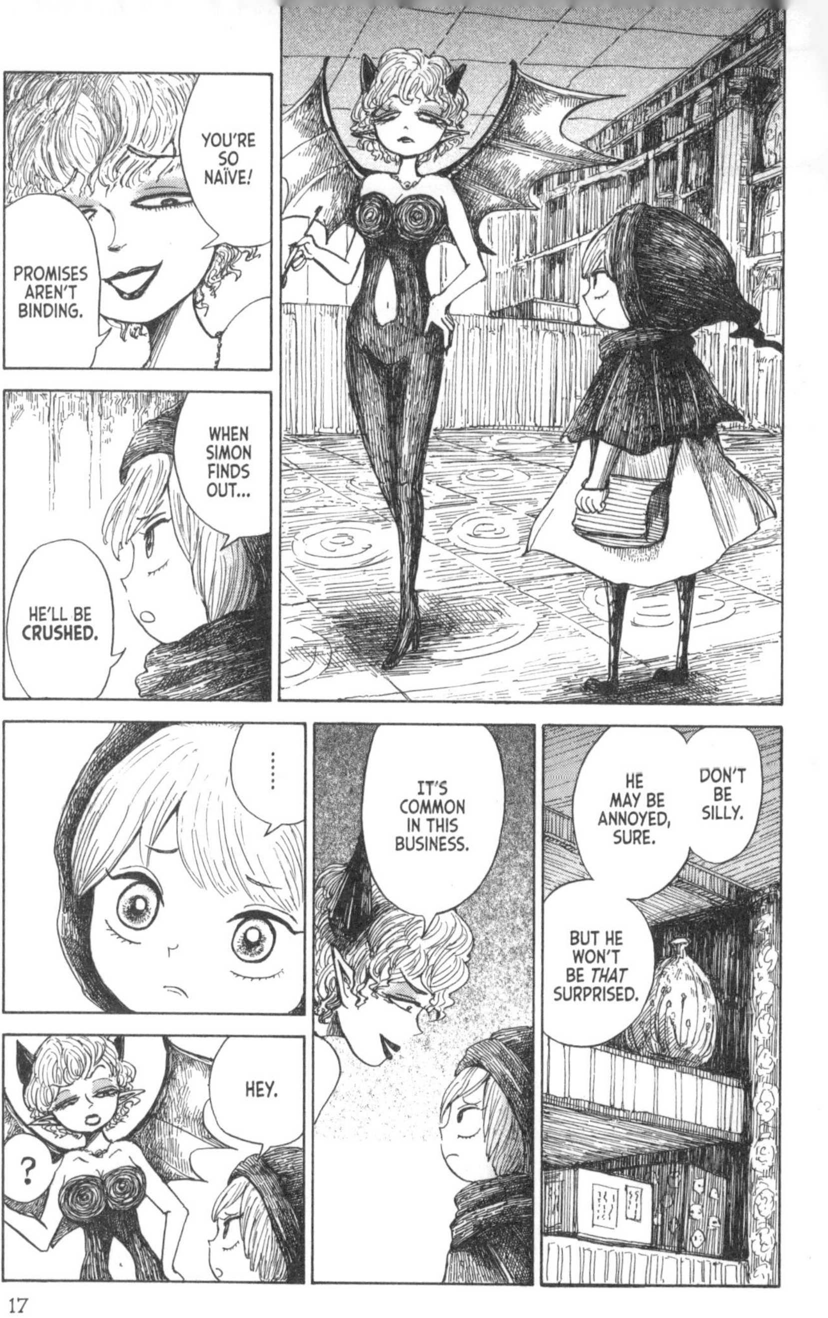
YOU'RE SO NAÏVE!
PROMISES AREN'T BINDING.
WHEN SIMON FINDS OUT...
HE'LL BE CRUSHED.
DON'T BE SILLY.
HE MAY BE ANNOYED, SURE.
BUT HE WON'T BE *THAT* SURPRISED.
IT'S COMMON IN THIS BUSINESS.
......
HEY.
?

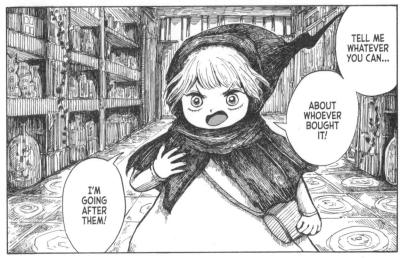

TELL ME WHATEVER YOU CAN...
ABOUT WHOEVER BOUGHT IT!
I'M GOING AFTER THEM!
HUH? WHAT DO YOU MEAN?
IT WON'T HELP.
WHAT DO THEY LOOK LIKE?!
WHOA!
WHERE'D THEY GO?!
RAR!
FINE!
LET ME THINK.
HE WAS A FLUFF MONSTER WITH A GRAY TURBAN.
I DON'T KNOW WHERE HE WENT, THOUGH.
GOT IT! THANKS!
DASH
SLAM
WHAT'S *HER* PROBLEM?

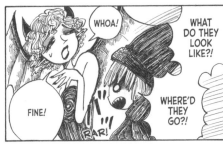

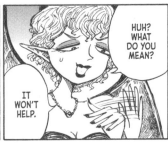

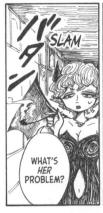

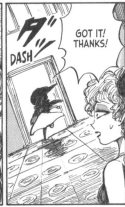

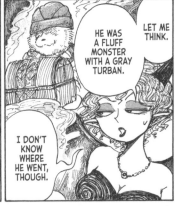

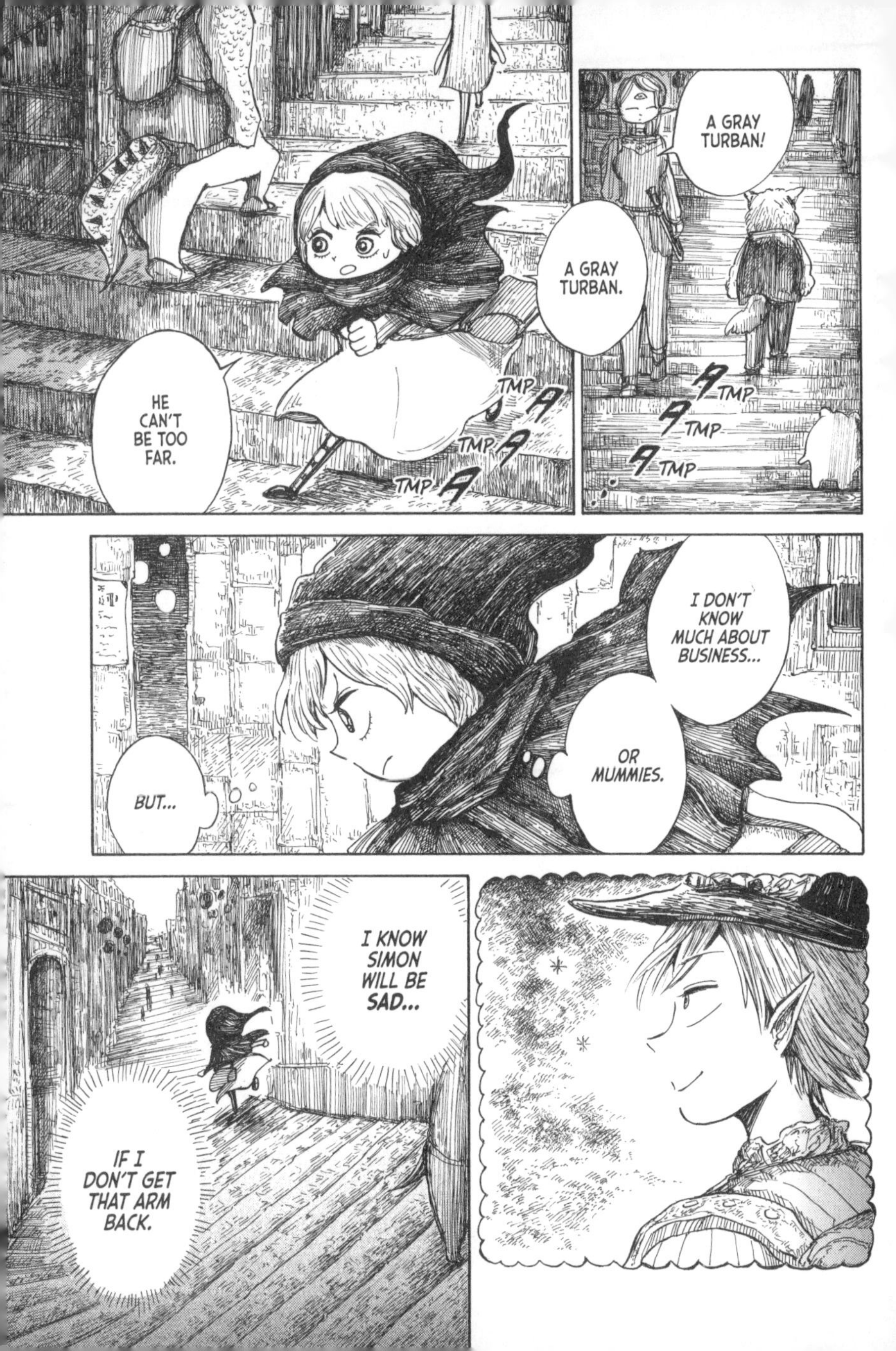
A GRAY TURBAN!
TMP TMP TMP
A GRAY TURBAN.
HE CAN'T BE TOO FAR.
TMP TMP TMP
I DON'T KNOW MUCH ABOUT BUSINESS...
OR MUMMIES.
BUT...
I KNOW SIMON WILL BE SAD...
IF I DON'T GET THAT ARM BACK.

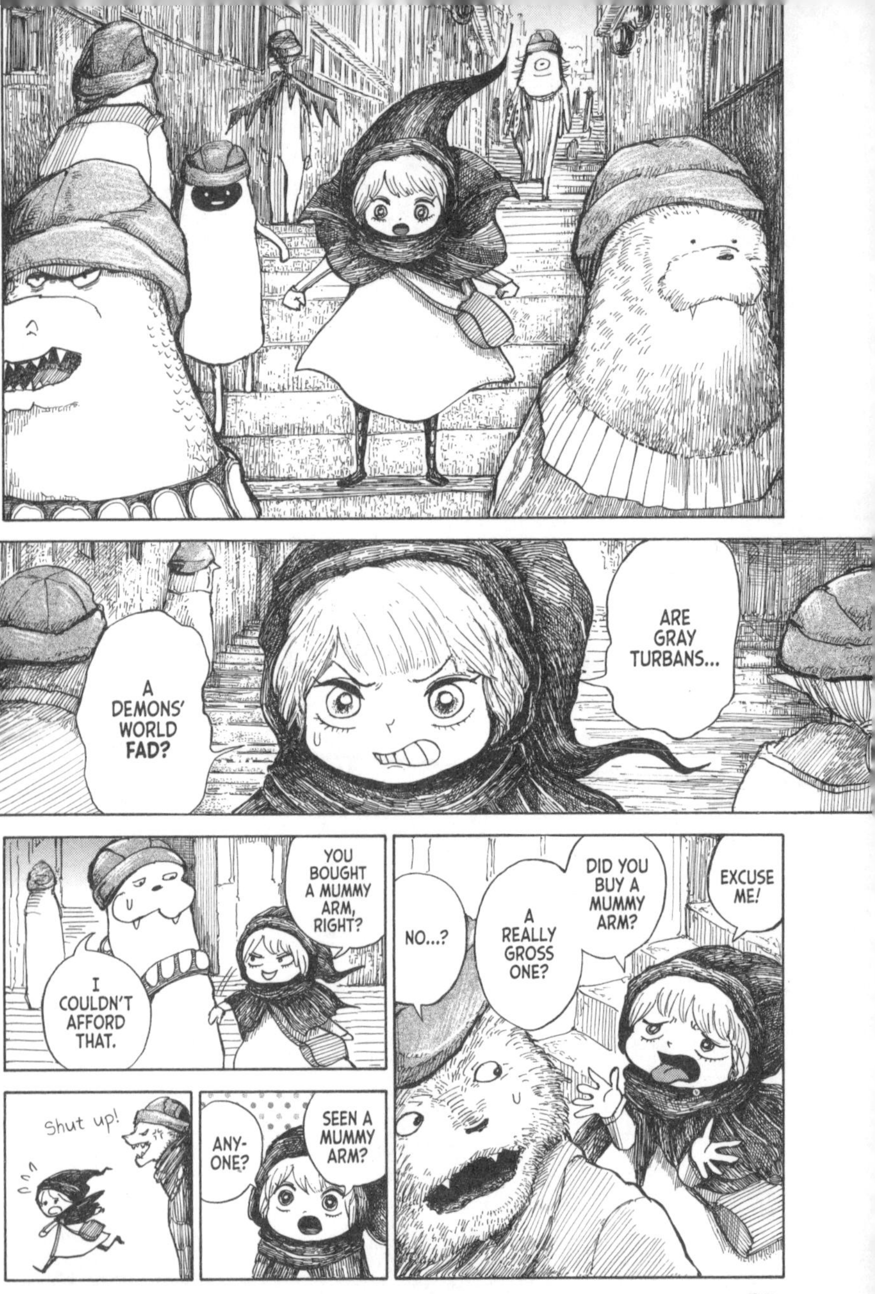
ARE GRAY TURBANS...
A DEMONS' WORLD FAD?
EXCUSE ME!
DID YOU BUY A MUMMY ARM?
A REALLY GROSS ONE?
NO...?
YOU BOUGHT A MUMMY ARM, RIGHT?
I COULDN'T AFFORD THAT.
SEEN A MUMMY ARM?
ANY-ONE?
Shut up!

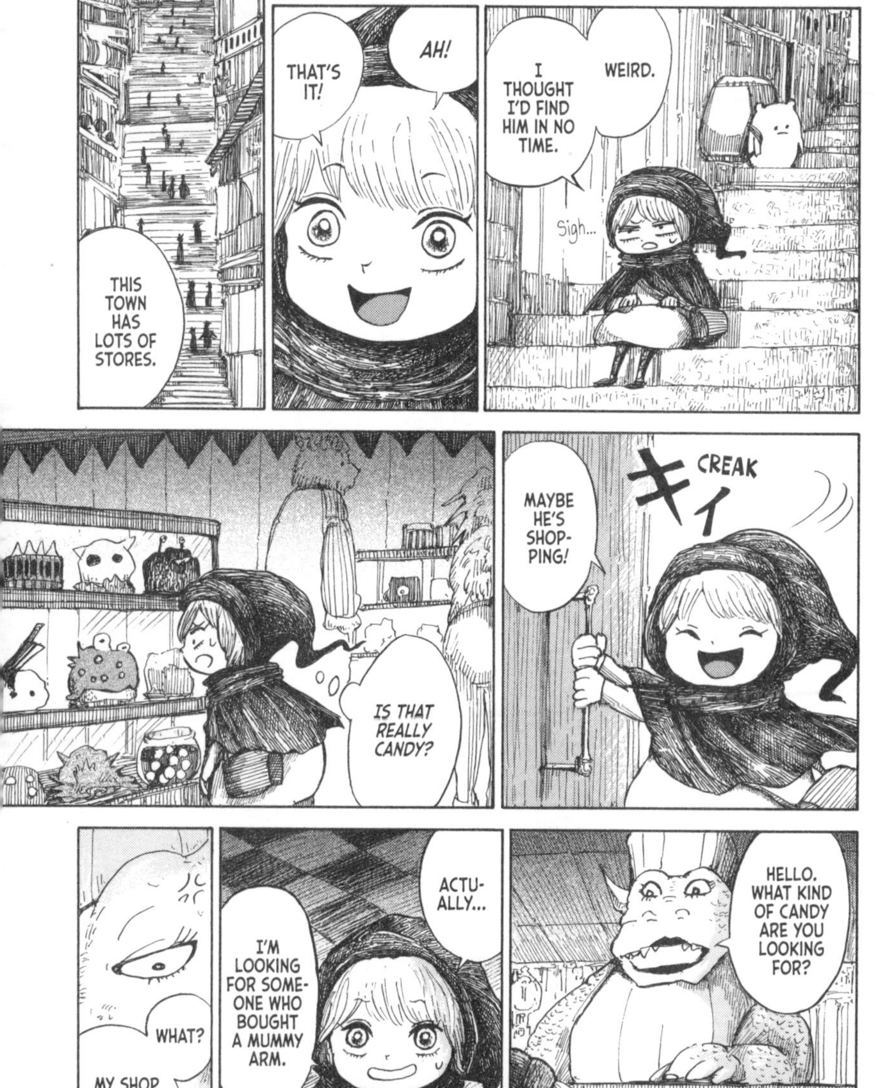
WEIRD.
I THOUGHT I'D FIND HIM IN NO TIME.
Sigh...
AH!
THAT'S IT!
THIS TOWN HAS LOTS OF STORES.
キイ CREAK
MAYBE HE'S SHOP-PING!
IS THAT REALLY CANDY?
HELLO. WHAT KIND OF CANDY ARE YOU LOOKING FOR?
ACTU-ALLY...
I'M LOOKING FOR SOME-ONE WHO BOUGHT A MUMMY ARM.
WHAT?
MY SHOP DOESN'T SELL MUMMY PARTS!

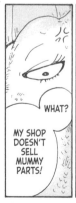

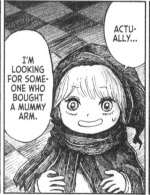

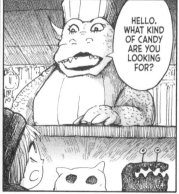

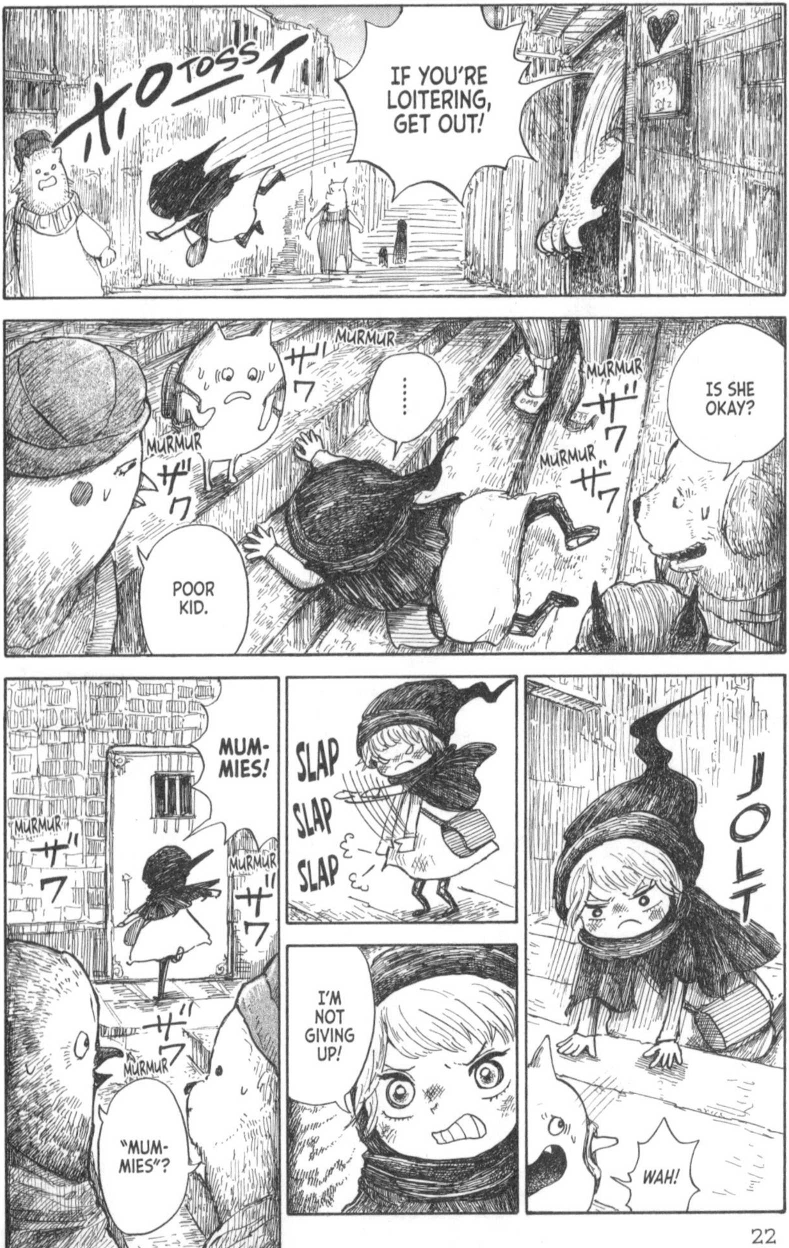
IF YOU'RE LOITERING, GET OUT!
TOSS
IS SHE OKAY?
MURMUR
MURMUR
......
MURMUR
MURMUR
POOR KID.
JOLT
WAH!
SLAP
SLAP
SLAP
I'M NOT GIVING UP!
MUM-MIES!
MURMUR
MURMUR
MURMUR
"MUM-MIES"?

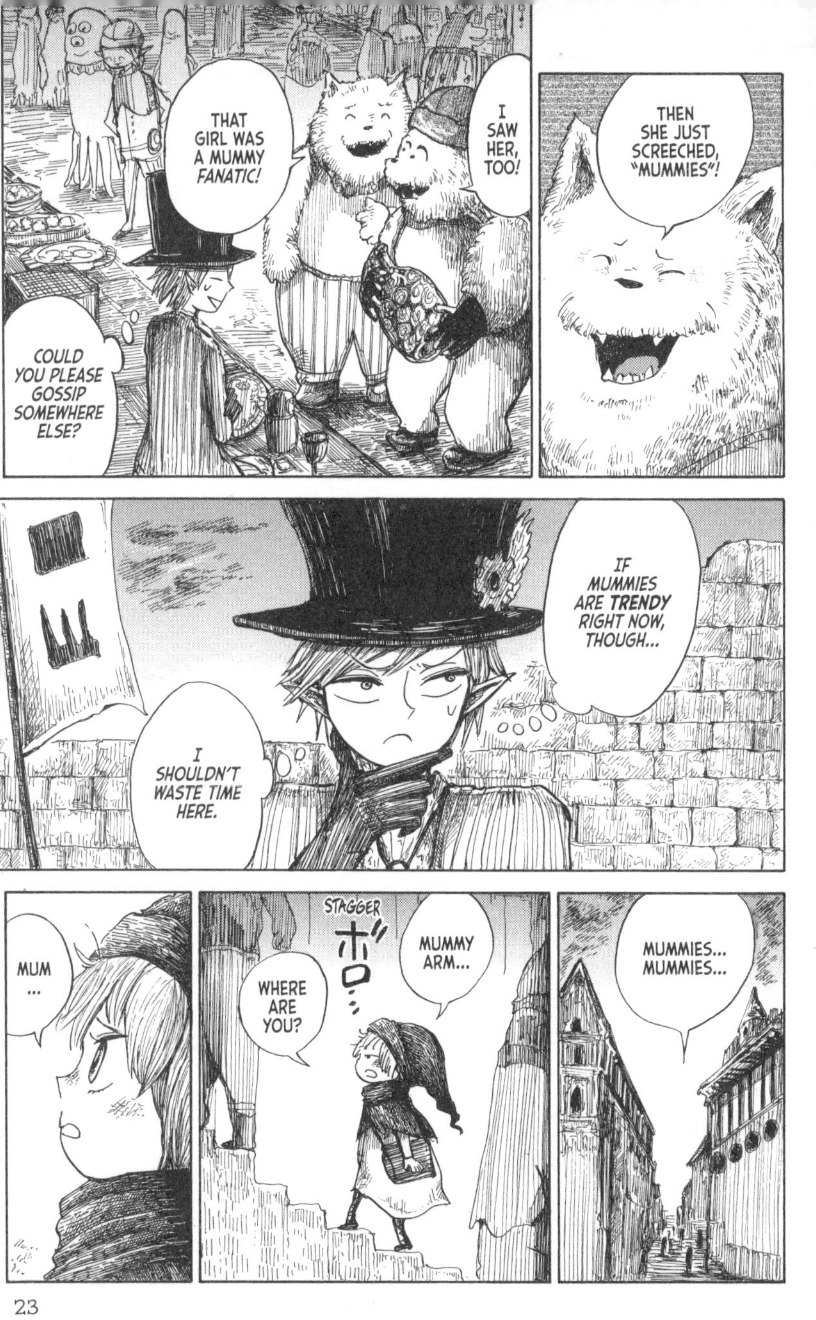
THEN SHE JUST SCREECHED, "MUMMIES"!
I SAW HER, TOO!
THAT GIRL WAS A MUMMY *FANATIC!*
COULD YOU PLEASE GOSSIP SOMEWHERE ELSE?
*IF MUMMIES ARE **TRENDY** RIGHT NOW, THOUGH...*
I SHOULDN'T WASTE TIME HERE.
MUMMIES... MUMMIES...
STAGGER
MUMMY ARM...
WHERE ARE YOU?
MUM ...

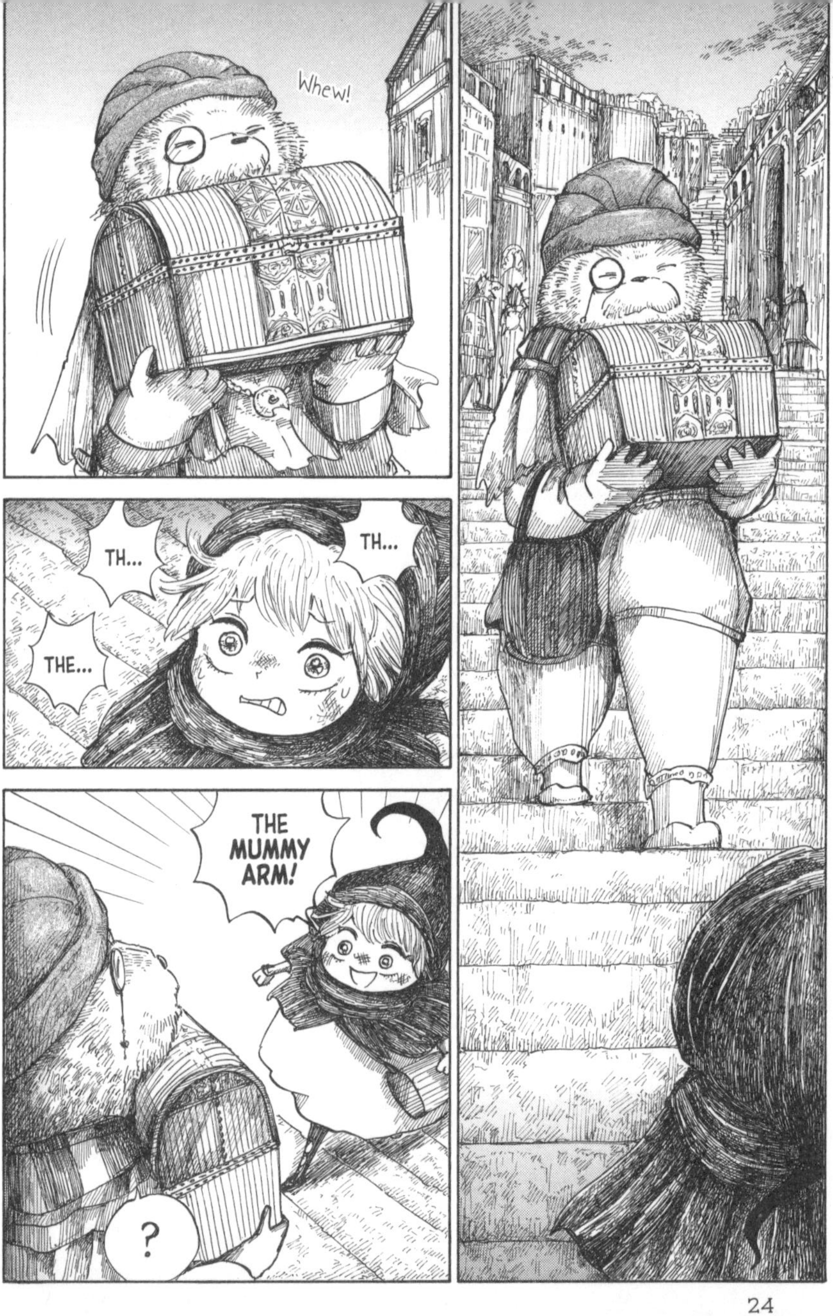
Whew!
TH...
TH...
THE...
THE MUMMY ARM!
?

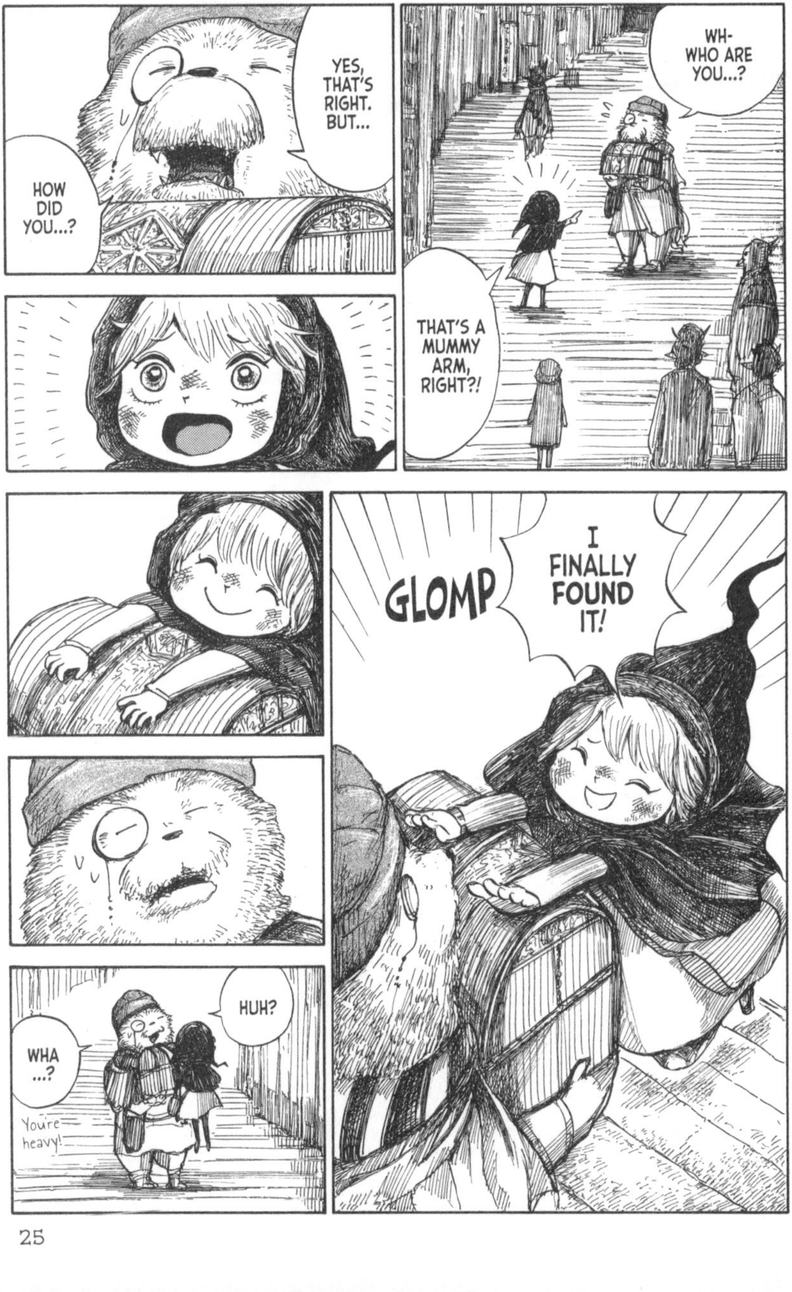

WH- WHO ARE YOU...?
THAT'S A MUMMY ARM, RIGHT?!
YES, THAT'S RIGHT. BUT...
HOW DID YOU...?
I FINALLY FOUND IT!
GLOMP
HUH?
WHA ...?
You're heavy!

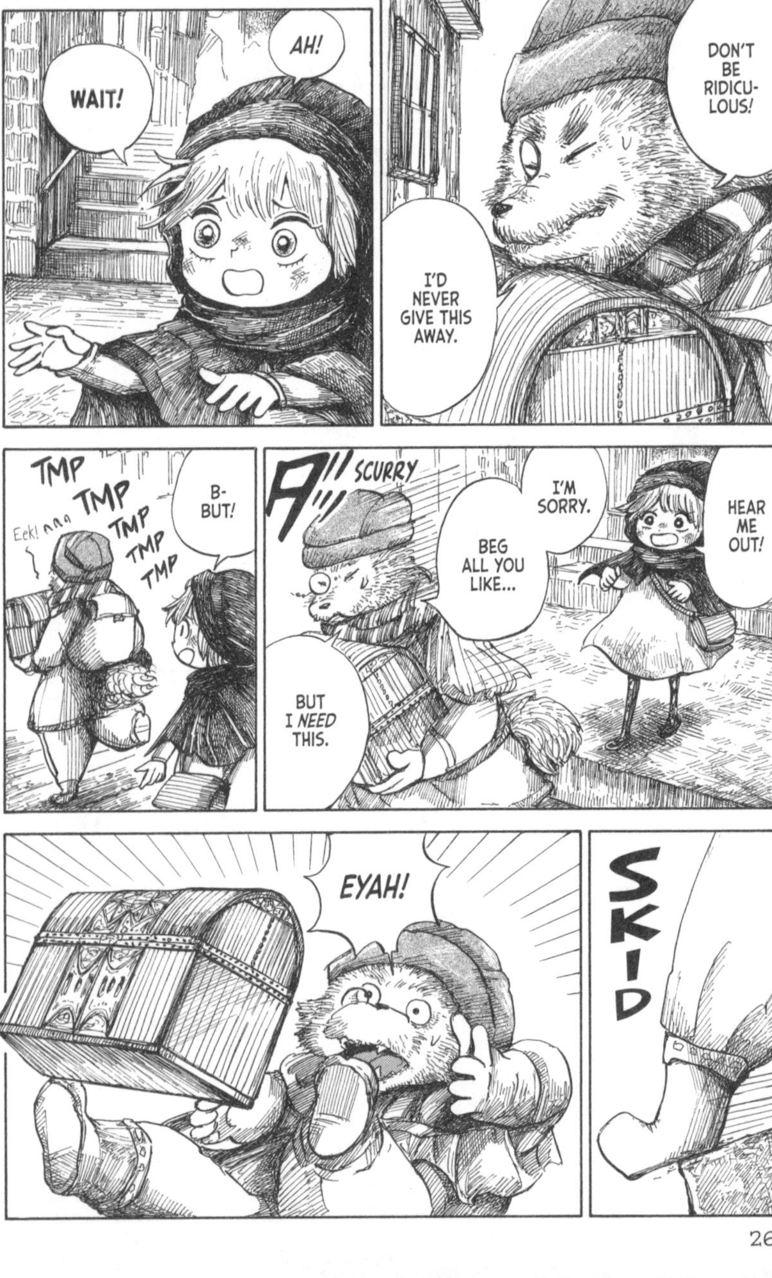
DON'T BE RIDICULOUS!
I'D NEVER GIVE THIS AWAY.
AH!
WAIT!
HEAR ME OUT!
I'M SORRY.
BEG ALL YOU LIKE...
SCURRY
BUT I NEED THIS.
B-BUT!
TMP TMP TMP TMP TMP
Eek!
SKID
EYAH!

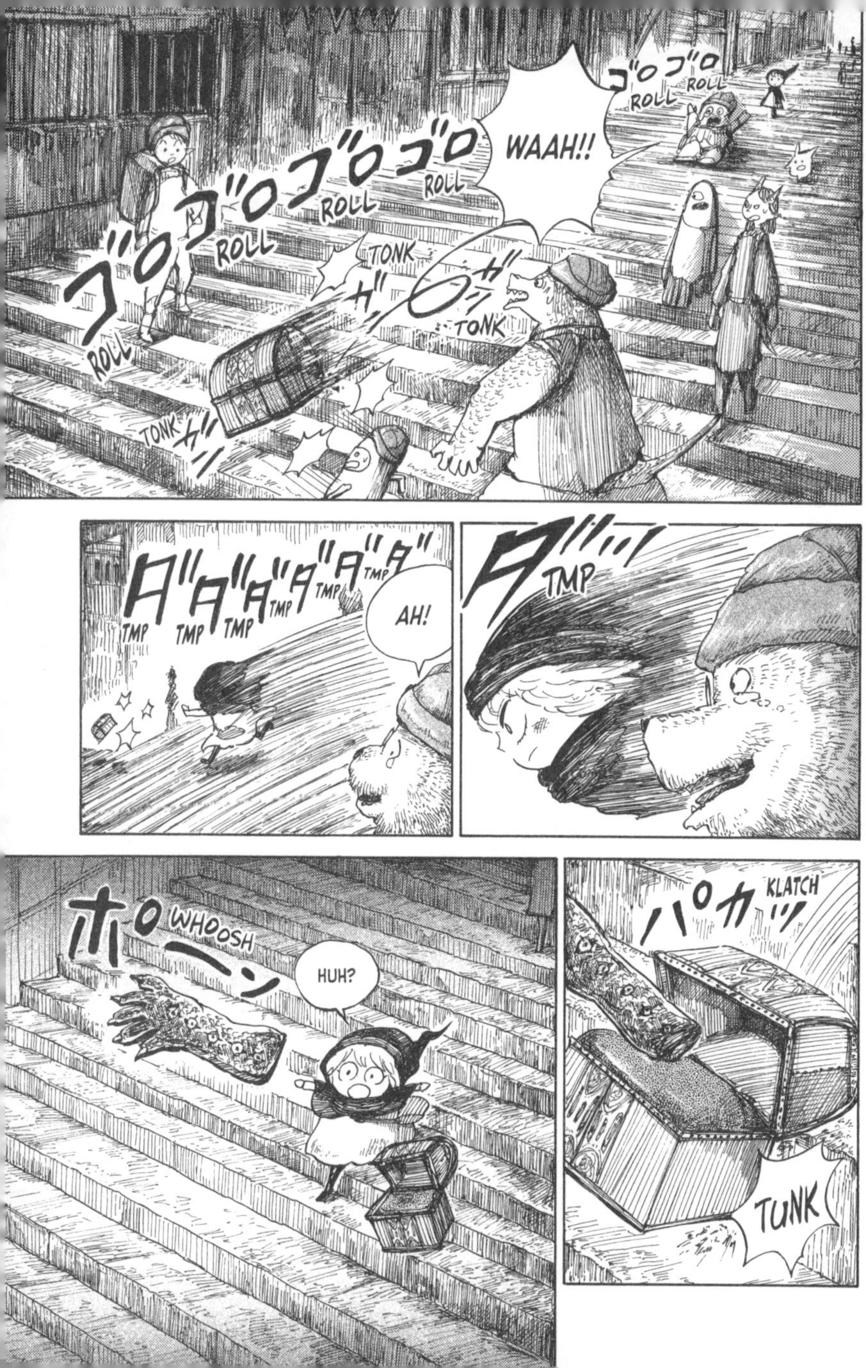
ゴロゴロ
ROLL ROLL
WAAH!!
ROLL
ROLL
ROLL
ROLL
ROLL
TONK
TONK
TONK
TMP
AH!
TMP TMP TMP TMP TMP TMP
KLATCH
TUNK
WHOOSH
HUH?

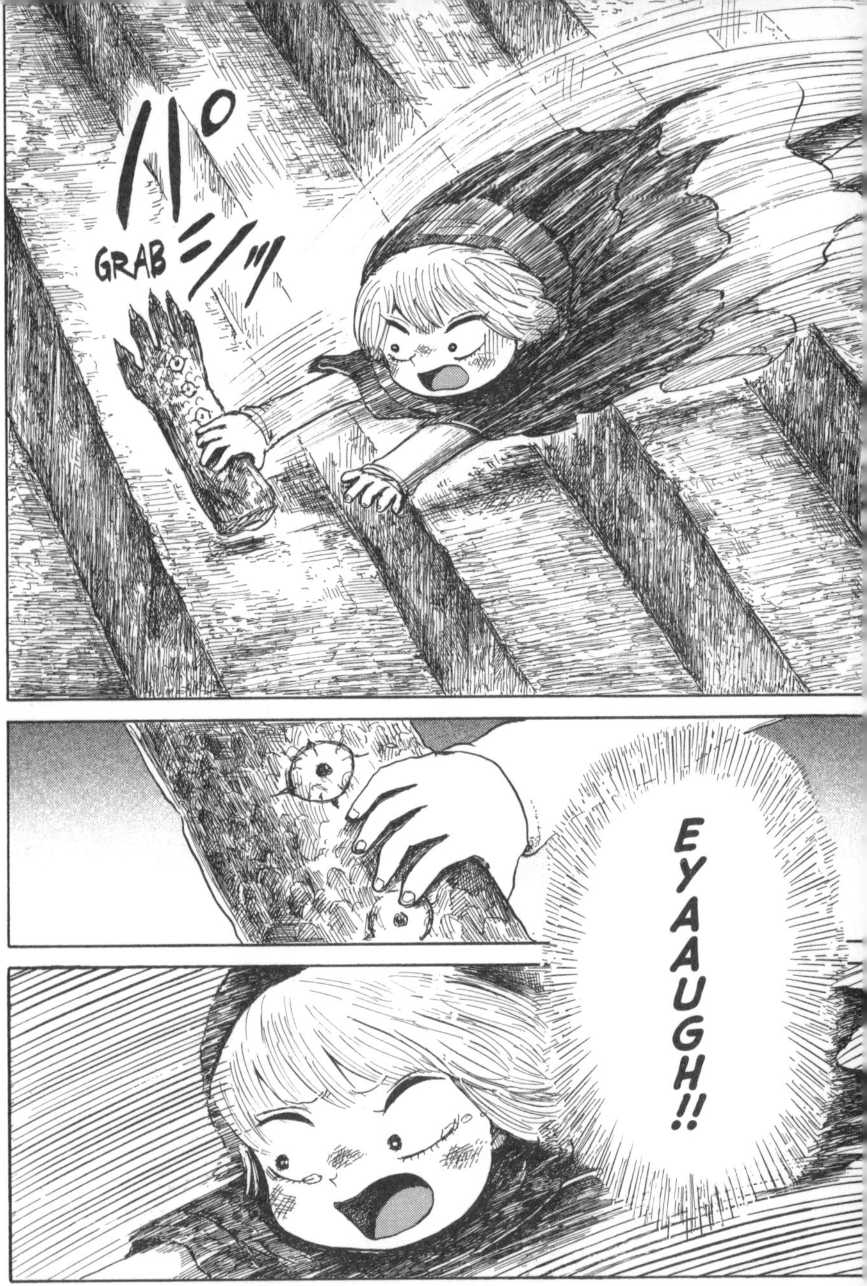
パシッ
GRAB
EYAAAUGH!!

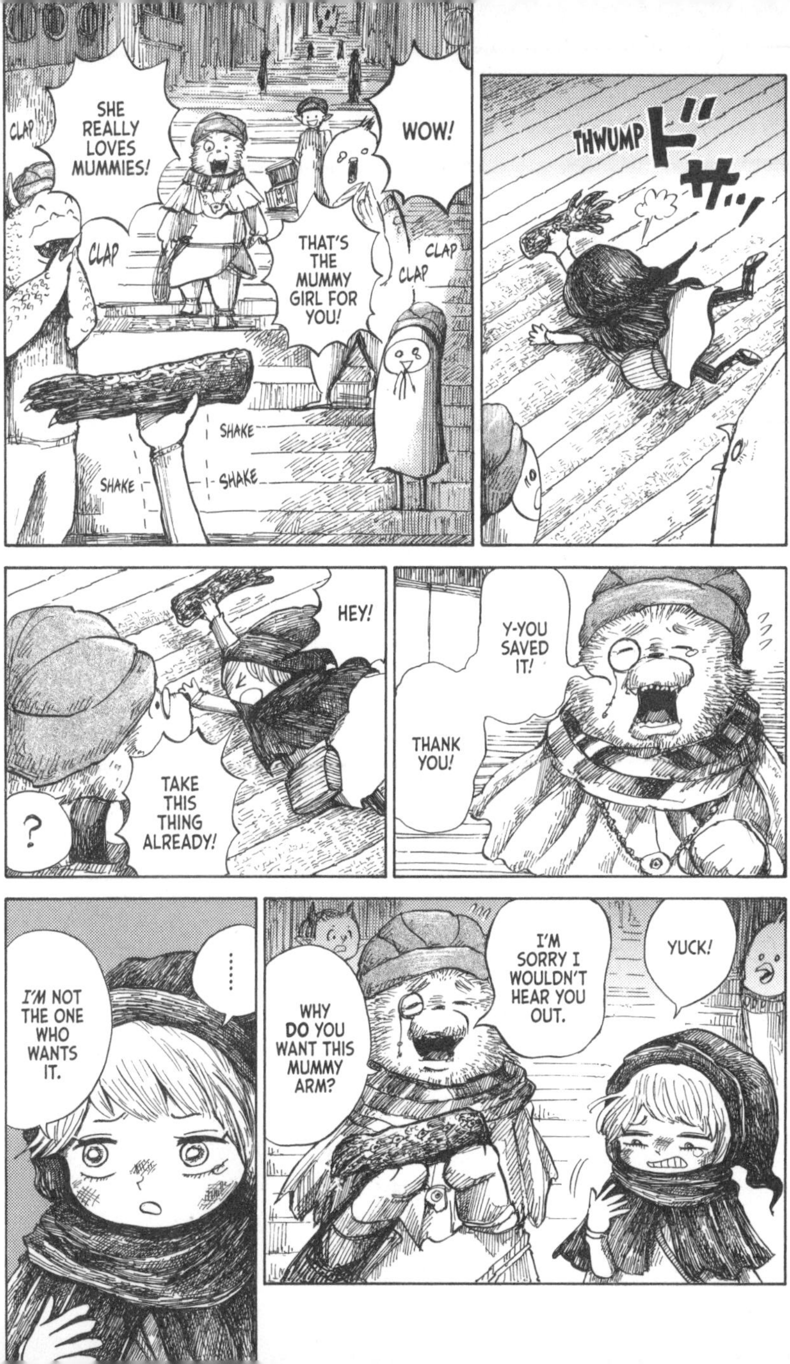
THWUMP
ドサッ
WOW!
SHE REALLY LOVES MUMMIES!
CLAP
CLAP
CLAP
CLAP
THAT'S THE MUMMY GIRL FOR YOU!
SHAKE
SHAKE
SHAKE
Y-YOU SAVED IT!
THANK YOU!
HEY!
TAKE THIS THING ALREADY!
?
YUCK!
I'M SORRY I WOULDN'T HEAR YOU OUT.
WHY DO YOU WANT THIS MUMMY ARM?
......
I'M NOT THE ONE WHO WANTS IT.

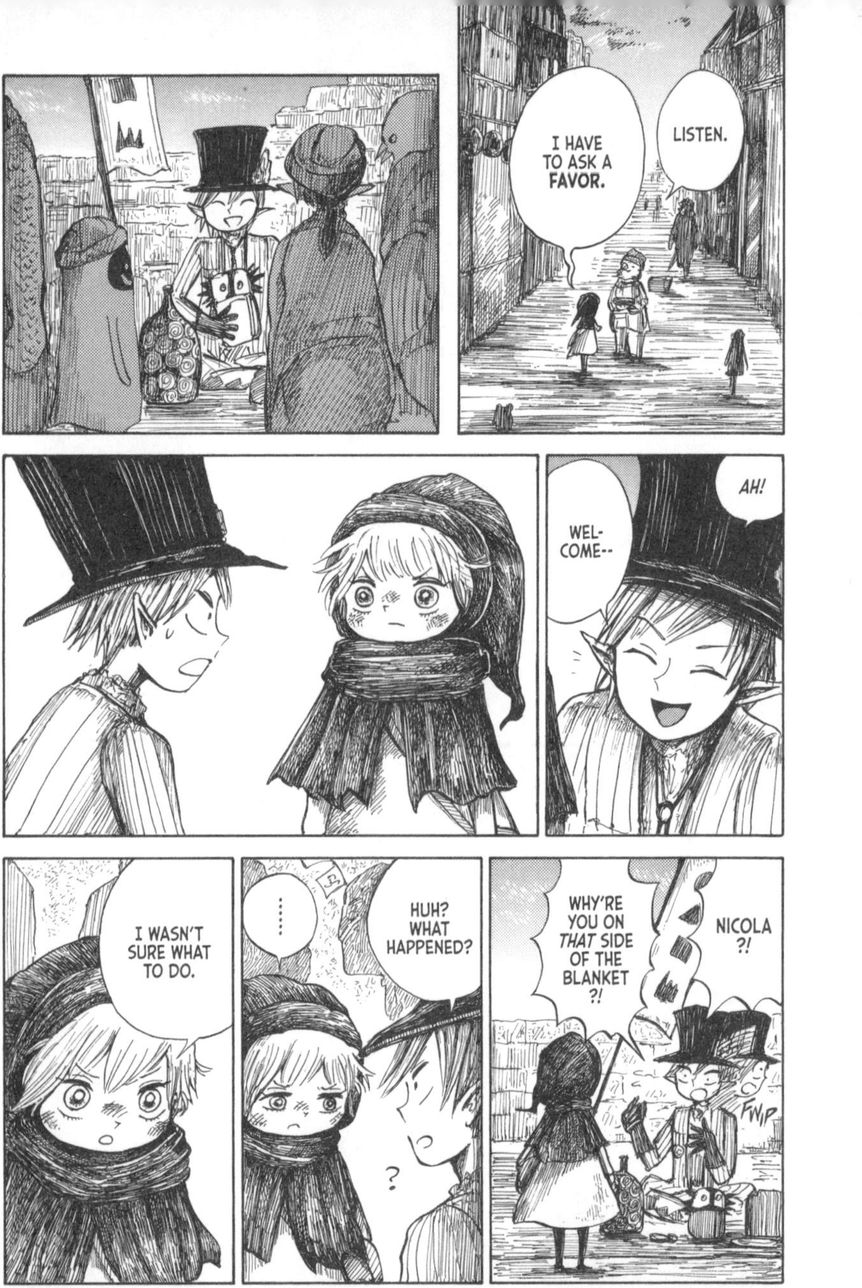
LISTEN.
I HAVE TO ASK A FAVOR.
AH!
WEL-COME--
NICOLA?!
WHY'RE YOU ON *THAT* SIDE OF THE BLANKET?!
FWIP
HUH? WHAT HAPPENED?
......
?
I WASN'T SURE WHAT TO DO.

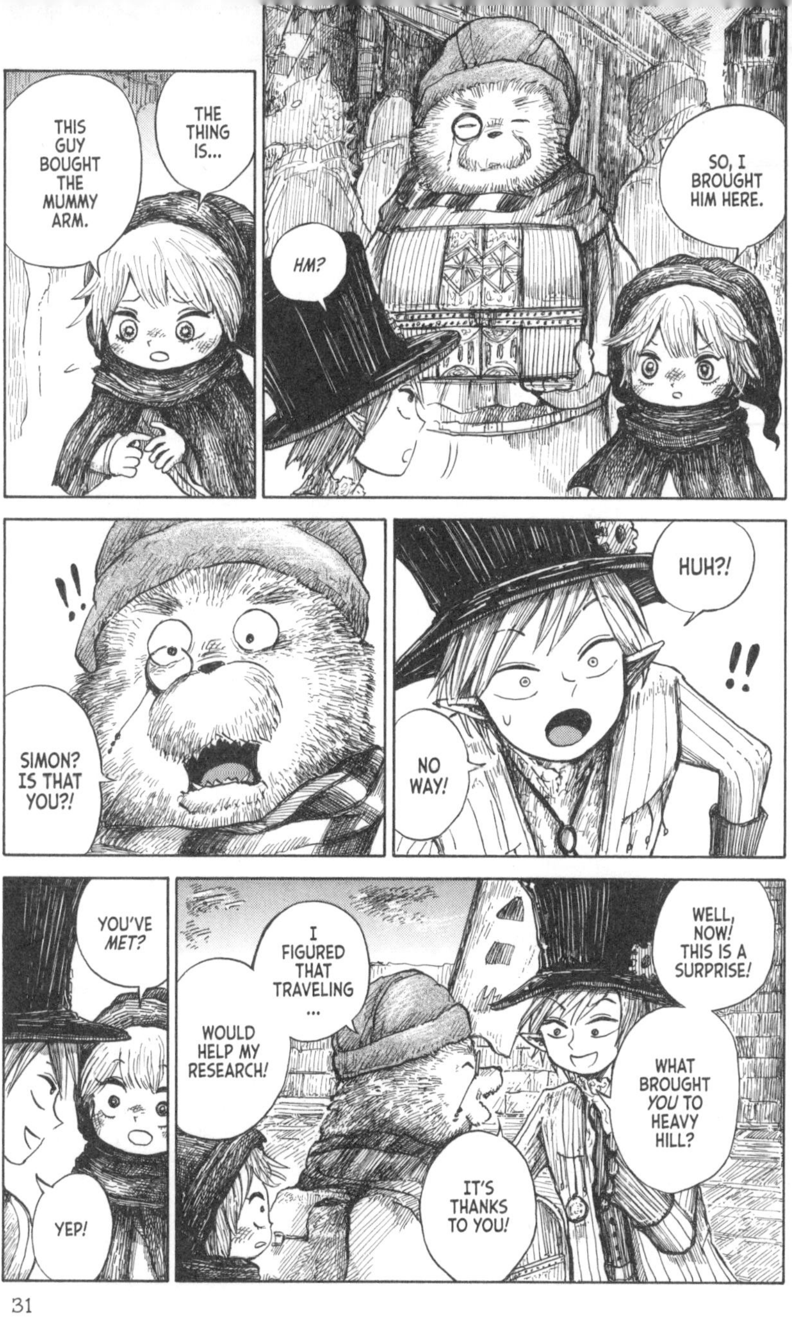
SO, I BROUGHT HIM HERE.
HM?
THE THING IS...
THIS GUY BOUGHT THE MUMMY ARM.
HUH?!
!!
NO WAY!
!!
SIMON? IS THAT YOU?!
WELL, NOW! THIS IS A SURPRISE!
WHAT BROUGHT YOU TO HEAVY HILL?
IT'S THANKS TO YOU!
I FIGURED THAT TRAVELING ...
WOULD HELP MY RESEARCH!
YOU'VE MET?
YEP!

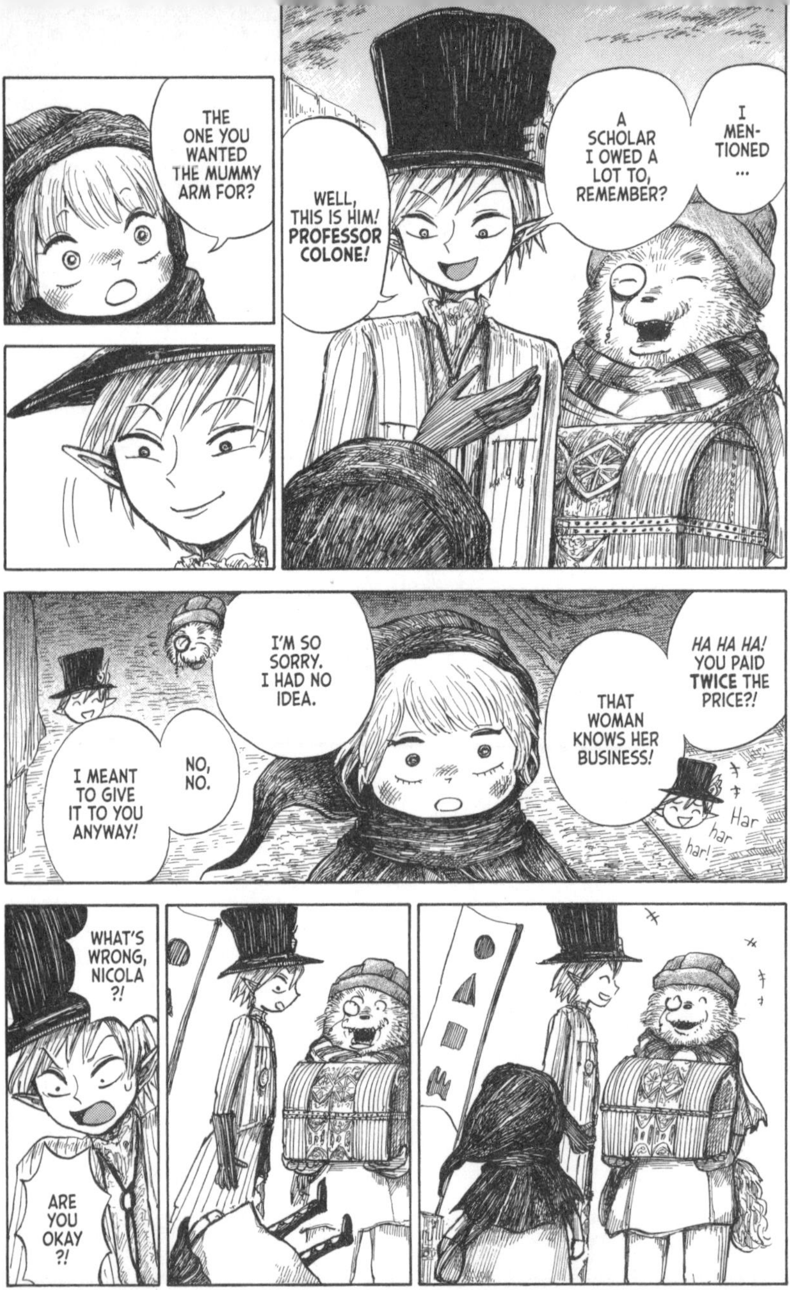
I MENTIONED ...
A SCHOLAR I OWED A LOT TO, REMEMBER?
WELL, THIS IS HIM! PROFESSOR COLONE!
THE ONE YOU WANTED THE MUMMY ARM FOR?
HA HA HA! YOU PAID TWICE THE PRICE?!
THAT WOMAN KNOWS HER BUSINESS!
Har har har!
I'M SO SORRY. I HAD NO IDEA.
NO, NO.
I MEANT TO GIVE IT TO YOU ANYWAY!
WHAT'S WRONG, NICOLA?!
ARE YOU OKAY?!

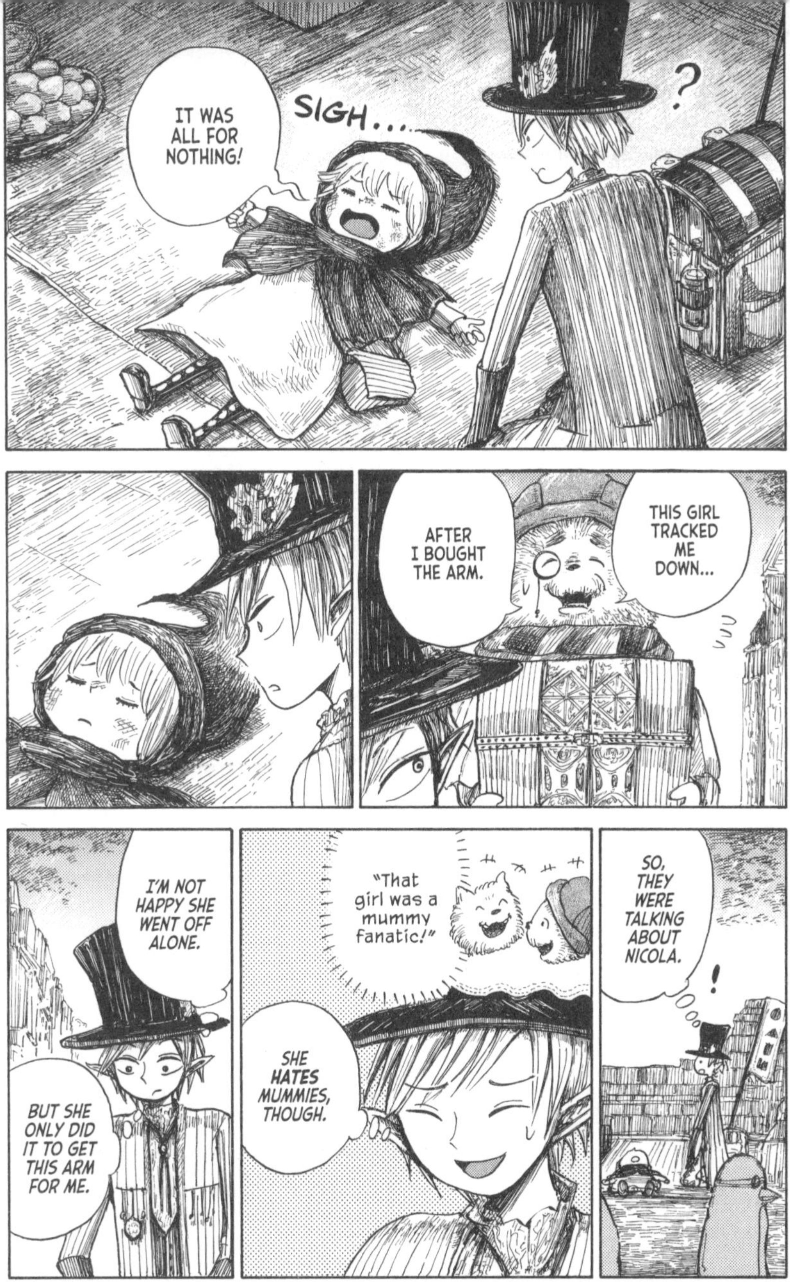
SIGH...
IT WAS ALL FOR NOTHING!
THIS GIRL TRACKED ME DOWN...
AFTER I BOUGHT THE ARM.
SO, THEY WERE TALKING ABOUT NICOLA.
"That girl was a mummy fanatic!"
SHE HATES MUMMIES, THOUGH.
I'M NOT HAPPY SHE WENT OFF ALONE.
BUT SHE ONLY DID IT TO GET THIS ARM FOR ME.

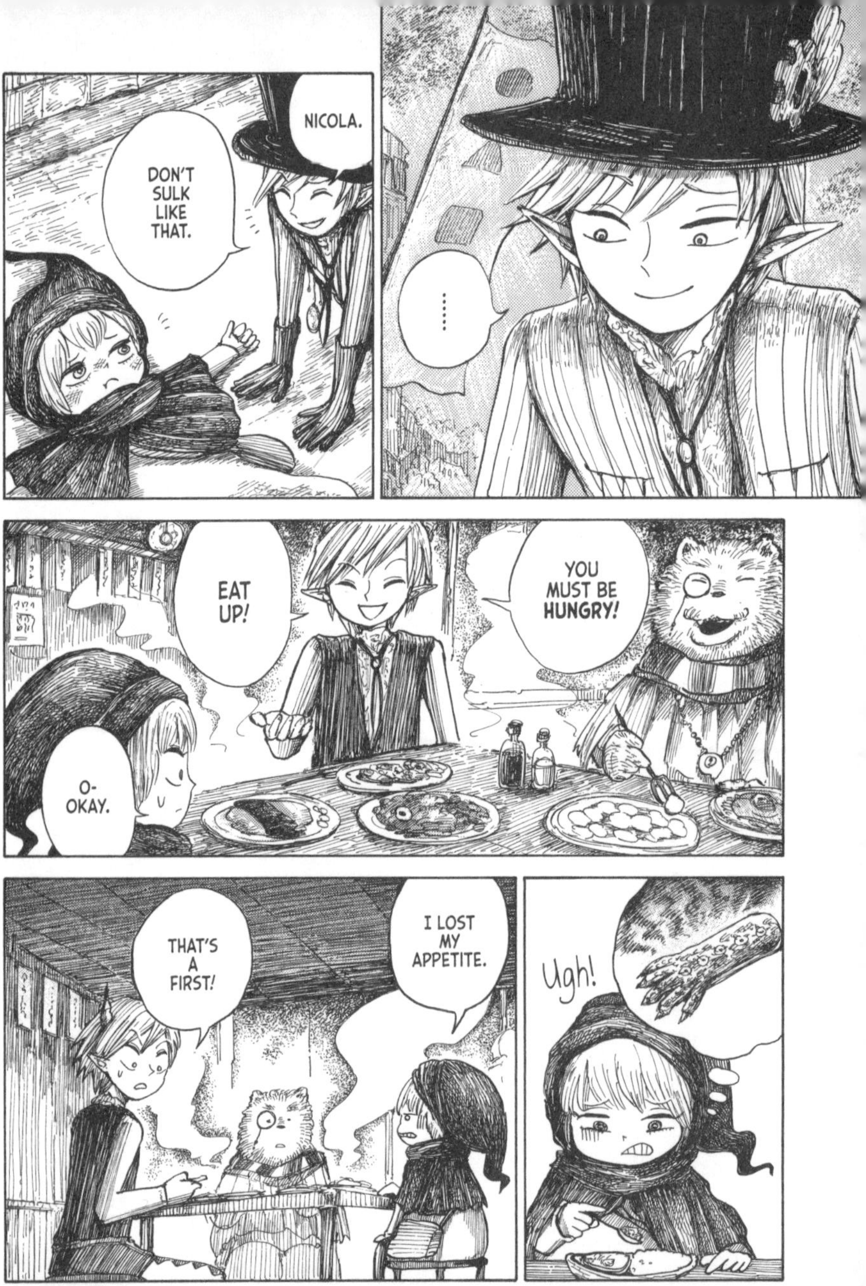
……
NICOLA.
DON'T SULK LIKE THAT.
YOU MUST BE HUNGRY!
EAT UP!
O- OKAY.
Ugh!
I LOST MY APPETITE.
THAT'S A FIRST!

Chapter 7 END

After the Visit 7

after that

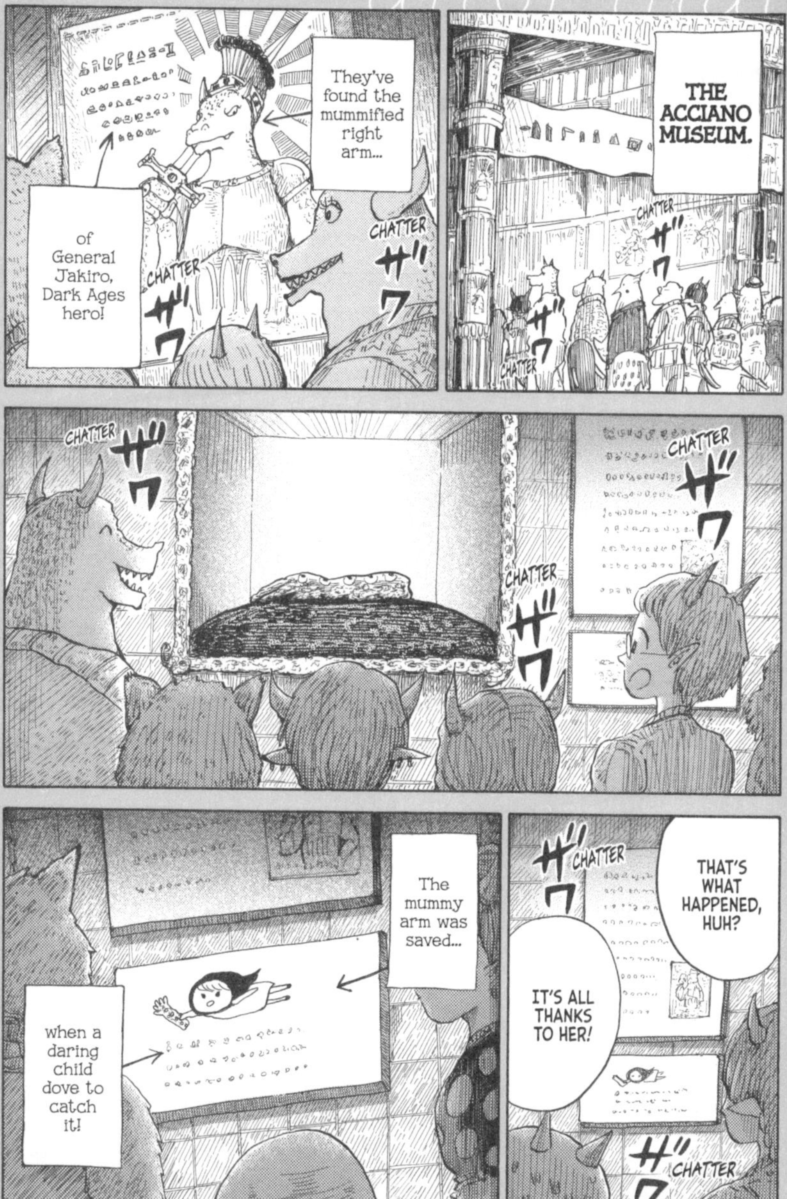
THE ACCIANO MUSEUM.
CHATTER ザワ
CHATTER ザワ
They've found the mummified right arm...
of General Jakiro, Dark Ages hero!
CHATTER ザワ
CHATTER ザワ
CHATTER ザワ
CHATTER ザワ
CHATTER ザワ
THAT'S WHAT HAPPENED, HUH?
IT'S ALL THANKS TO HER!
ザワ CHATTER
ザワ CHATTER
The mummy arm was saved...
when a daring child dove to catch it!

Nicola Traveling Around The Demons' World

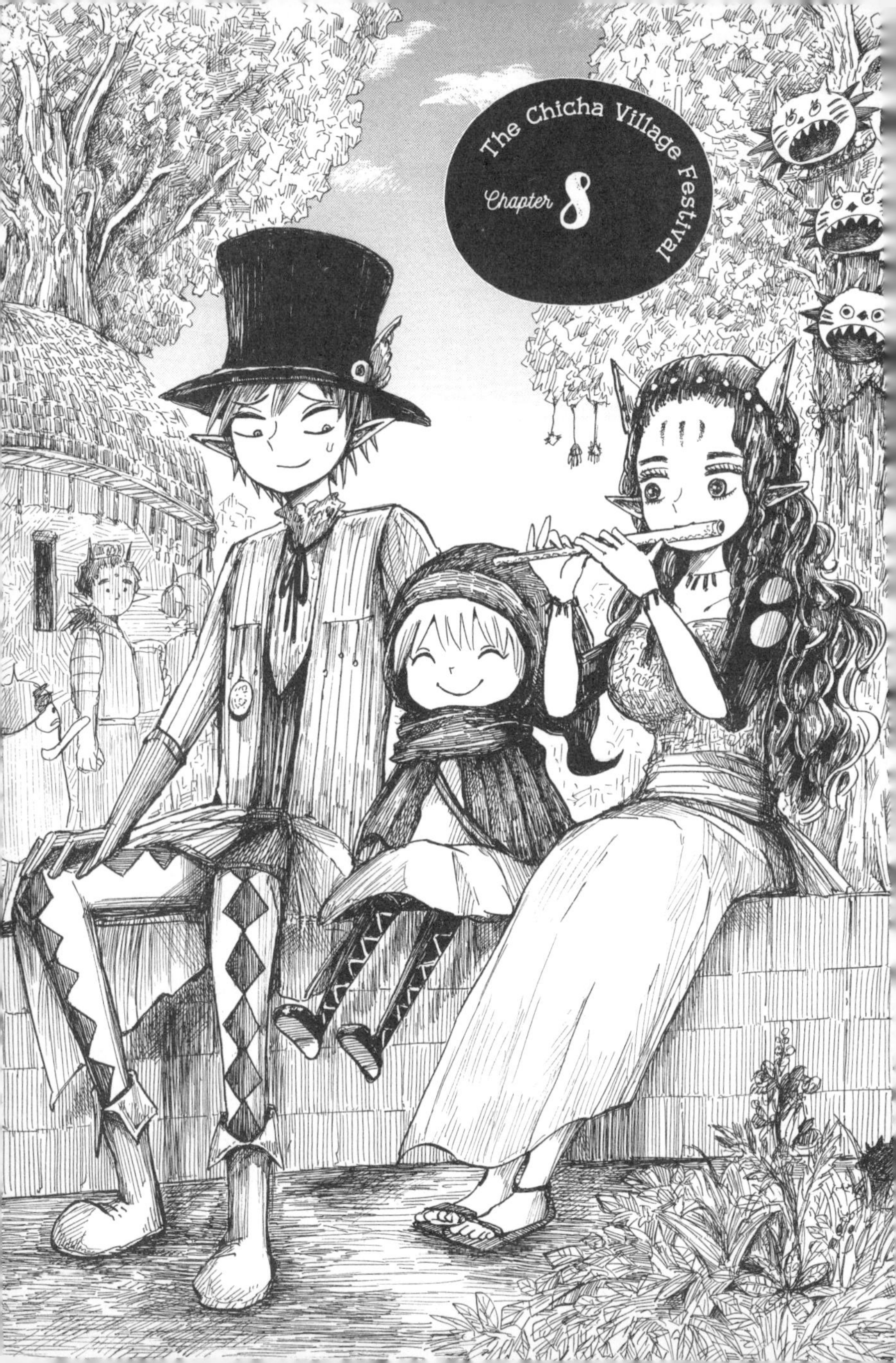
The Chicha Village Festival
Chapter 8

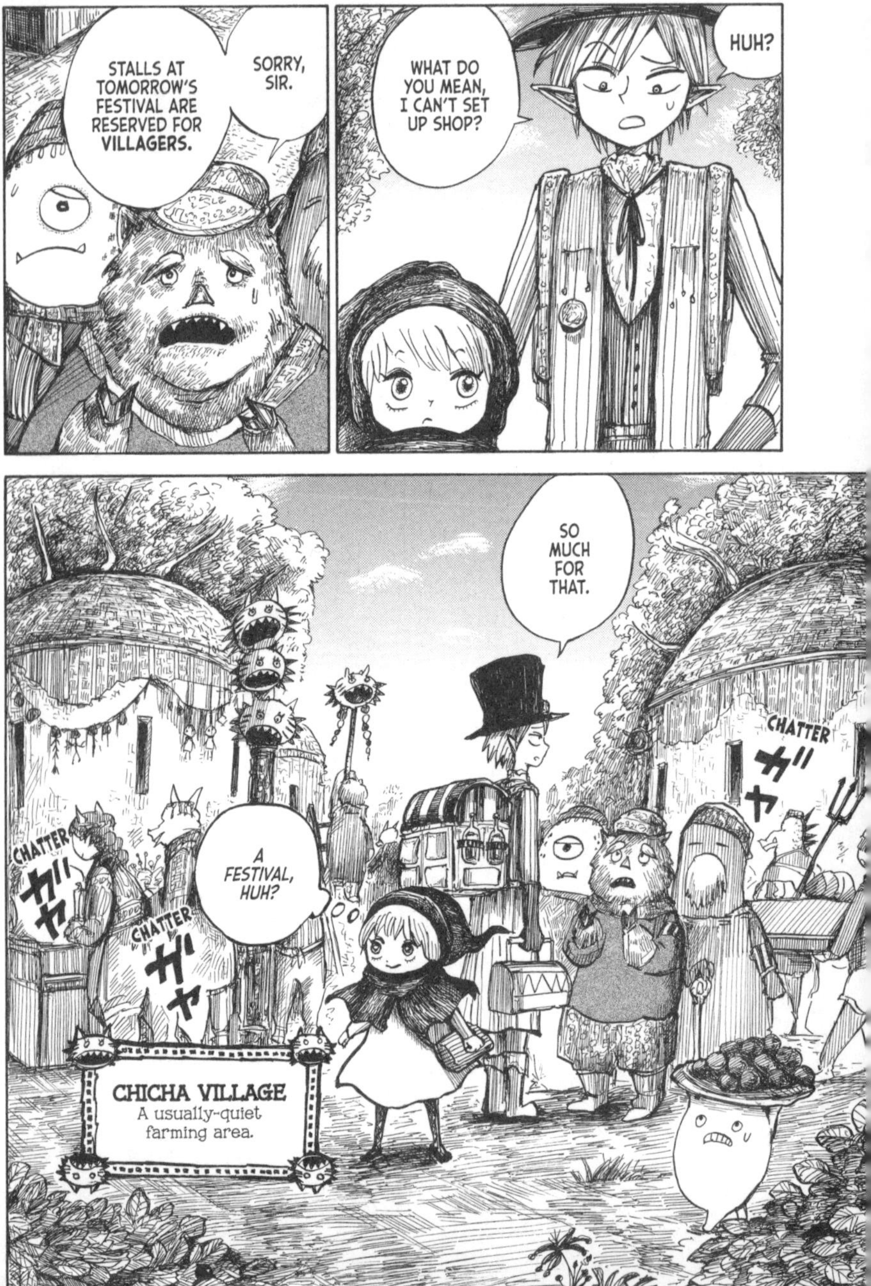
HUH?
WHAT DO YOU MEAN, I CAN'T SET UP SHOP?
SORRY, SIR.
STALLS AT TOMORROW'S FESTIVAL ARE RESERVED FOR **VILLAGERS.**
SO MUCH FOR THAT.
CHATTER
ガヤ
A FESTIVAL, HUH?
CHATTER
ガヤ
CHATTER
ガヤ
CHICHA VILLAGE
A usually-quiet farming area.

WHAT IS IT?

WE'RE LEAVING, NICOLA.

?

ARE YOU CRAZY, SIMON?!

TRUDGE

TRUDGE

TRUDGE

WHY SHOULD WE?!

I CAN'T *SELL* ANYTHING HERE!

TO HAVE FUN!

LET'S STAAAY!

BUT...

DRAAAAG

TMP

TMP

TMP

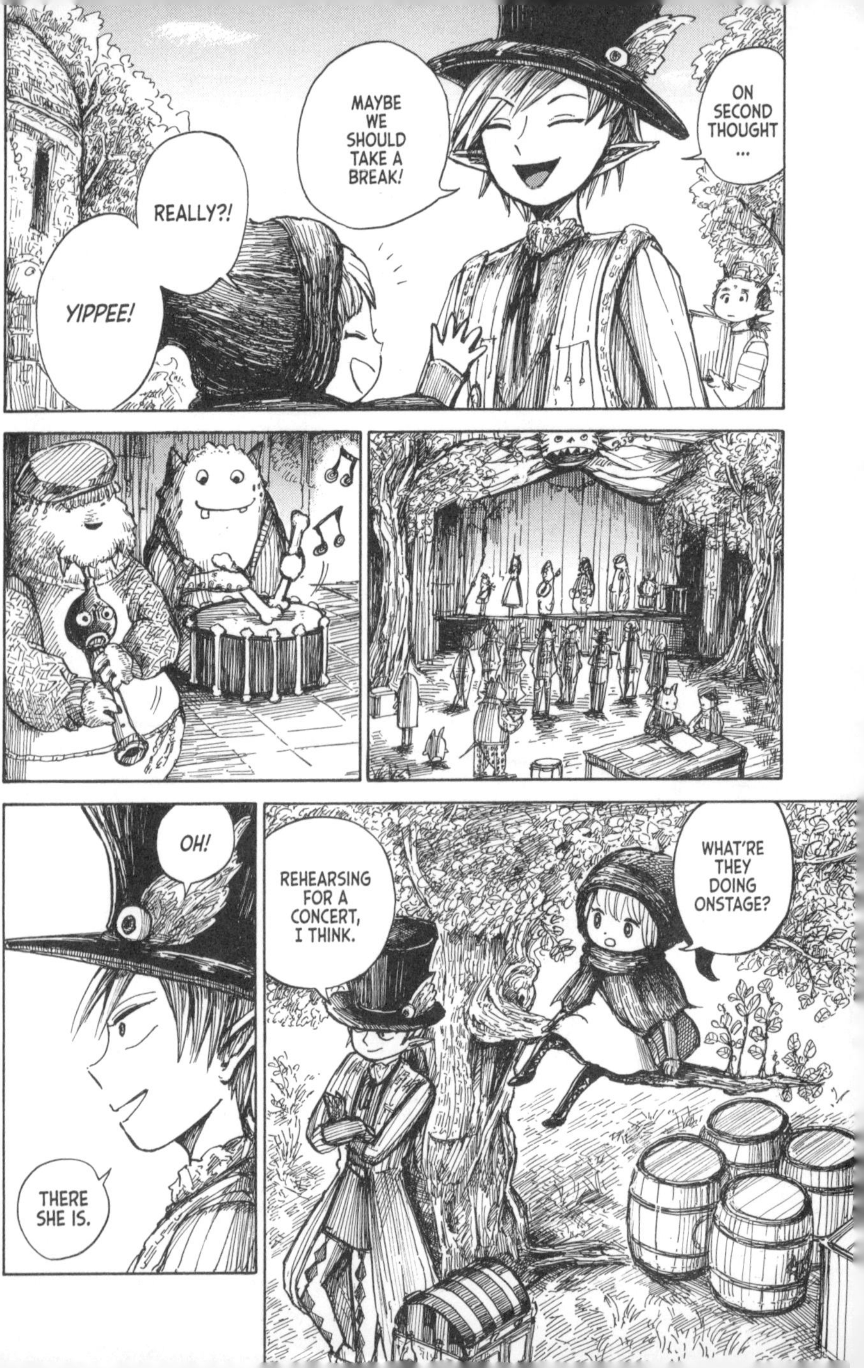
ON SECOND THOUGHT ...
MAYBE WE SHOULD TAKE A BREAK!
REALLY?!
YIPPEE!
WHAT'RE THEY DOING ONSTAGE?
REHEARSING FOR A CONCERT, I THINK.
OH!
THERE SHE IS.

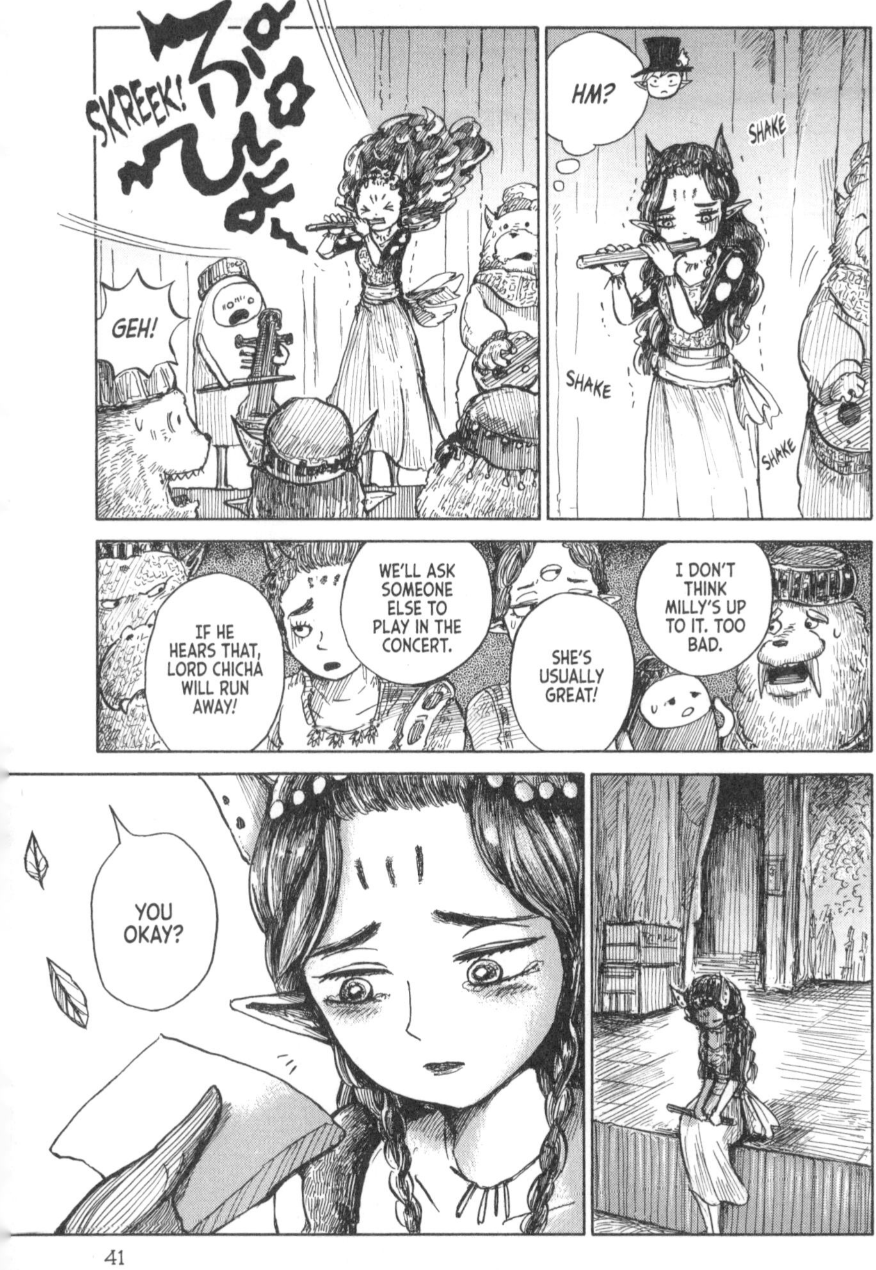
HM?
SHAKE
SHAKE
SHAKE
SKREEK!
GEH!
I DON'T THINK MILLY'S UP TO IT. TOO BAD.
SHE'S USUALLY GREAT!
WE'LL ASK SOMEONE ELSE TO PLAY IN THE CONCERT.
IF HE HEARS THAT, LORD CHICHA WILL RUN AWAY!
YOU OKAY?

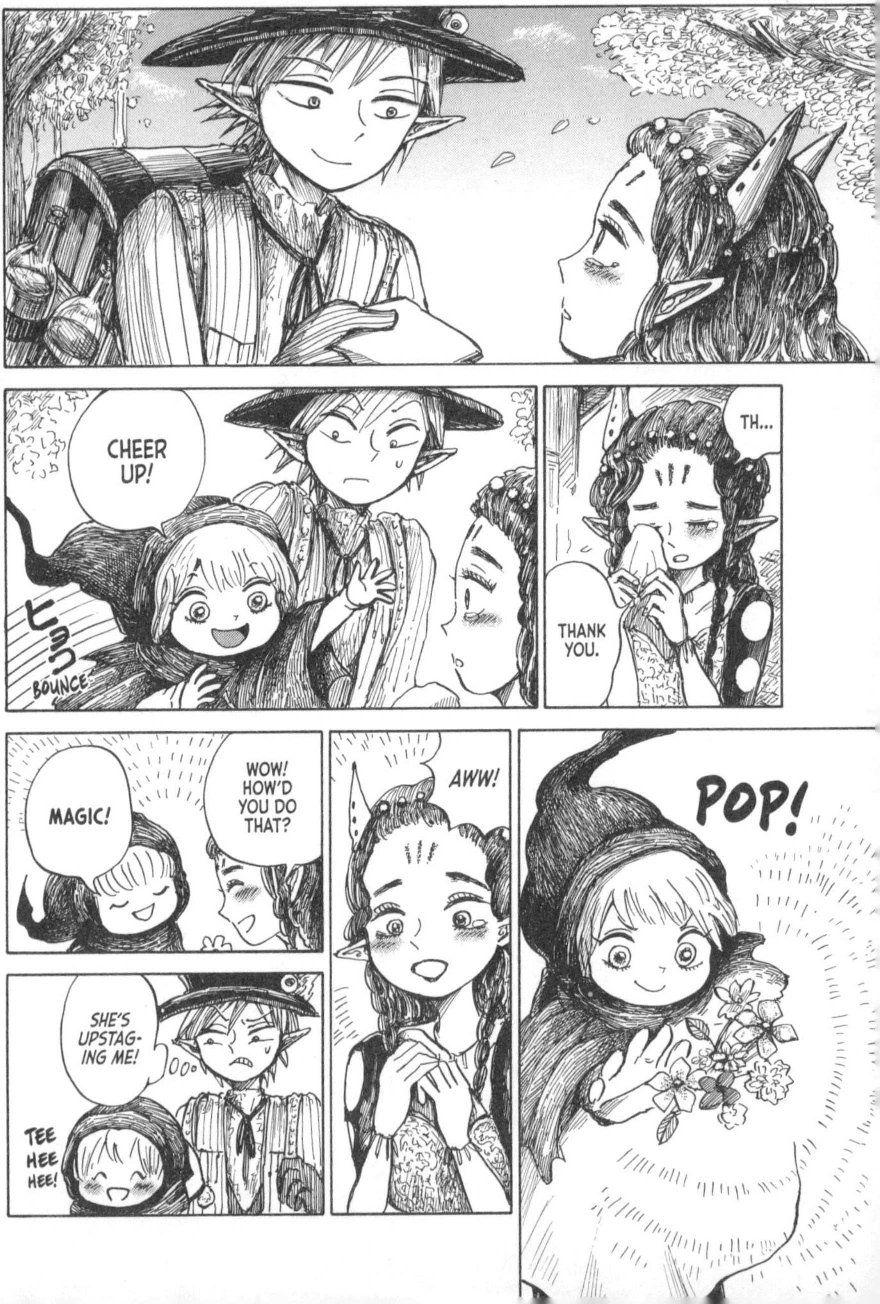
TH...
THANK YOU.
CHEER UP!
ヒョコ
BOUNCE
POP!
AWW!
WOW! HOW'D YOU DO THAT?
MAGIC!
SHE'S UPSTAG-ING ME!
TEE HEE HEE!

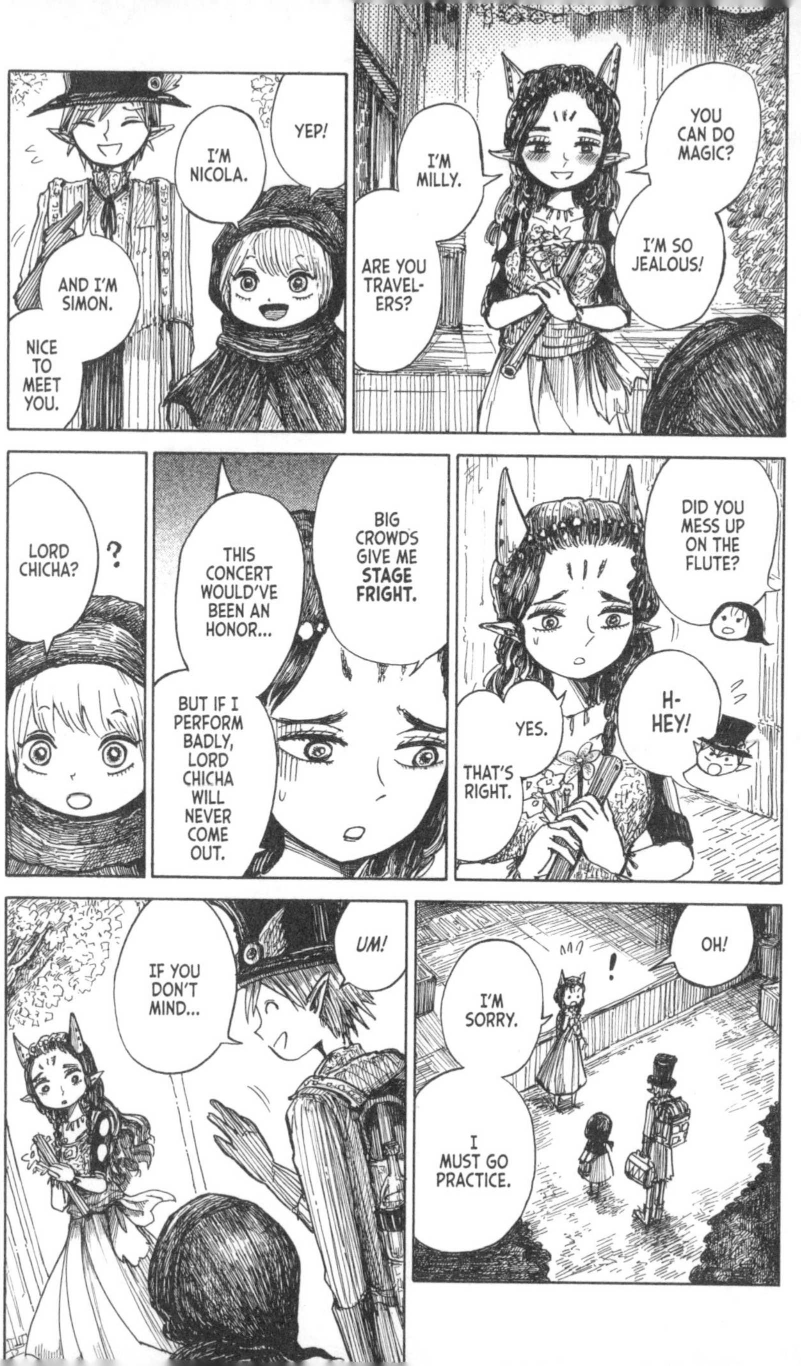
YOU CAN DO MAGIC?
I'M SO JEALOUS!
I'M MILLY.
ARE YOU TRAVELERS?
YEP!
I'M NICOLA.
AND I'M SIMON.
NICE TO MEET YOU.
DID YOU MESS UP ON THE FLUTE?
H-HEY!
YES.
THAT'S RIGHT.
BIG CROWDS GIVE ME **STAGE FRIGHT.**
THIS CONCERT WOULD'VE BEEN AN HONOR...
BUT IF I PERFORM BADLY, LORD CHICHA WILL NEVER COME OUT.
LORD CHICHA?
?
OH!
!
I'M SORRY.
I MUST GO PRACTICE.
UM!
IF YOU DON'T MIND...

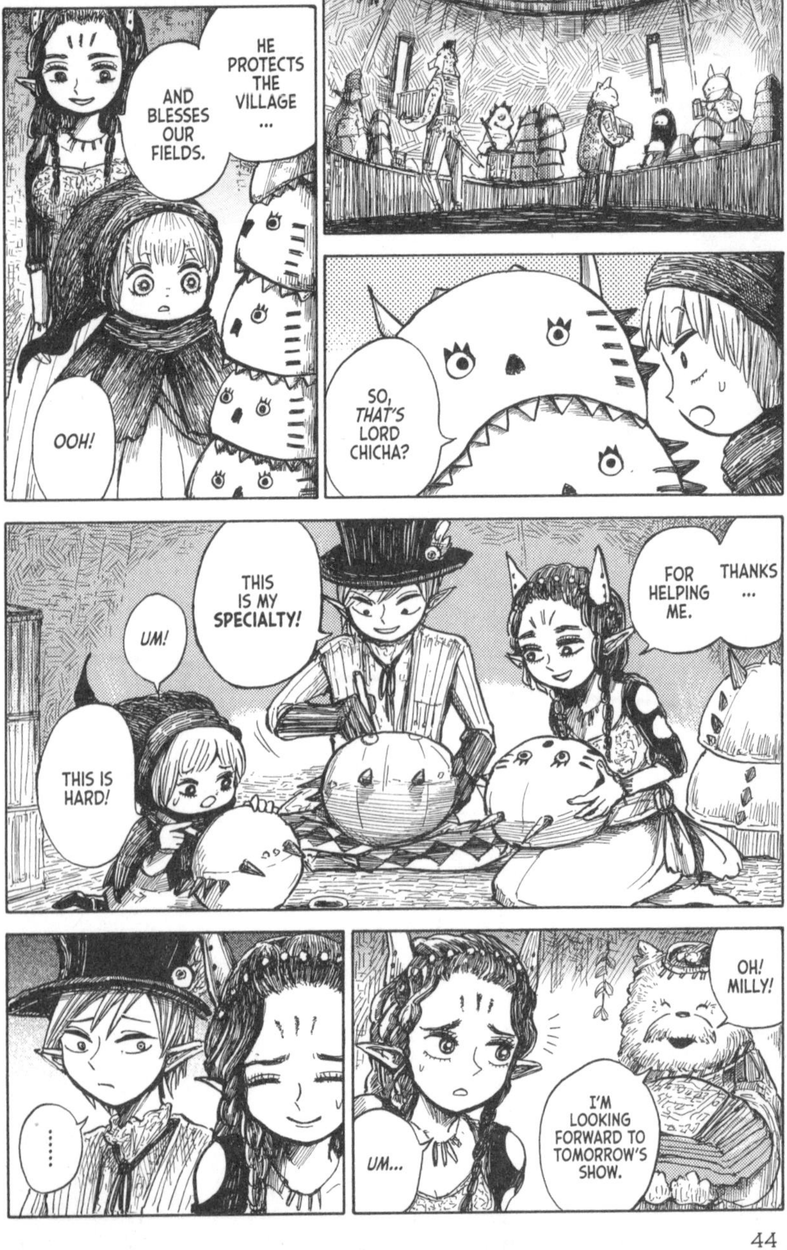
SO, THAT'S LORD CHICHA?
HE PROTECTS THE VILLAGE ...
AND BLESSES OUR FIELDS.
OOH!
THANKS ...
FOR HELPING ME.
THIS IS MY SPECIALTY!
UM!
THIS IS HARD!
OH! MILLY!
I'M LOOKING FORWARD TO TOMORROW'S SHOW.
UM...
......

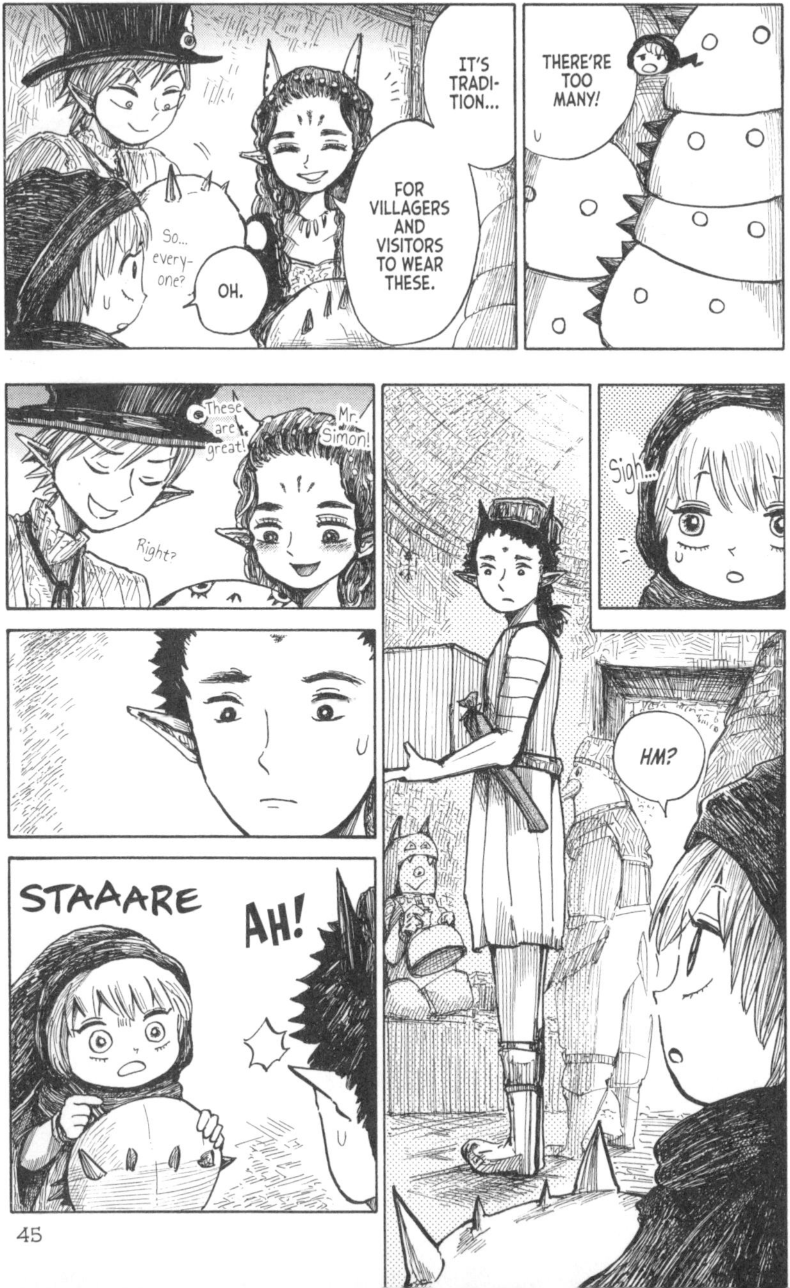
THERE'RE TOO MANY!
IT'S TRADITION...
FOR VILLAGERS AND VISITORS TO WEAR THESE.
OH.
So... everyone?
Sigh...
HM?
Mr. Simon!
These are great!
Right?
STAAARE
AH!

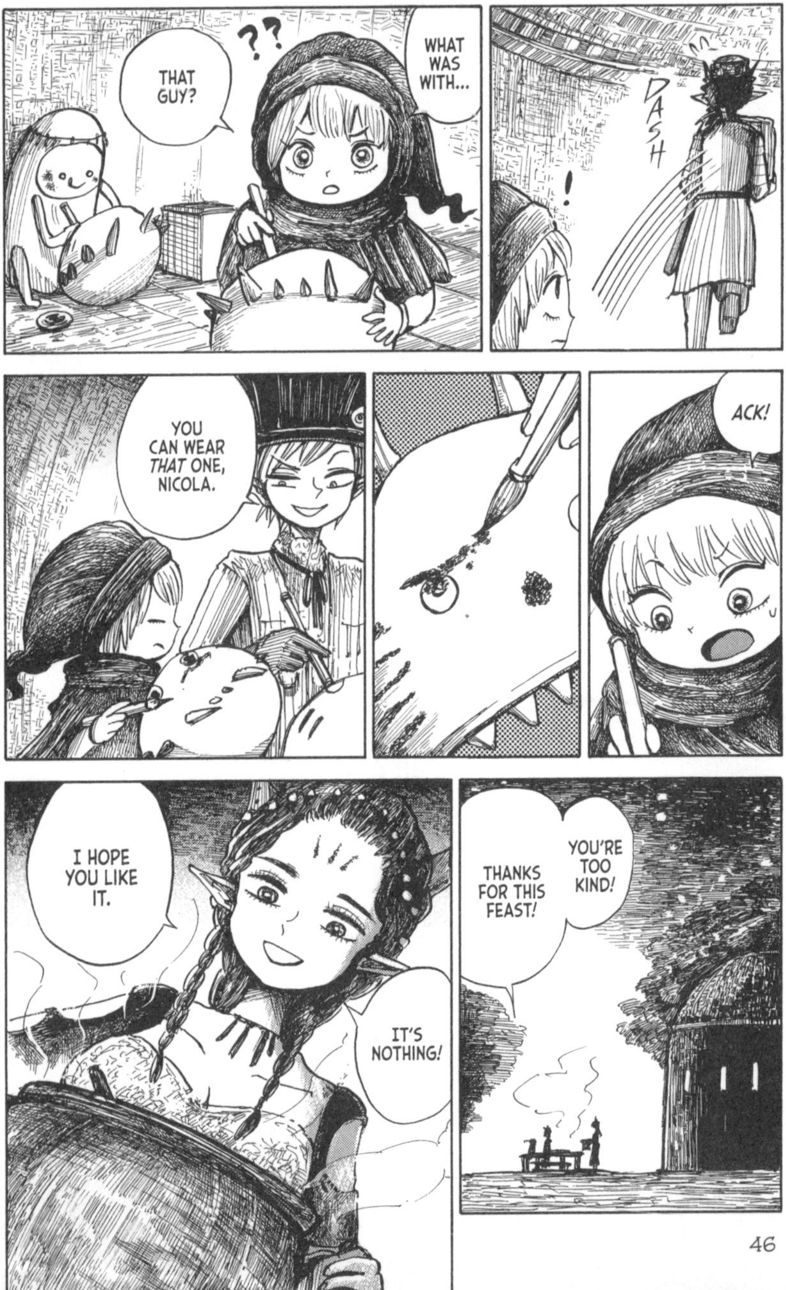
DASH
!
WHAT WAS WITH...
??
THAT GUY?
ACK!
YOU CAN WEAR *THAT* ONE, NICOLA.
YOU'RE TOO KIND!
THANKS FOR THIS FEAST!
I HOPE YOU LIKE IT.
IT'S NOTHING!

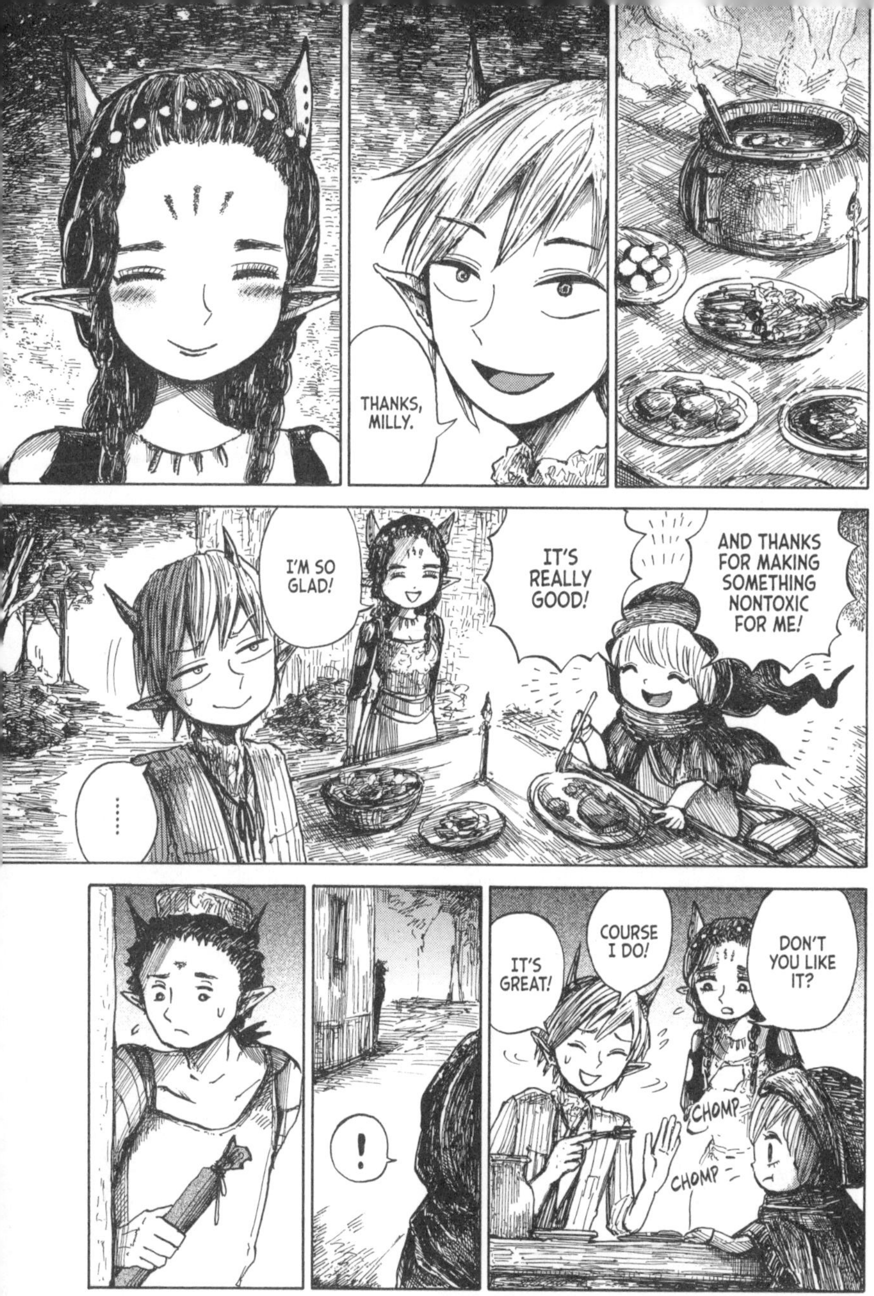
THANKS, MILLY.
AND THANKS FOR MAKING SOMETHING NONTOXIC FOR ME!
IT'S REALLY GOOD!
I'M SO GLAD!
......
DON'T YOU LIKE IT?
CHOMP
CHOMP
COURSE I DO!
IT'S GREAT!
!

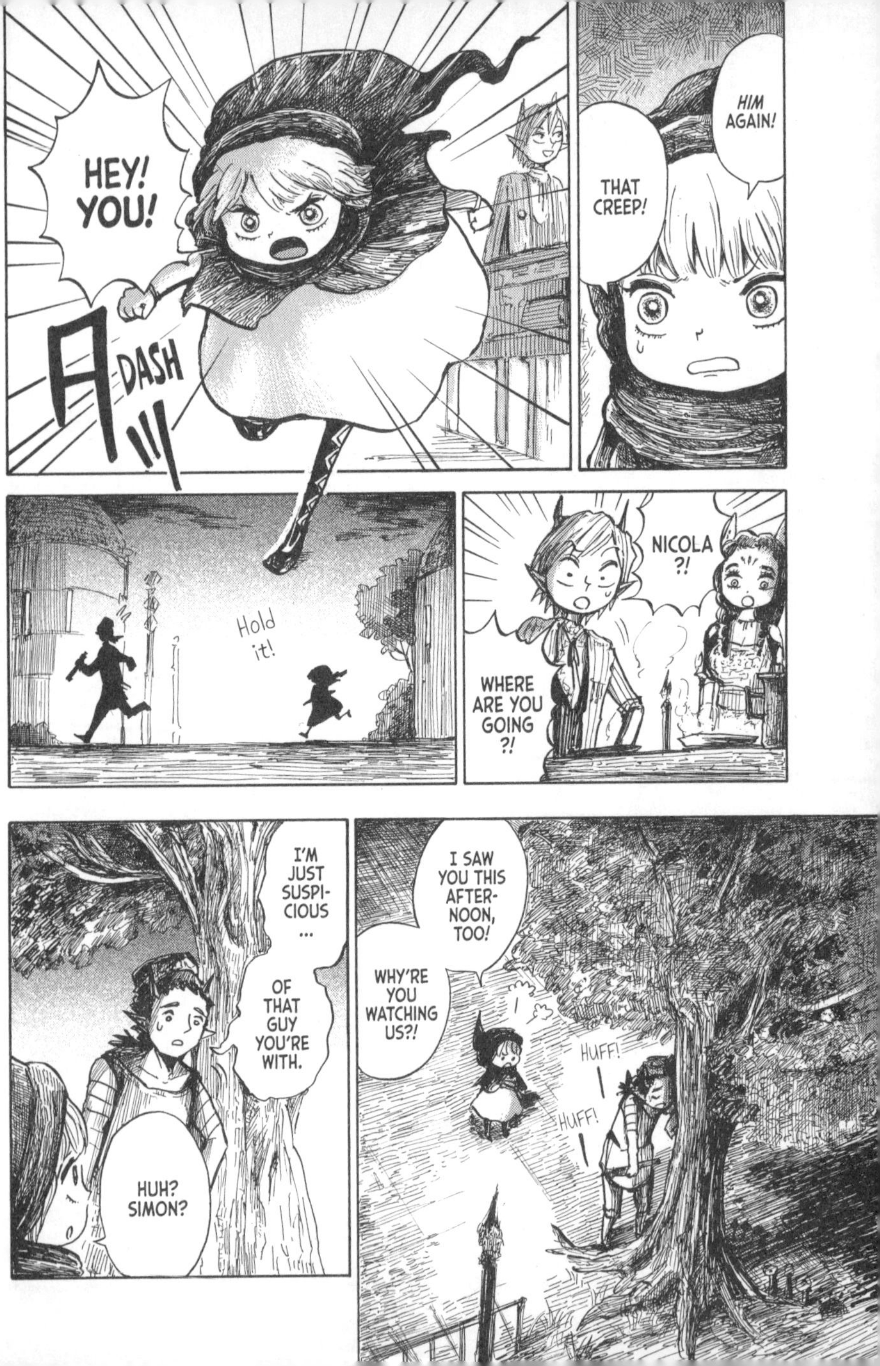
HIM AGAIN!
THAT CREEP!
HEY! YOU!
DASH
NICOLA ?!
WHERE ARE YOU GOING ?!
Hold it!
I SAW YOU THIS AFTERNOON, TOO!
WHY'RE YOU WATCHING US?!
HUFF!
HUFF!
I'M JUST SUSPICIOUS...
OF THAT GUY YOU'RE WITH.
HUH? SIMON?

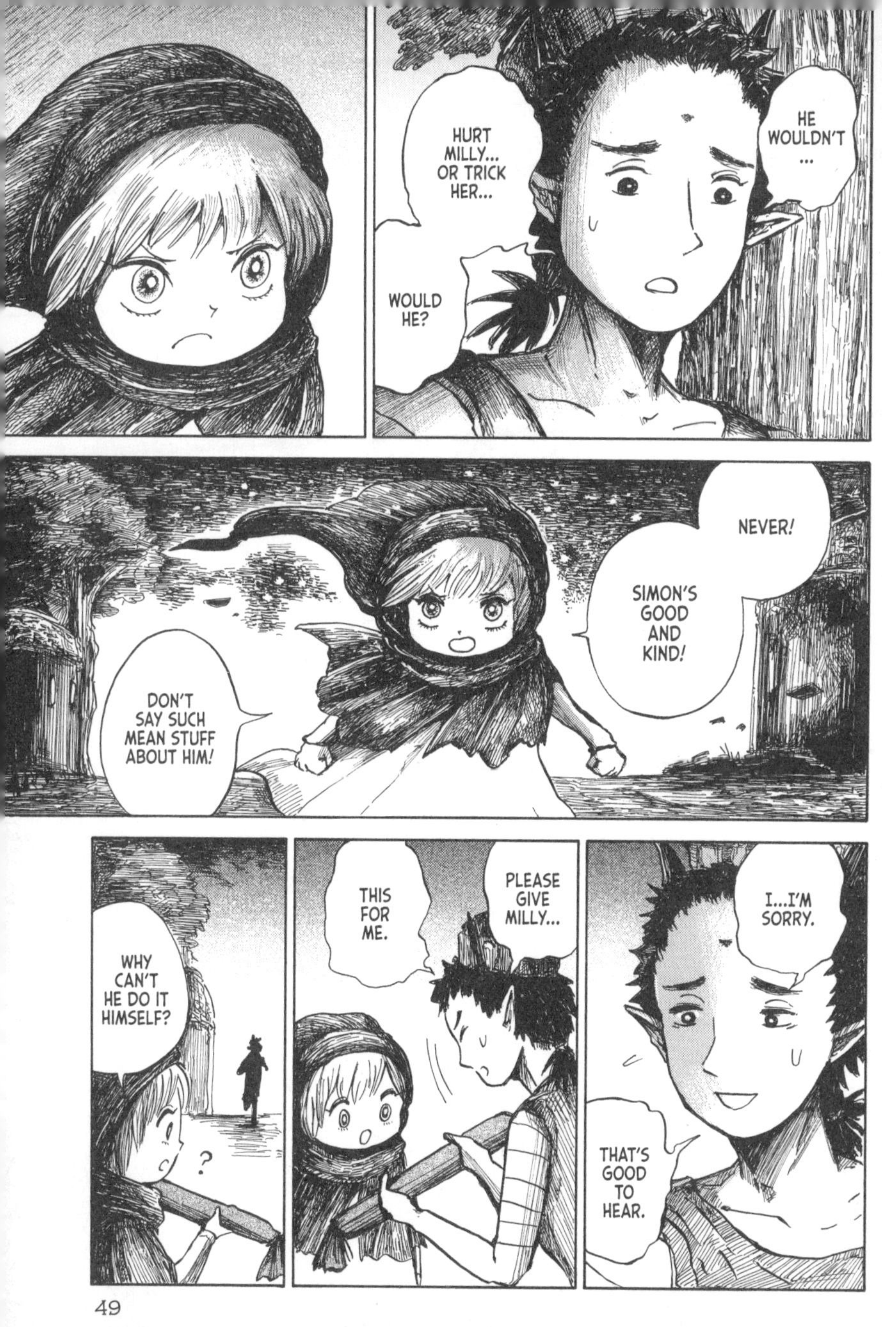
HE WOULDN'T ...
HURT MILLY... OR TRICK HER...
WOULD HE?
NEVER!
SIMON'S GOOD AND KIND!
DON'T SAY SUCH MEAN STUFF ABOUT HIM!
I...I'M SORRY.
THAT'S GOOD TO HEAR.
PLEASE GIVE MILLY...
THIS FOR ME.
WHY CAN'T HE DO IT HIMSELF?
?

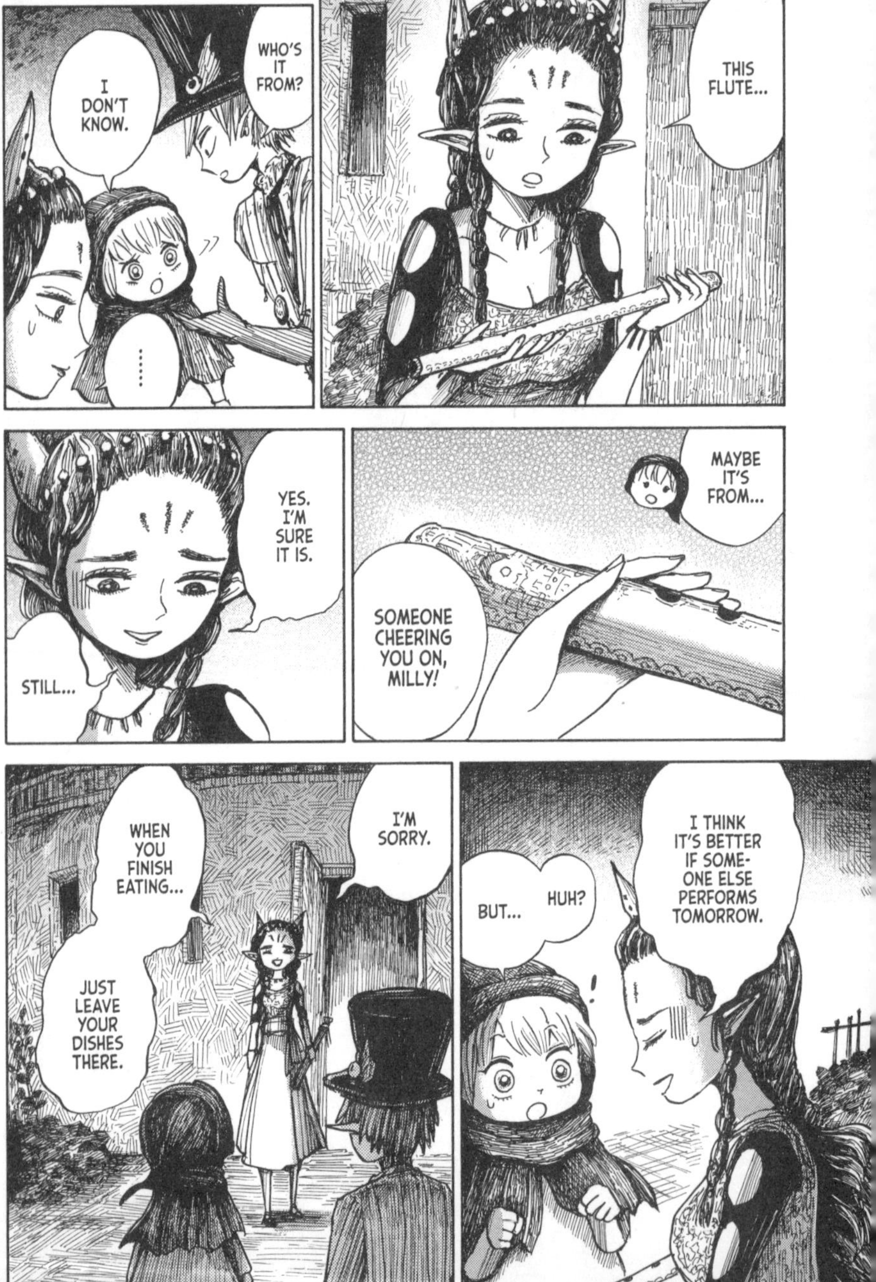
THIS FLUTE...
WHO'S IT FROM?
I DON'T KNOW.
......
MAYBE IT'S FROM...
SOMEONE CHEERING YOU ON, MILLY!
YES. I'M SURE IT IS.
STILL...
I THINK IT'S BETTER IF SOME-ONE ELSE PERFORMS TOMORROW.
HUH?
BUT...
!
I'M SORRY.
WHEN YOU FINISH EATING...
JUST LEAVE YOUR DISHES THERE.

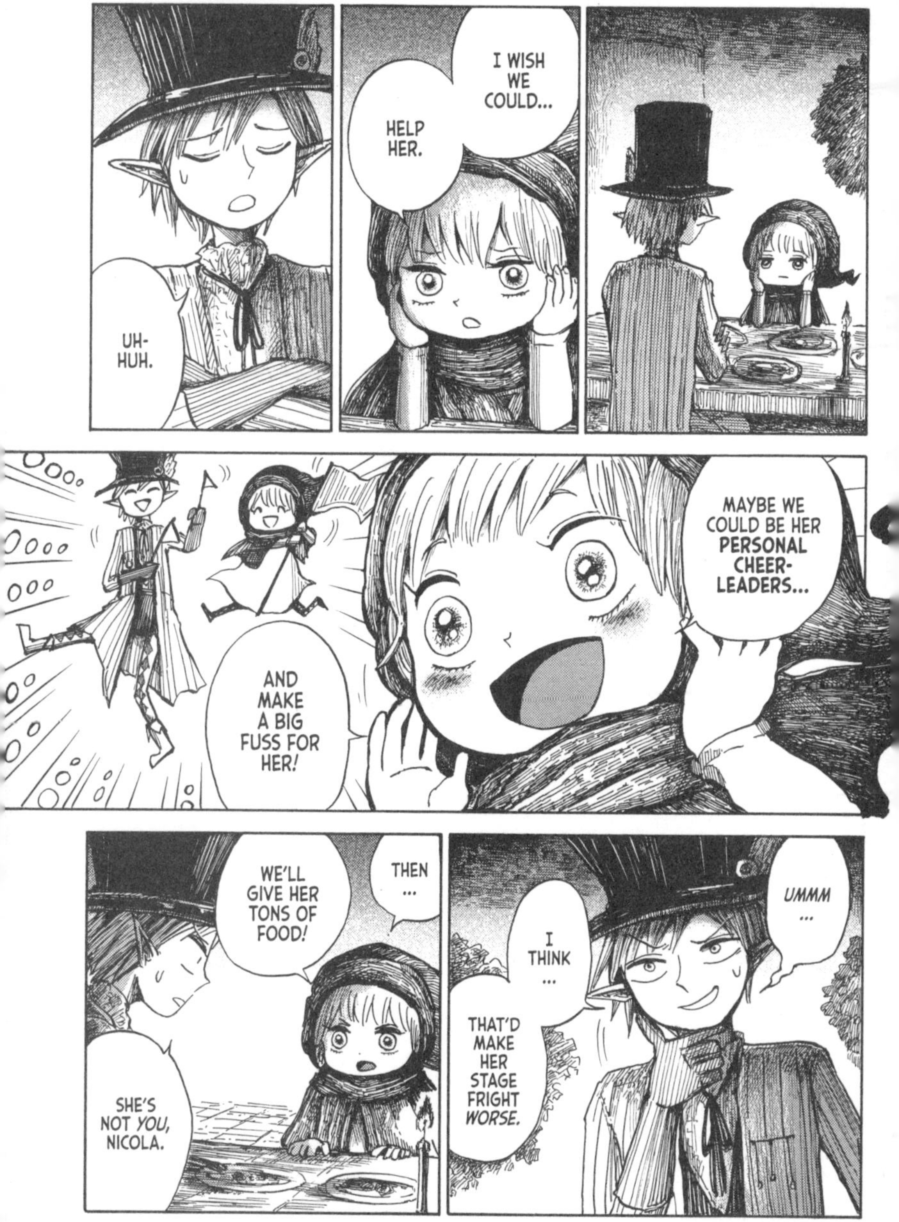
I WISH WE COULD...
HELP HER.
UH-HUH.
MAYBE WE COULD BE HER PERSONAL CHEER-LEADERS...
AND MAKE A BIG FUSS FOR HER!
UMMM ...
I THINK ...
THAT'D MAKE HER STAGE FRIGHT *WORSE.*
THEN ...
WE'LL GIVE HER TONS OF FOOD!
SHE'S NOT *YOU,* NICOLA.

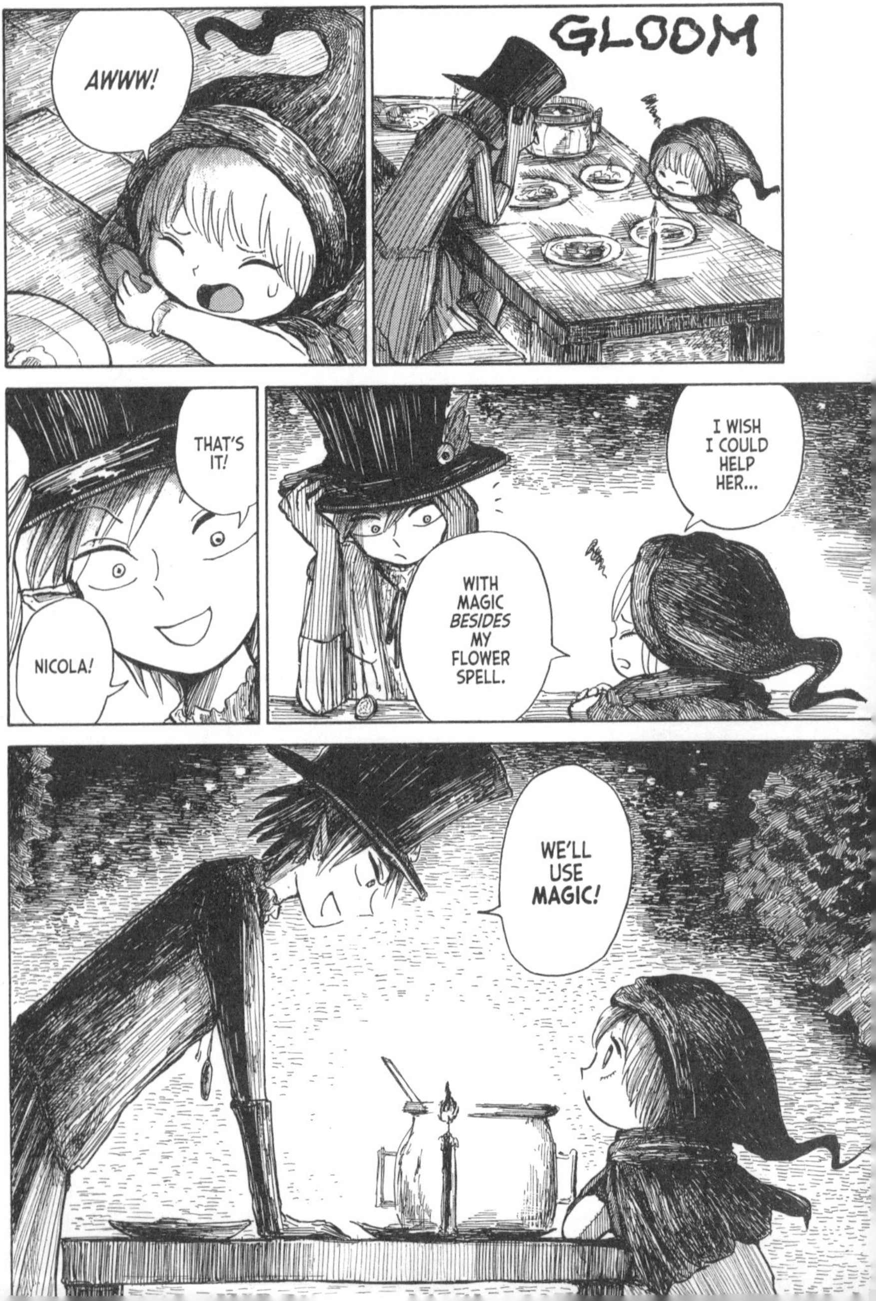
GLOOM
AWWW!
I WISH I COULD HELP HER...
WITH MAGIC *BESIDES* MY FLOWER SPELL.
THAT'S IT!
NICOLA!
WE'LL USE **MAGIC!**

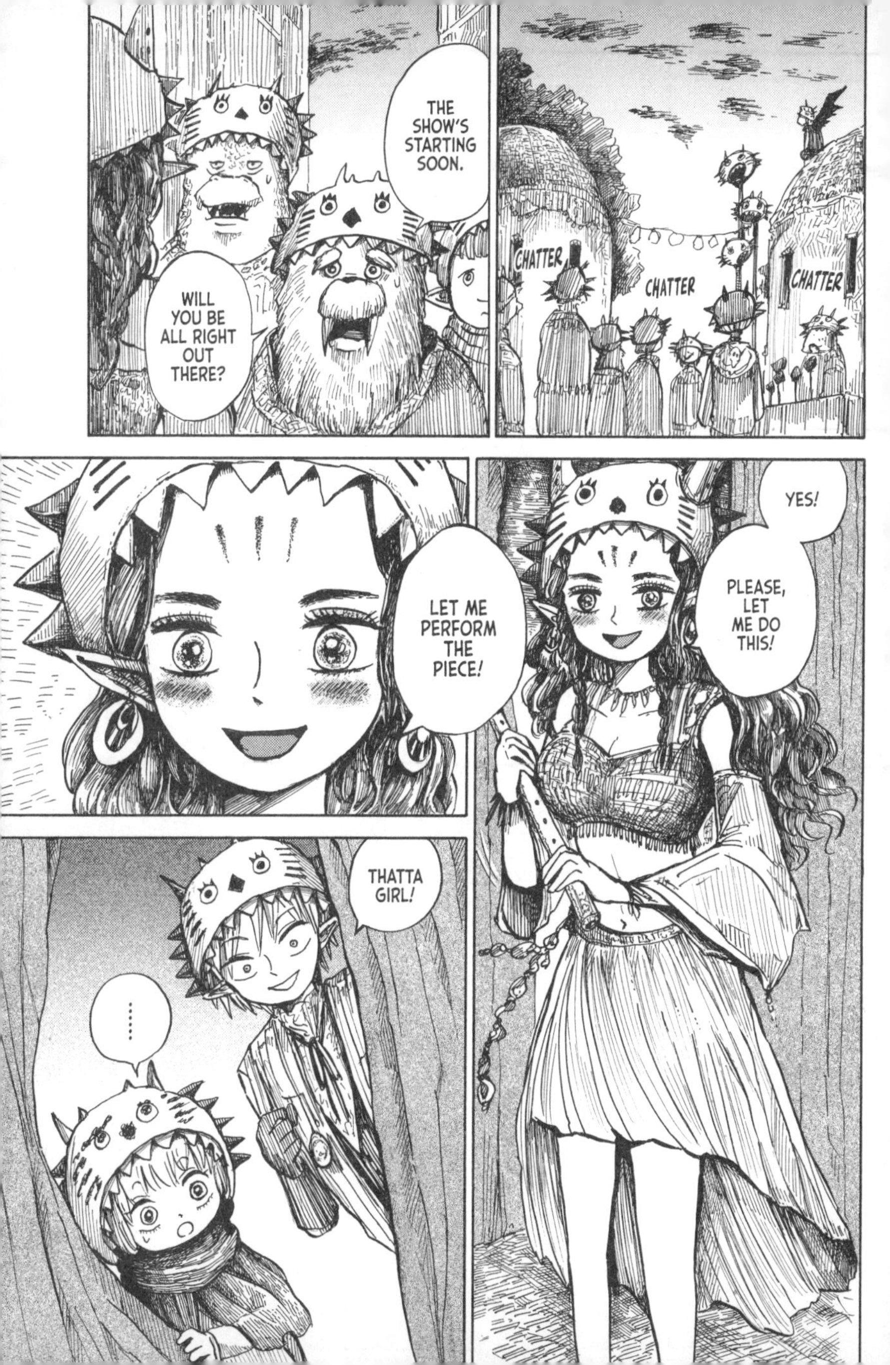
CHATTER
CHATTER
CHATTER
THE SHOW'S STARTING SOON.
WILL YOU BE ALL RIGHT OUT THERE?
YES!
PLEASE, LET ME DO THIS!
LET ME PERFORM THE PIECE!
THATTA GIRL!
……

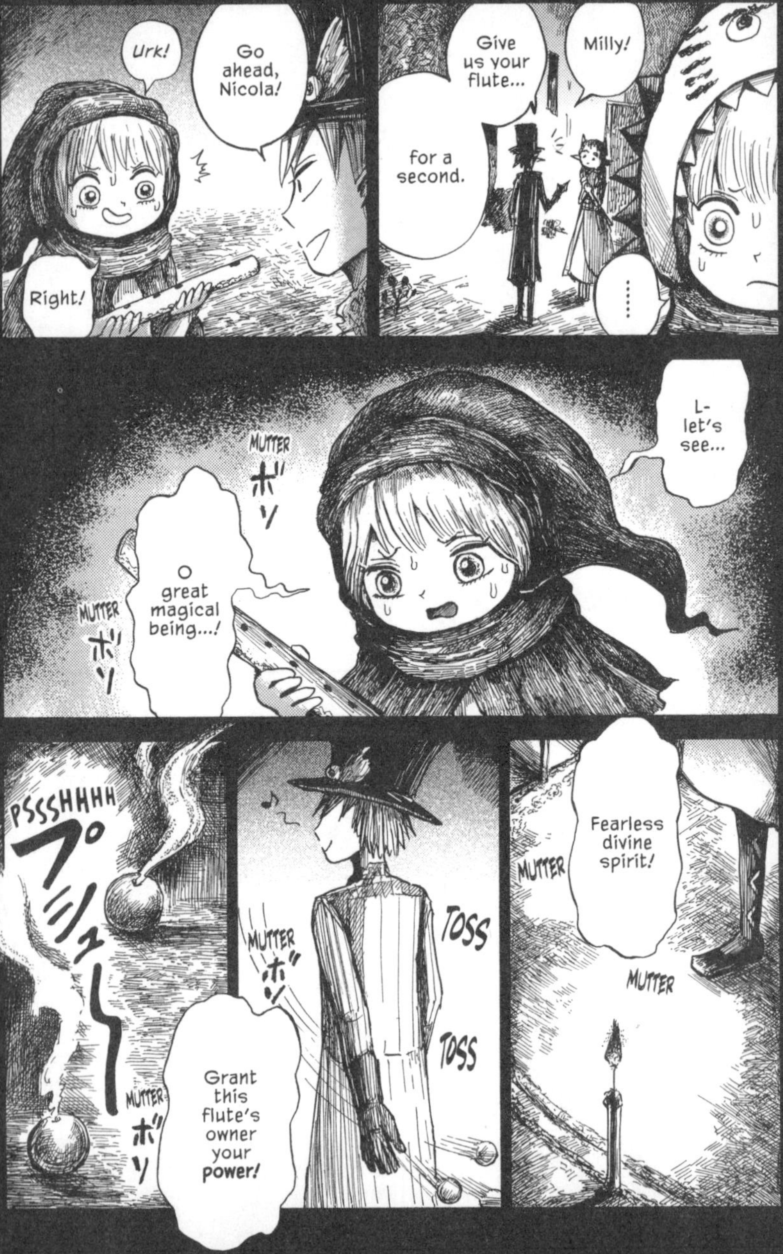
Milly!
Give us your flute...
for a second.
......
Go ahead, Nicola!
Urk!
Right!
L- let's see...
MUTTER
ボソ
O great magical being...!
MUTTER
ボソ
Fearless divine spirit!
MUTTER
MUTTER
TOSS
TOSS
MUTTER
ボソ
Grant this flute's owner your power!
PSSSHHHH
プシュ～
MUTTER
ボソ

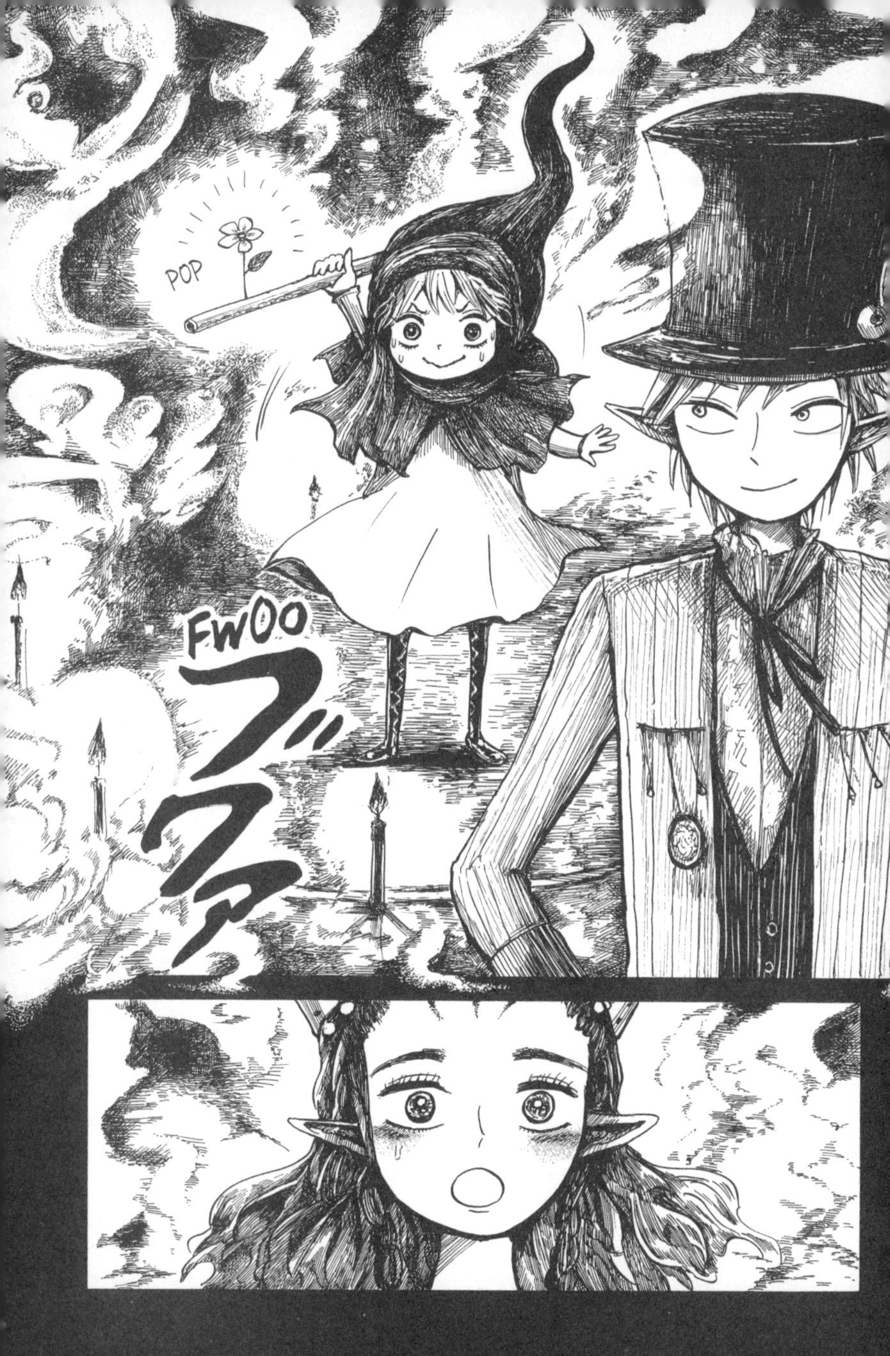
POP
FWOO
ブワァ

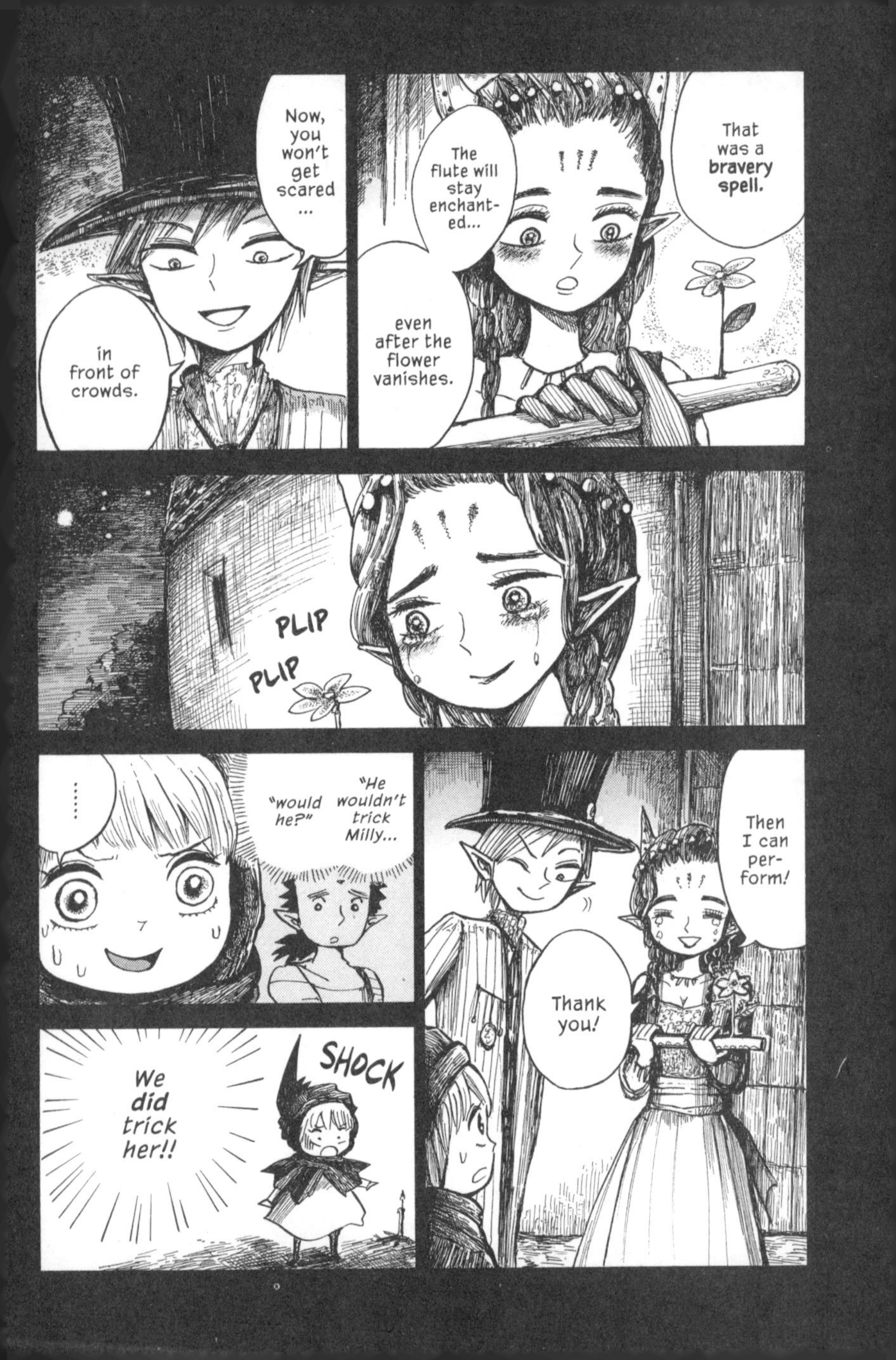
That was a bravery spell.
The flute will stay enchant-ed...
even after the flower vanishes.
Now, you won't get scared ...
in front of crowds.
PLIP
PLIP
Then I can per-form!
Thank you!
"He wouldn't trick Milly...
"would he?"
......
SHOCK
We did trick her!!

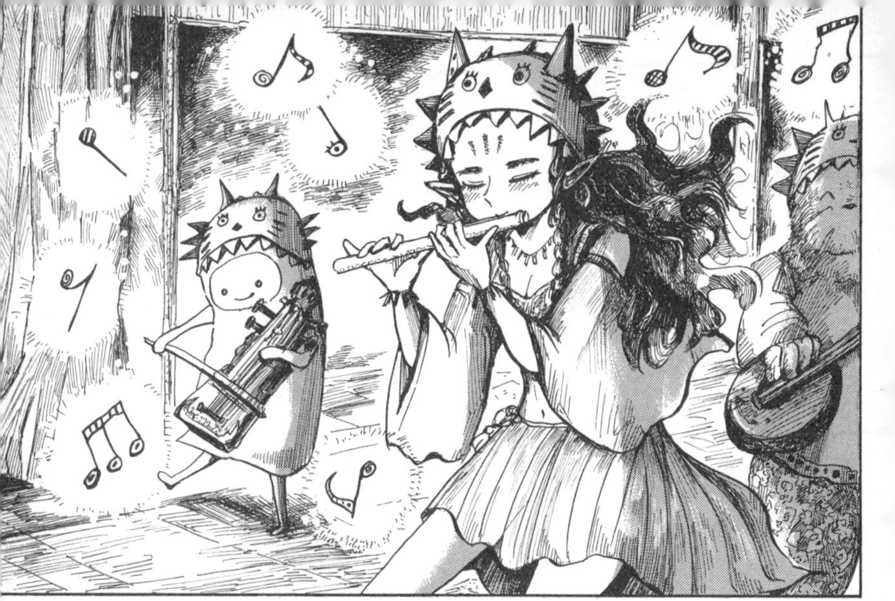

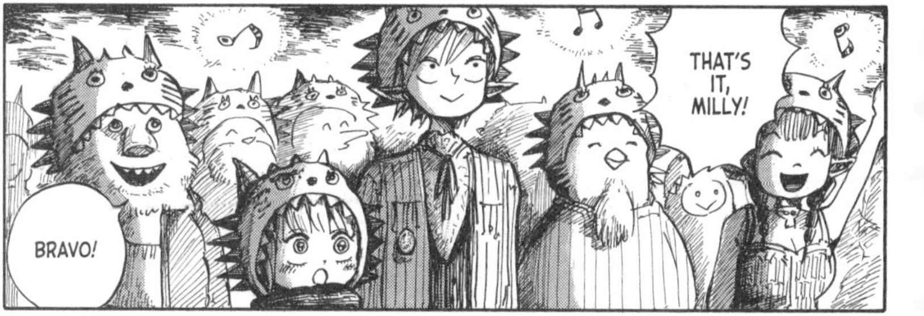
THAT'S IT, MILLY!
BRAVO!

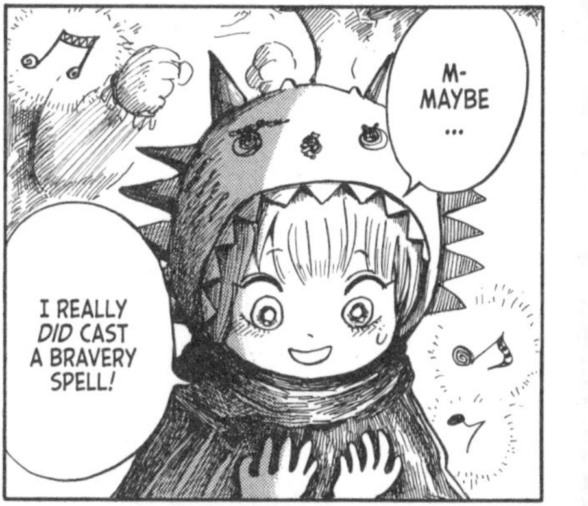
M-MAYBE ...
I REALLY *DID* CAST A BRAVERY SPELL!

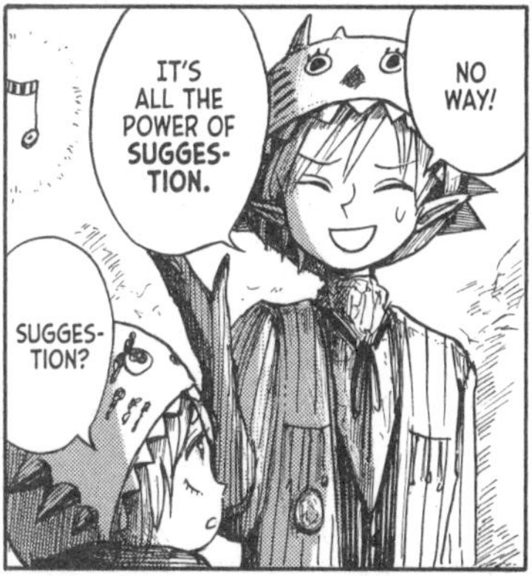
NO WAY!
IT'S ALL THE POWER OF **SUGGESTION.**
SUGGESTION?

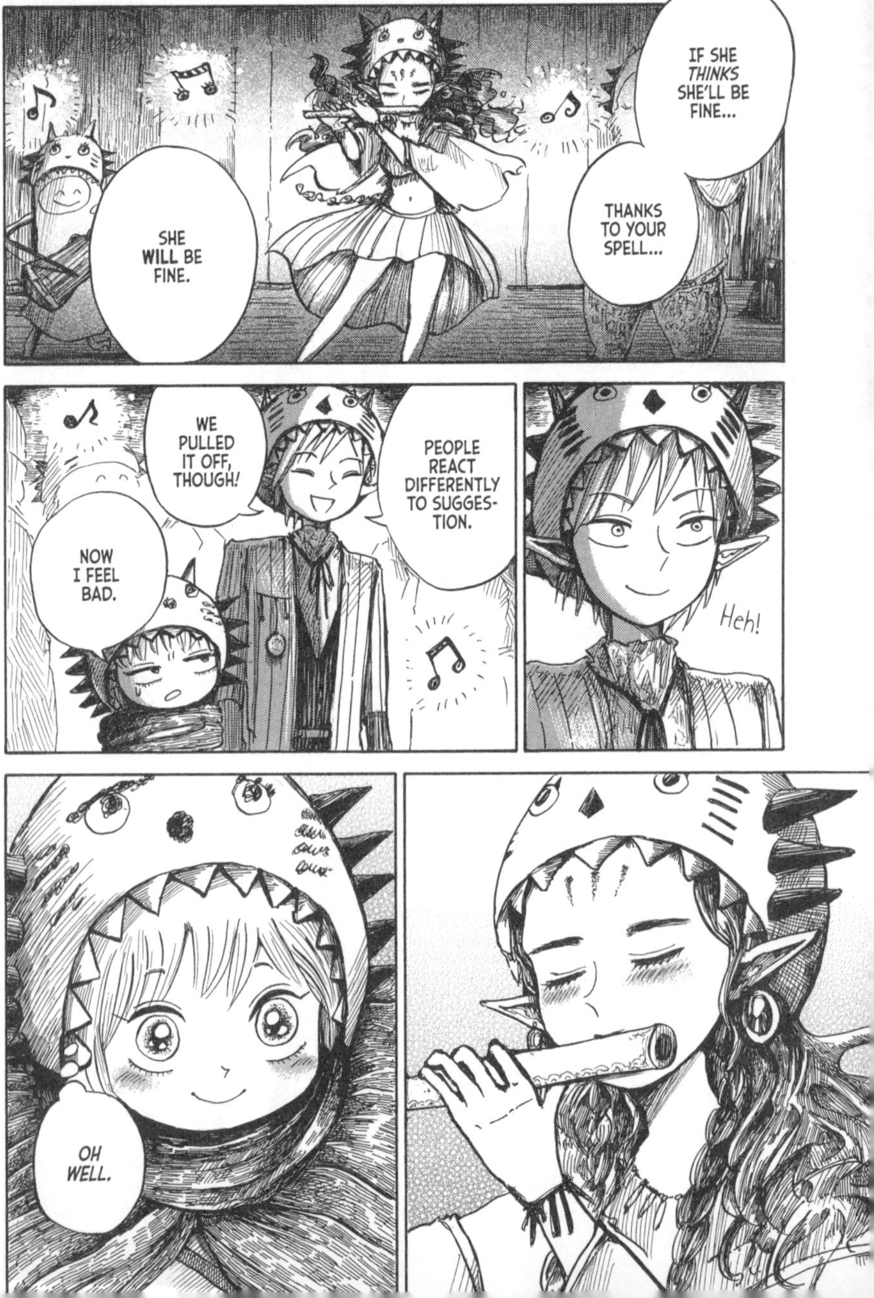
IF SHE THINKS SHE'LL BE FINE...
THANKS TO YOUR SPELL...
SHE WILL BE FINE.
Heh!
PEOPLE REACT DIFFERENTLY TO SUGGES-TION.
WE PULLED IT OFF, THOUGH!
NOW I FEEL BAD.
OH WELL.

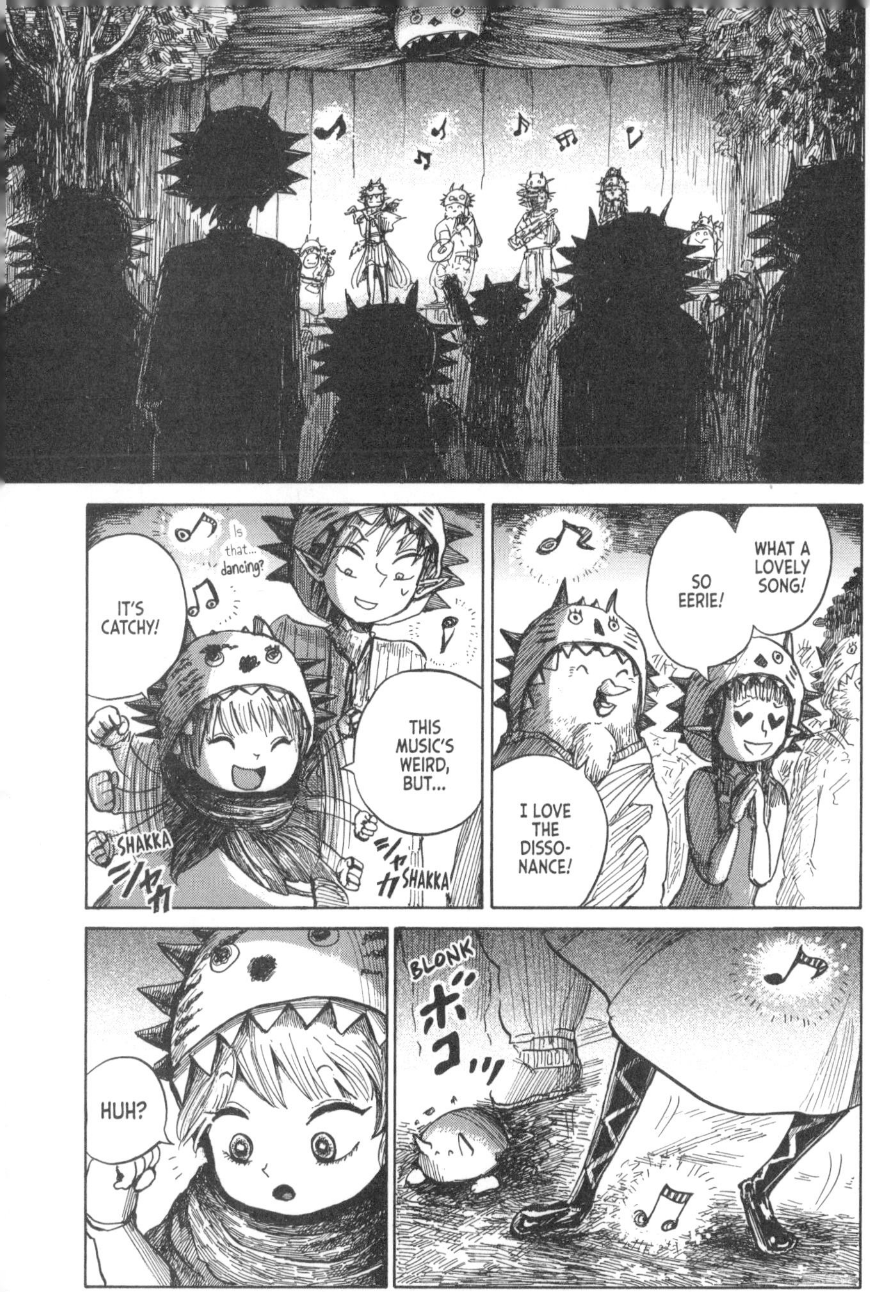
WHAT A LOVELY SONG!
SO EERIE!
I LOVE THE DISSONANCE!
Is that... dancing?
IT'S CATCHY!
THIS MUSIC'S WEIRD, BUT...
シャカ SHAKKA!
SHAKKA シャカ
BLONK ボコッ
HUH?

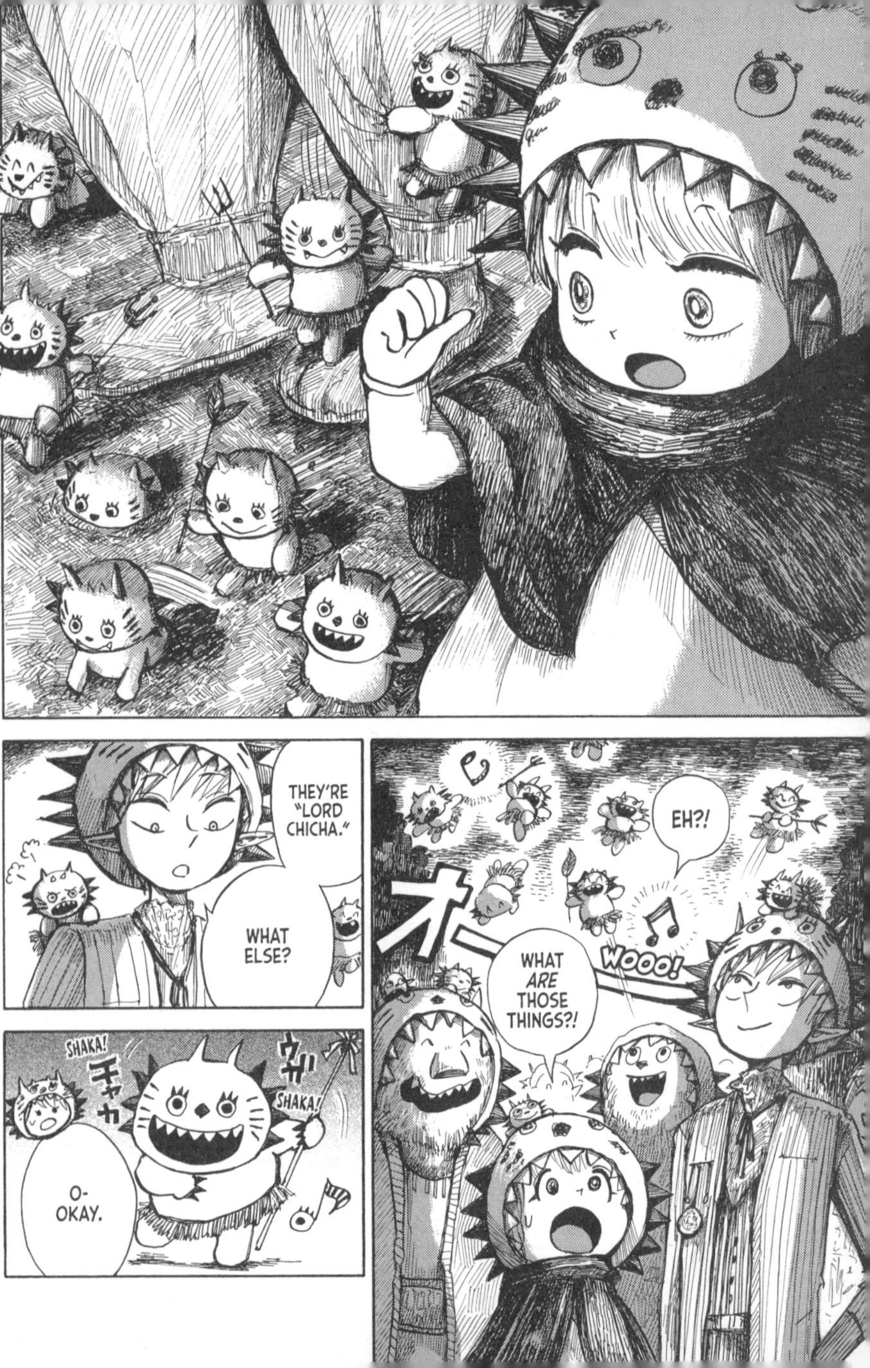
EH?!
WOOO!
WHAT *ARE* THOSE THINGS?!
オー
THEY'RE "LORD CHICHA."
WHAT ELSE?
SHAKA!
ウガ
SHAKA!
チャカ
O-OKAY.

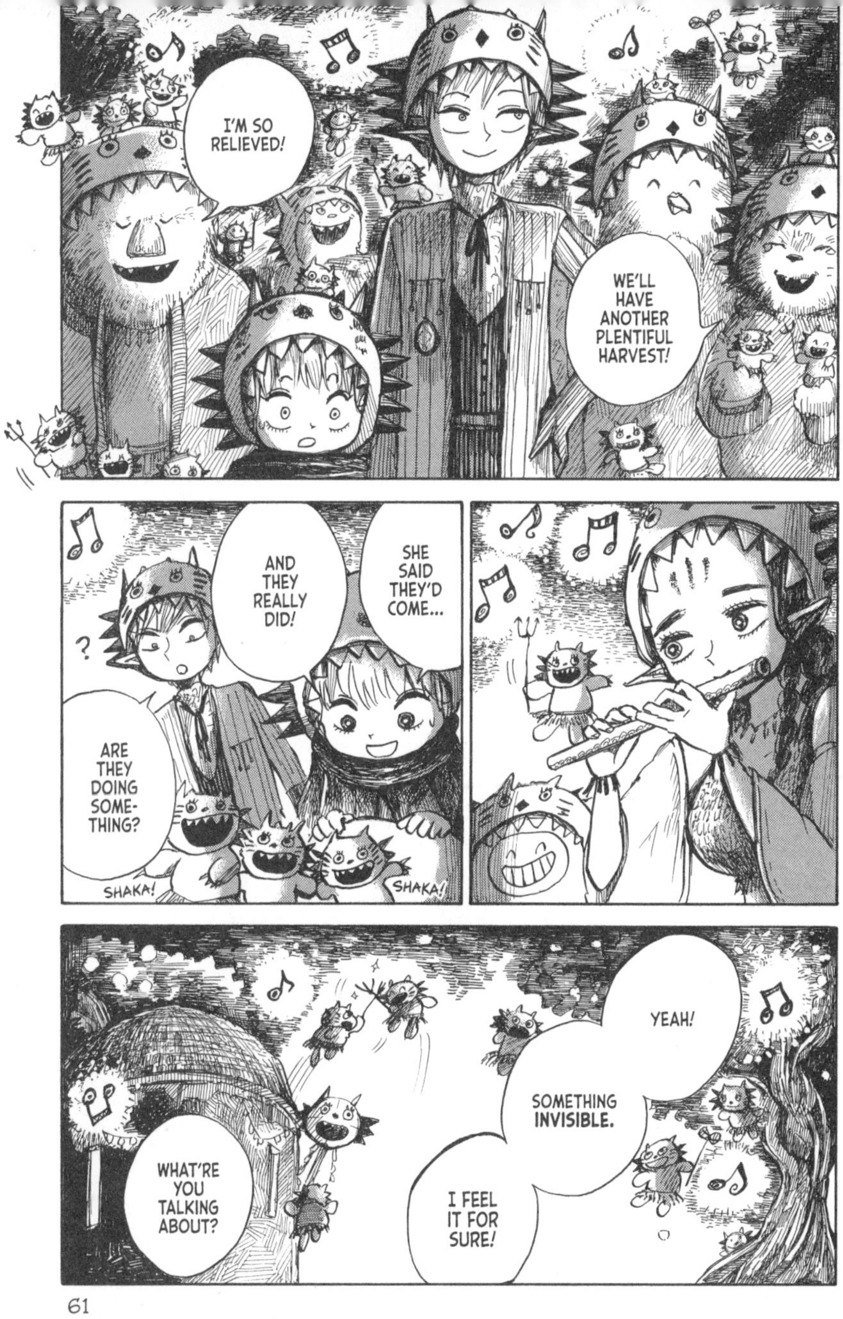
WE'LL HAVE ANOTHER PLENTIFUL HARVEST!
I'M SO RELIEVED!
SHE SAID THEY'D COME...
AND THEY REALLY DID!
ARE THEY DOING SOME-THING?
SHAKA!
SHAKA!
YEAH!
SOMETHING INVISIBLE.
I FEEL IT FOR SURE!
WHAT'RE YOU TALKING ABOUT?

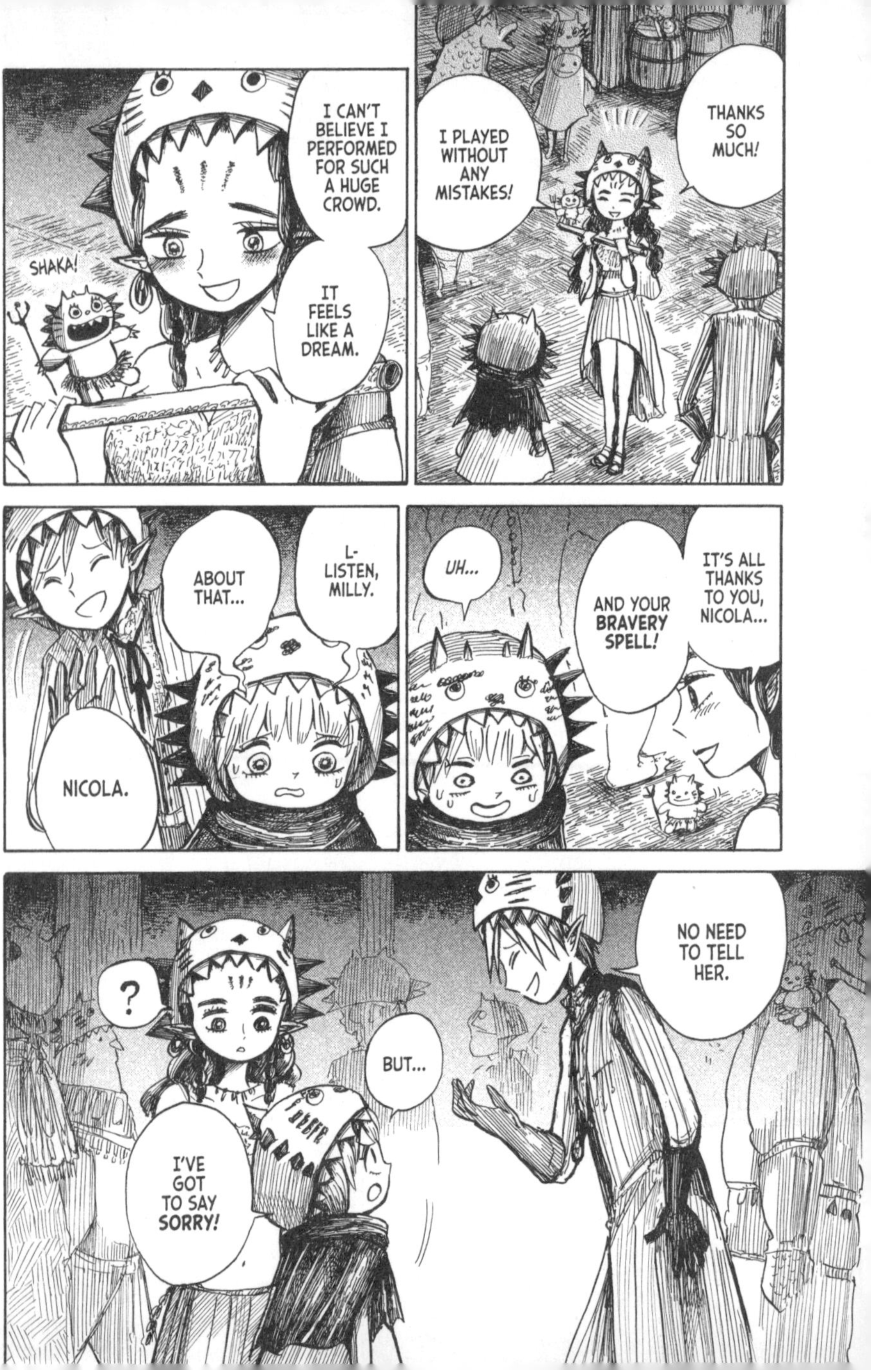
THANKS SO MUCH!
I PLAYED WITHOUT ANY MISTAKES!
I CAN'T BELIEVE I PERFORMED FOR SUCH A HUGE CROWD.
IT FEELS LIKE A DREAM.
SHAKA!
IT'S ALL THANKS TO YOU, NICOLA...
AND YOUR BRAVERY SPELL!
UH...
L-LISTEN, MILLY.
ABOUT THAT...
NICOLA.
NO NEED TO TELL HER.
BUT...
?
I'VE GOT TO SAY SORRY!

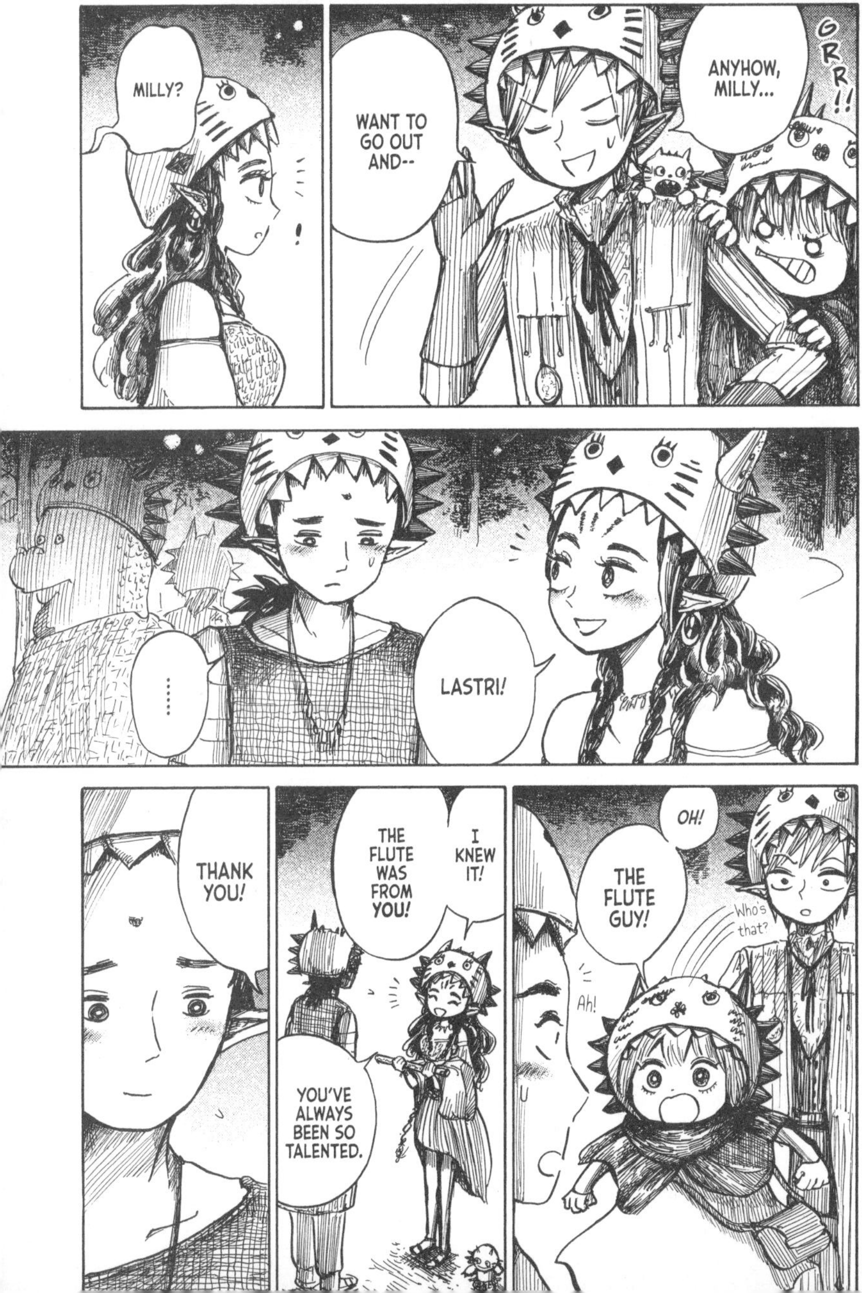
ANYHOW, MILLY...
GRR!!
WANT TO GO OUT AND--
MILLY?
!
LASTRI!
......
OH!
THE FLUTE GUY!
Who's that?
Ah!
I KNEW IT!
THE FLUTE WAS FROM YOU!
YOU'VE ALWAYS BEEN SO TALENTED.
THANK YOU!

AH!

UM...

NICOLA ACTUALLY...

CAST A **BRAVERY SPELL** ON THIS *FLUTE!*

MM-HMM!

THAT'S WHY I PLAYED FINE.

HUH?

A SPELL?

?

CLENCH

FOR A SEC?

CAN I SEE IT...

UM?

64

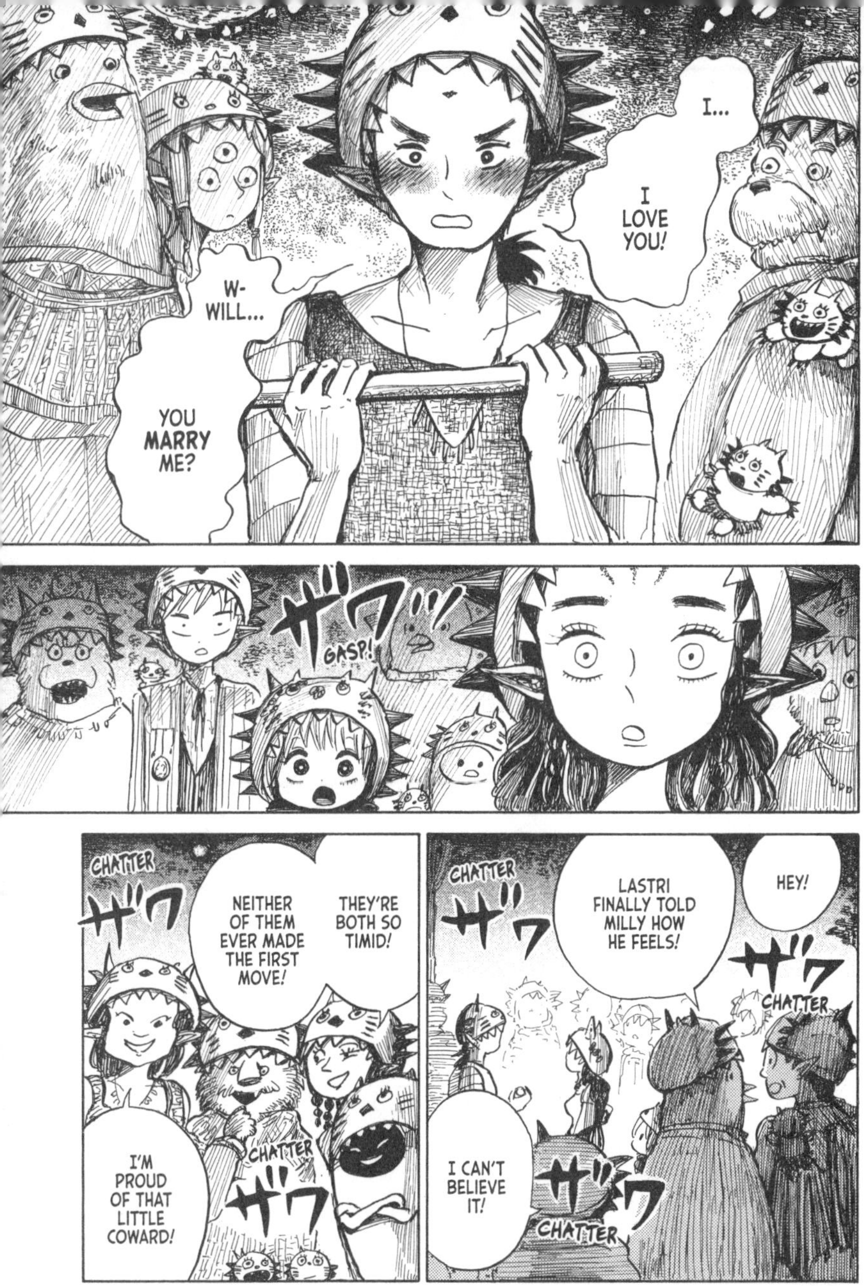
I...
I LOVE YOU!
W- WILL...
YOU MARRY ME?
ザワ!!
GASP!
HEY!
LASTRI FINALLY TOLD MILLY HOW HE FEELS!
ザワ
CHATTER
CHATTER
ザワ
ザワ
CHATTER
I CAN'T BELIEVE IT!
THEY'RE BOTH SO TIMID!
NEITHER OF THEM EVER MADE THE FIRST MOVE!
CHATTER
ザワ
CHATTER
ザワ
I'M PROUD OF THAT LITTLE COWARD!

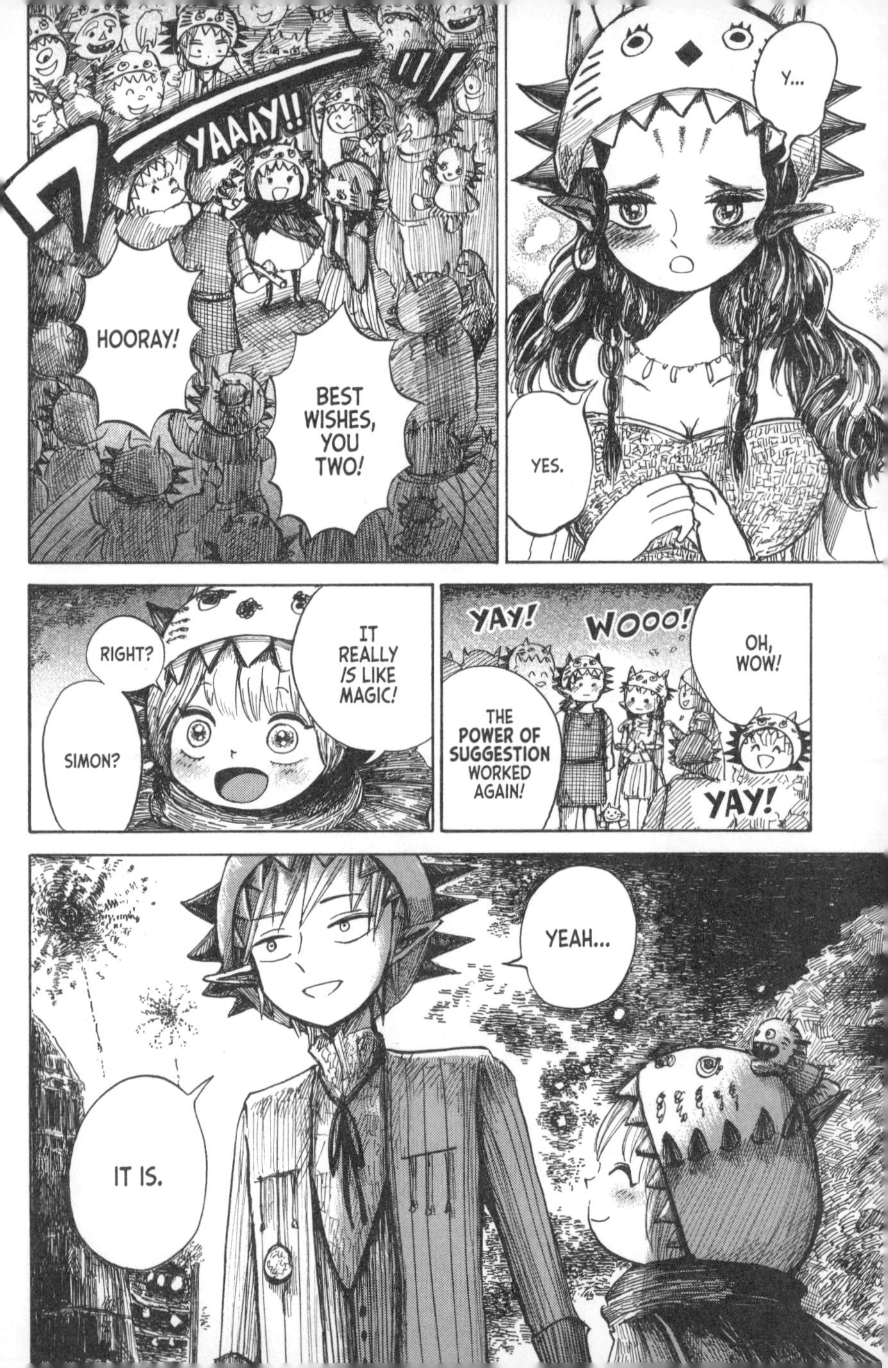
Y...
YES.
YAAAY!!
HOORAY!
BEST WISHES, YOU TWO!
OH, WOW!
WOOO!
YAY!
THE POWER OF SUGGESTION WORKED AGAIN!
YAY!
IT REALLY *IS* LIKE MAGIC!
RIGHT?
SIMON?
YEAH...
IT IS.

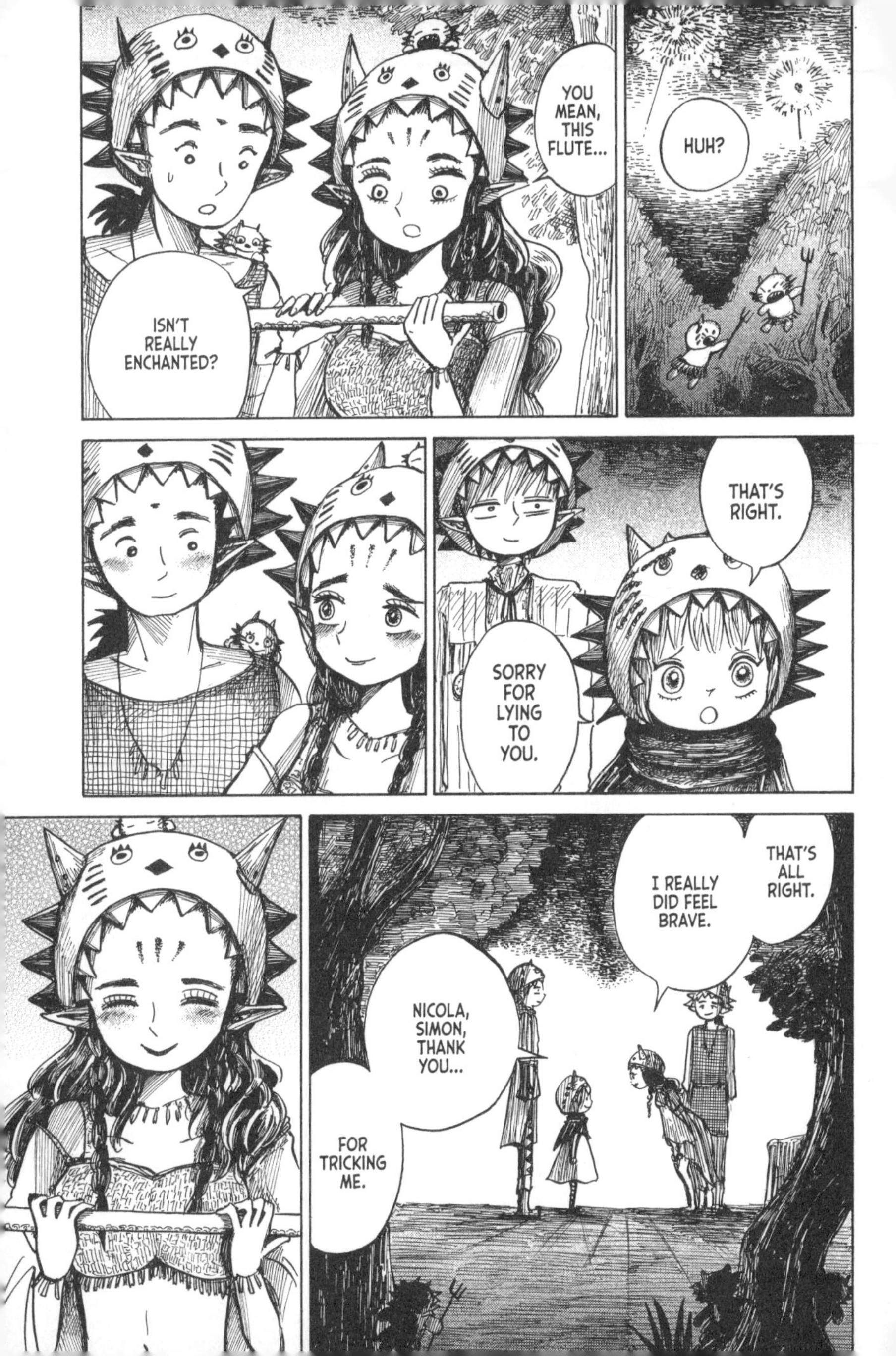
HUH?
YOU MEAN, THIS FLUTE...
ISN'T REALLY ENCHANTED?
THAT'S RIGHT.
SORRY FOR LYING TO YOU.
THAT'S ALL RIGHT.
I REALLY DID FEEL BRAVE.
NICOLA, SIMON, THANK YOU...
FOR TRICKING ME.

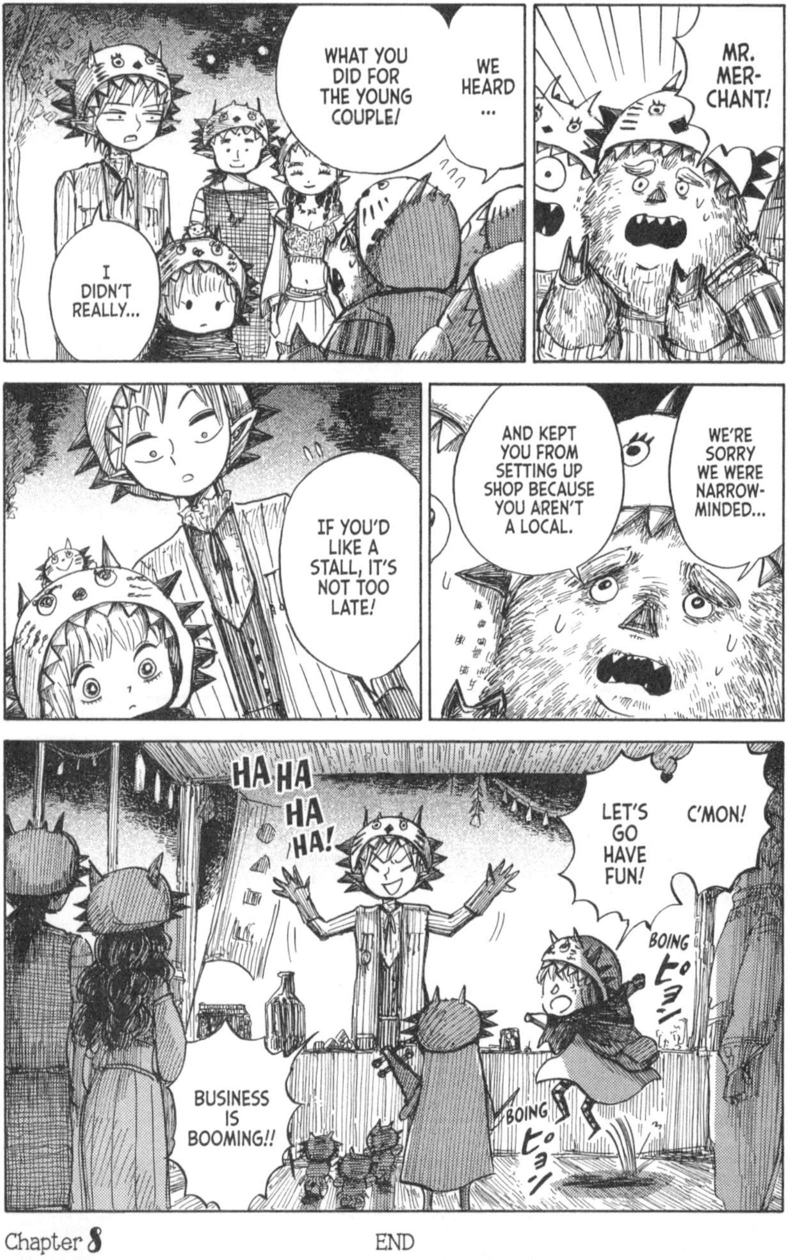
MR. MER-CHANT!
WE HEARD ...
WHAT YOU DID FOR THE YOUNG COUPLE!
I DIDN'T REALLY...
WE'RE SORRY WE WERE NARROW-MINDED...
AND KEPT YOU FROM SETTING UP SHOP BECAUSE YOU AREN'T A LOCAL.
IF YOU'D LIKE A STALL, IT'S NOT TOO LATE!
C'MON!
LET'S GO HAVE FUN!
HA HA HA HA!
BOING
ピョン
BUSINESS IS BOOMING!!
BOING
ピョン

Chapter 8 END

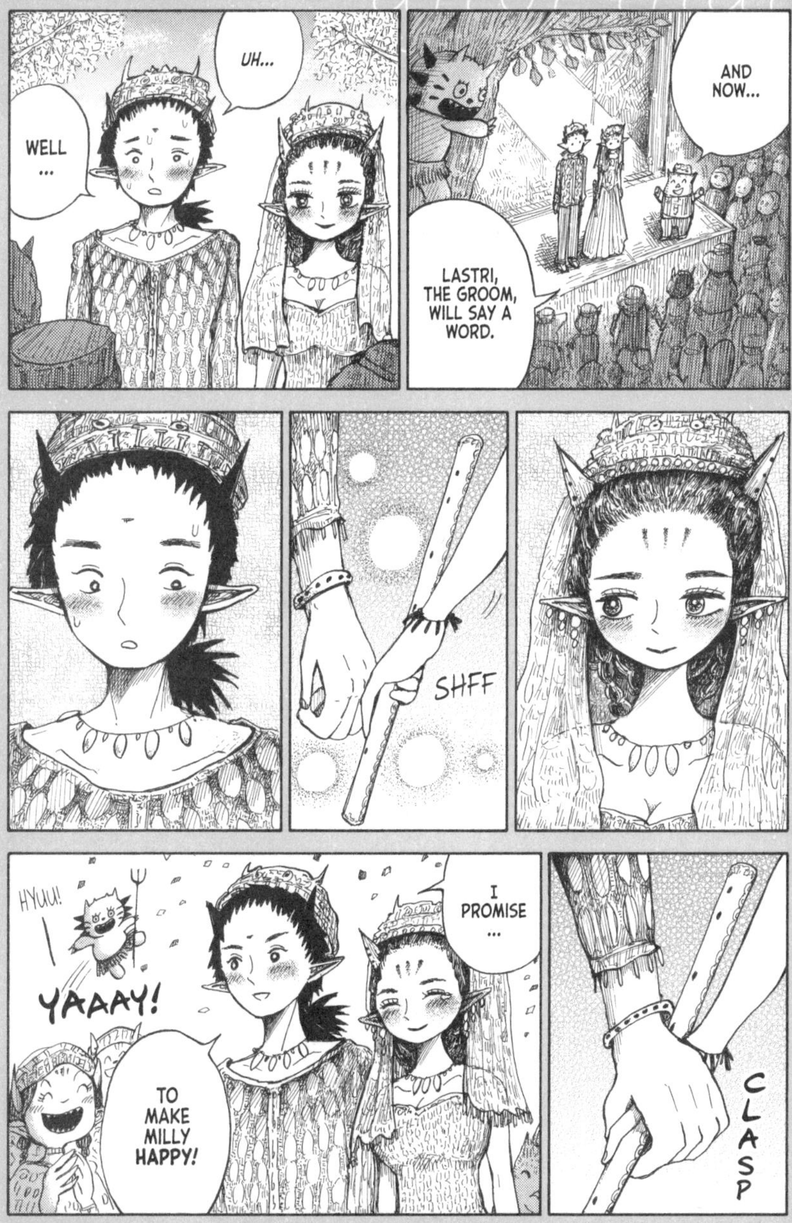
AND NOW...
LASTRI, THE GROOM, WILL SAY A WORD.
UH...
WELL ...
SHFF
CLASP
I PROMISE ...
HYUU!
YAAAY!
TO MAKE MILLY HAPPY!

Nicola Traveling Around The Demons' World.

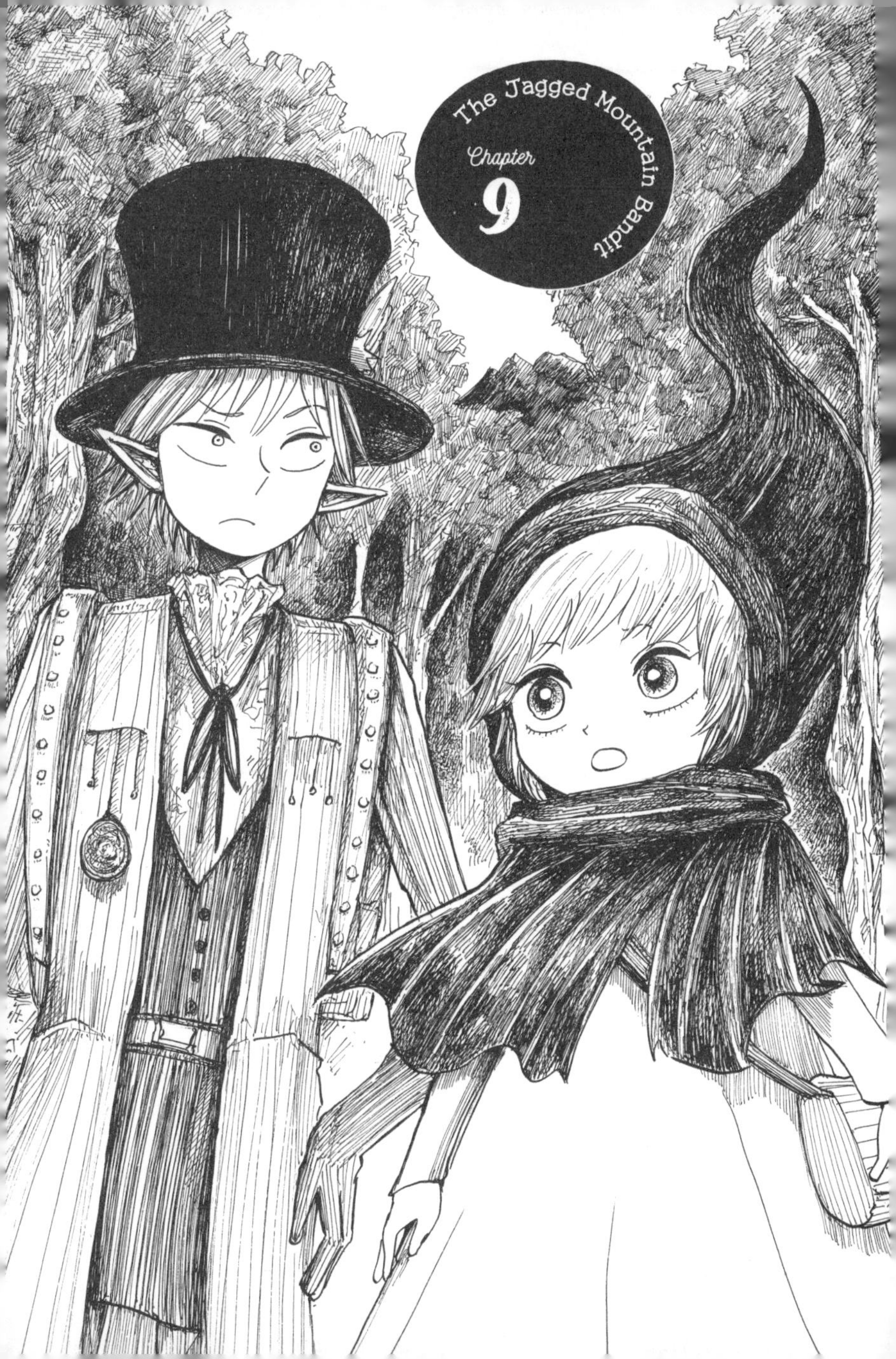
The Jagged Mountain Bandit
Chapter
9

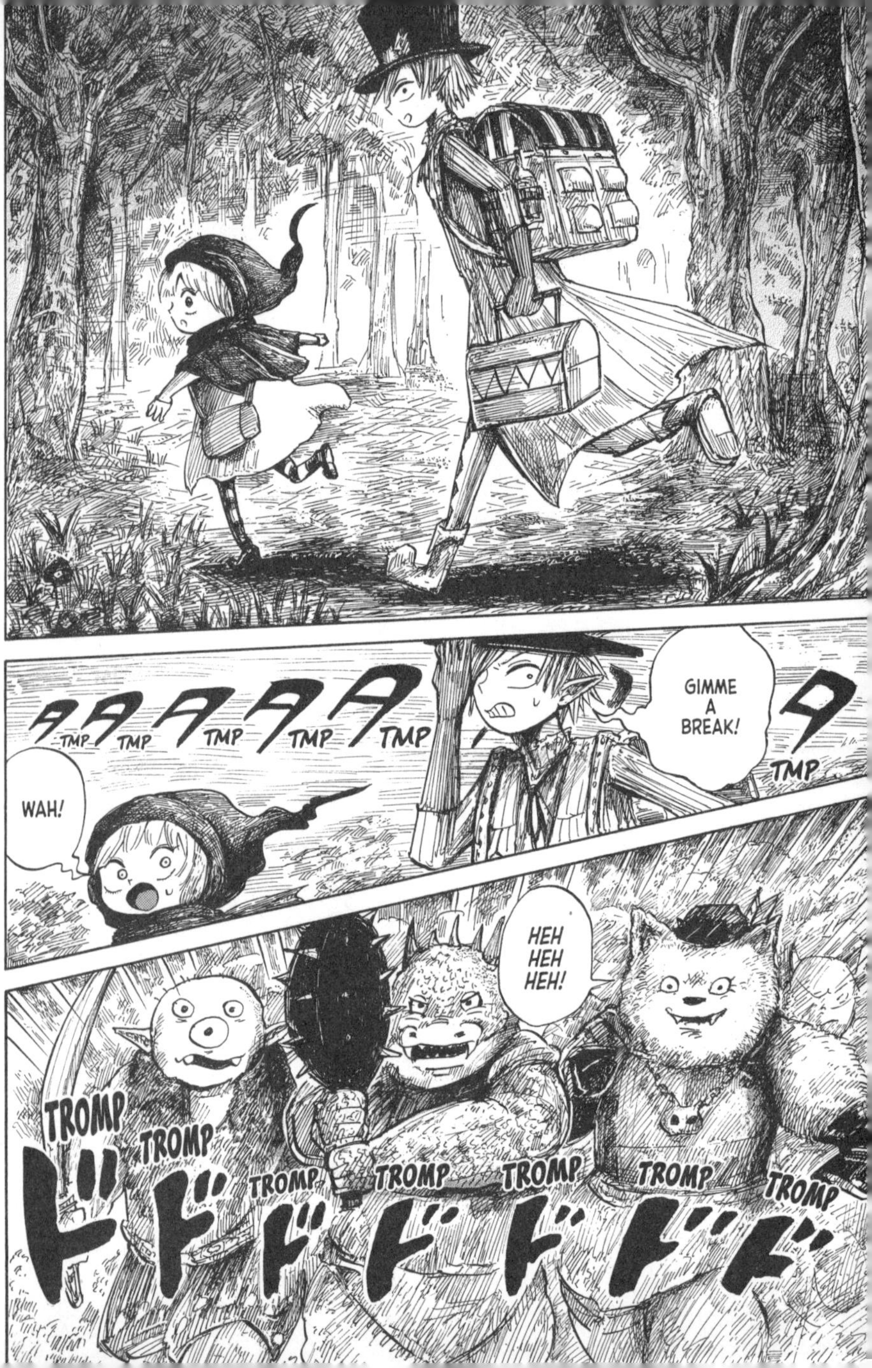
TMP
GIMME A BREAK!
TMP
TMP
TMP
TMP
TMP
WAH!
HEH HEH HEH!
TROMP
TROMP
TROMP
TROMP
TROMP
TROMP
TROMP
ドドドドドドド

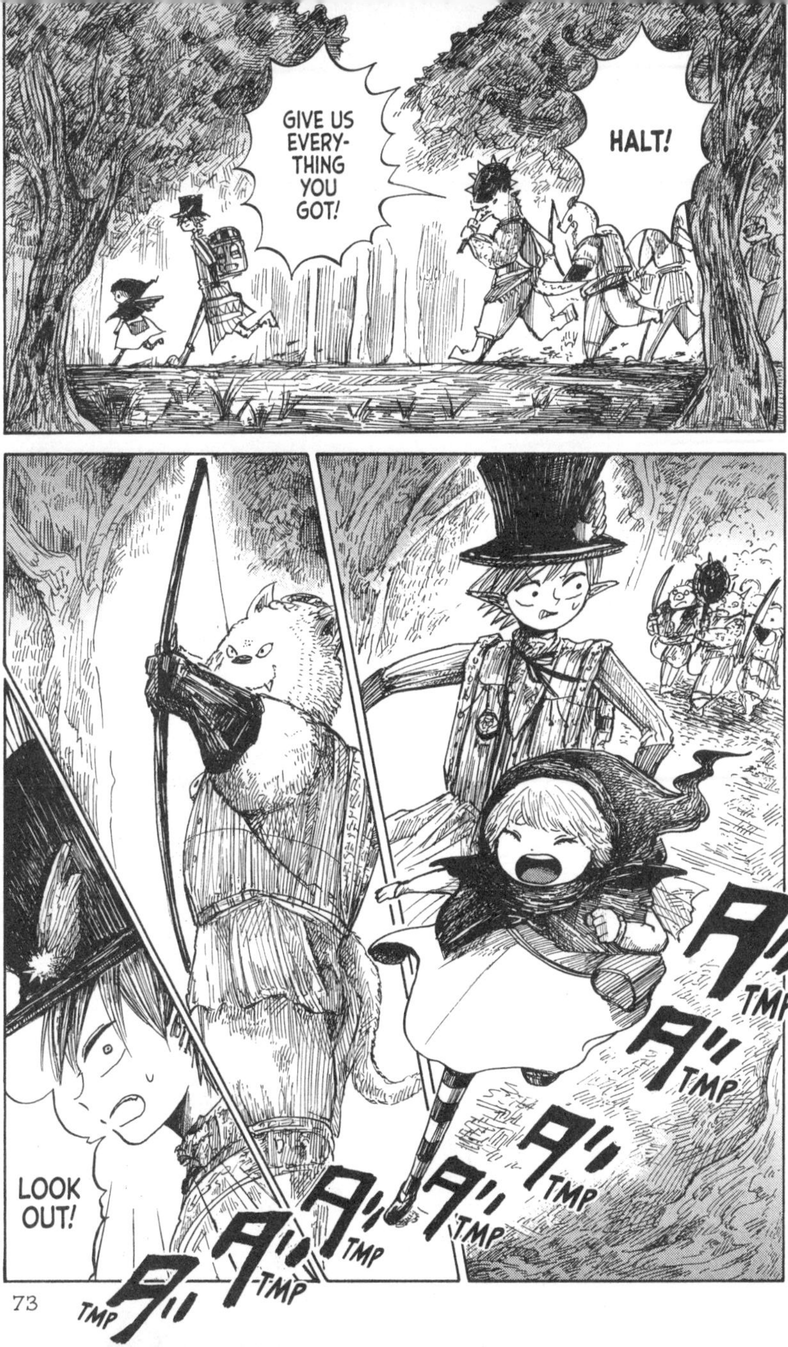
HALT!
GIVE US EVERY-THING YOU GOT!
ダッ TMP
ダッ TMP
ダッ TMP
ダッ TMP
ダッ TMP
ダッ TMP
ダッ TMP
LOOK OUT!

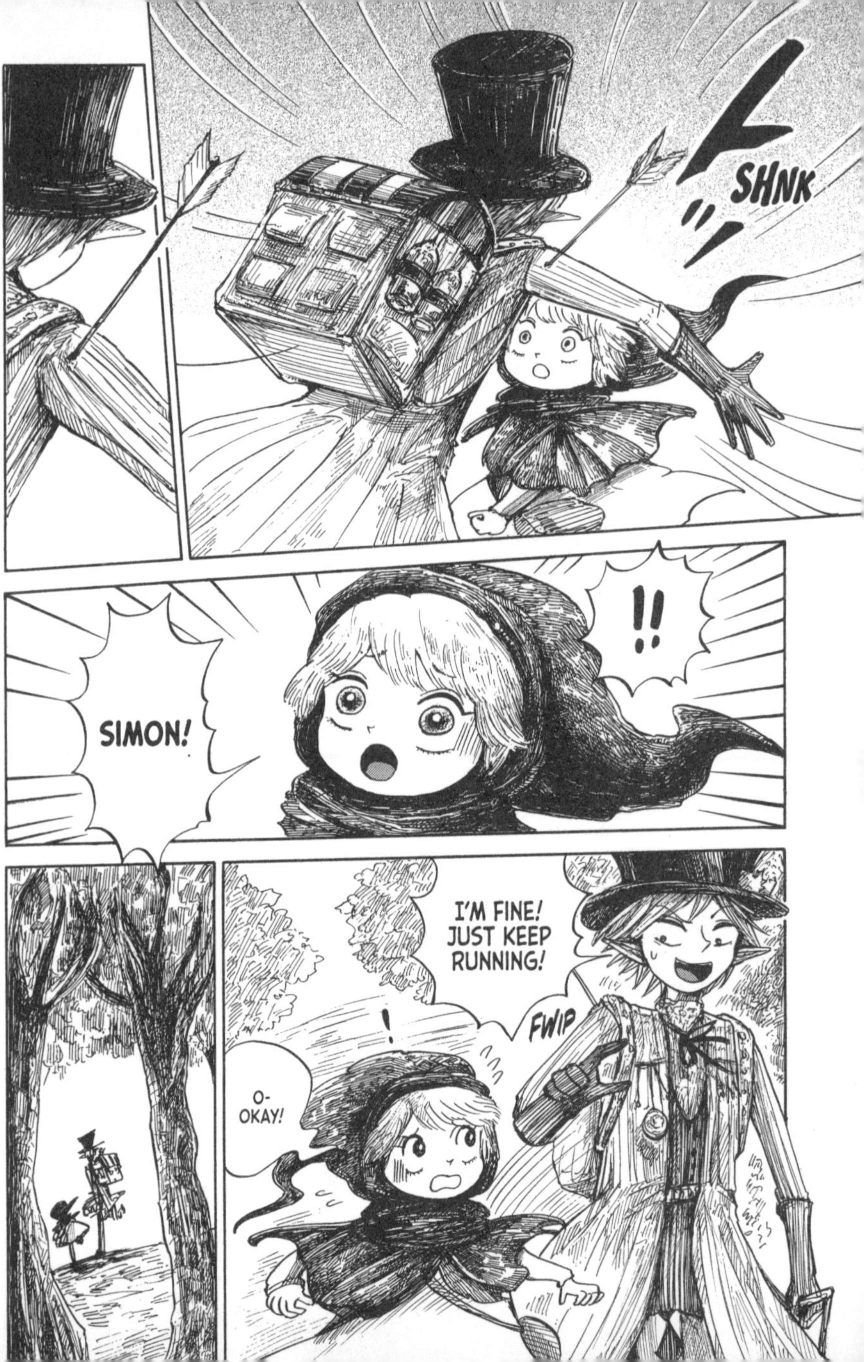
SHNK
!!
SIMON!
I'M FINE! JUST KEEP RUNNING!
FWIP
!
O-OKAY!

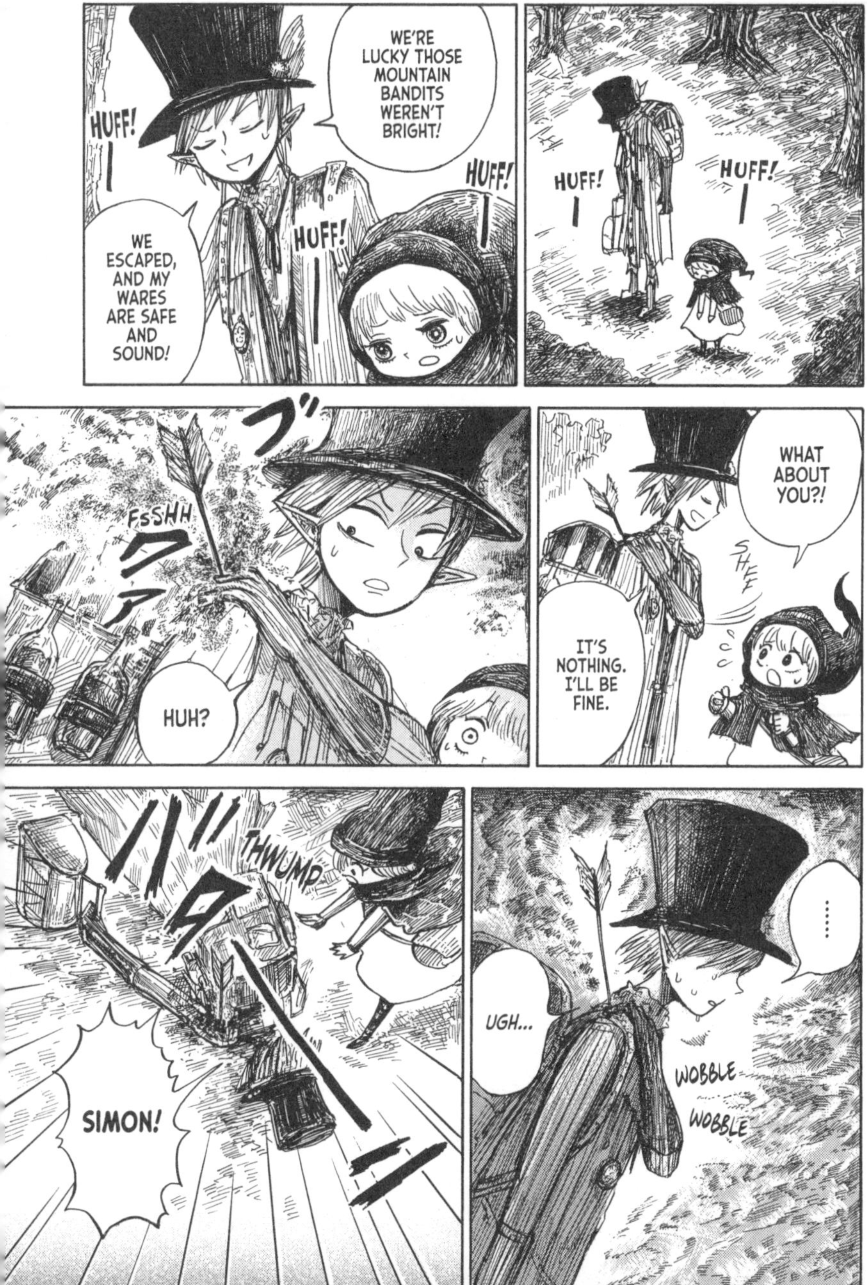
HUFF!
HUFF!
WE'RE LUCKY THOSE MOUNTAIN BANDITS WEREN'T BRIGHT!
HUFF!
HUFF!
HUFF!
WE ESCAPED, AND MY WARES ARE SAFE AND SOUND!
WHAT ABOUT YOU?!
SHFF
IT'S NOTHING. I'LL BE FINE.
FSSHH
HUH?
......
UGH...
WOBBLE
WOBBLE
THWUMP
SIMON!

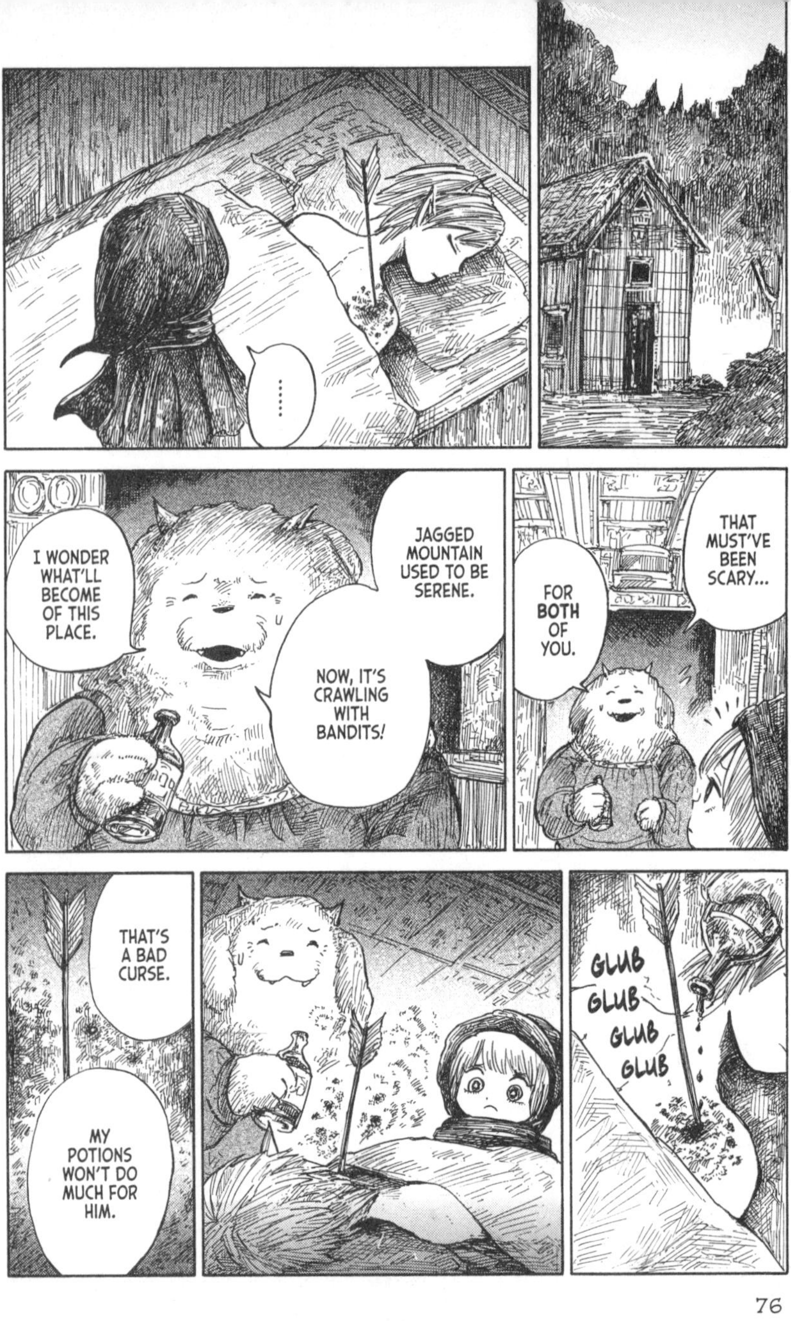
……
THAT MUST'VE BEEN SCARY...
FOR BOTH OF YOU.
JAGGED MOUNTAIN USED TO BE SERENE.
NOW, IT'S CRAWLING WITH BANDITS!
I WONDER WHAT'LL BECOME OF THIS PLACE.
GLUB GLUB GLUB GLUB
THAT'S A BAD CURSE.
MY POTIONS WON'T DO MUCH FOR HIM.

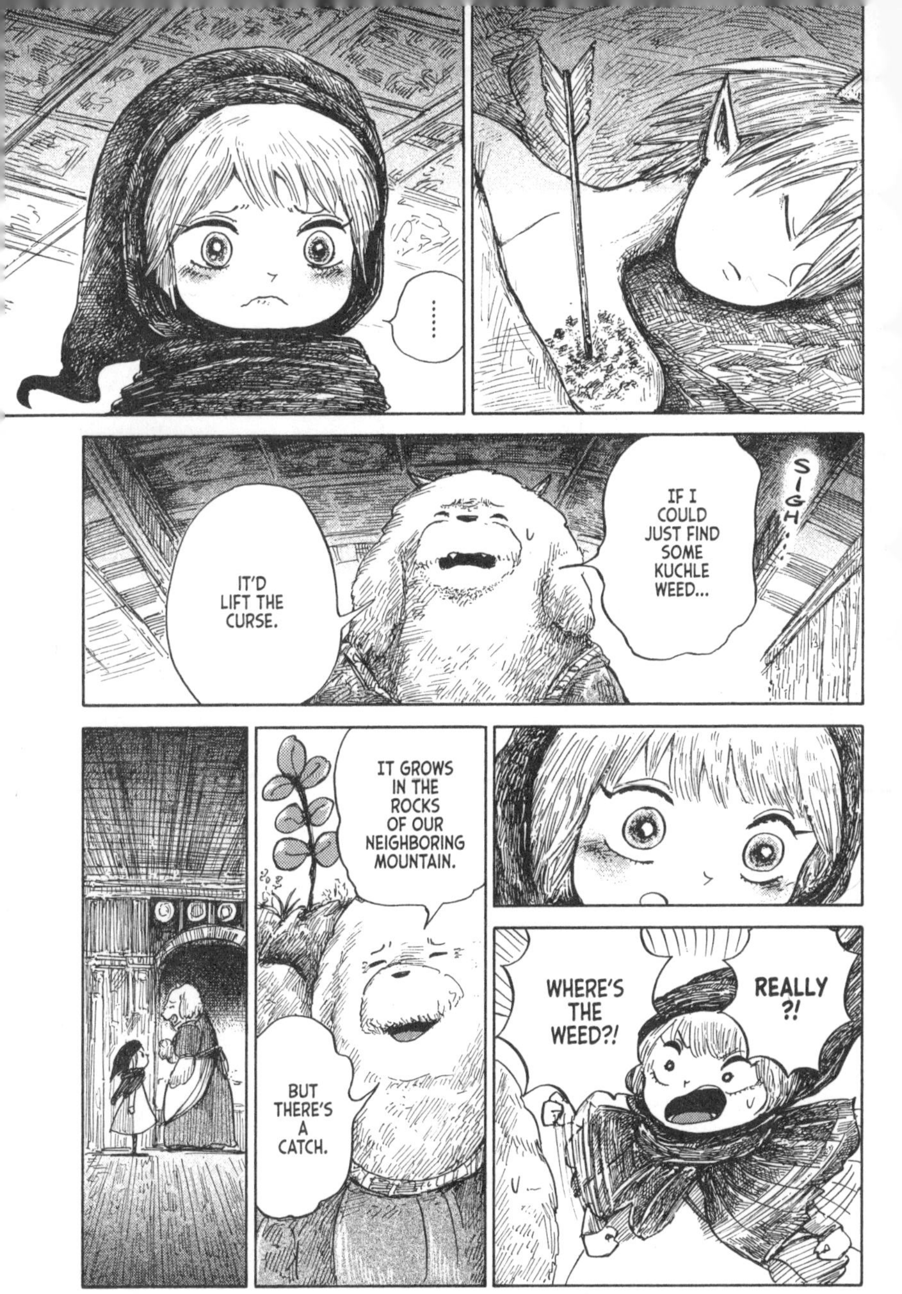
……
SIGH...
IF I COULD JUST FIND SOME KUCHLE WEED...
IT'D LIFT THE CURSE.
REALLY ?!
WHERE'S THE WEED?!
IT GROWS IN THE ROCKS OF OUR NEIGHBORING MOUNTAIN.
BUT THERE'S A CATCH.

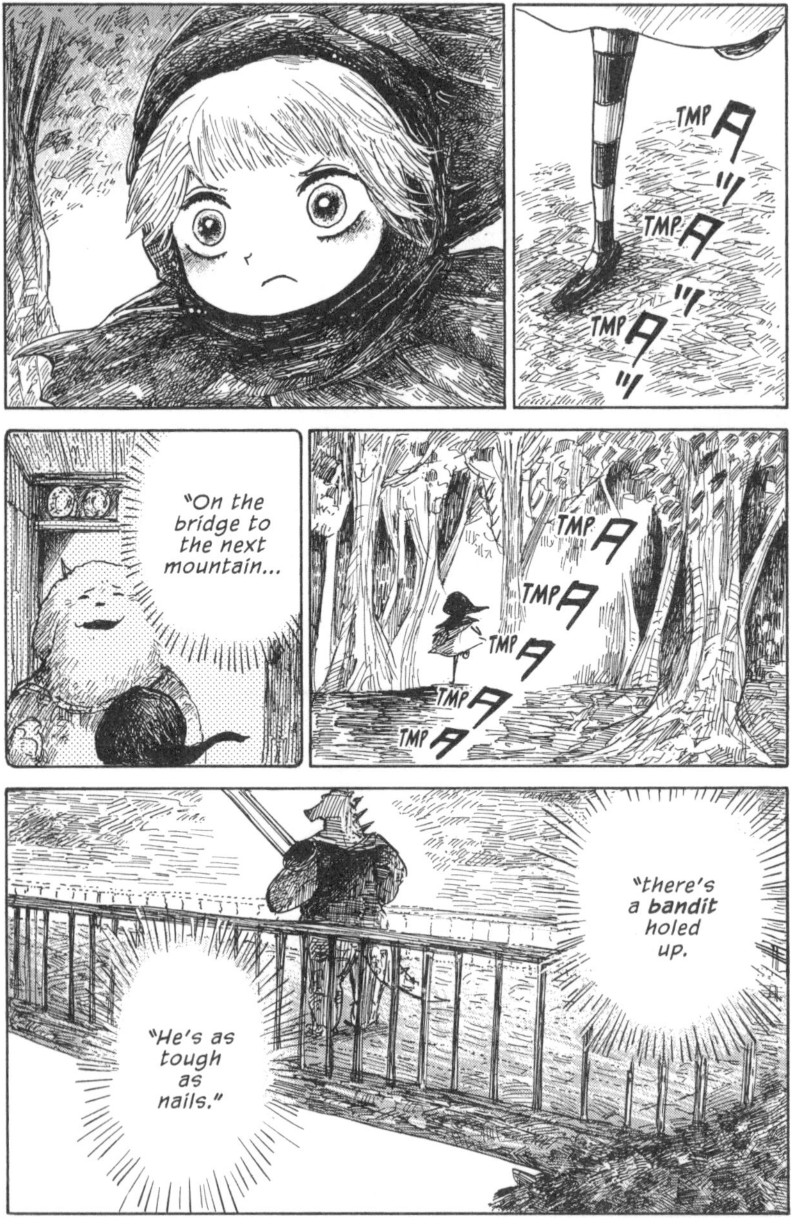

TMP タッ
TMP タッ
TMP タッ
TMP タッ
TMP タッ
TMP タ
TMP タ
TMP タ
"On the bridge to the next mountain...
"there's a **bandit** holed up.
"He's as tough as nails."

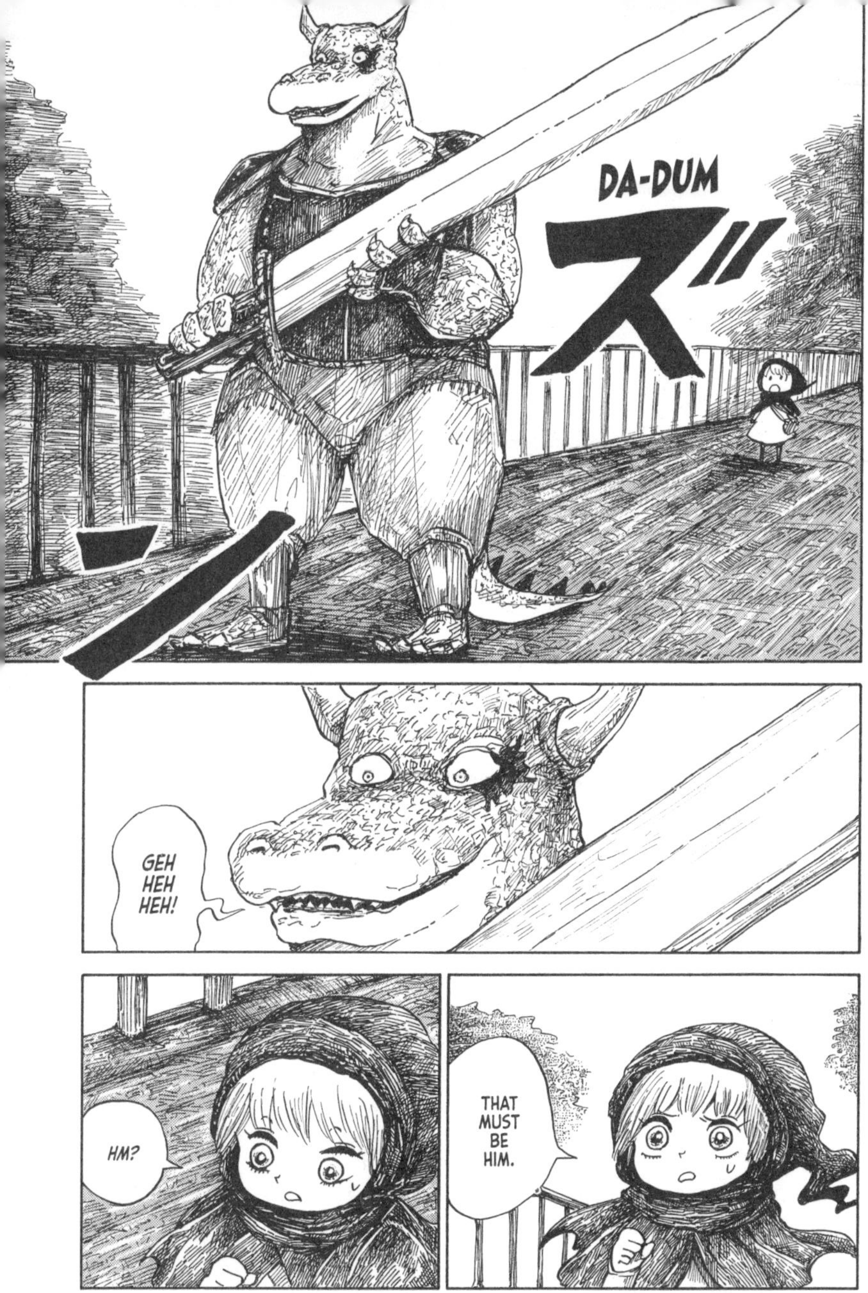
DA-DUM
ズ
GEH HEH HEH!
THAT MUST BE HIM.
HM?

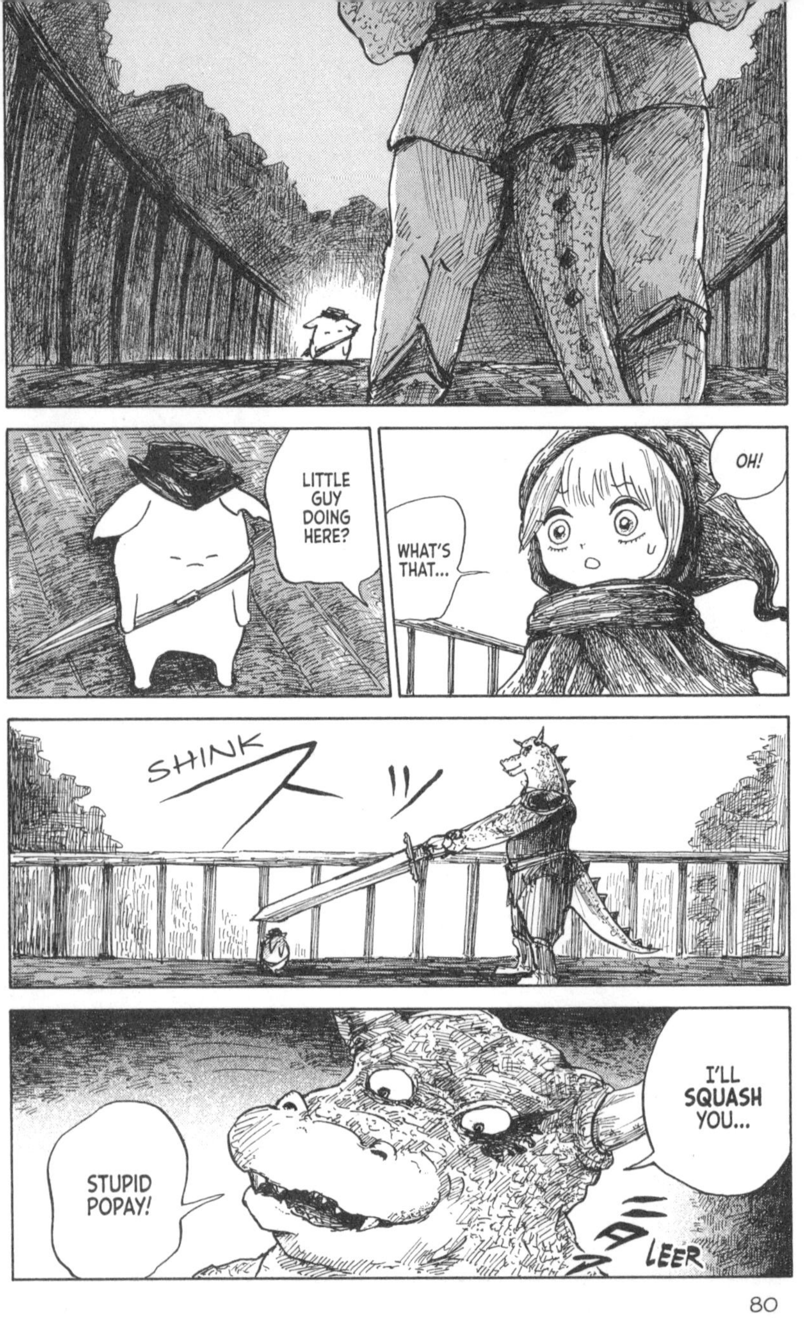
OH!
WHAT'S THAT...
LITTLE GUY DOING HERE?
SHINK
I'LL SQUASH YOU...
STUPID POPAY!
LEER

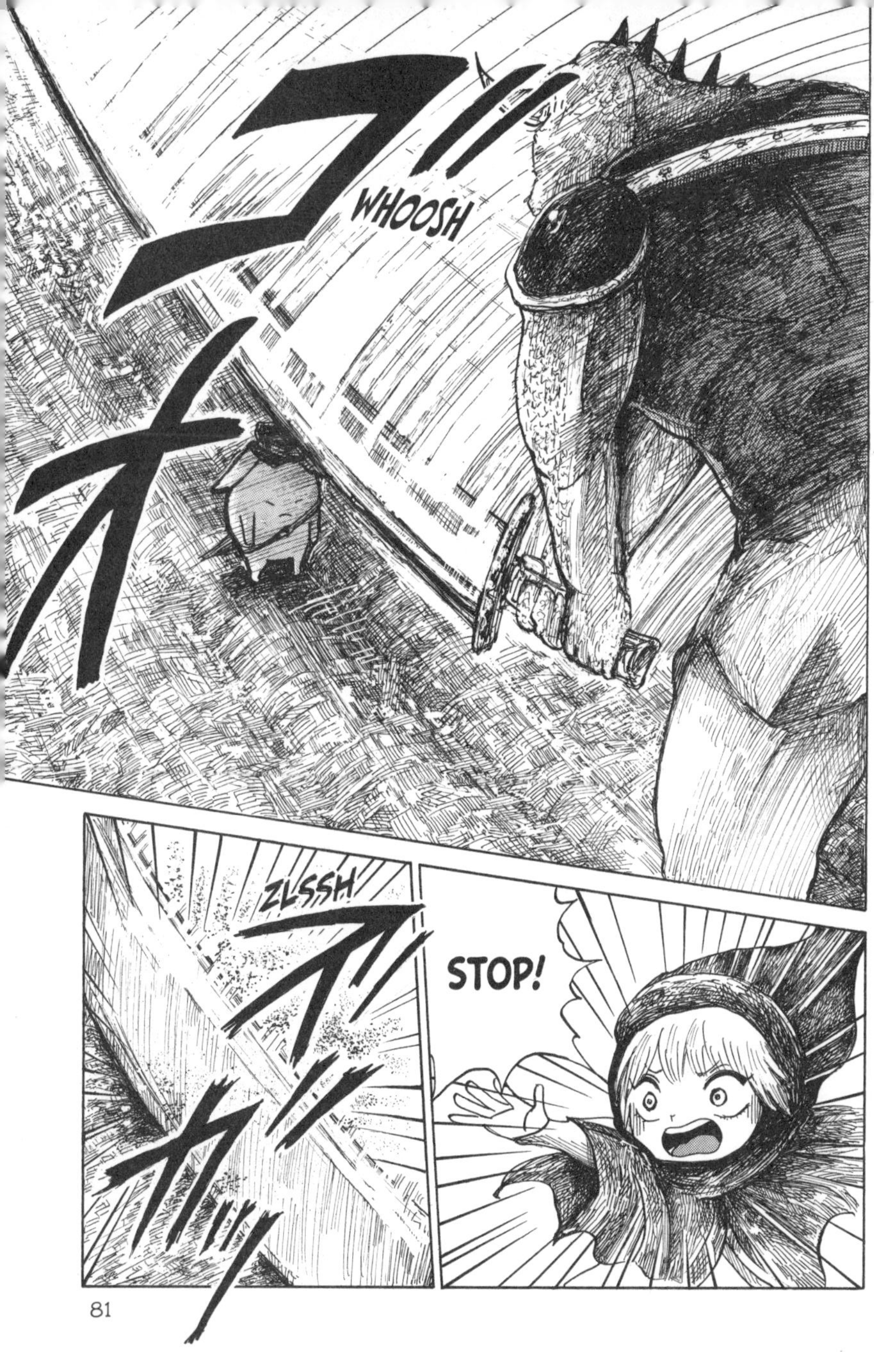
WHOOSH
STOP!
ZLSSH

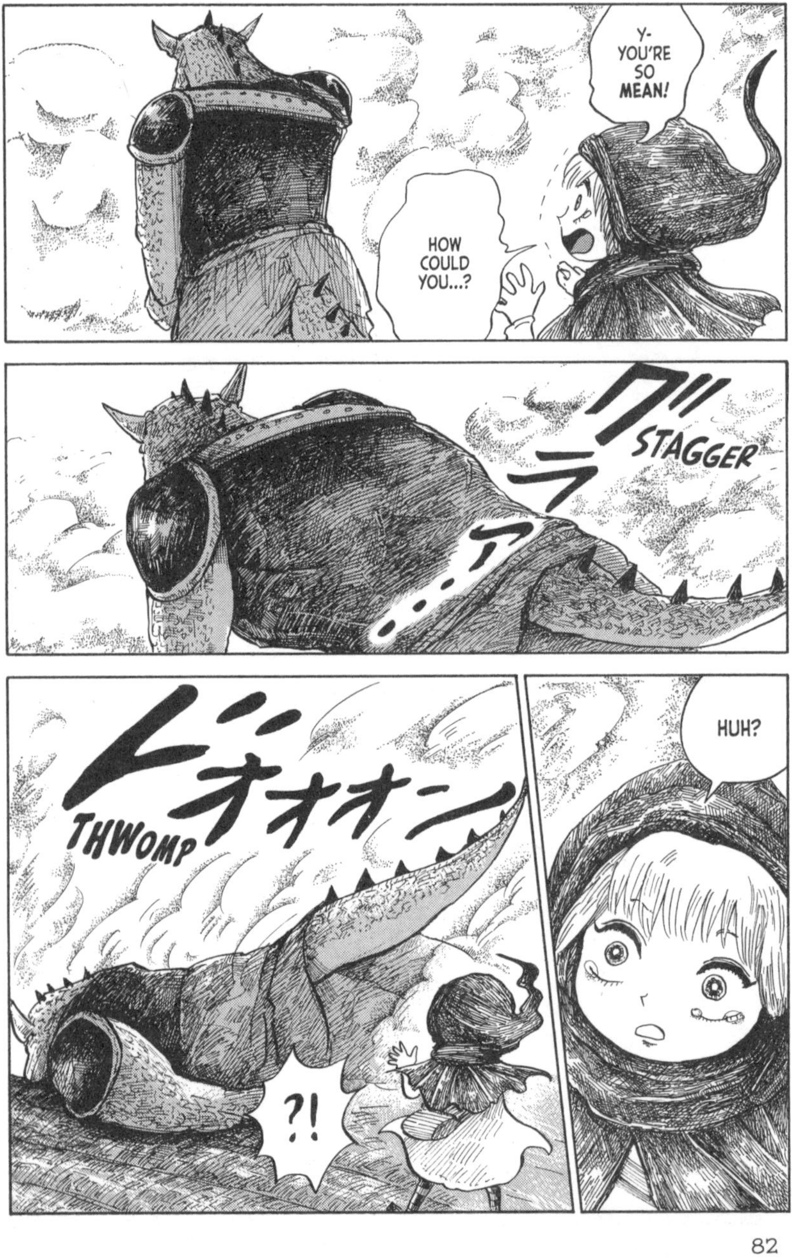

Y- YOU'RE SO MEAN!
HOW COULD YOU...?
STAGGER
HUH?
THWOMP
?!

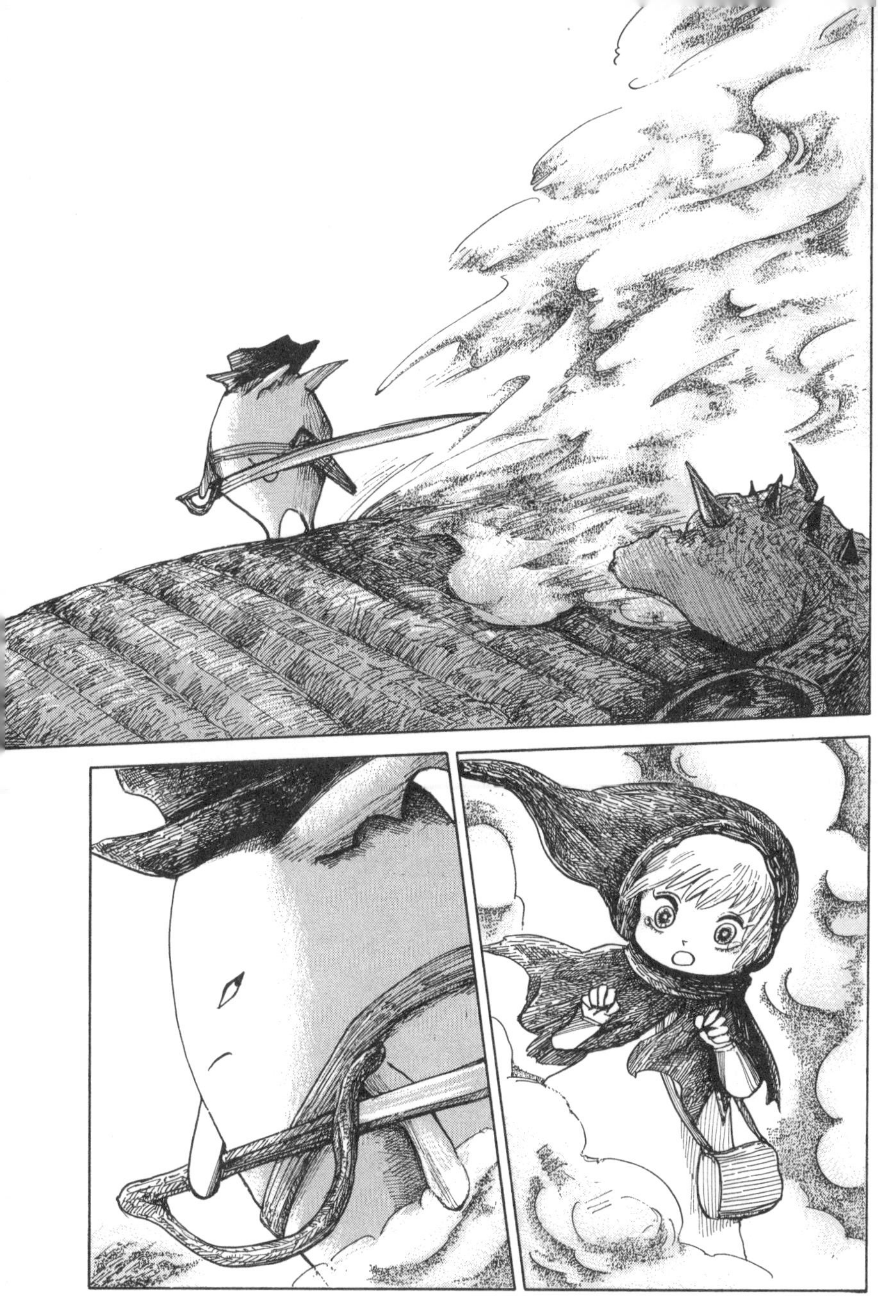

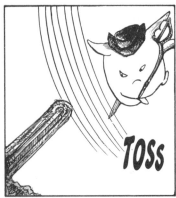

TOSS

HUP

YOU.

KLANG

IF YOU WANT TO CROSS THIS BRIDGE...

YOU'LL HAVE TO GO THROUGH *ME.*

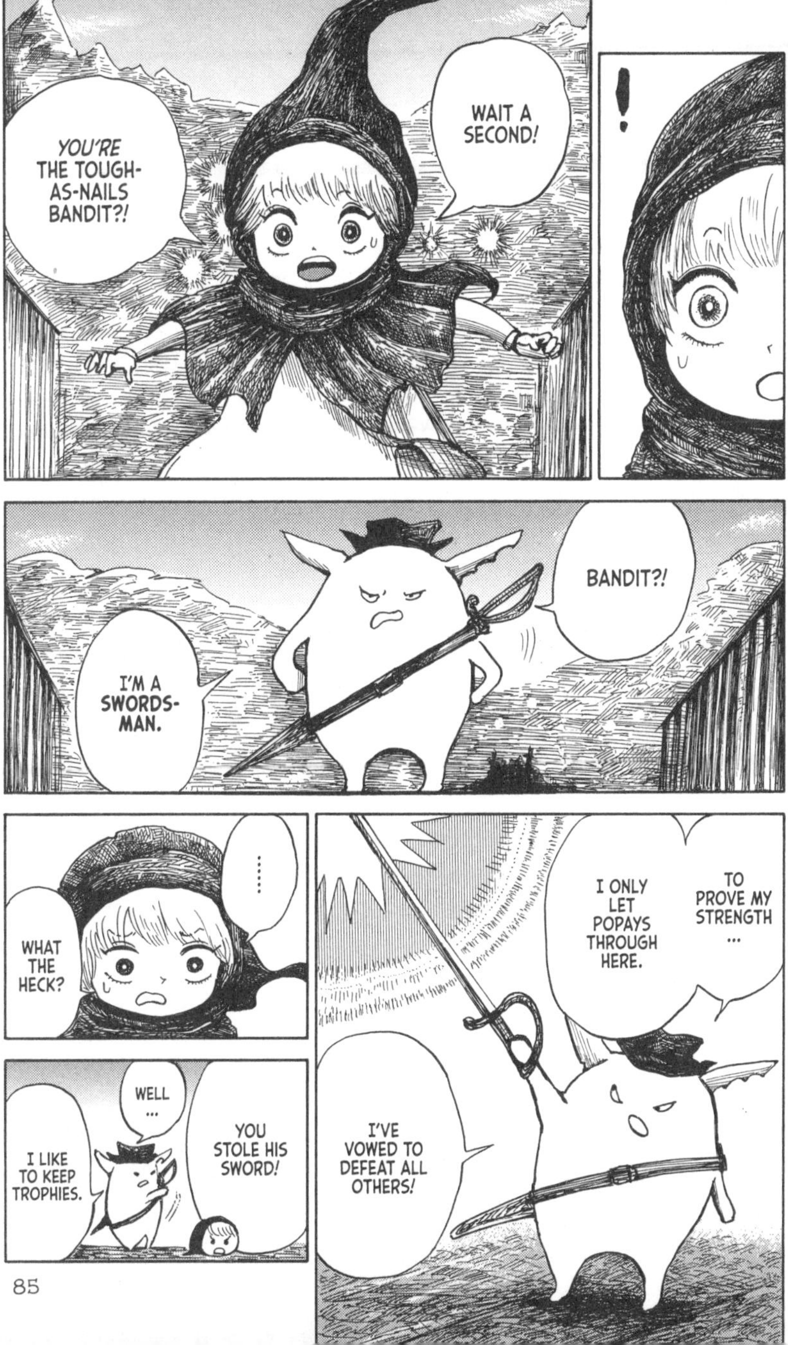
!
WAIT A SECOND!
YOU'RE THE TOUGH-AS-NAILS BANDIT?!
BANDIT?!
I'M A SWORDS-MAN.
TO PROVE MY STRENGTH ...
I ONLY LET POPAYS THROUGH HERE.
I'VE VOWED TO DEFEAT ALL OTHERS!
......
WHAT THE HECK?
YOU STOLE HIS SWORD!
WELL ...
I LIKE TO KEEP TROPHIES.

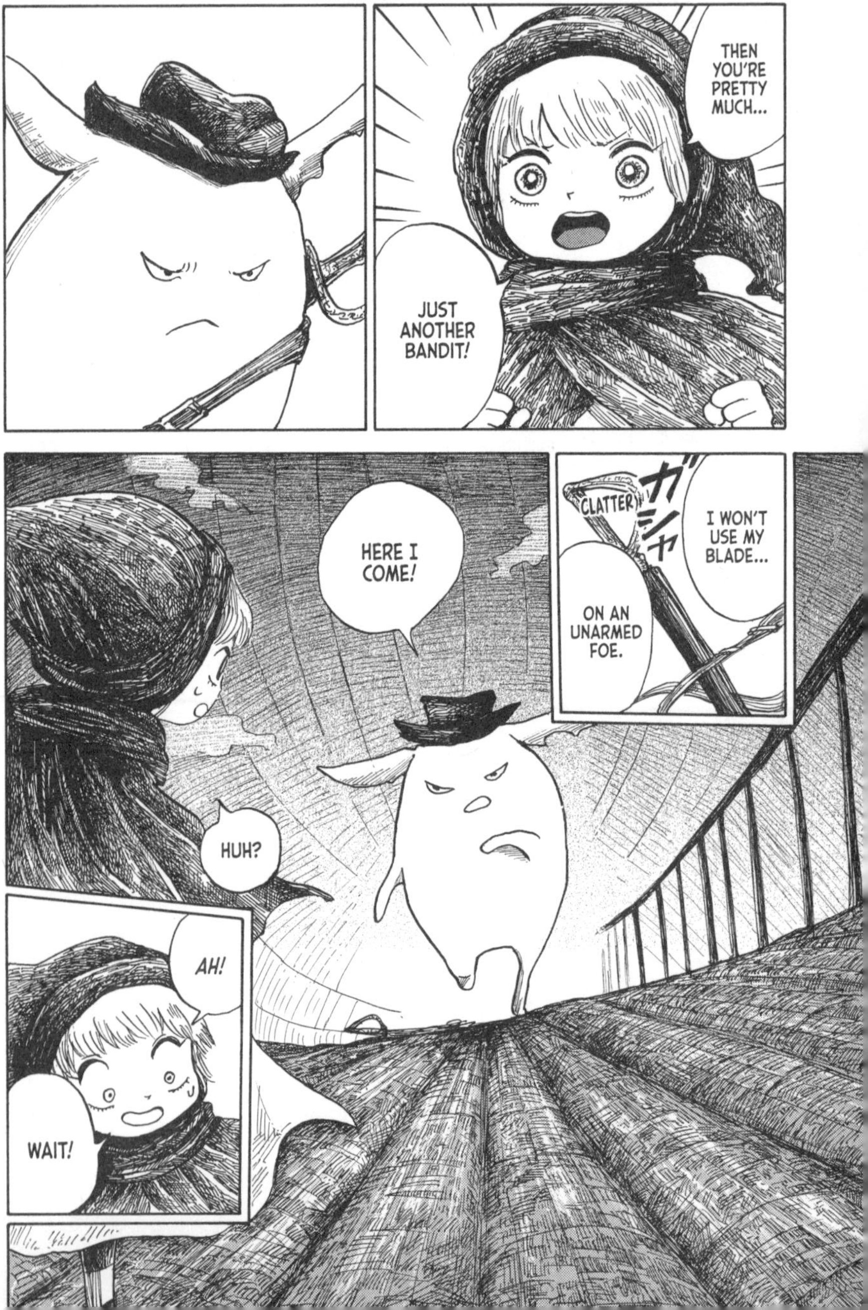
THEN YOU'RE PRETTY MUCH...
JUST ANOTHER BANDIT!
CLATTER
ガシャ
I WON'T USE MY BLADE...
ON AN UNARMED FOE.
HERE I COME!
HUH?
AH!
WAIT!

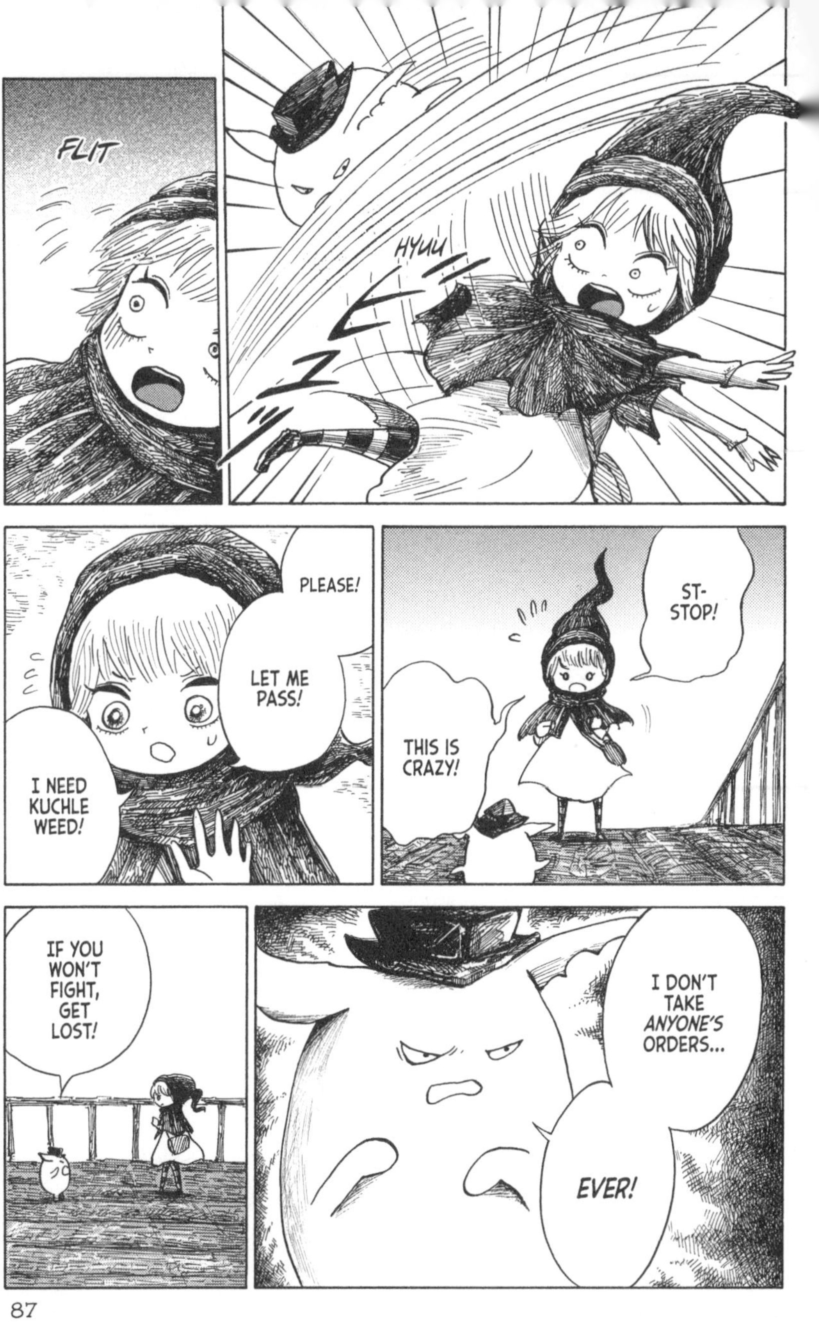
HYUU
FLIT
ST- STOP!
THIS IS CRAZY!
PLEASE!
LET ME PASS!
I NEED KUCHLE WEED!
I DON'T TAKE ANYONE'S ORDERS...
EVER!
IF YOU WON'T FIGHT, GET LOST!

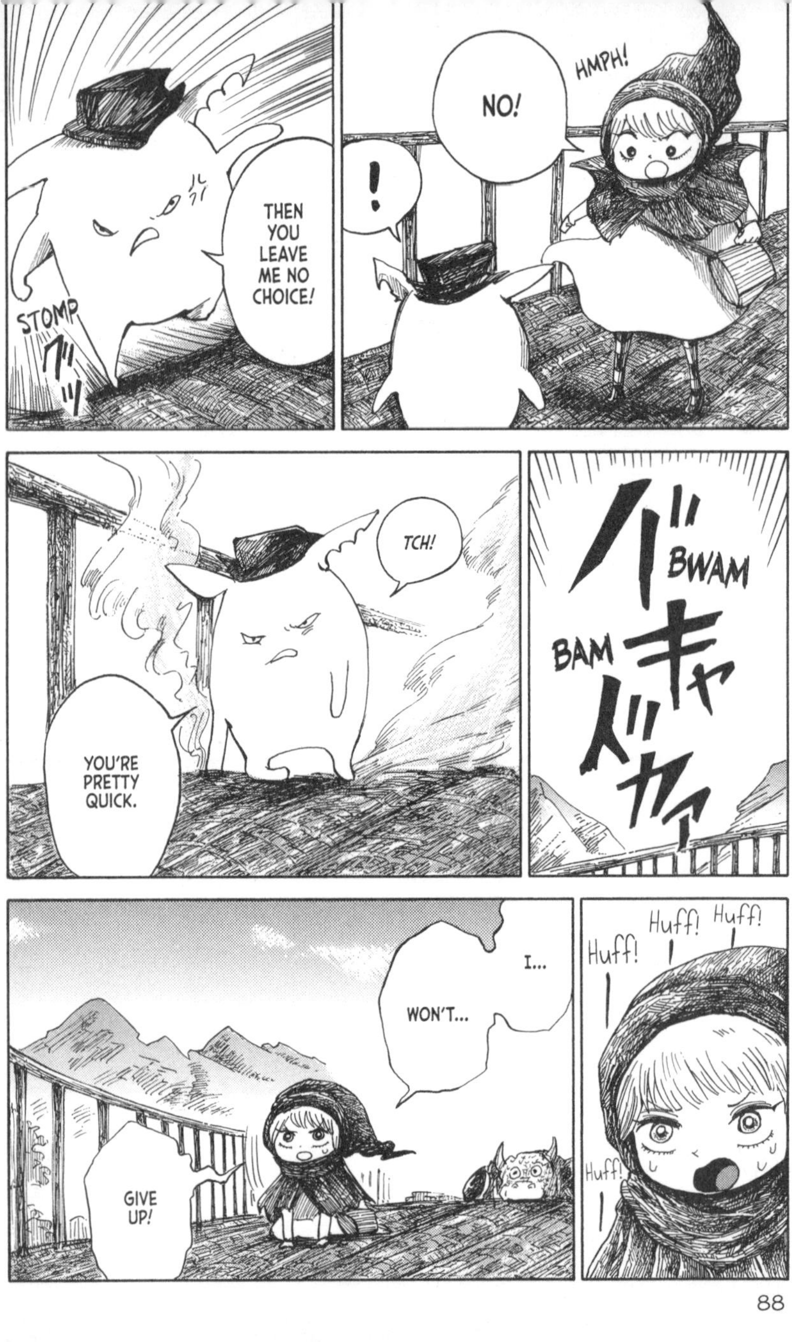
HMPH!
NO!
!
THEN YOU LEAVE ME NO CHOICE!
STOMP
BWAM
BAM
TCH!
YOU'RE PRETTY QUICK.
Huff!
Huff!
Huff!
Huff!
I...
WON'T...
GIVE UP!

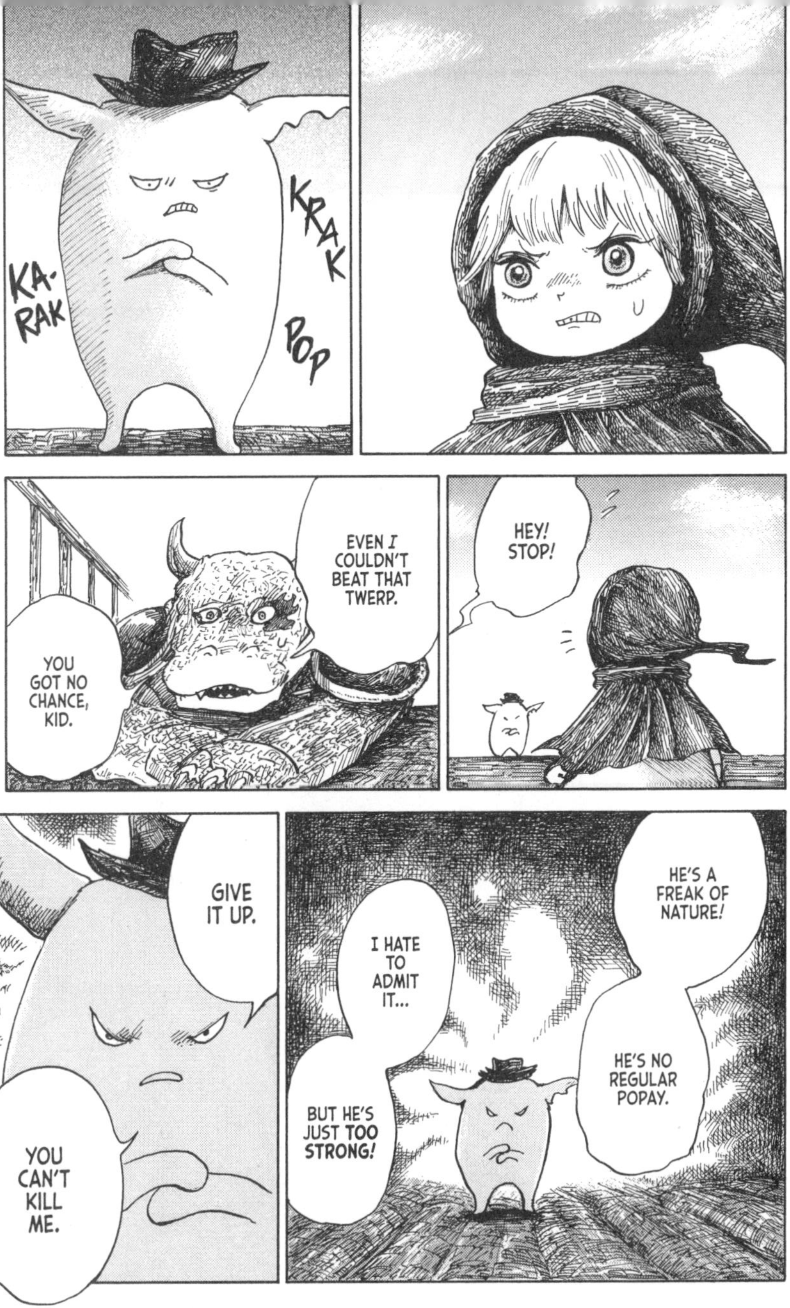

KRAK
KA-RAK
POP
HEY! STOP!
EVEN *I* COULDN'T BEAT THAT TWERP.
YOU GOT NO CHANCE, KID.
HE'S A FREAK OF NATURE!
I HATE TO ADMIT IT...
HE'S NO REGULAR POPAY.
BUT HE'S JUST **TOO STRONG!**
GIVE IT UP.
YOU CAN'T KILL ME.

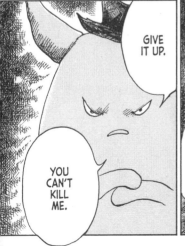

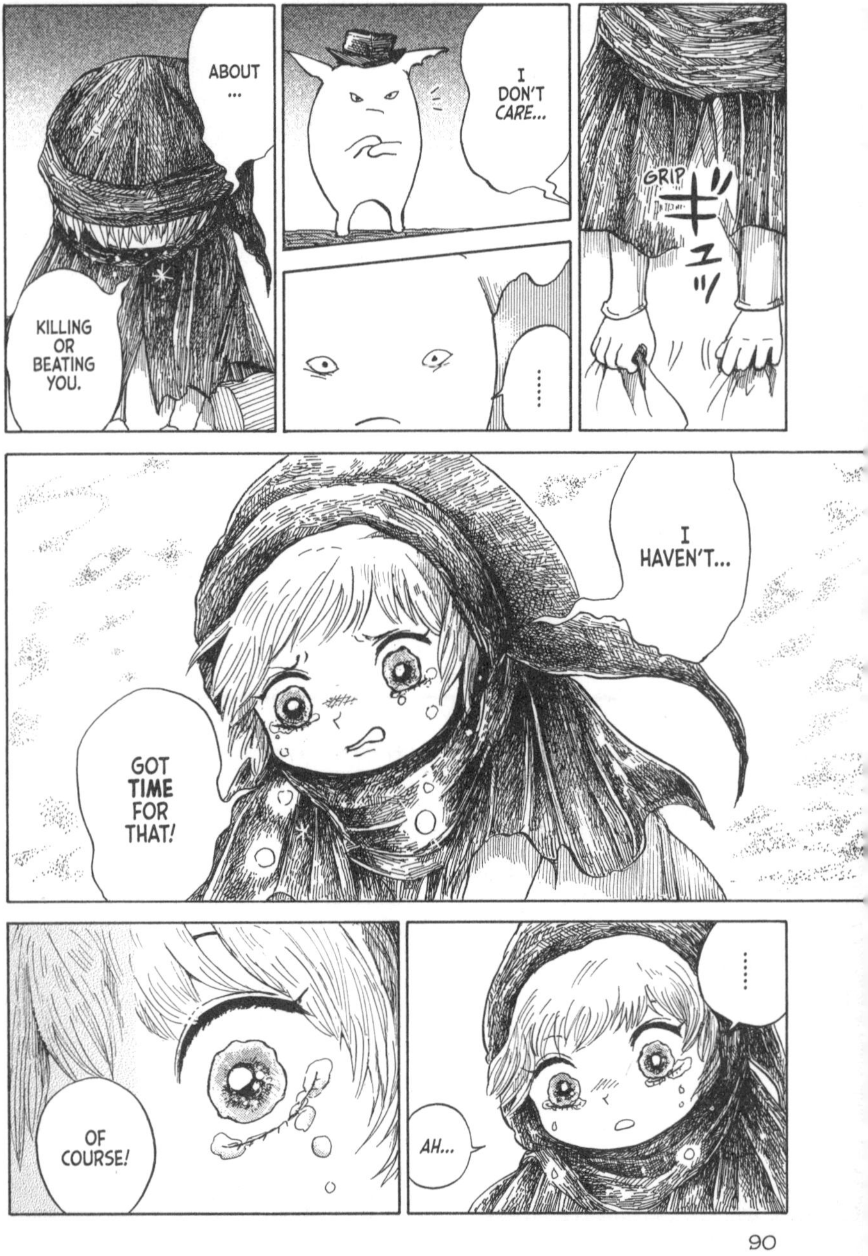
GRIP
ギュッ
I DON'T CARE...
......
ABOUT ...
KILLING OR BEATING YOU.
I HAVEN'T...
GOT TIME FOR THAT!
......
AH...
OF COURSE!

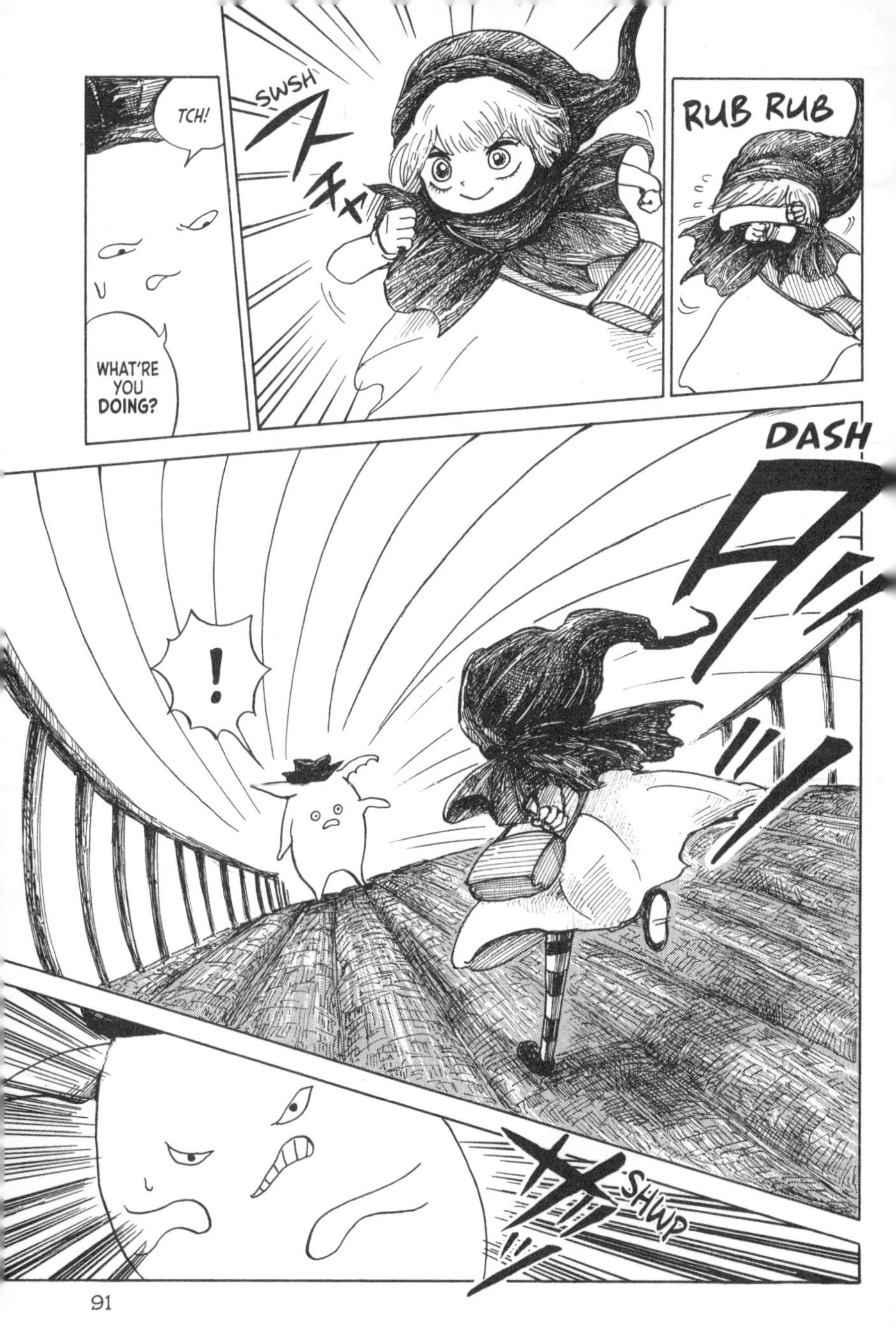
RUB RUB
SWSH
TCH!
WHAT'RE YOU DOING?
DASH
!
SHWP

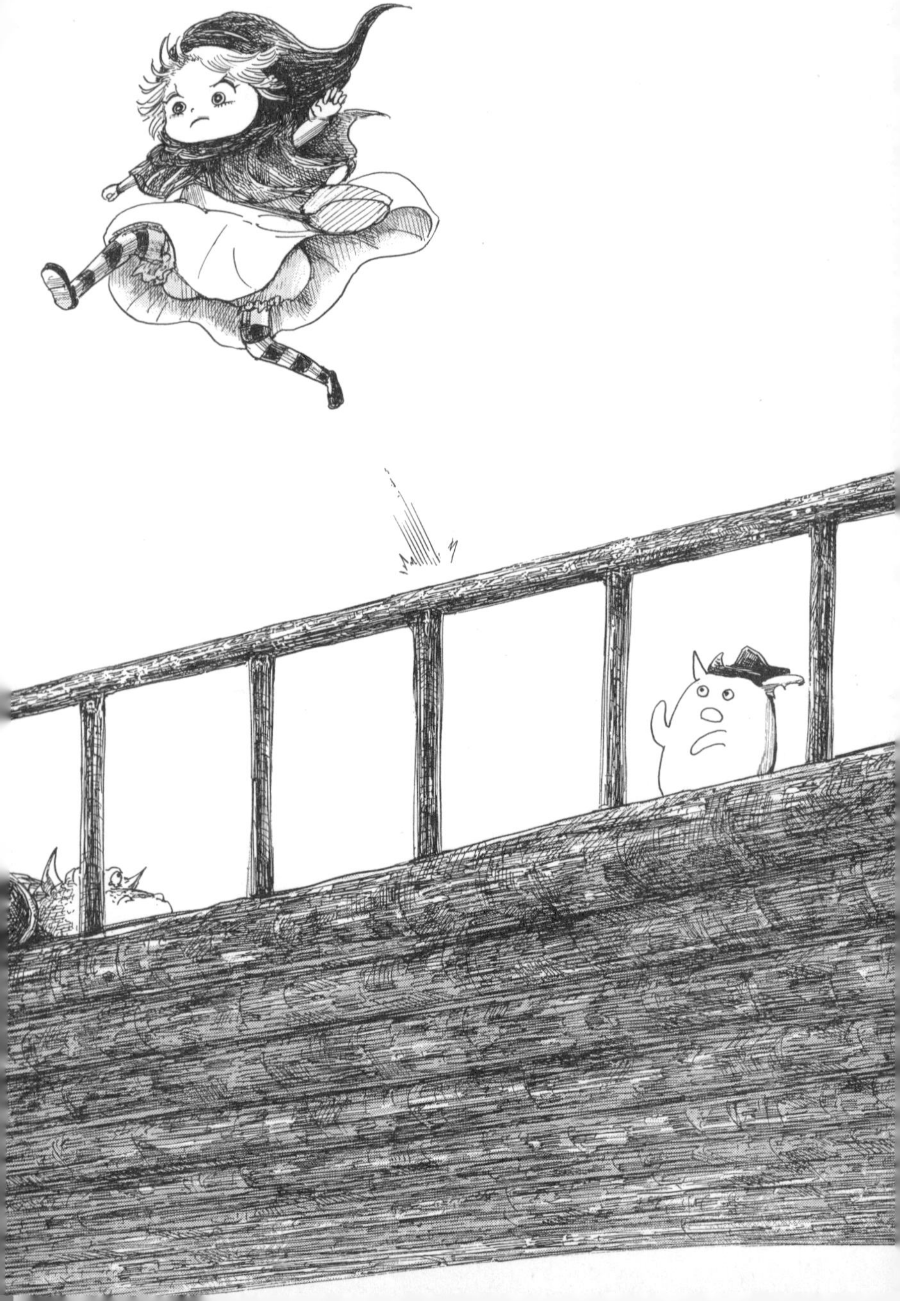

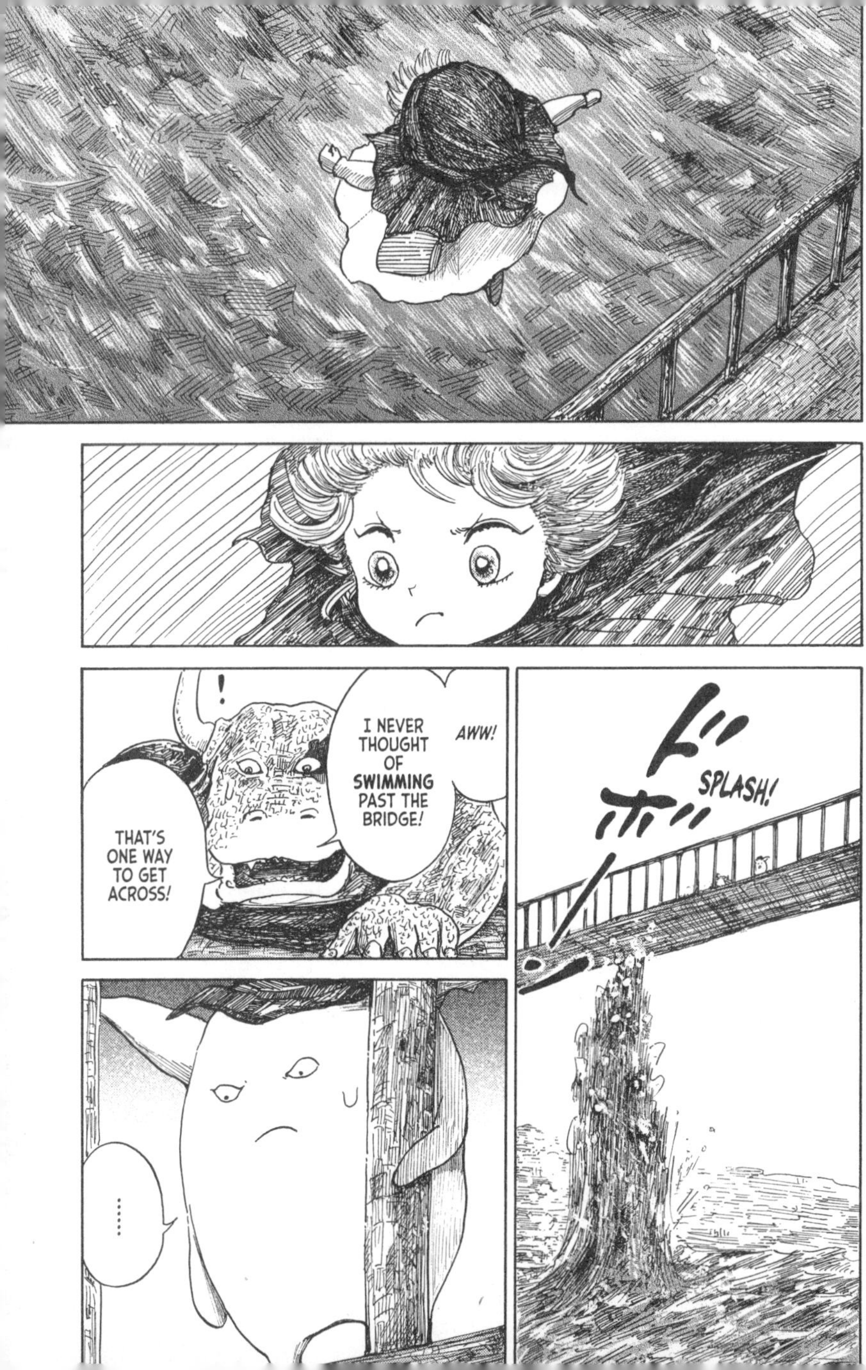
SPLASH!
AWW!
I NEVER THOUGHT OF **SWIMMING** PAST THE BRIDGE!
!
THAT'S ONE WAY TO GET ACROSS!
......

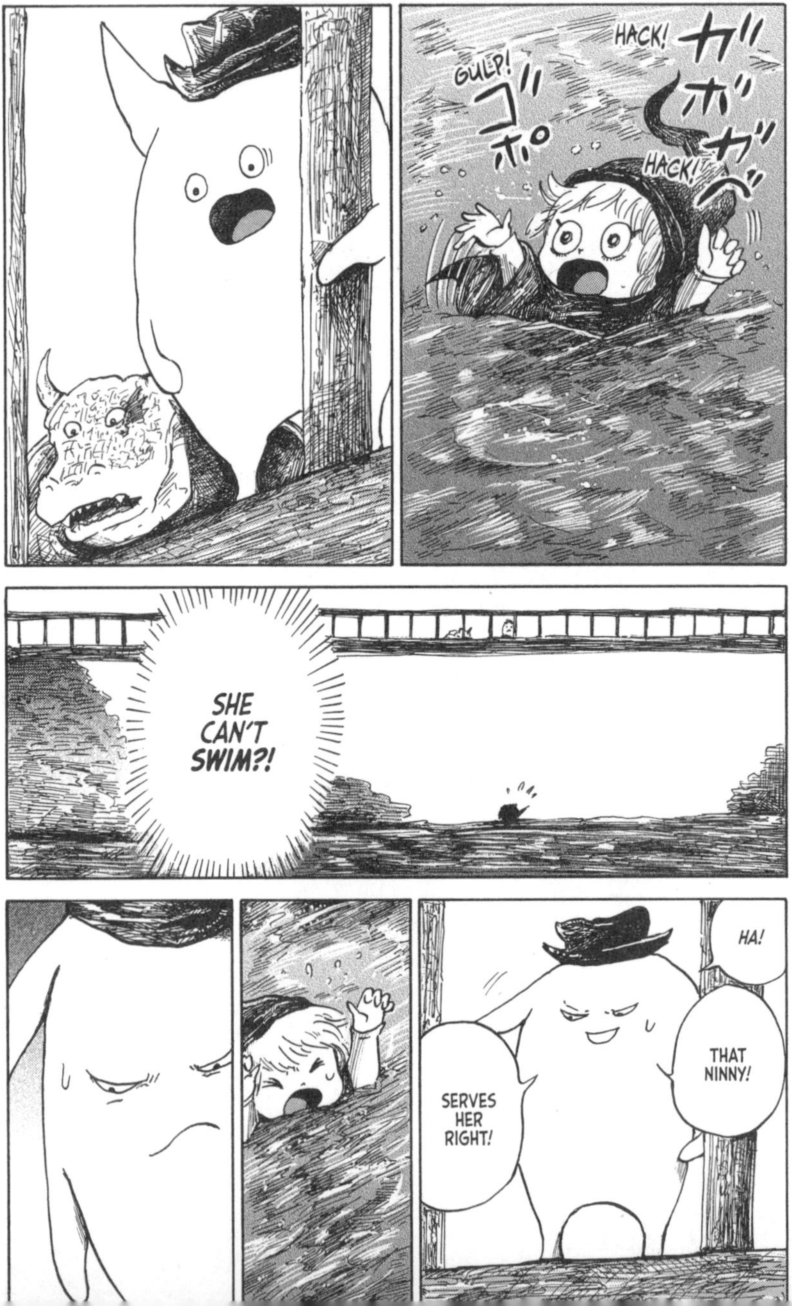
HACK!
ガボガベ
GULP!
ゴポ
HACK!
SHE CAN'T SWIM?!
HA!
THAT NINNY!
SERVES HER RIGHT!

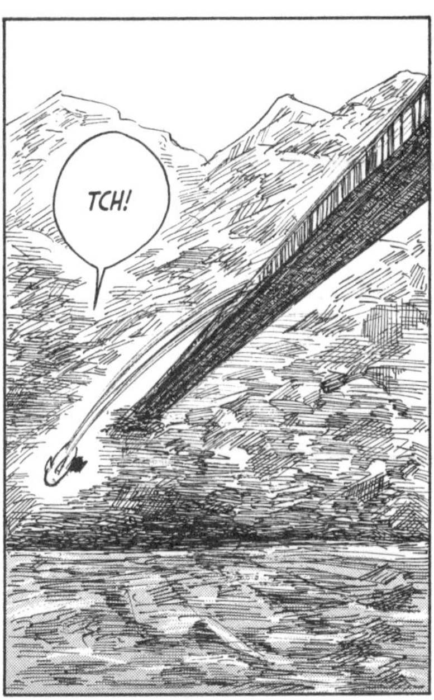
TCH!
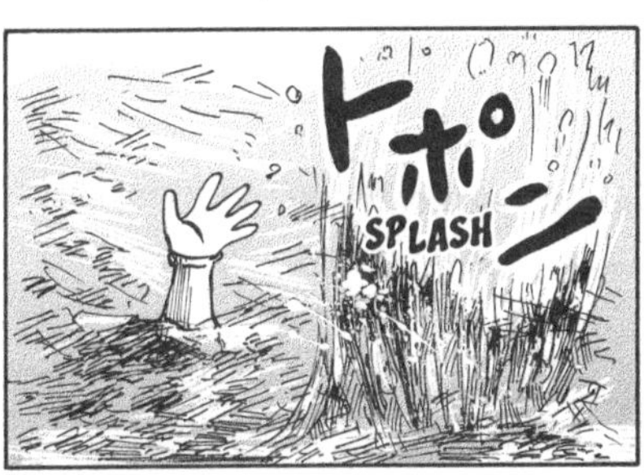
トポーン
SPLASH
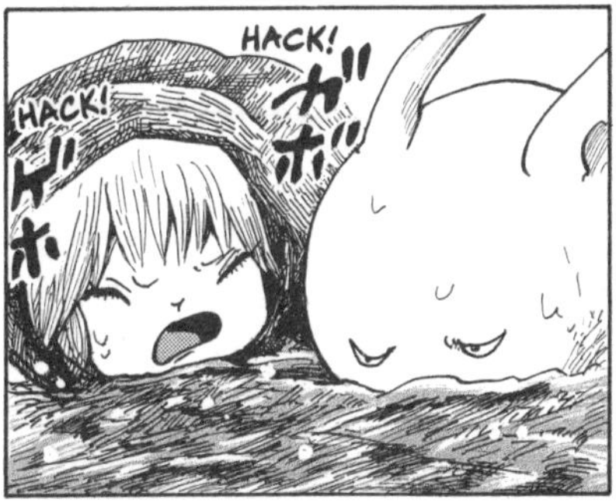
HACK!
ガボ
HACK!
ゲホ
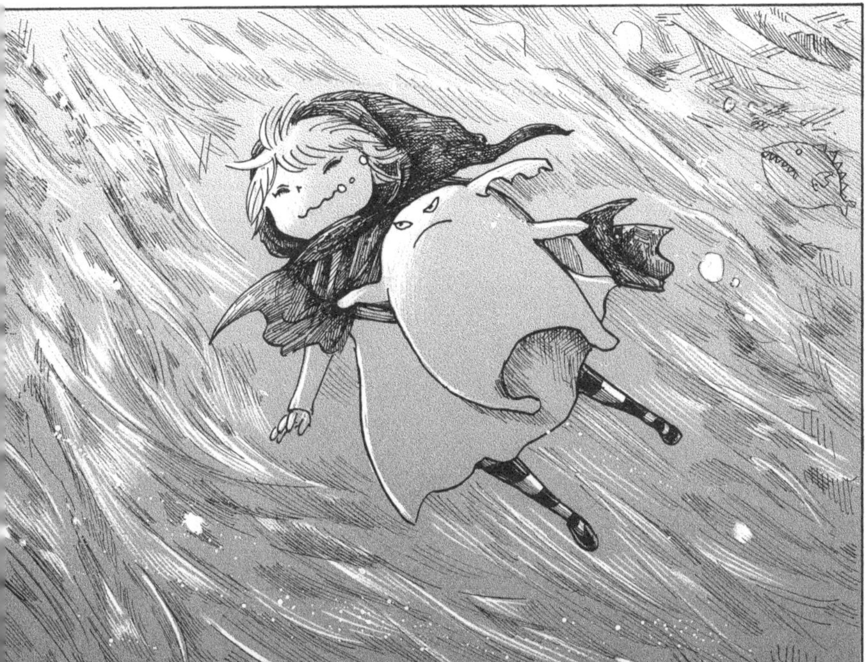

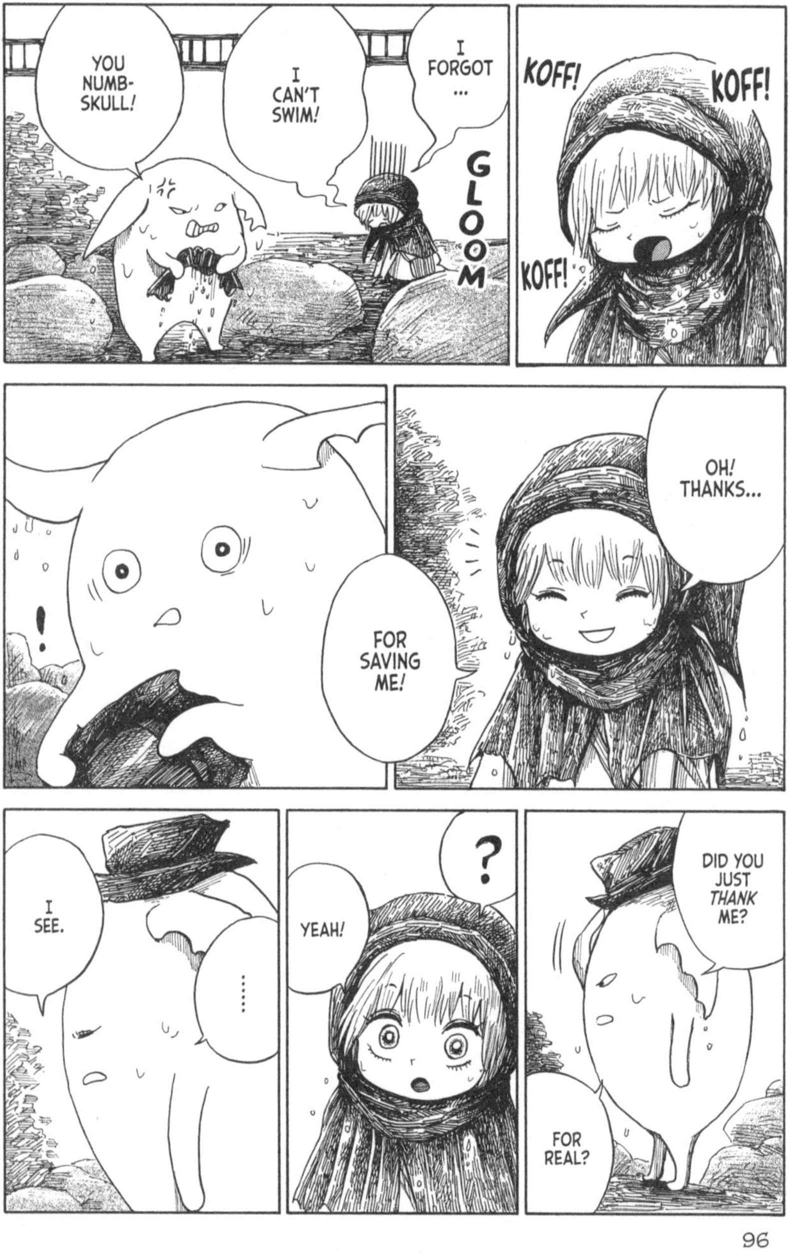
KOFF!
KOFF!
KOFF!
GLOOM
I FORGOT ...
I CAN'T SWIM!
YOU NUMBSKULL!
OH! THANKS...
FOR SAVING ME!
!
DID YOU JUST *THANK* ME?
FOR REAL?
?
YEAH!
......
I SEE.

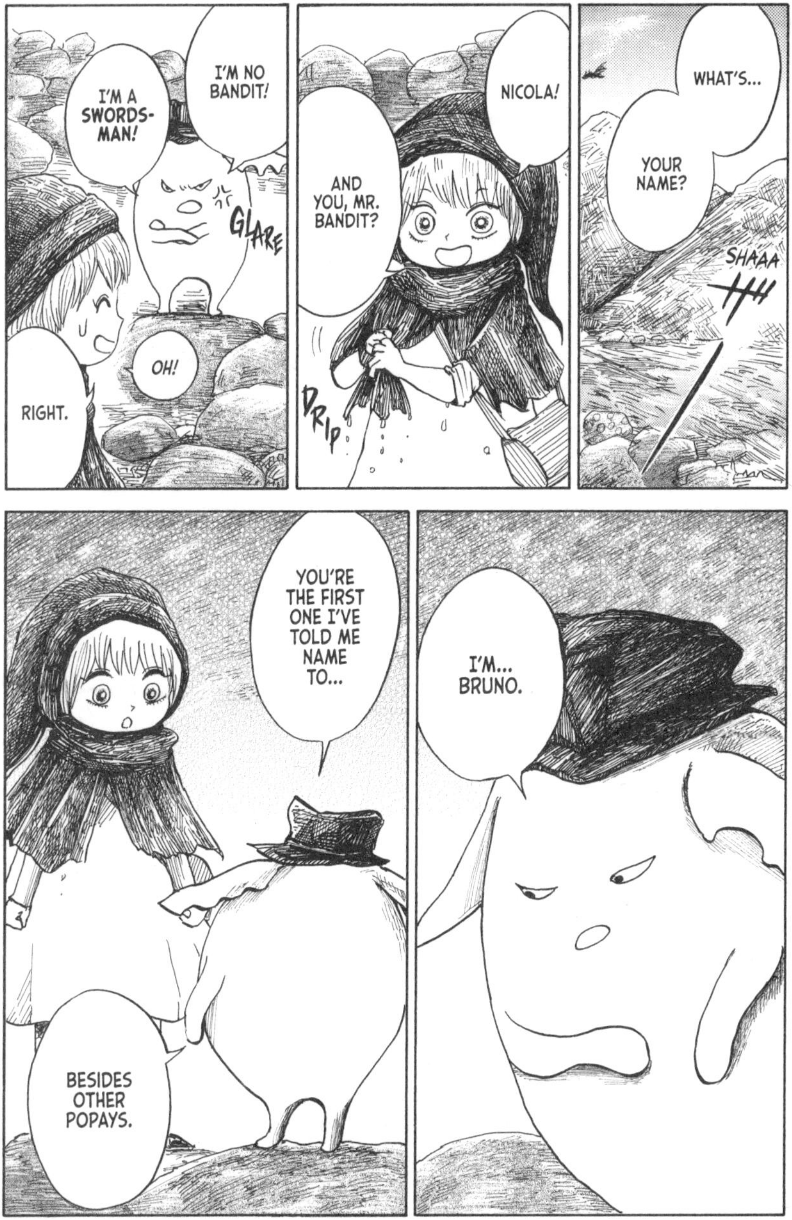
WHAT'S...
YOUR NAME?
SHAAA
NICOLA!
AND YOU, MR. BANDIT?
DRIP
I'M NO BANDIT!
I'M A SWORDS-MAN!
GLARE
OH!
RIGHT.
I'M... BRUNO.
YOU'RE THE FIRST ONE I'VE TOLD ME NAME TO...
BESIDES OTHER POPAYS.

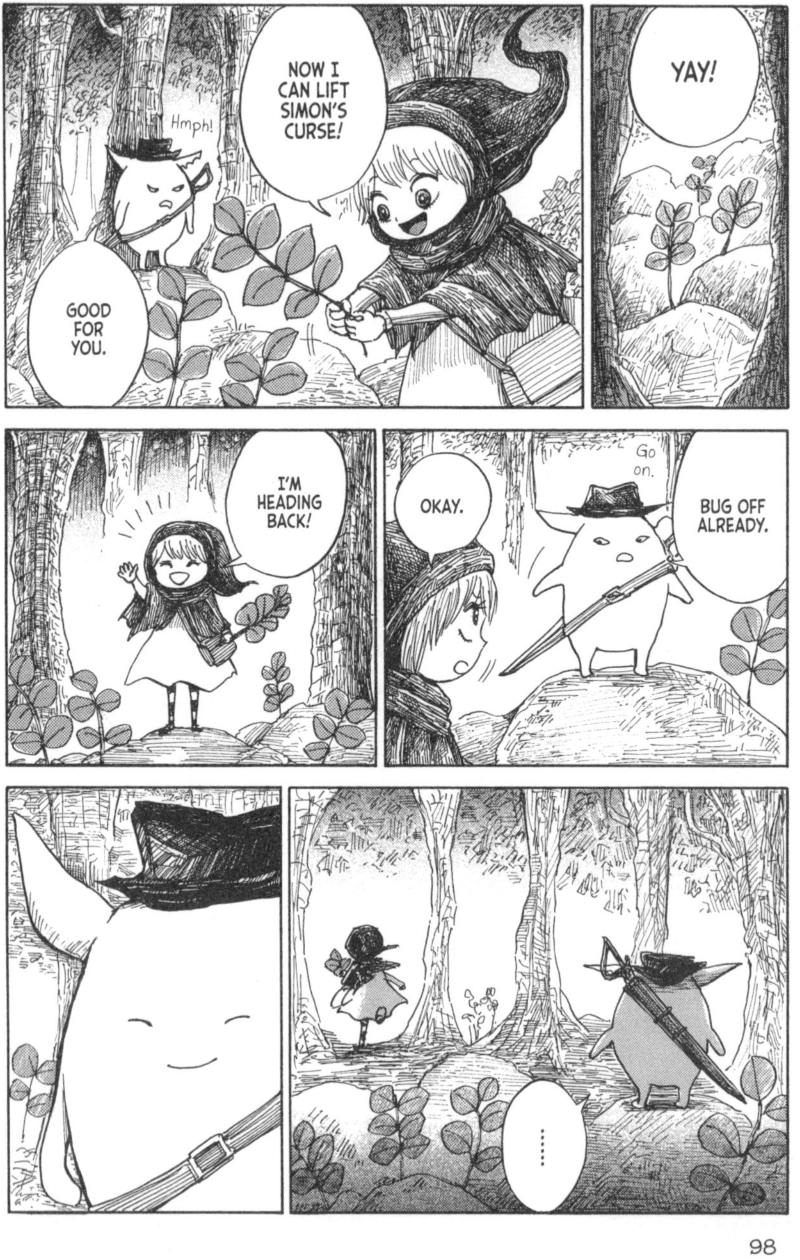
YAY!
NOW I CAN LIFT SIMON'S CURSE!
Hmph!
GOOD FOR YOU.
BUG OFF ALREADY.
Go on.
OKAY.
I'M HEADING BACK!
......

TWITCH

THOSE GOONS ....!

DASH

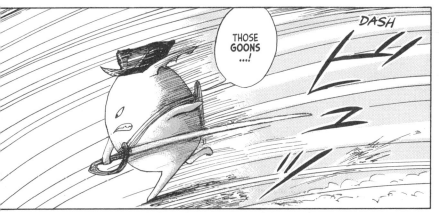

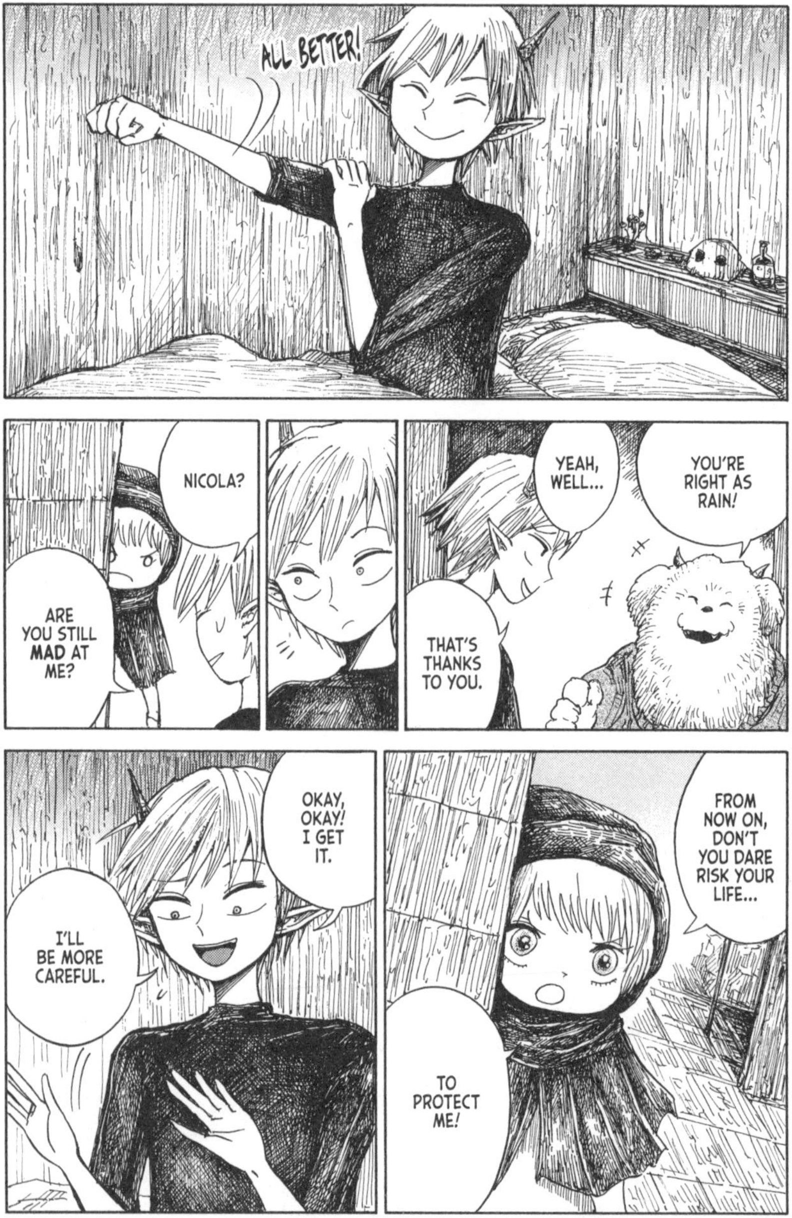
ALL BETTER!
YOU'RE RIGHT AS RAIN!
YEAH, WELL...
THAT'S THANKS TO YOU.
NICOLA?
ARE YOU STILL MAD AT ME?
FROM NOW ON, DON'T YOU DARE RISK YOUR LIFE...
TO PROTECT ME!
OKAY, OKAY! I GET IT.
I'LL BE MORE CAREFUL.

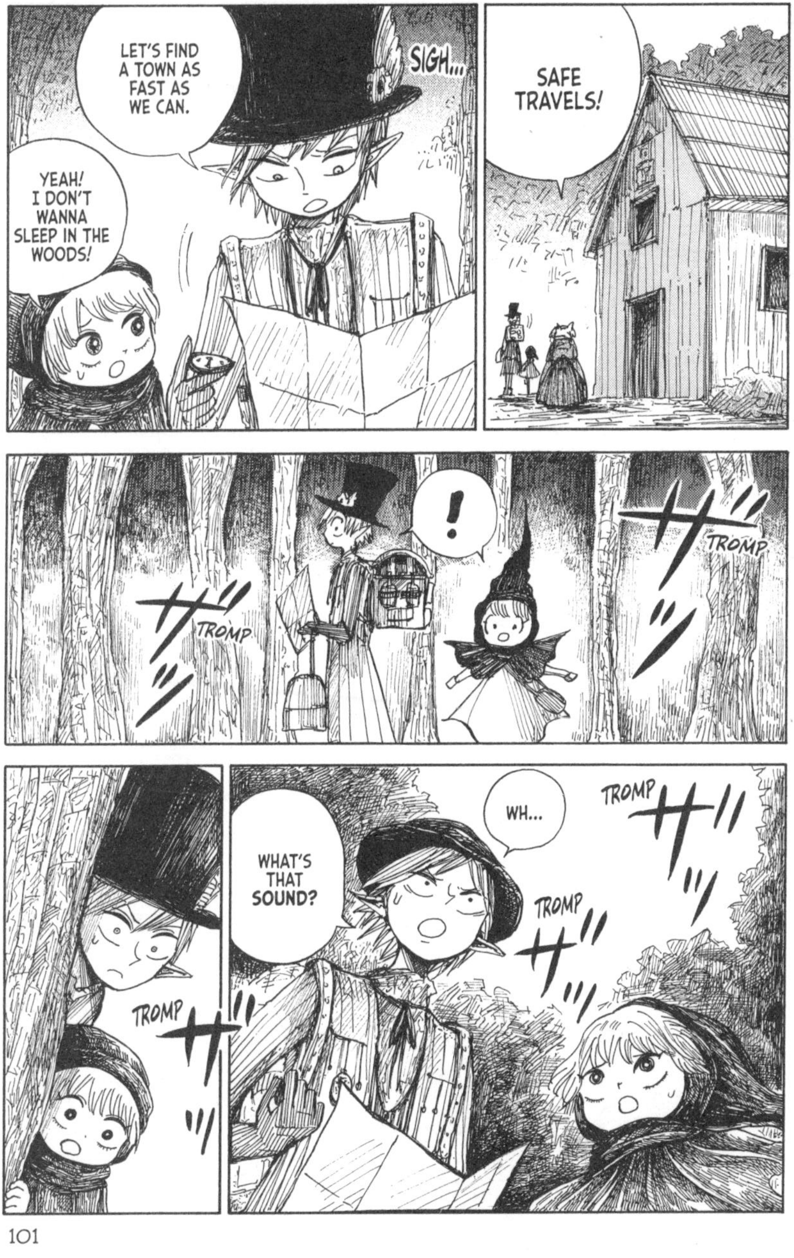

SAFE TRAVELS!
SIGH...
LET'S FIND A TOWN AS FAST AS WE CAN.
YEAH! I DON'T WANNA SLEEP IN THE WOODS!
TROMP
!
TROMP
TROMP
WH...
TROMP
WHAT'S THAT SOUND?
TROMP

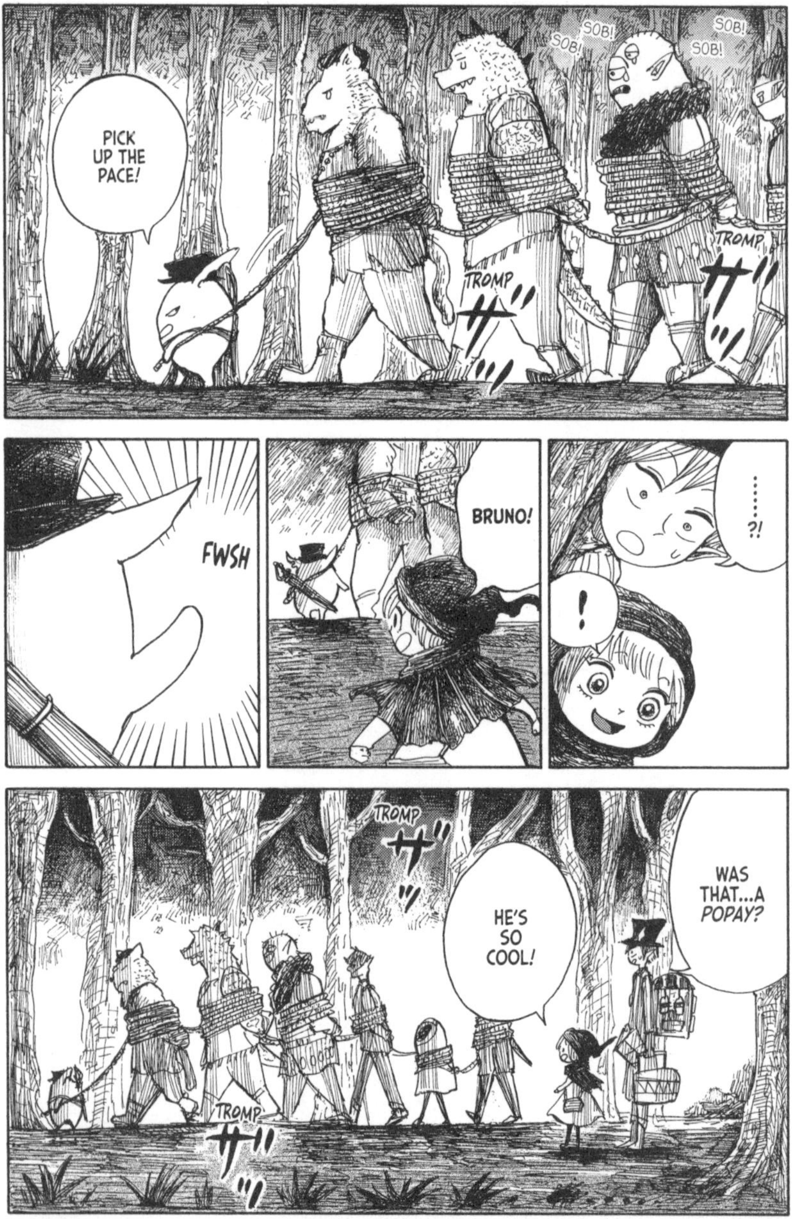
SOB!
SOB!
SOB!
SOB!
PICK UP THE PACE!
TROMP
TROMP
......?!
!
BRUNO!
FWSH
WAS THAT...A *POPAY*?
HE'S SO COOL!
TROMP
TROMP

Chapter 9 END

After the Visit 9

after that

PSST!
PSST!
HAVE YOU HEARD ABOUT THAT REALLY TOUGH POPAY?!
PERK
HE USED TO BE A BANDIT ON JAGGED MOUNTAIN...
What?!
SHOCK!
B-BANDIT?!
BUT NOW HE'S A PROPER SWORDS-MAN...
PROTECTING US!
!
ISN'T THAT COOL?
I... I WONDER IF WE COULD EVER DO THAT!
......
♪
BOING
BOING

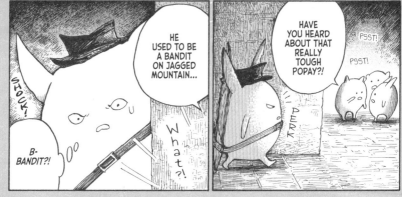

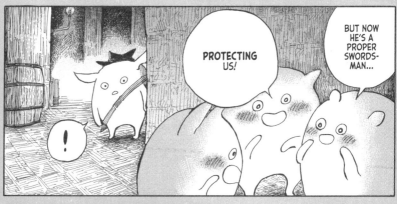

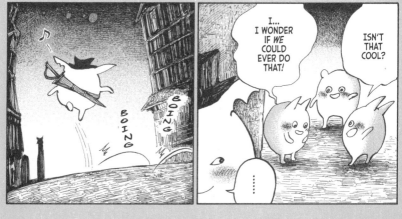

Nicola Traveling Around The Demons' World.

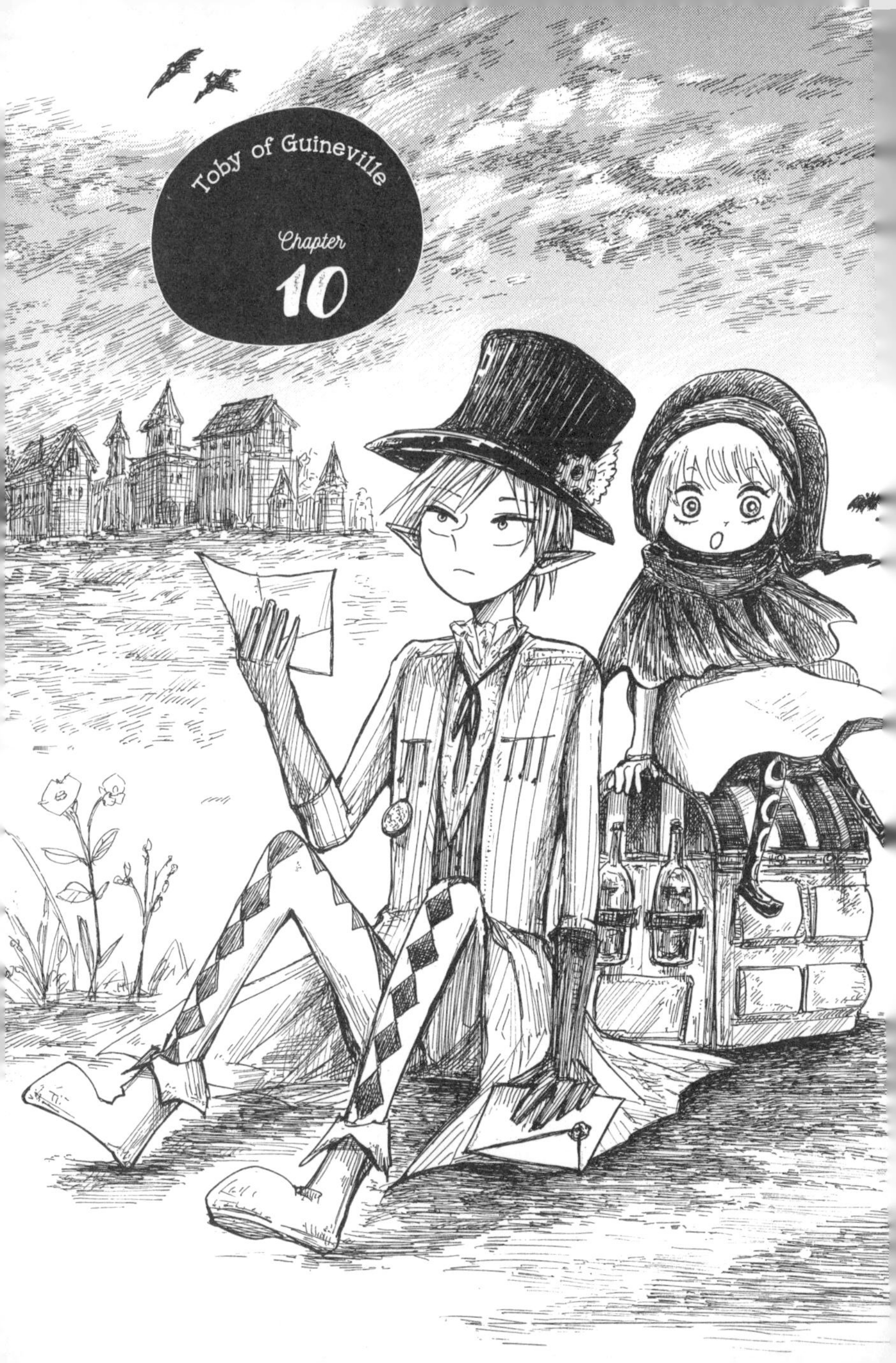
Toby of Guineville
Chapter
10

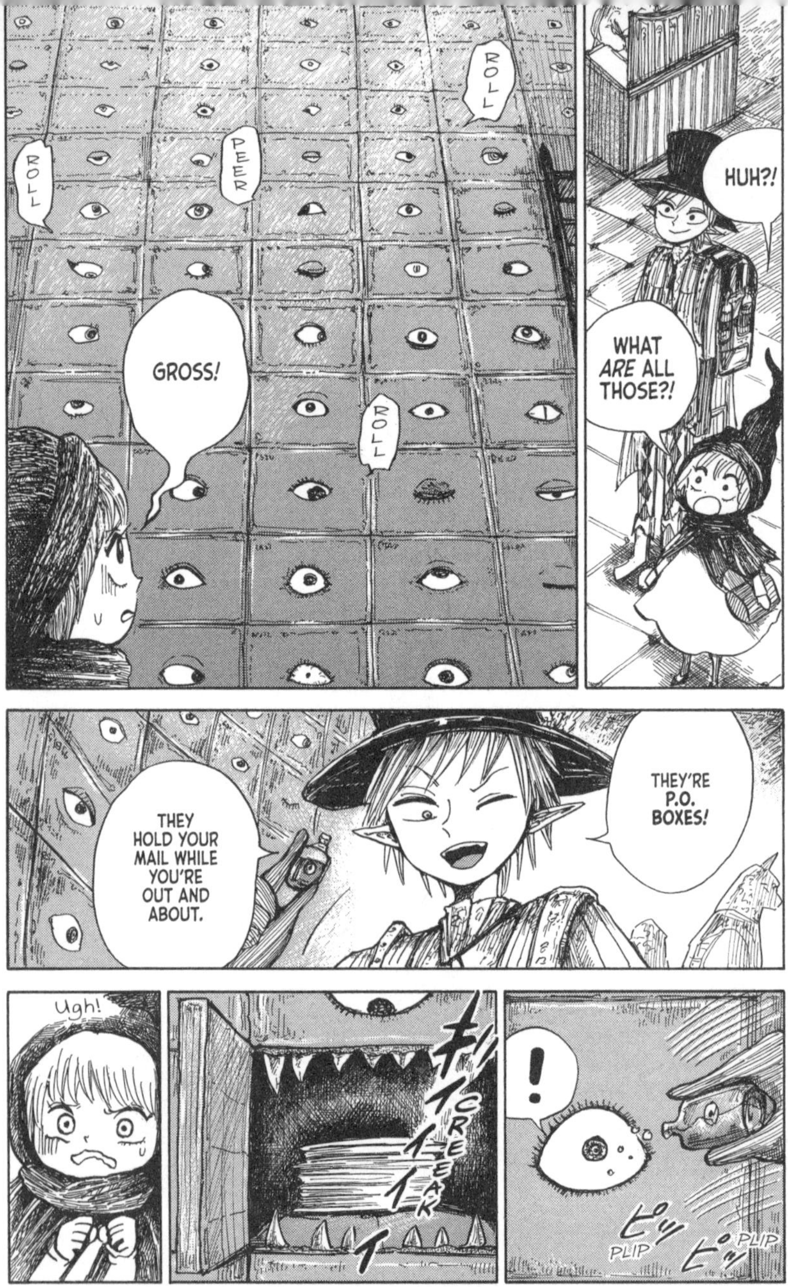
HUH?!
WHAT ARE ALL THOSE?!
ROLL
PEER
ROLL
GROSS!
ROLL
THEY'RE P.O. BOXES!
THEY HOLD YOUR MAIL WHILE YOU'RE OUT AND ABOUT.
!
ピッ PLIP
ピッ PLIP
CREEAK
Ugh!

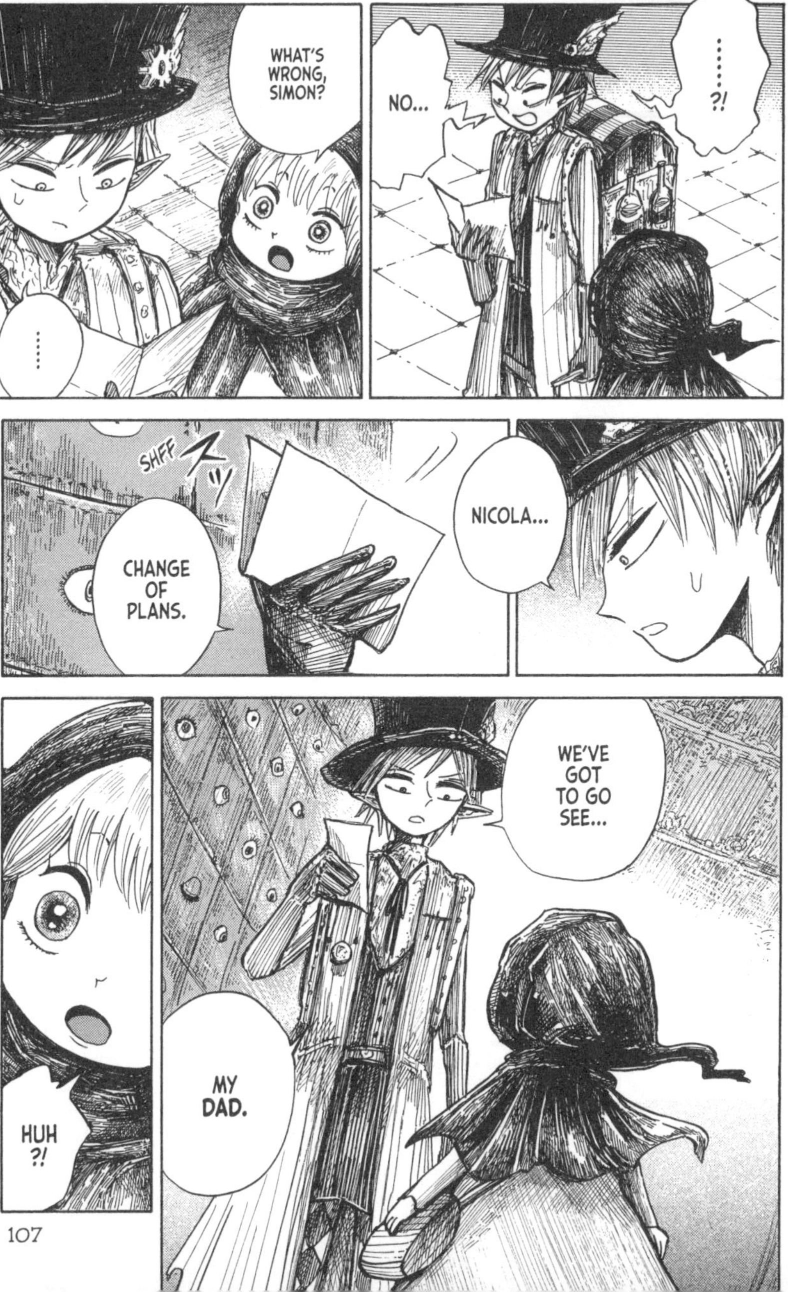
......?!
NO...
WHAT'S WRONG, SIMON?
......
NICOLA...
SHFF
CHANGE OF PLANS.
WE'VE GOT TO GO SEE...
MY DAD.
HUH?!

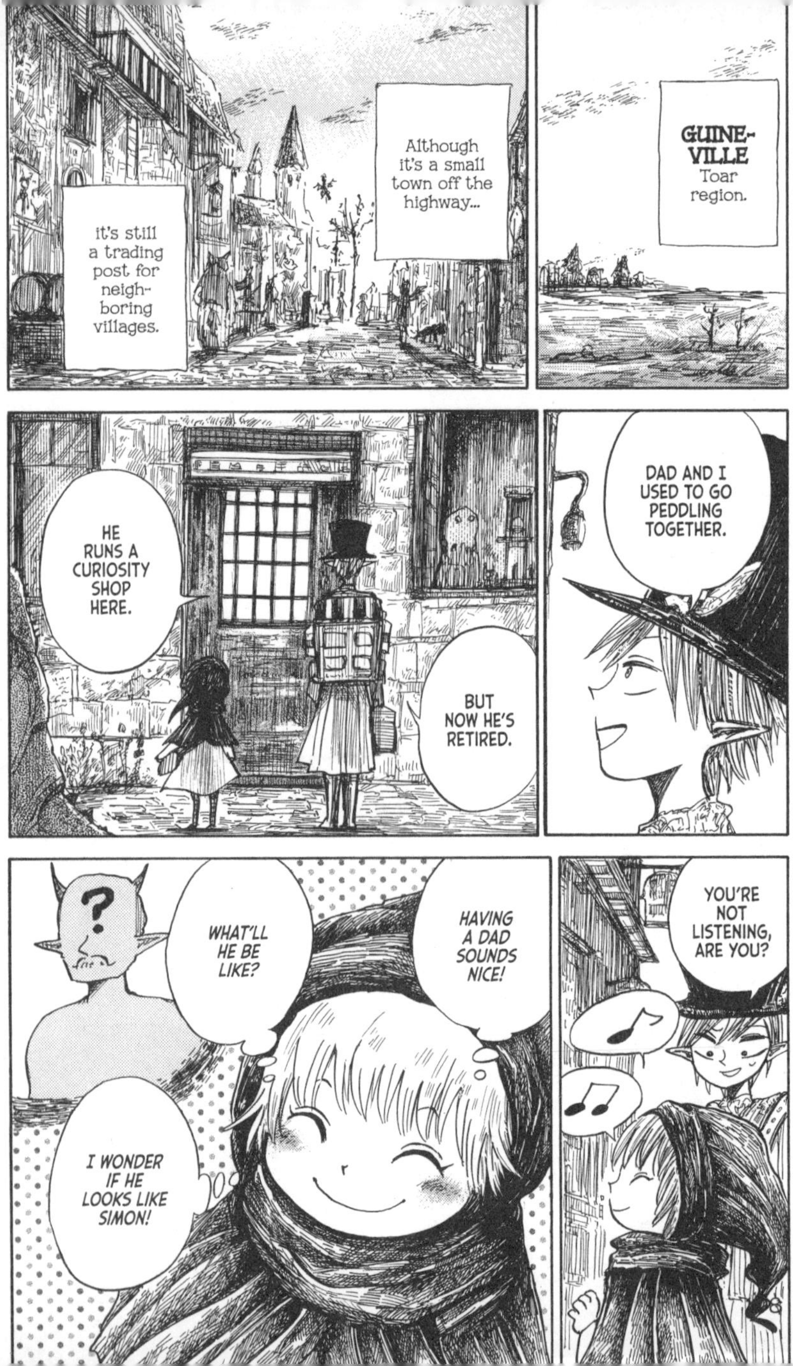
GUINE-VILLE
Toar region.
Although it's a small town off the highway...
it's still a trading post for neighboring villages.
DAD AND I USED TO GO PEDDLING TOGETHER.
HE RUNS A CURIOSITY SHOP HERE.
BUT NOW HE'S RETIRED.
YOU'RE NOT LISTENING, ARE YOU?
HAVING A DAD SOUNDS NICE!
WHAT'LL HE BE LIKE?
?
I WONDER IF HE LOOKS LIKE SIMON!

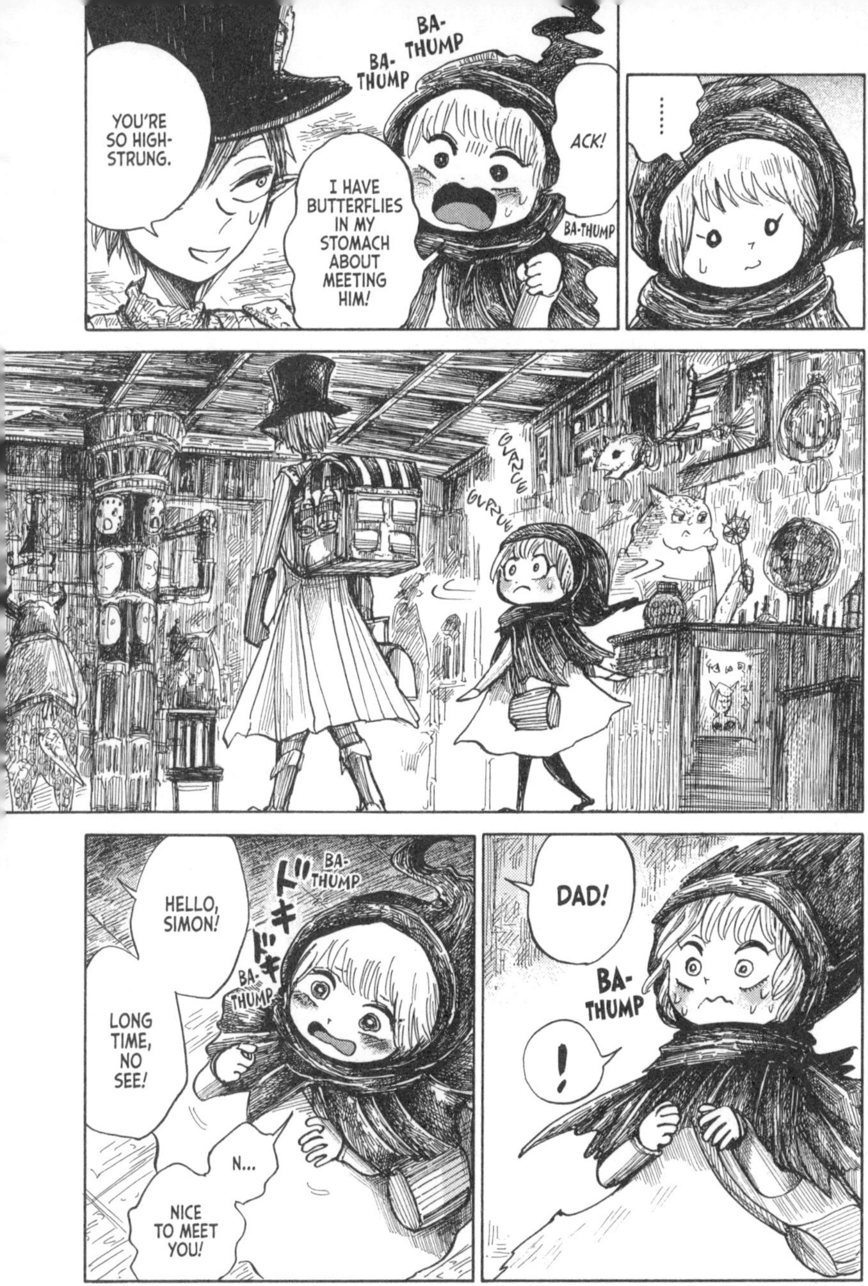
......
BA-THUMP
BA-THUMP
ACK!
BA-THUMP
I HAVE BUTTERFLIES IN MY STOMACH ABOUT MEETING HIM!
YOU'RE SO HIGH-STRUNG.
GLANCE
GLANCE
DAD!
BA-THUMP
!
BA-THUMP
ドキドキ
HELLO, SIMON!
BA-THUMP
LONG TIME, NO SEE!
N...
NICE TO MEET YOU!

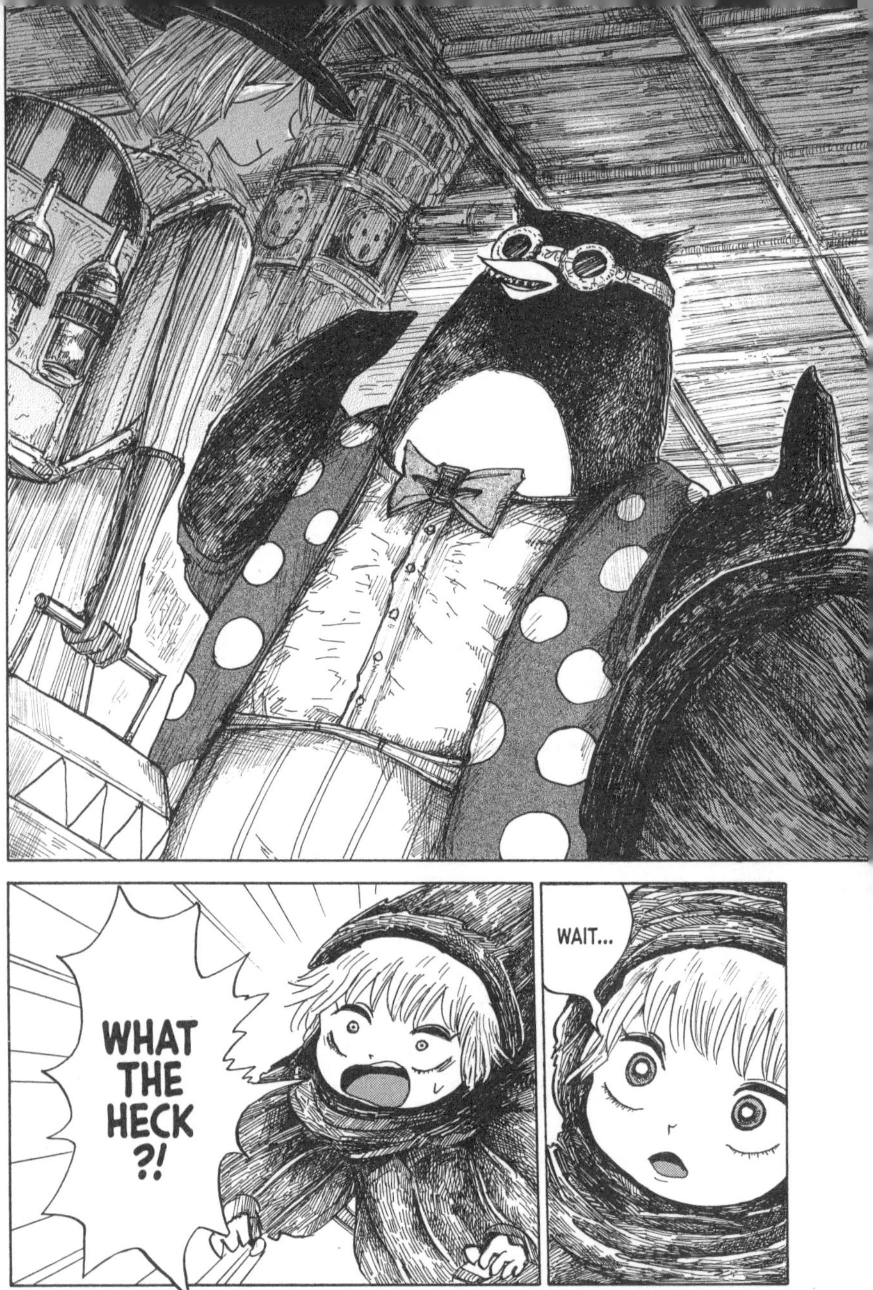
WAIT...
WHAT THE HECK ?!

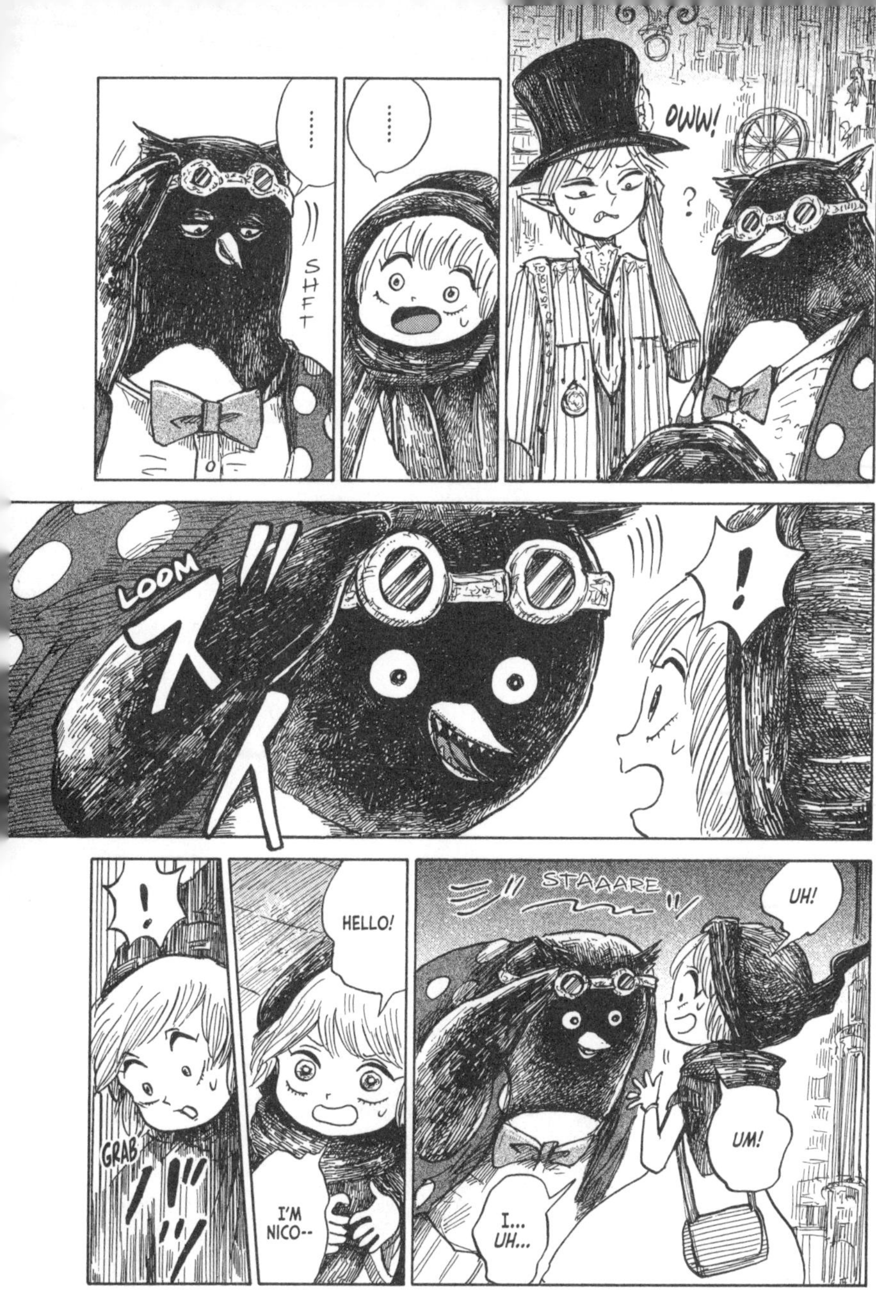
OWW!
?
......
......
SHFT
!
LOOM
ズイ
STAAARE
UH!
UM!
I... UH...
HELLO!
I'M NICO--
!
GRAB

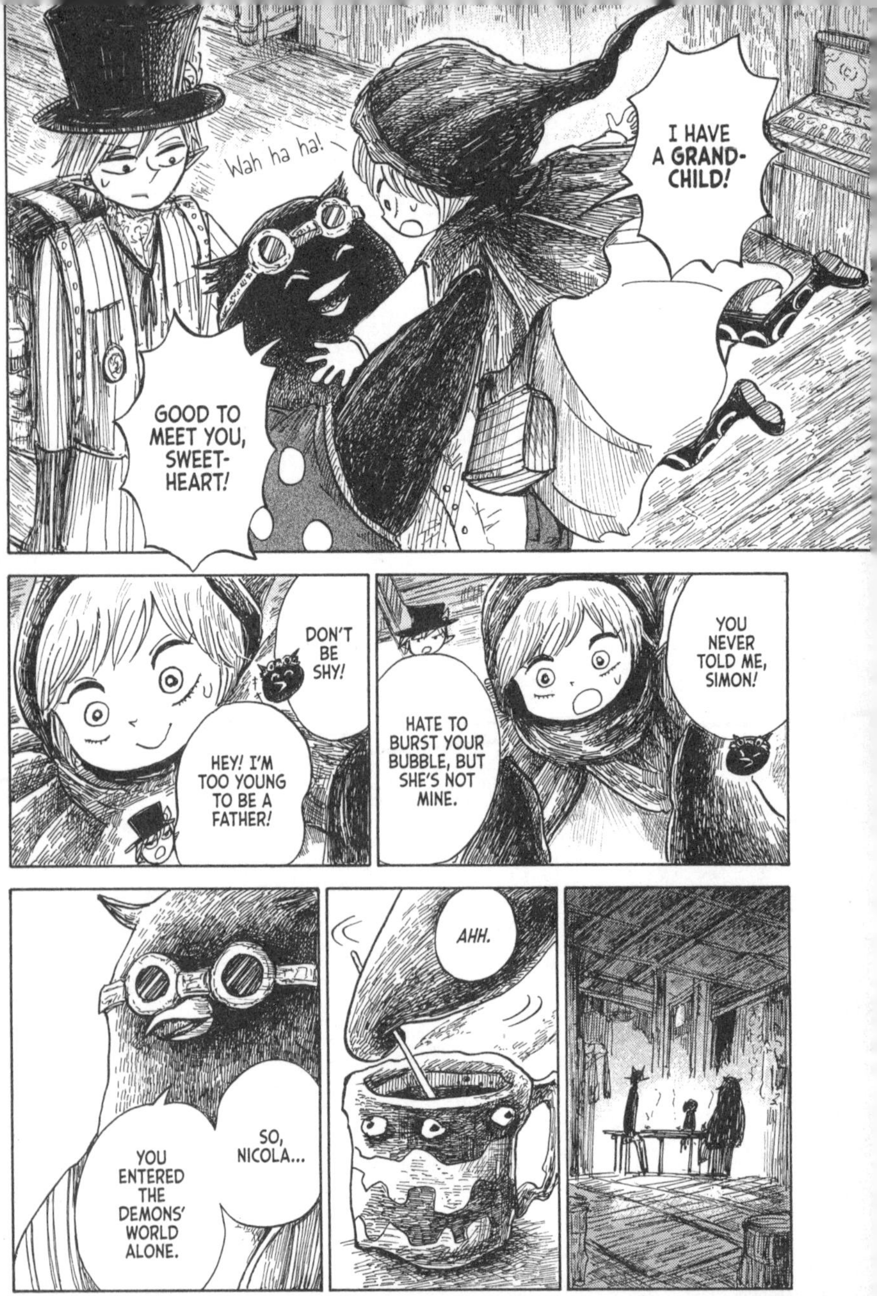
I HAVE A GRAND-CHILD!
Wah ha ha!
GOOD TO MEET YOU, SWEET-HEART!
YOU NEVER TOLD ME, SIMON!
HATE TO BURST YOUR BUBBLE, BUT SHE'S NOT MINE.
DON'T BE SHY!
HEY! I'M TOO YOUNG TO BE A FATHER!
AHH.
SO, NICOLA...
YOU ENTERED THE DEMONS' WORLD ALONE.

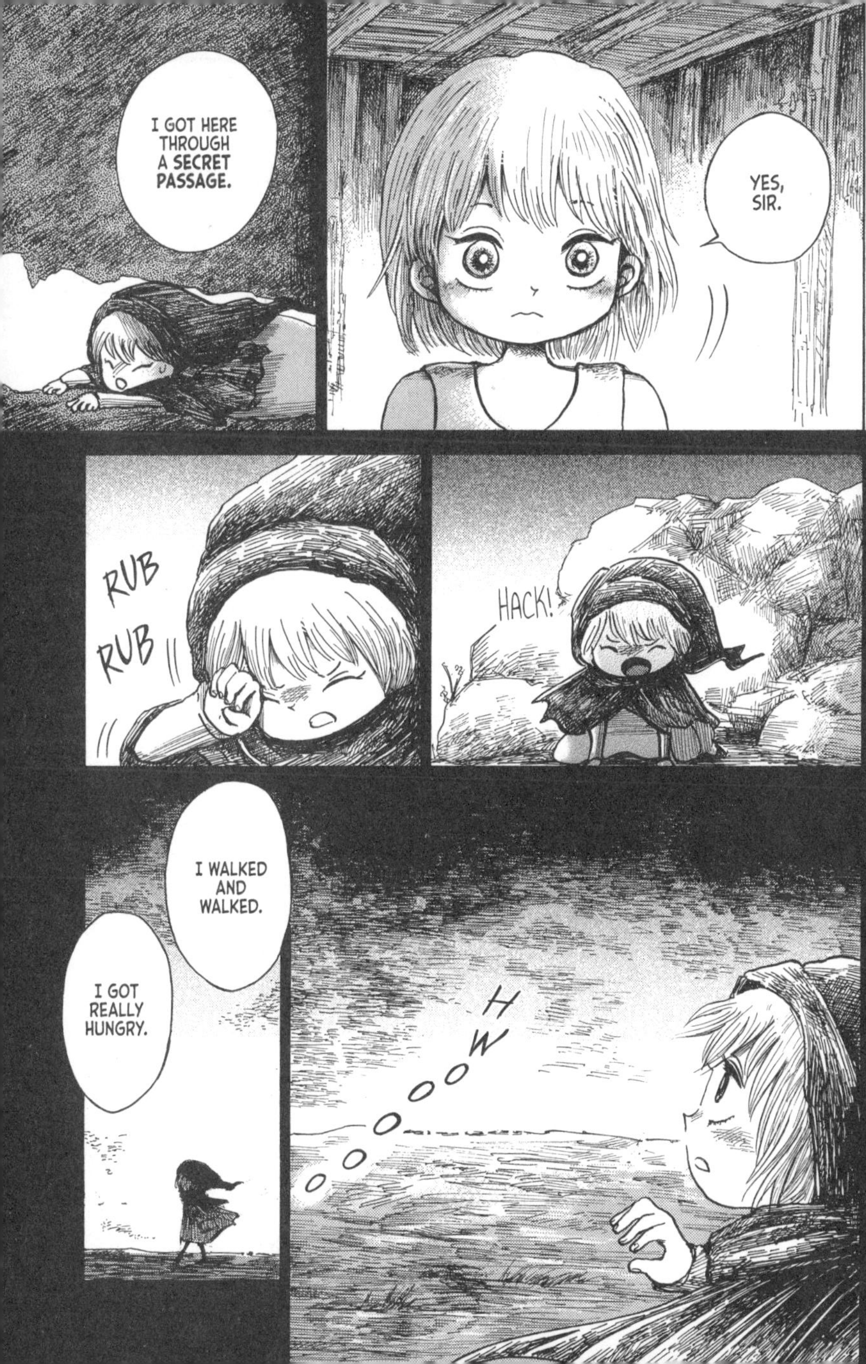
YES, SIR.
I GOT HERE THROUGH A SECRET PASSAGE.
HACK!
RUB
RUB
I WALKED AND WALKED.
I GOT REALLY HUNGRY.
HWOOOOOOO

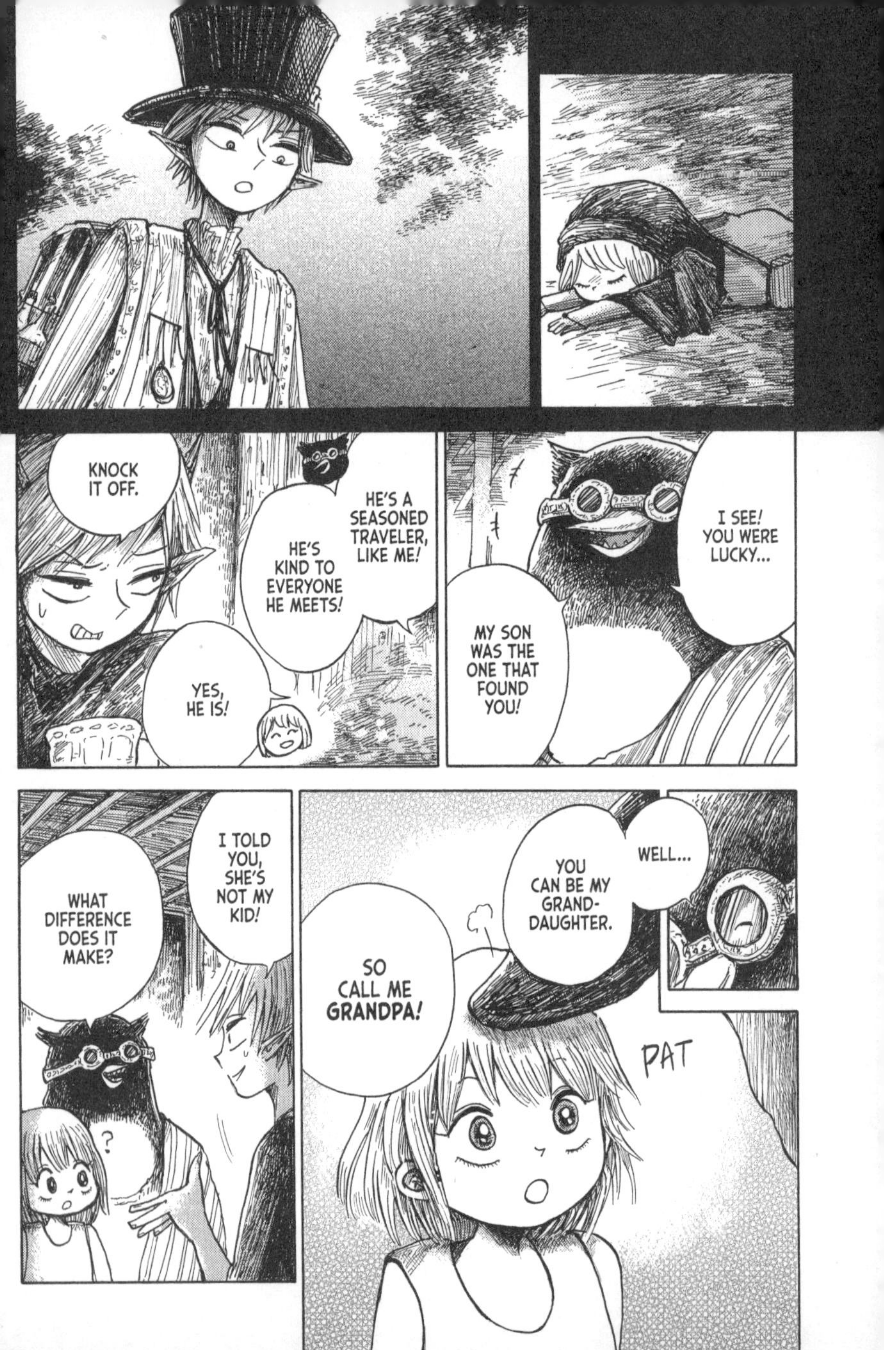
I SEE! YOU WERE LUCKY...
MY SON WAS THE ONE THAT FOUND YOU!
HE'S A SEASONED TRAVELER, LIKE ME!
HE'S KIND TO EVERYONE HE MEETS!
YES, HE IS!
KNOCK IT OFF.
WELL...
YOU CAN BE MY GRAND-DAUGHTER.
SO CALL ME **GRANDPA!**
PAT
I TOLD YOU, SHE'S NOT MY KID!
WHAT DIFFERENCE DOES IT MAKE?
?

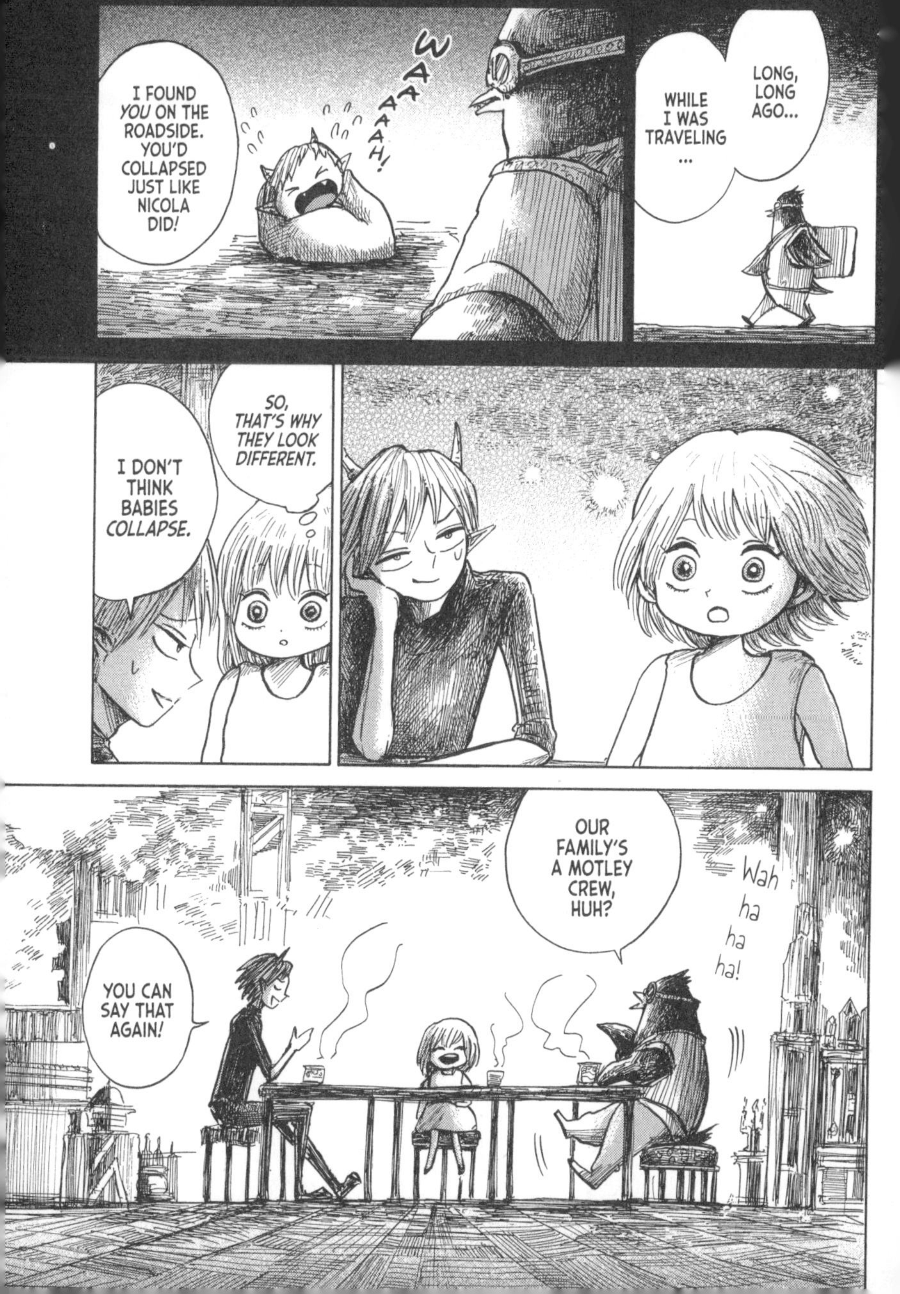
LONG, LONG AGO...
WHILE I WAS TRAVELING ...
WAAAAAH!
I FOUND *YOU* ON THE ROADSIDE. YOU'D COLLAPSED JUST LIKE NICOLA DID!
SO, THAT'S WHY THEY LOOK DIFFERENT.
I DON'T THINK BABIES *COLLAPSE.*
Wah ha ha ha!
OUR FAMILY'S A MOTLEY CREW, HUH?
YOU CAN SAY THAT AGAIN!

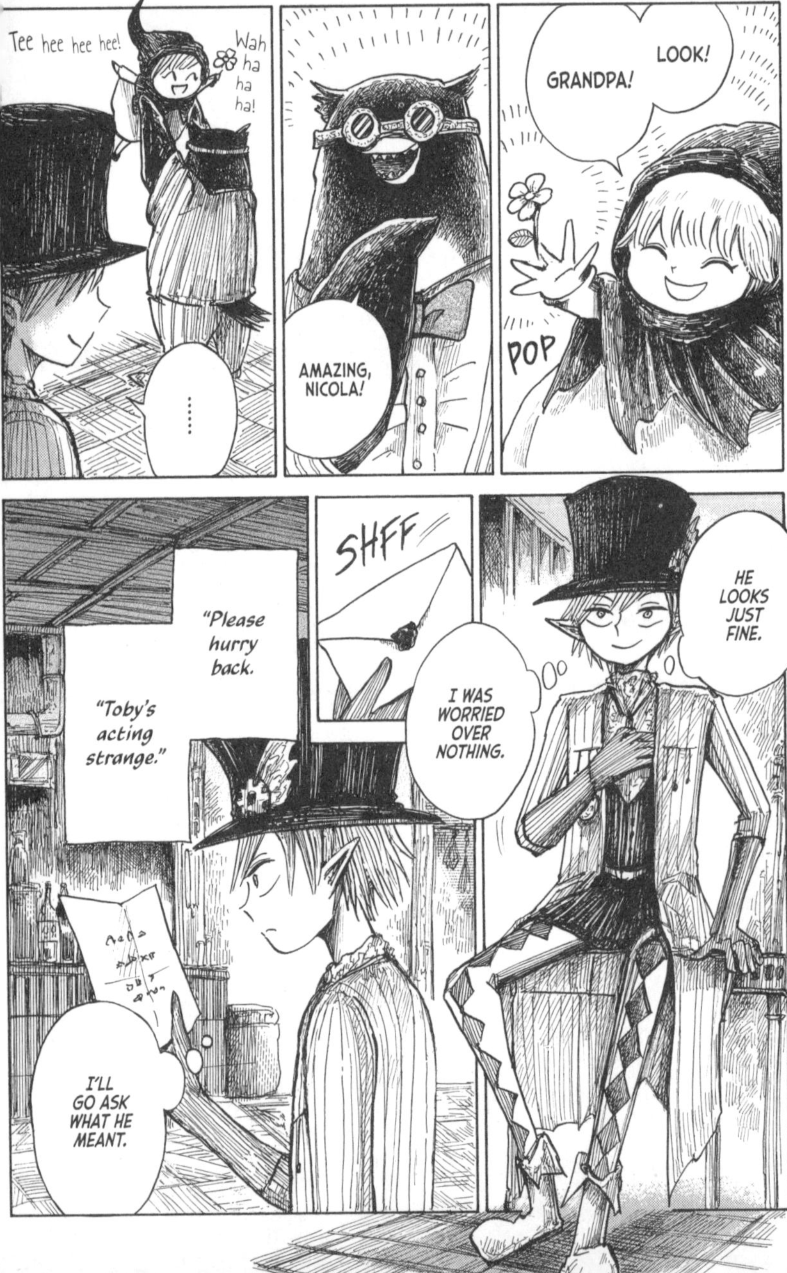
GRANDPA! LOOK!
POP
AMAZING, NICOLA!
Wah ha ha ha!
Tee hee hee hee!
......
HE LOOKS JUST FINE.
I WAS WORRIED OVER NOTHING.
SHFF
"Please hurry back.
"Toby's acting strange."
I'LL GO ASK WHAT HE MEANT.

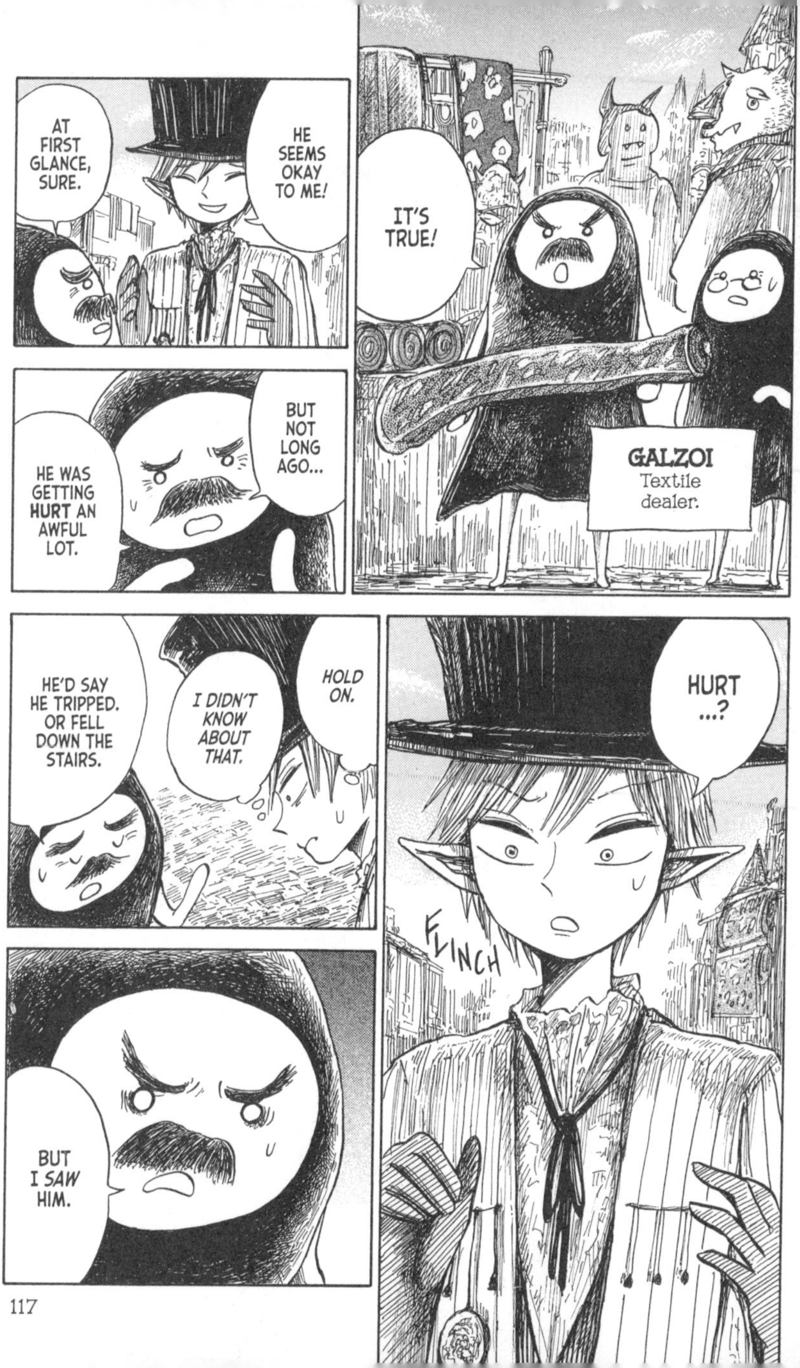
IT'S TRUE!
GALZOI
Textile dealer.
HE SEEMS OKAY TO ME!
AT FIRST GLANCE, SURE.
BUT NOT LONG AGO...
HE WAS GETTING HURT AN AWFUL LOT.
HURT ...?
FLINCH
HOLD ON.
I DIDN'T KNOW ABOUT THAT.
HE'D SAY HE TRIPPED. OR FELL DOWN THE STAIRS.
BUT I SAW HIM.

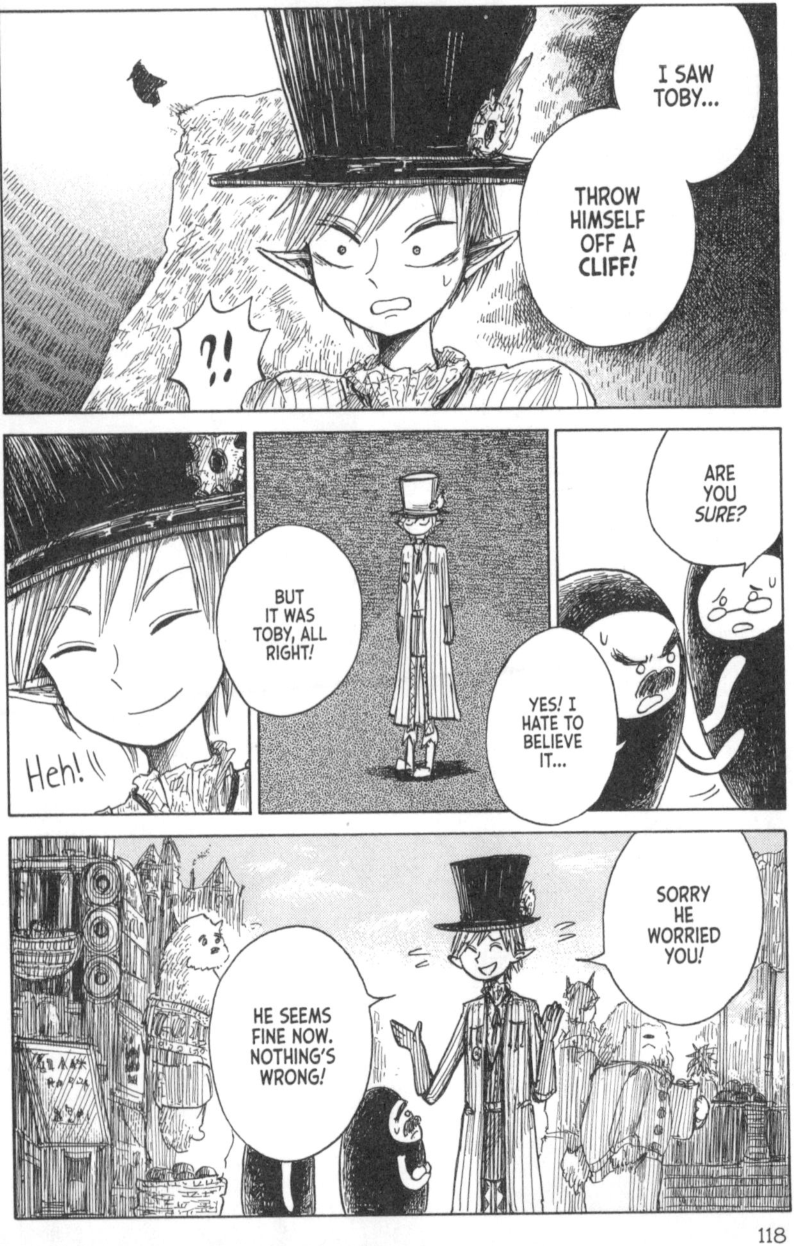

I SAW TOBY...
THROW HIMSELF OFF A CLIFF!
?!
ARE YOU *SURE?*
YES! I HATE TO BELIEVE IT...
BUT IT WAS TOBY, ALL RIGHT!
Heh!
SORRY HE WORRIED YOU!
HE SEEMS FINE NOW. NOTHING'S WRONG!

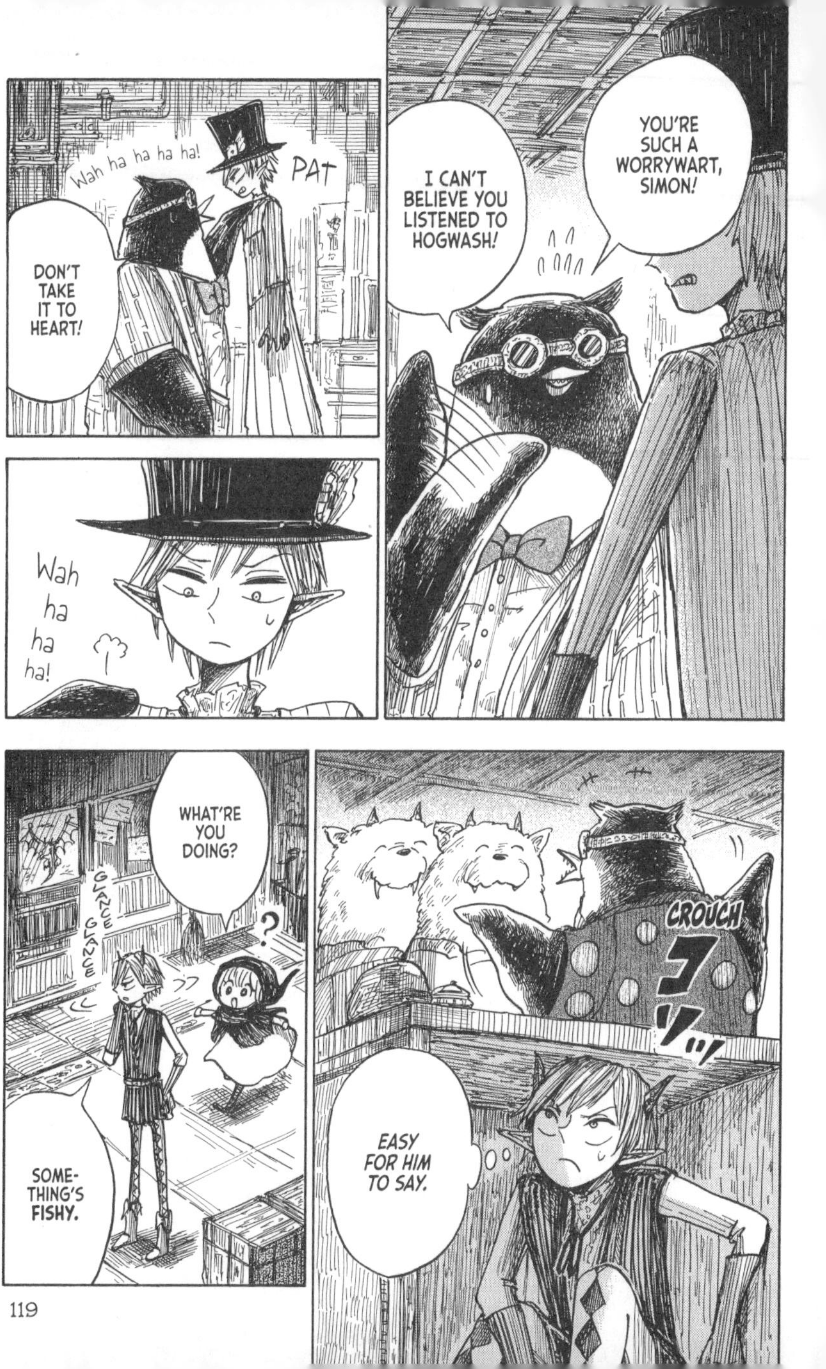
YOU'RE SUCH A WORRYWART, SIMON!
I CAN'T BELIEVE YOU LISTENED TO HOGWASH!
PAT
Wah ha ha ha ha!
DON'T TAKE IT TO HEART!
Wah ha ha ha!
CROUCH
EASY FOR HIM TO SAY.
WHAT'RE YOU DOING?
?
GLANCE GLANCE
SOME-THING'S FISHY.

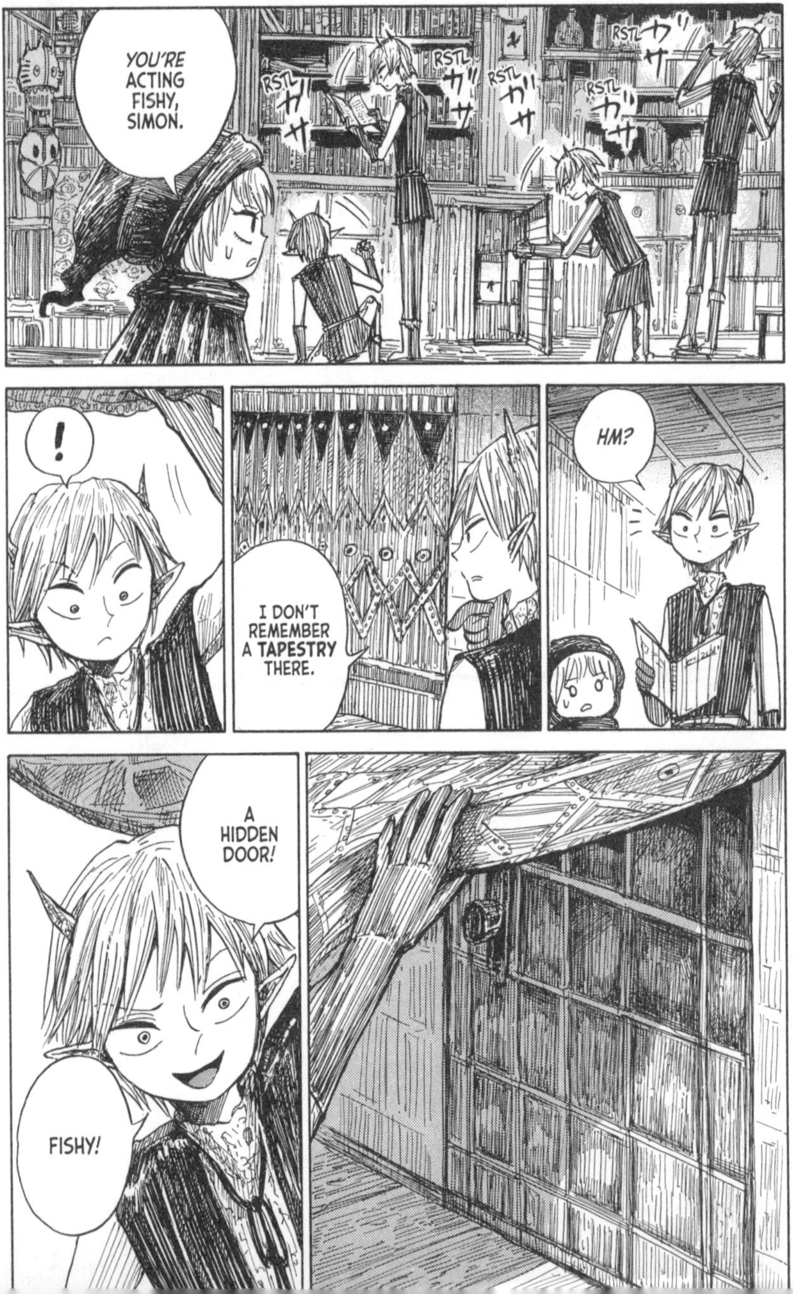
RSTL ガサ
RSTL ガサ
RSTL ガサ
RSTL ガサ
RSTL ガサ
YOU'RE ACTING FISHY, SIMON.
HM?
I DON'T REMEMBER A TAPESTRY THERE.
!
A HIDDEN DOOR!
FISHY!

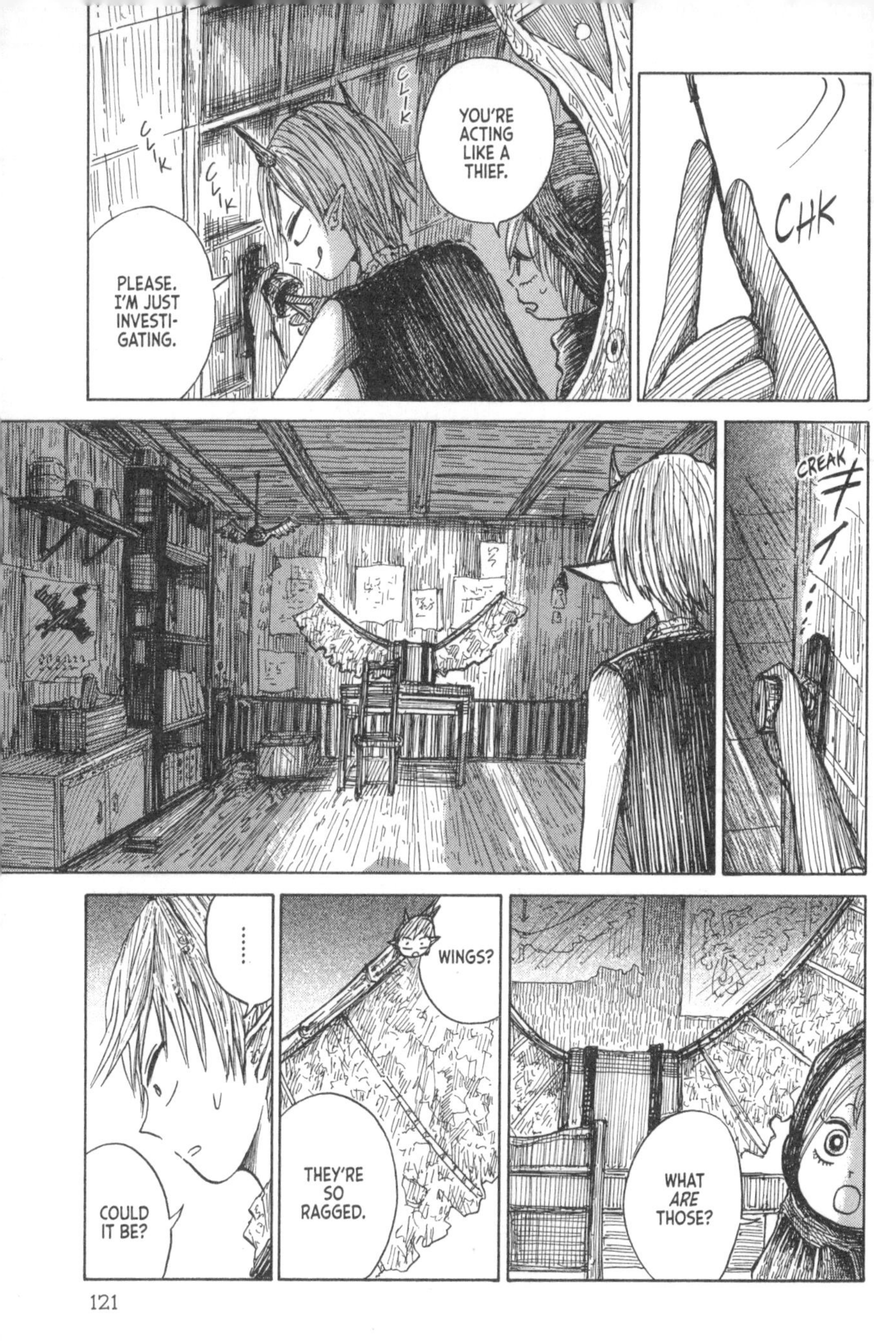
CHK
CLIK
YOU'RE ACTING LIKE A THIEF.
CLIK
CLIK
PLEASE. I'M JUST INVESTI-GATING.
CREAK
WHAT *ARE* THOSE?
WINGS?
THEY'RE SO RAGGED.
……
COULD IT BE?

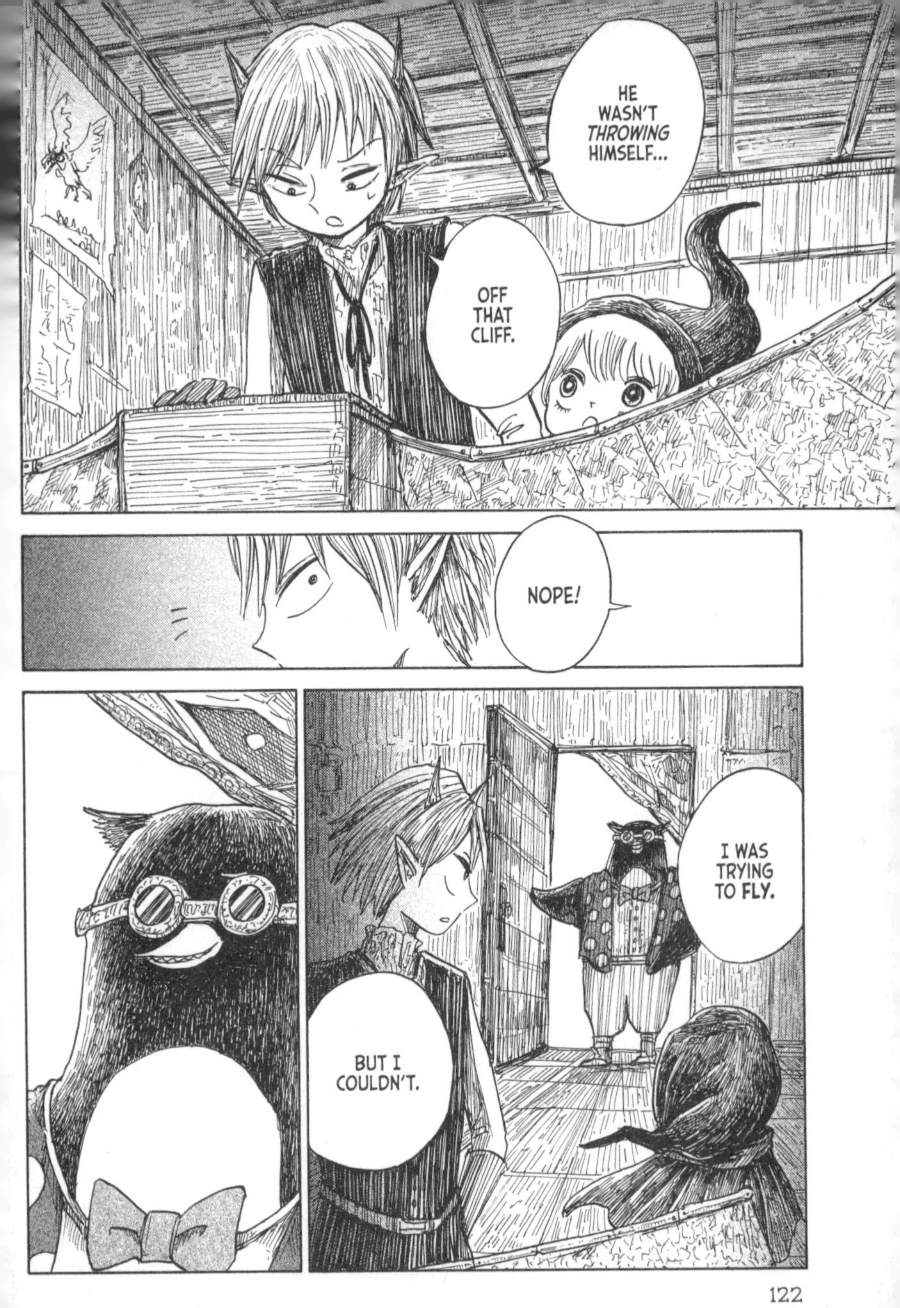
HE WASN'T *THROWING* HIMSELF...
OFF THAT CLIFF.
NOPE!
I WAS TRYING TO FLY.
BUT I COULDN'T.

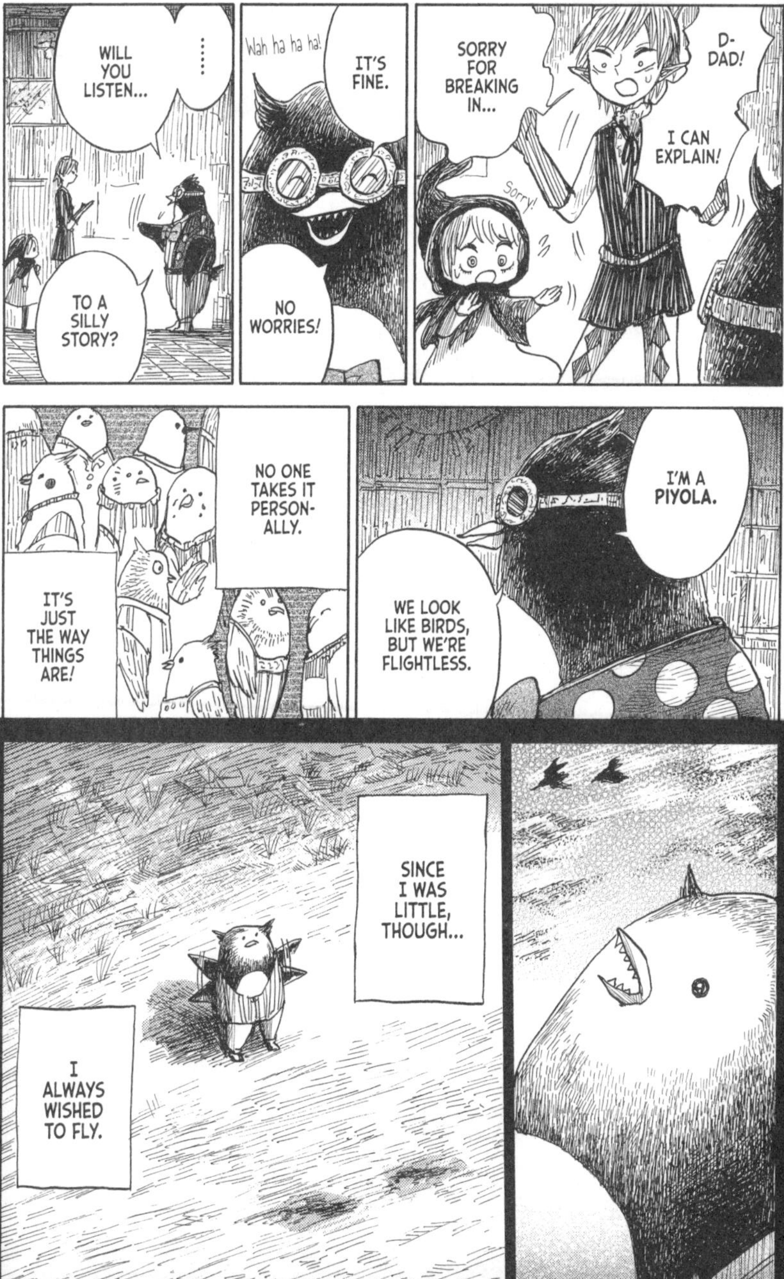
D-DAD!
I CAN EXPLAIN!
SORRY FOR BREAKING IN...
Sorry!
IT'S FINE.
Wah ha ha ha!
NO WORRIES!
......
WILL YOU LISTEN...
TO A SILLY STORY?
I'M A PIYOLA.
WE LOOK LIKE BIRDS, BUT WE'RE FLIGHTLESS.
NO ONE TAKES IT PERSON-ALLY.
IT'S JUST THE WAY THINGS ARE!
SINCE I WAS LITTLE, THOUGH...
I ALWAYS WISHED TO FLY.

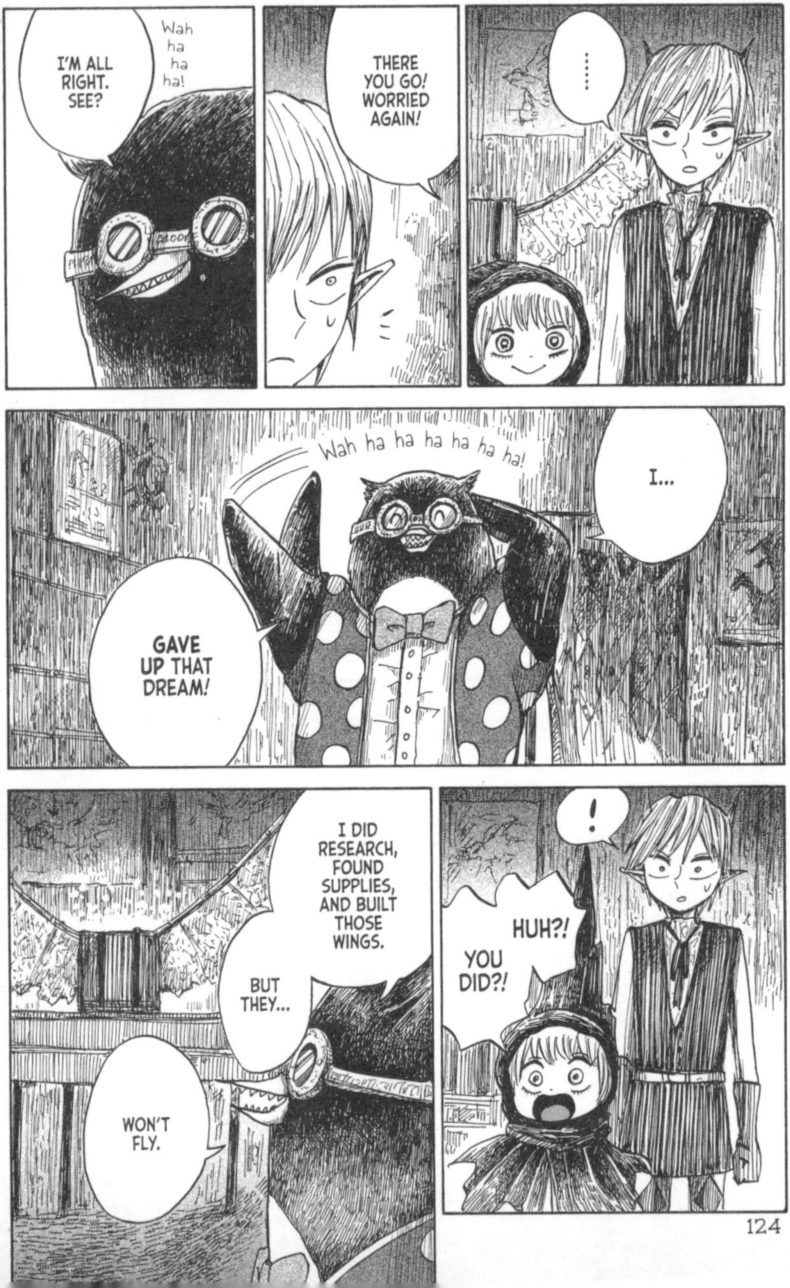
……
THERE YOU GO! WORRIED AGAIN!
Wah ha ha ha!
I'M ALL RIGHT. SEE?
I...
Wah ha ha ha ha ha ha!
GAVE UP THAT DREAM!
!
HUH?!
YOU DID?!
I DID RESEARCH, FOUND SUPPLIES, AND BUILT THOSE WINGS.
BUT THEY...
WON'T FLY.

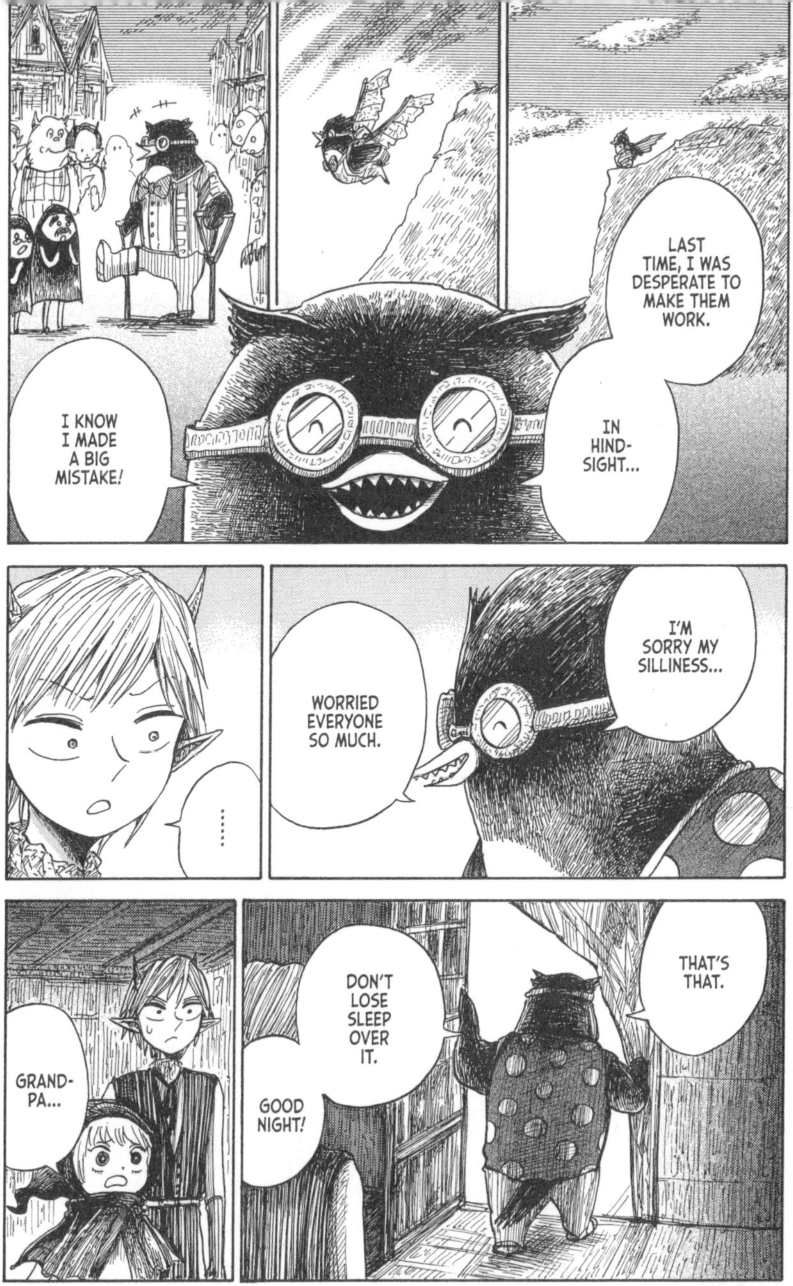
LAST TIME, I WAS DESPERATE TO MAKE THEM WORK.
IN HINDSIGHT...
I KNOW I MADE A BIG MISTAKE!
I'M SORRY MY SILLINESS...
WORRIED EVERYONE SO MUCH.
......
THAT'S THAT.
DON'T LOSE SLEEP OVER IT.
GOOD NIGHT!
GRANDPA...

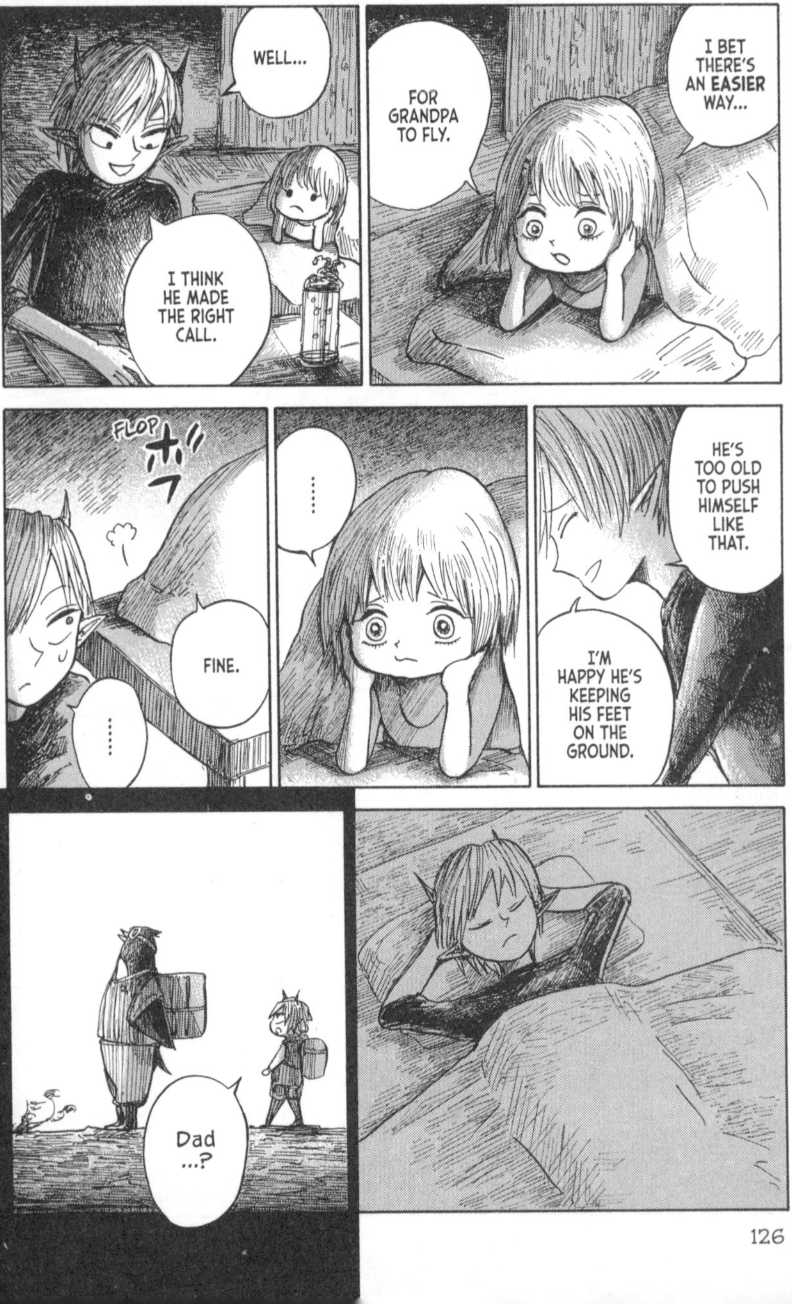
I BET THERE'S AN EASIER WAY...
FOR GRANDPA TO FLY.
WELL...
I THINK HE MADE THE RIGHT CALL.
HE'S TOO OLD TO PUSH HIMSELF LIKE THAT.
I'M HAPPY HE'S KEEPING HIS FEET ON THE GROUND.
......
FLOP
FINE.
......
Dad ...?

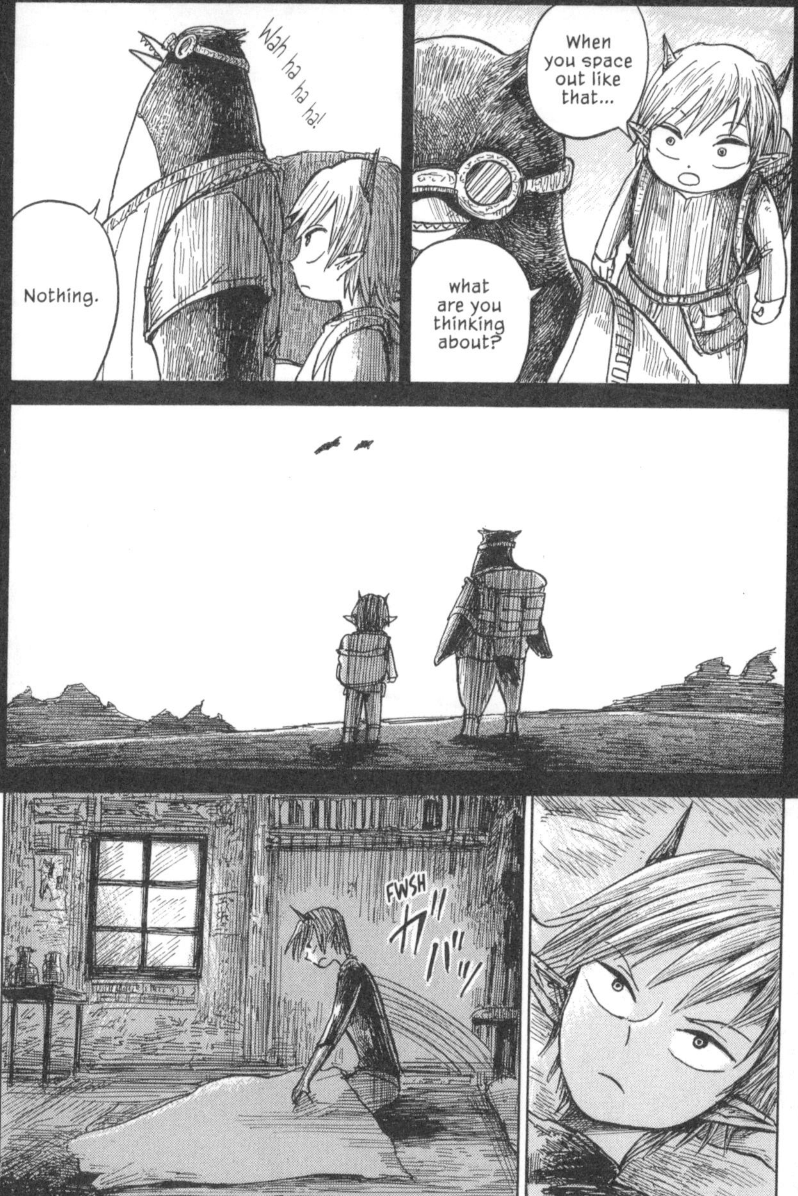
When you space out like that...
what are you thinking about?
Wah ha ha ha!
Nothing.
FWSH
ガバッ

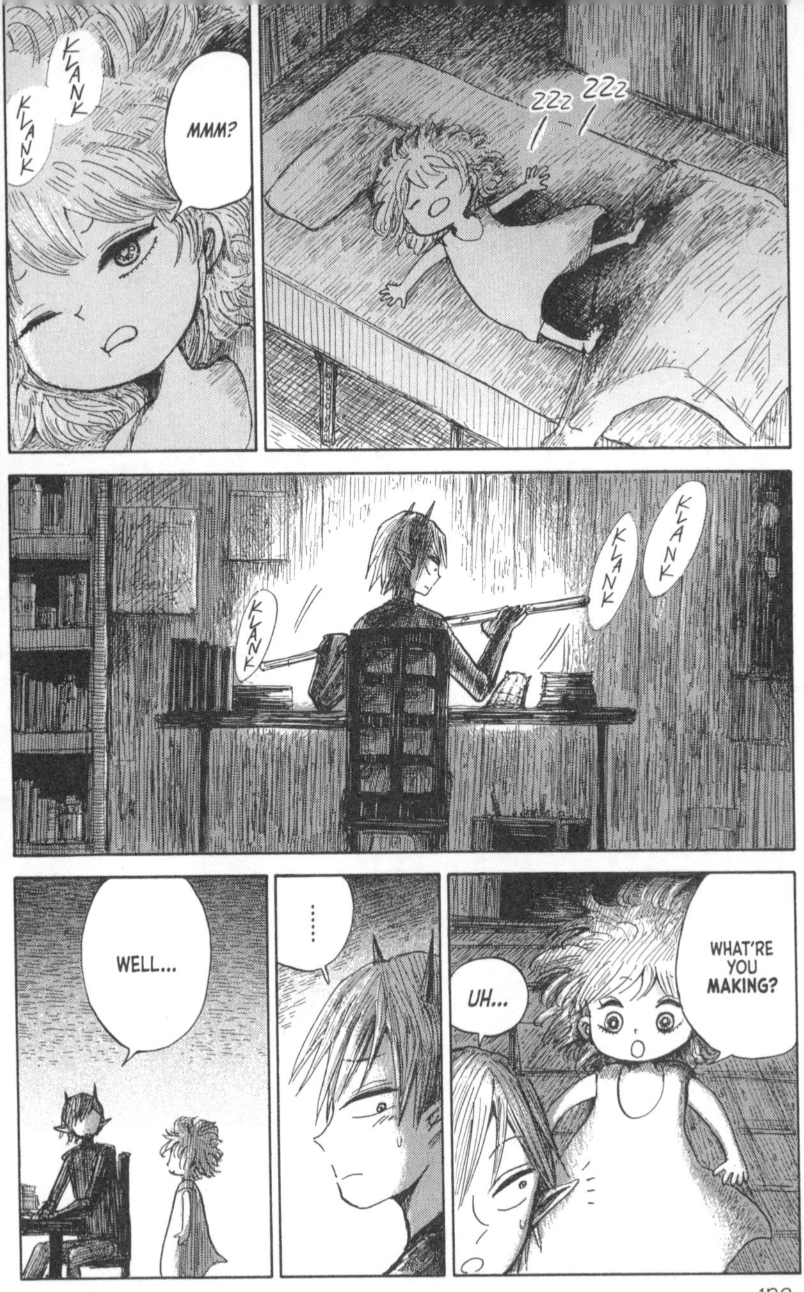
ZZZ
ZZZ
KLANK
KLANK
MMM?
KLANK
KLANK
KLANK
WHAT'RE YOU MAKING?
UH...
......
WELL...

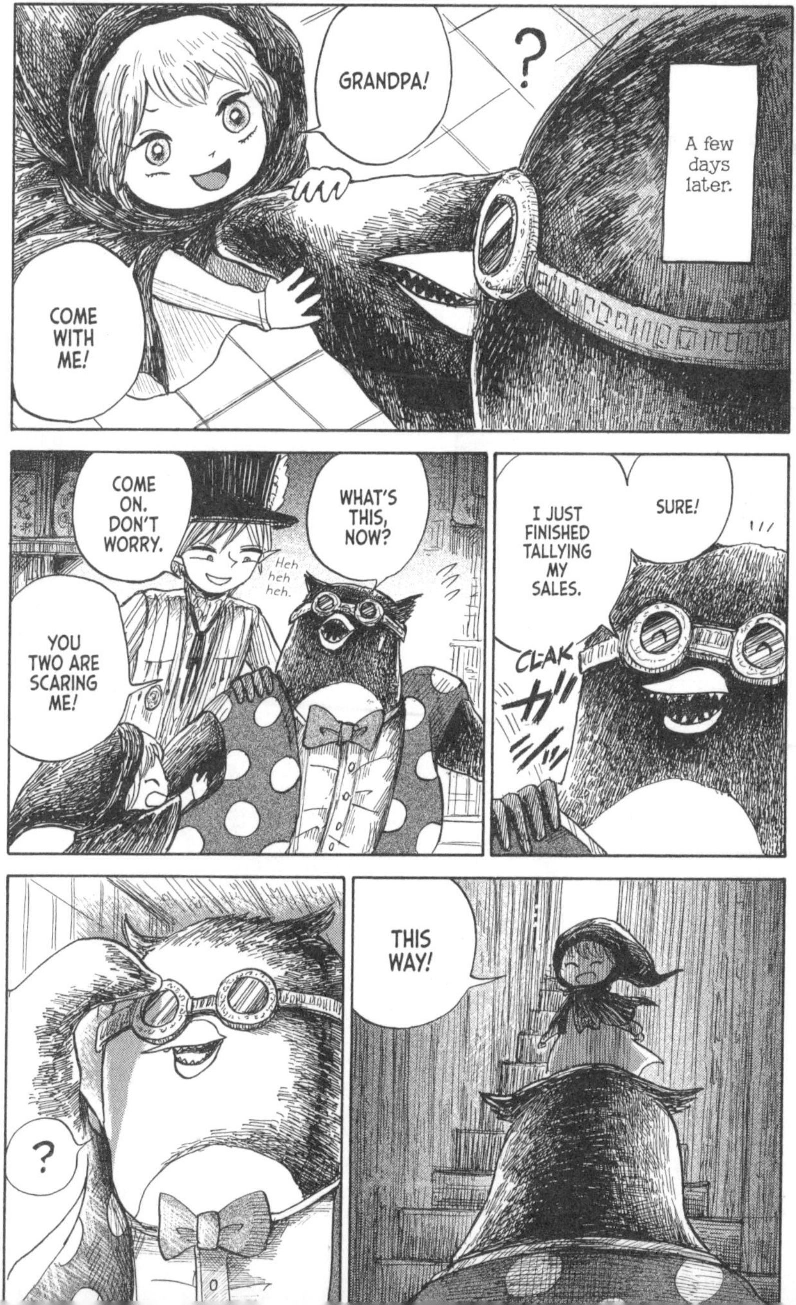
A few days later.
?
GRANDPA!
COME WITH ME!
SURE!
I JUST FINISHED TALLYING MY SALES.
CLAK
ガシッ
WHAT'S THIS, NOW?
COME ON. DON'T WORRY.
Heh heh heh.
YOU TWO ARE SCARING ME!
THIS WAY!
?

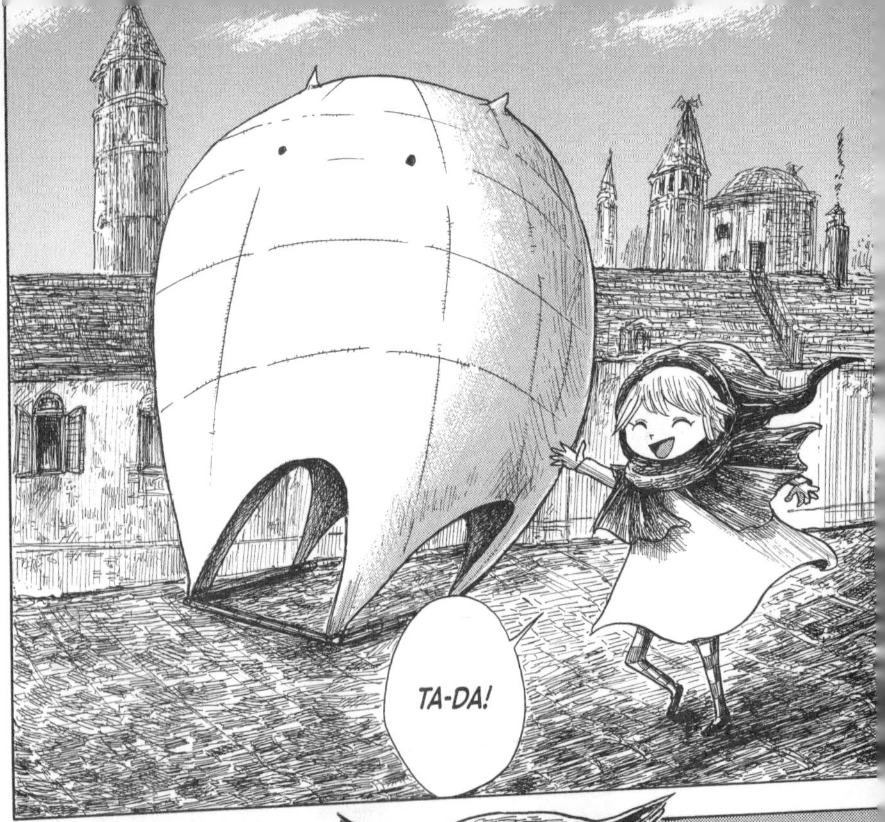
TA-DA!

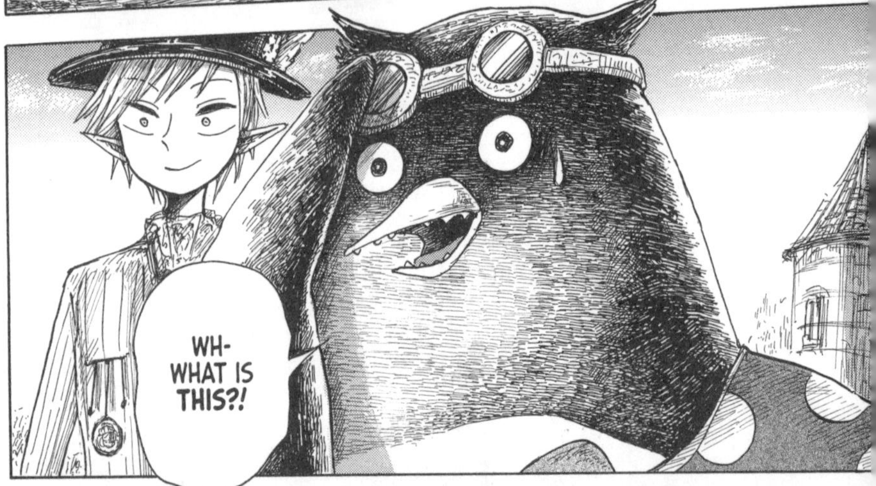
WH-
WHAT IS
THIS?!

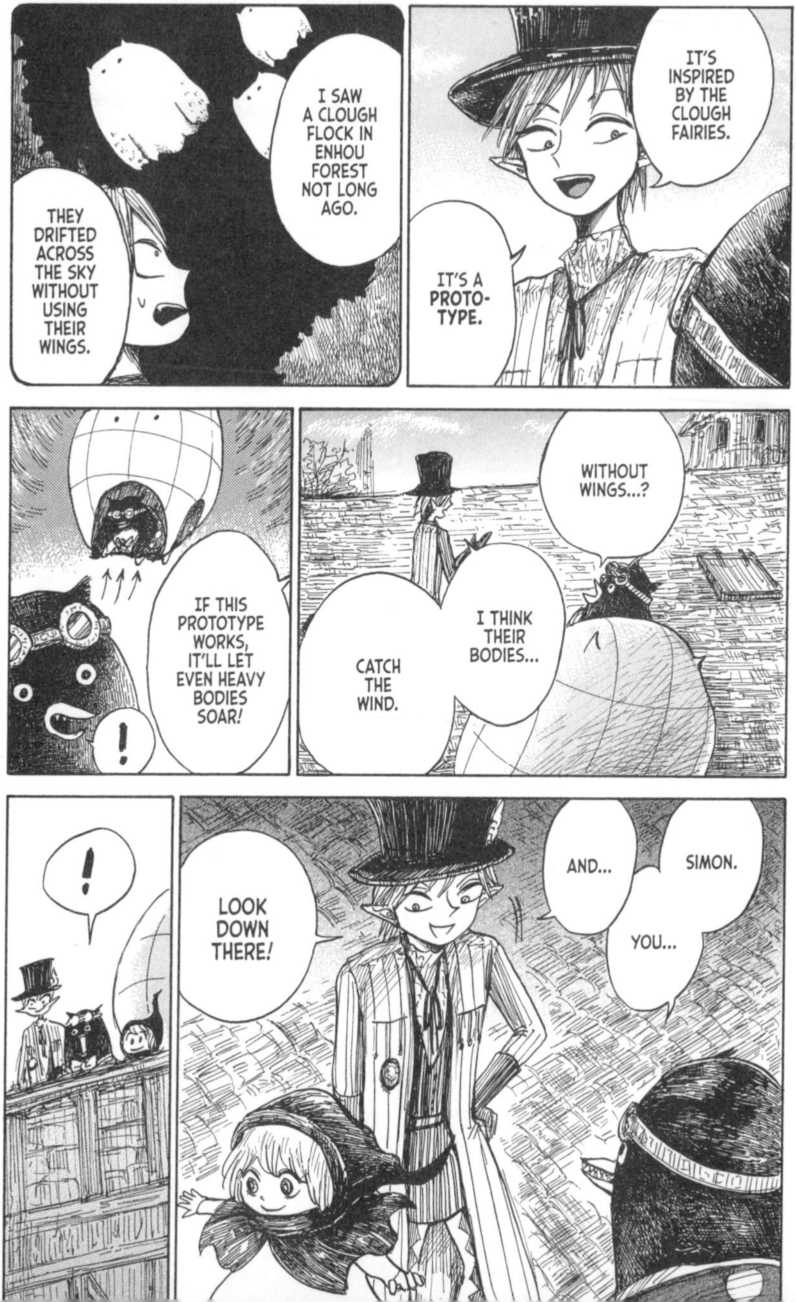
IT'S INSPIRED BY THE CLOUGH FAIRIES.
IT'S A PROTO-TYPE.
I SAW A CLOUGH FLOCK IN ENHOU FOREST NOT LONG AGO.
THEY DRIFTED ACROSS THE SKY WITHOUT USING THEIR WINGS.
WITHOUT WINGS...?
I THINK THEIR BODIES...
CATCH THE WIND.
IF THIS PROTOTYPE WORKS, IT'LL LET EVEN HEAVY BODIES SOAR!
!
SIMON.
YOU...
AND...
LOOK DOWN THERE!
!

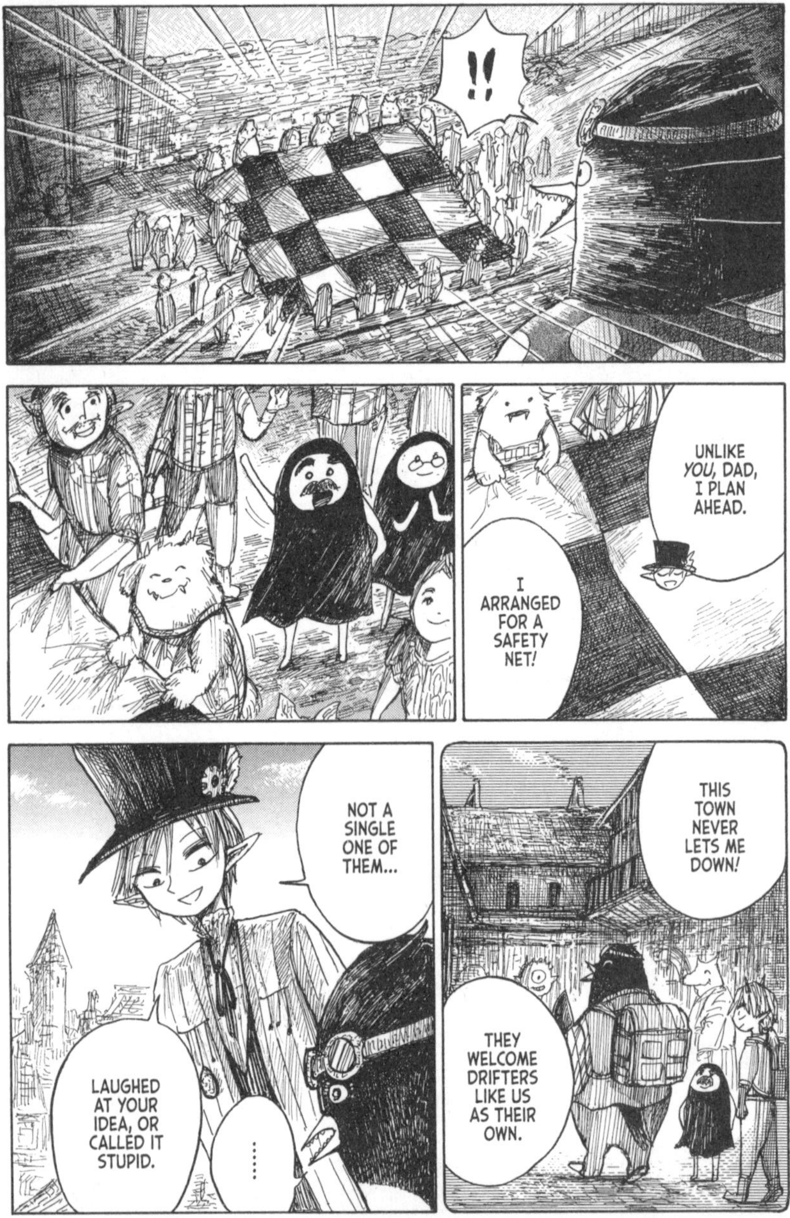
!!
UNLIKE *YOU,* DAD, I PLAN AHEAD.
I ARRANGED FOR A SAFETY NET!
THIS TOWN NEVER LETS ME DOWN!
THEY WELCOME DRIFTERS LIKE US AS THEIR OWN.
NOT A SINGLE ONE OF THEM...
LAUGHED AT YOUR IDEA, OR CALLED IT STUPID.
......

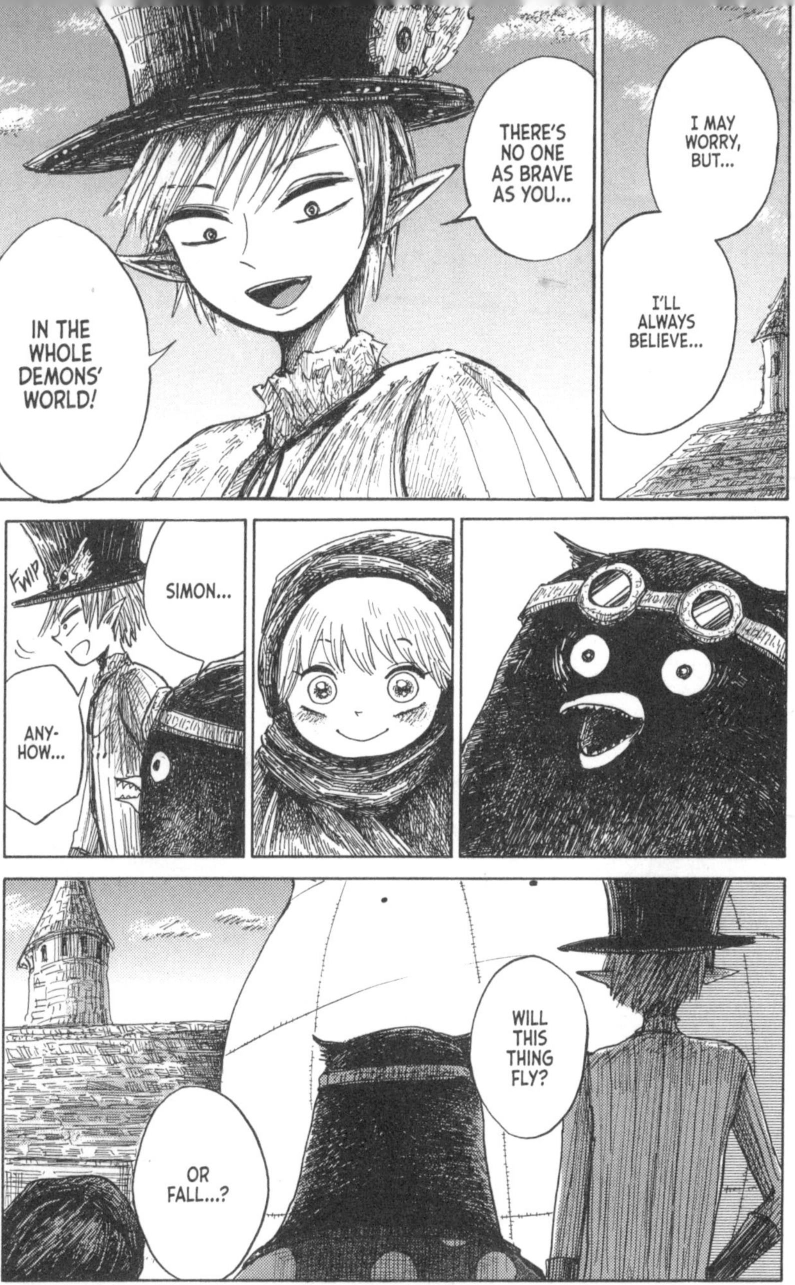
I MAY WORRY, BUT...
I'LL ALWAYS BELIEVE...
THERE'S NO ONE AS BRAVE AS YOU...
IN THE WHOLE DEMONS' WORLD!
FWIP
SIMON...
ANY-HOW...
WILL THIS THING FLY?
OR FALL...?

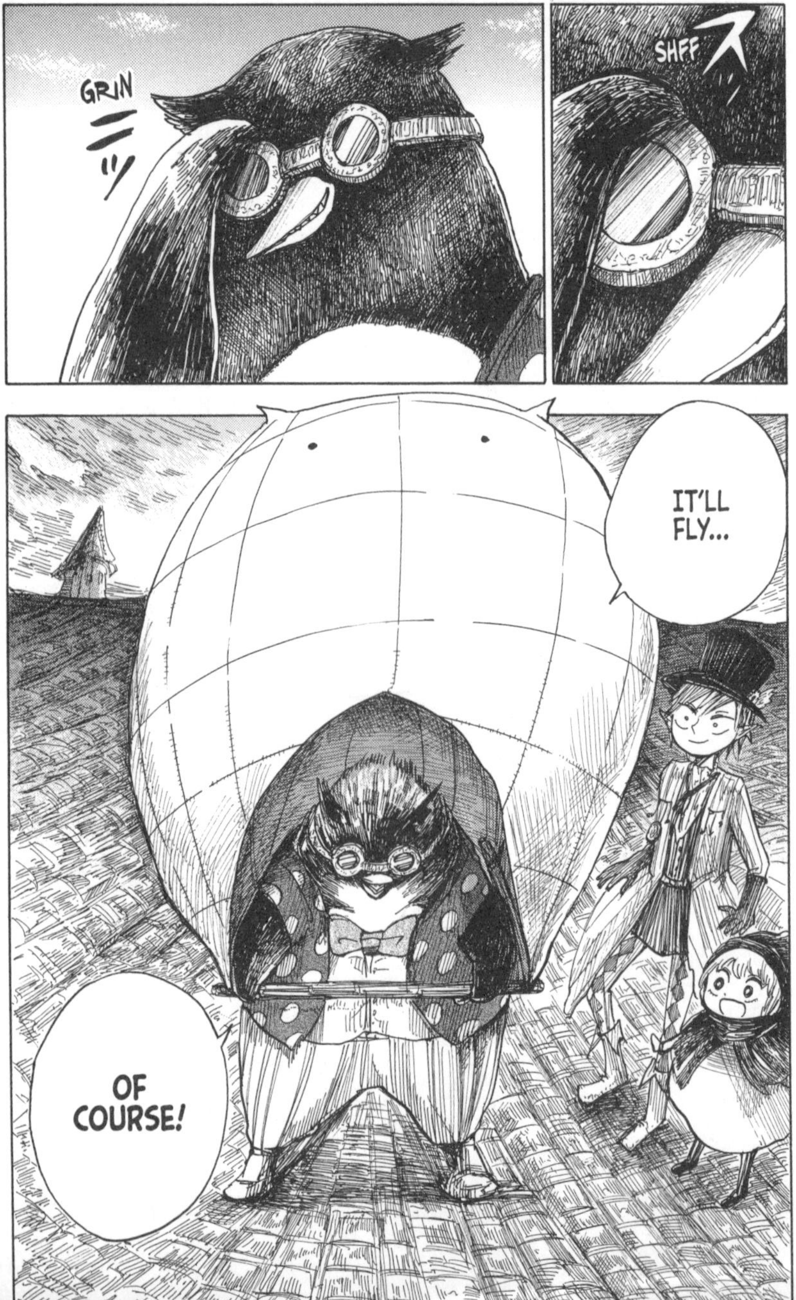
SHFF
GRIN
IT'LL FLY...
OF COURSE!

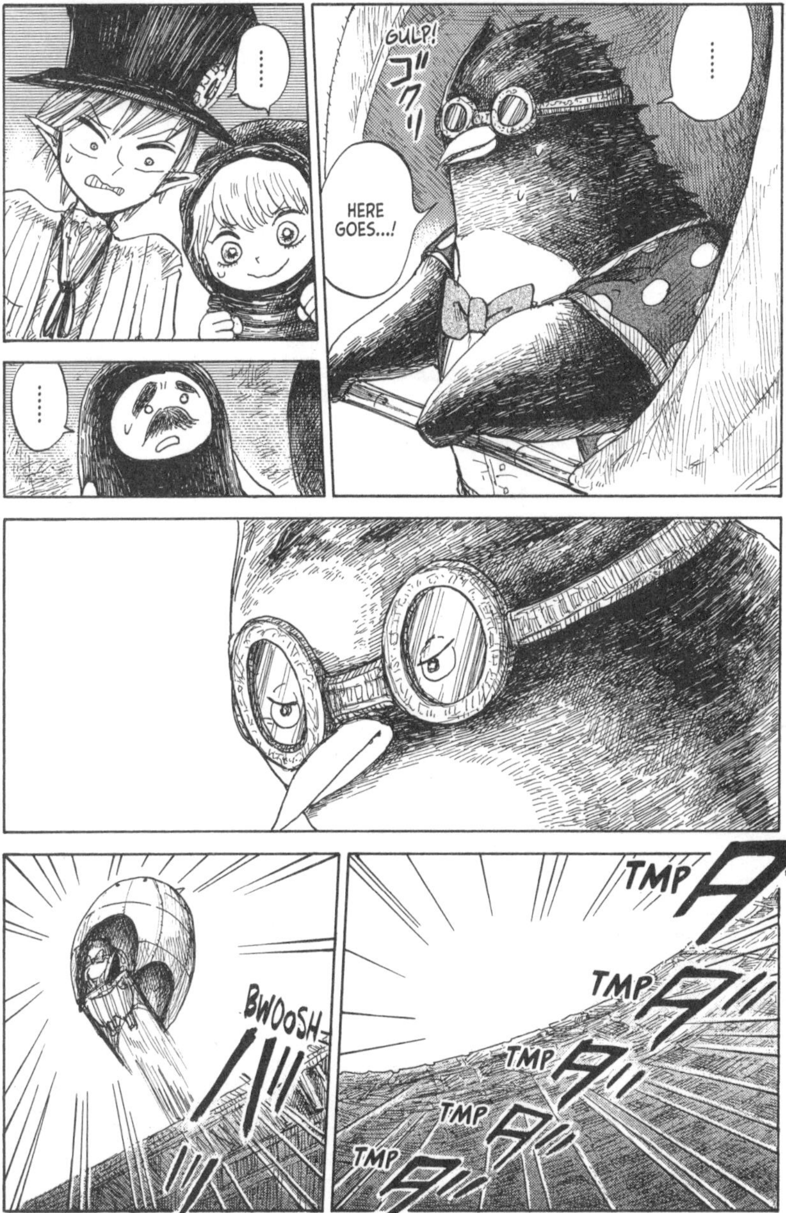
……
GULP!
ゴクリ
HERE GOES...!
……
……
TMP タ
TMP タ
TMP タ
TMP タ
TMP タ
BWOOSH
バ

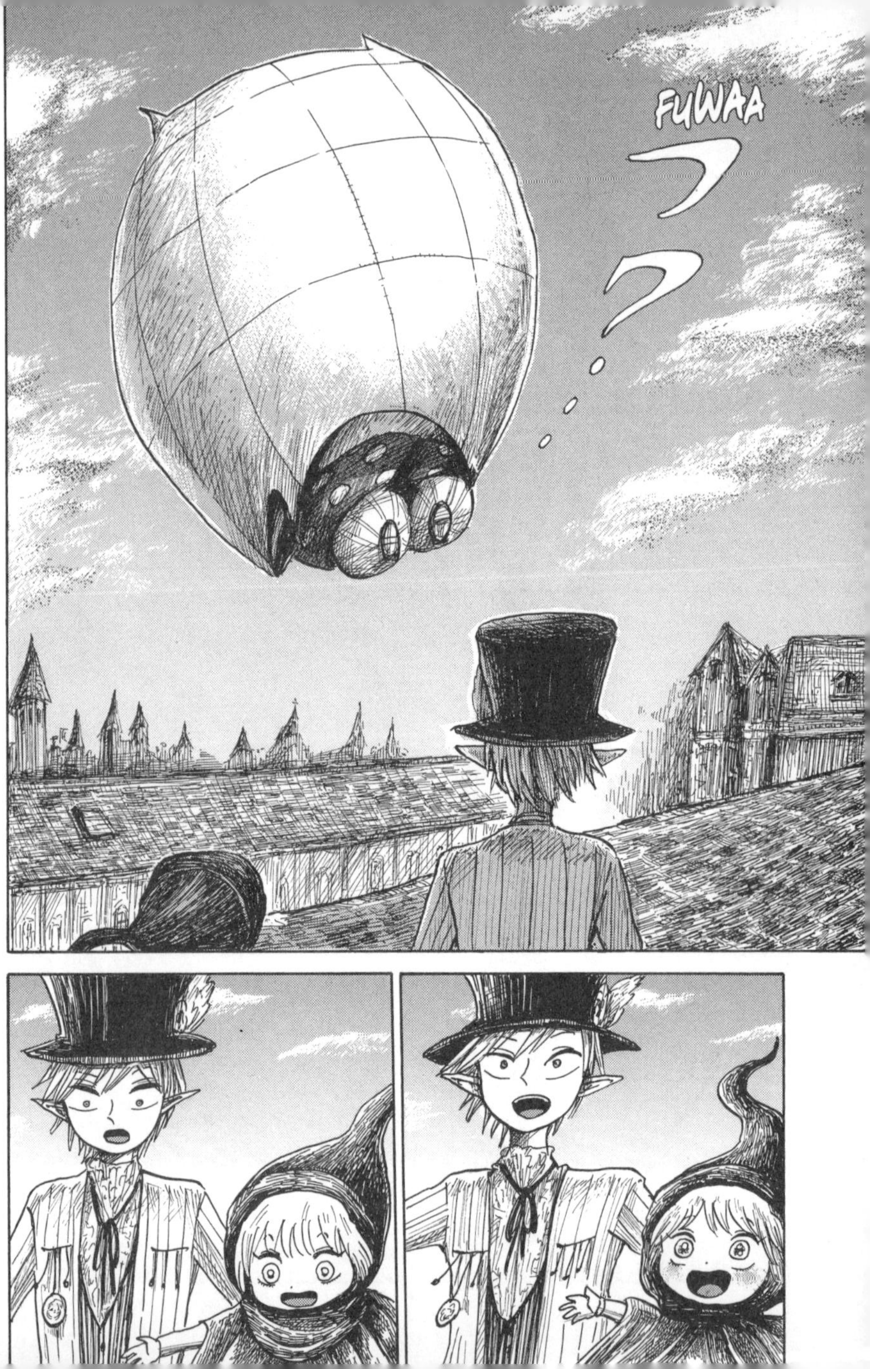
FUWAA

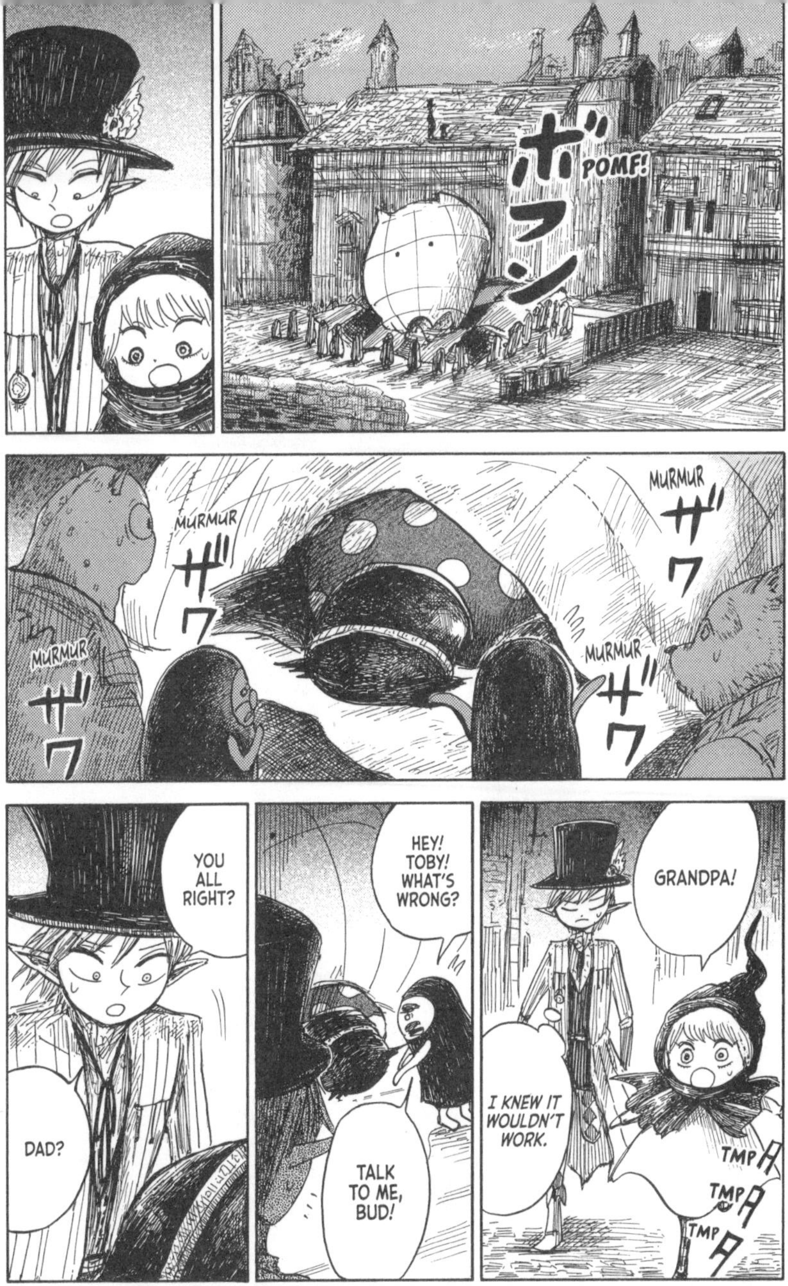
ボン
POMF!
MURMUR
ザワ
MURMUR
ザワ
MURMUR
ザワ
MURMUR
ザワ
GRANDPA!
I KNEW IT WOULDN'T WORK.
TMP
タ
TMP
タ
TMP
タ
HEY! TOBY! WHAT'S WRONG?
TALK TO ME, BUD!
YOU ALL RIGHT?
DAD?

SHFF

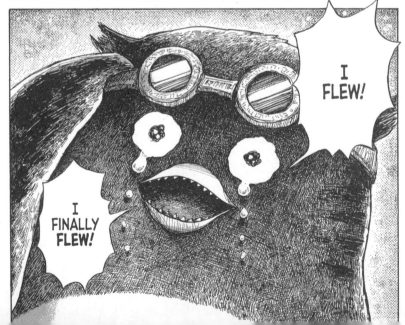

I FLEW!

I FINALLY FLEW!

YOU SAW, RIGHT?

FOR A MOMENT, I FELT THE WIND!

ポ PLIP

ポ PLIP

HUH?

MURMUR!

ザワ

WOO-HOOO!

SUBLIME!!

SO, THAT'S...

WHAT IT'S LIKE TO FLY!

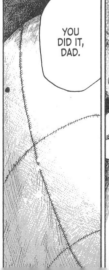

YOU DID IT, DAD.

WHEEEEE!

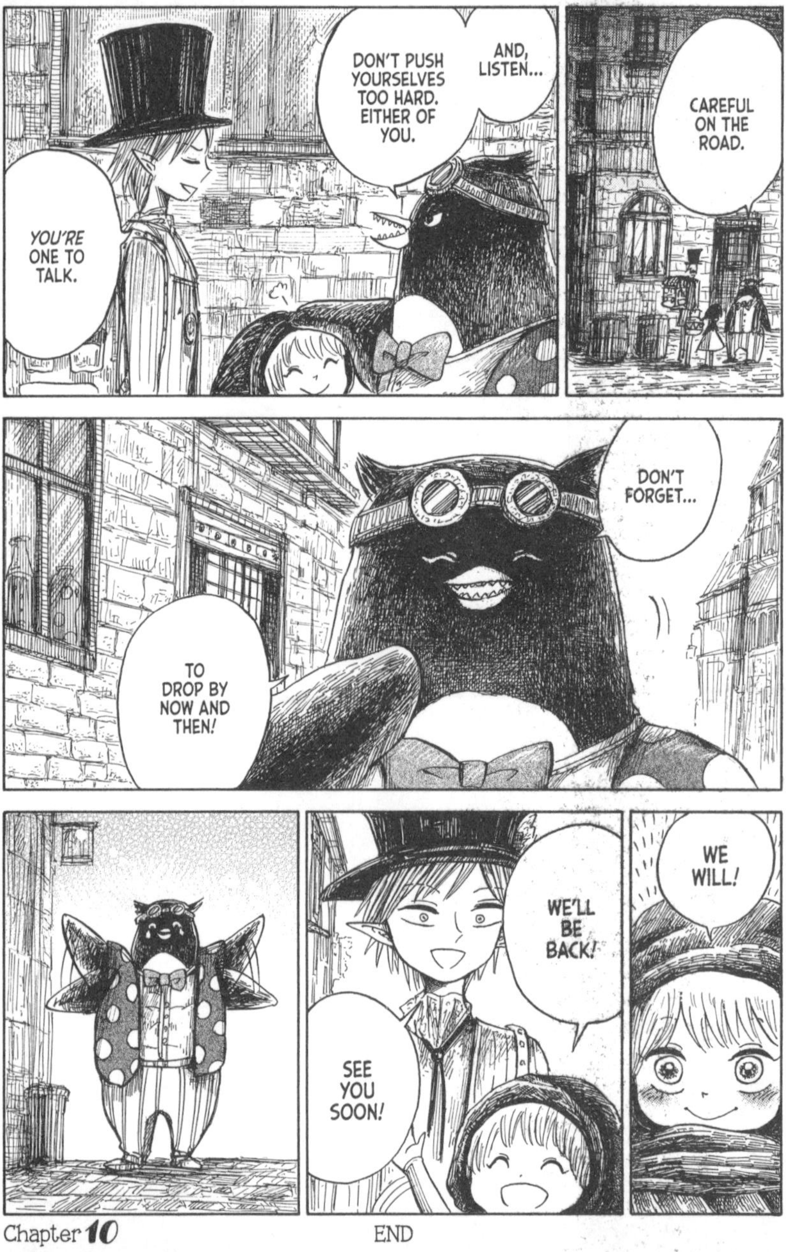
CAREFUL ON THE ROAD.
AND, LISTEN...
DON'T PUSH YOURSELVES TOO HARD. EITHER OF YOU.
YOU'RE ONE TO TALK.
DON'T FORGET...
TO DROP BY NOW AND THEN!
WE WILL!
WE'LL BE BACK!
SEE YOU SOON!

Chapter 10 END

After the Visit 10

after that

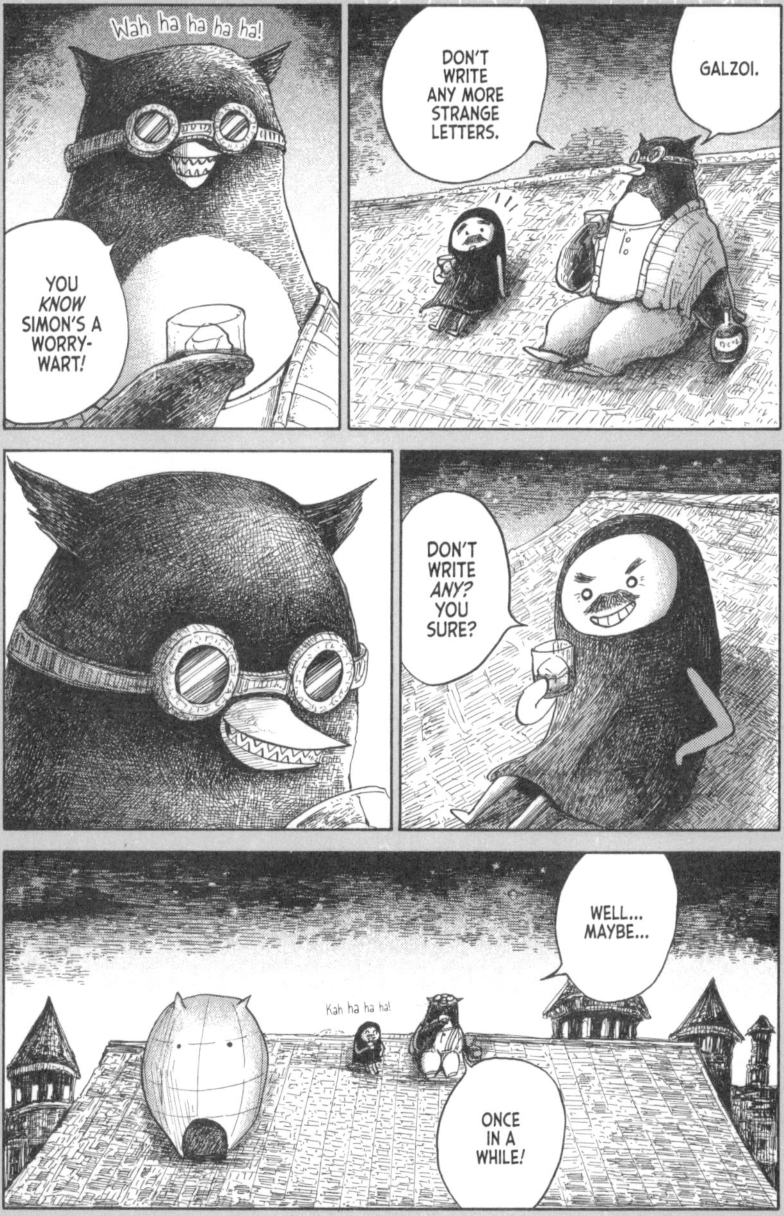

GALZOI.
DON'T WRITE ANY MORE STRANGE LETTERS.
Wah ha ha ha ha!
YOU *KNOW* SIMON'S A WORRY-WART!
DON'T WRITE *ANY?* YOU SURE?
WELL... MAYBE...
Kah ha ha ha!
ONCE IN A WHILE!

Nicola Traveling Around The Demons' World.

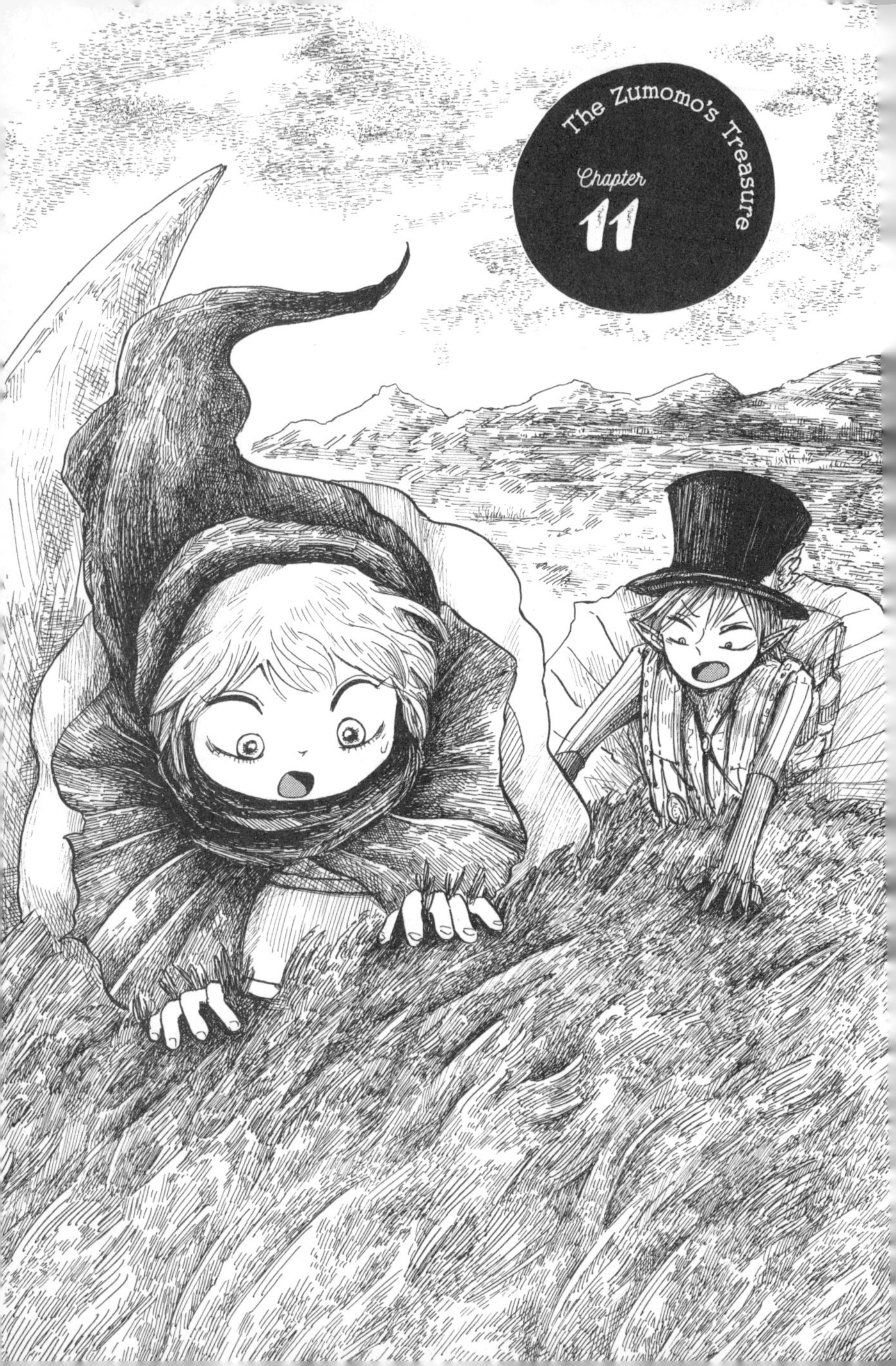
The Zumomo's Treasure
Chapter
11

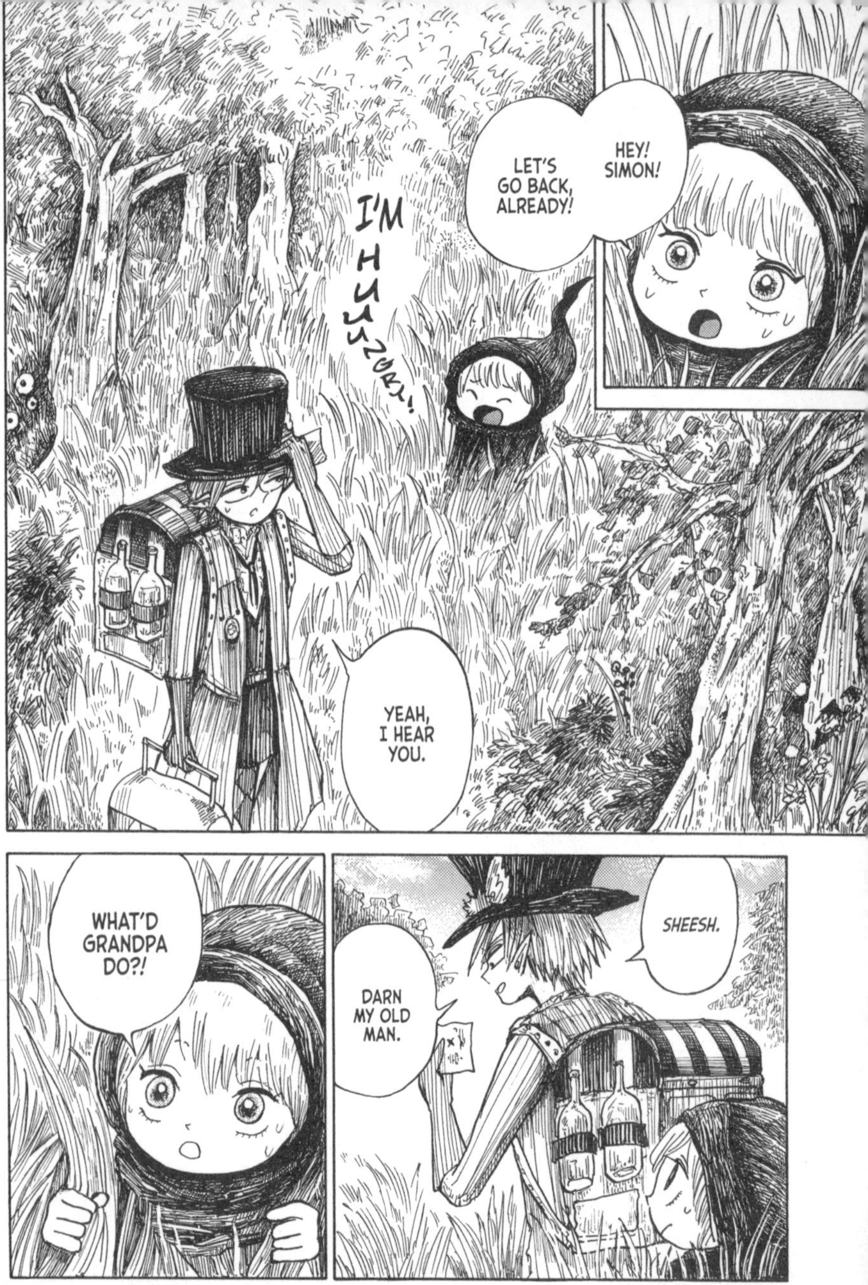
HEY! SIMON!
LET'S GO BACK, ALREADY!
I'M HUUUNGRY!
YEAH, I HEAR YOU.
SHEESH.
DARN MY OLD MAN.
WHAT'D GRANDPA DO?!

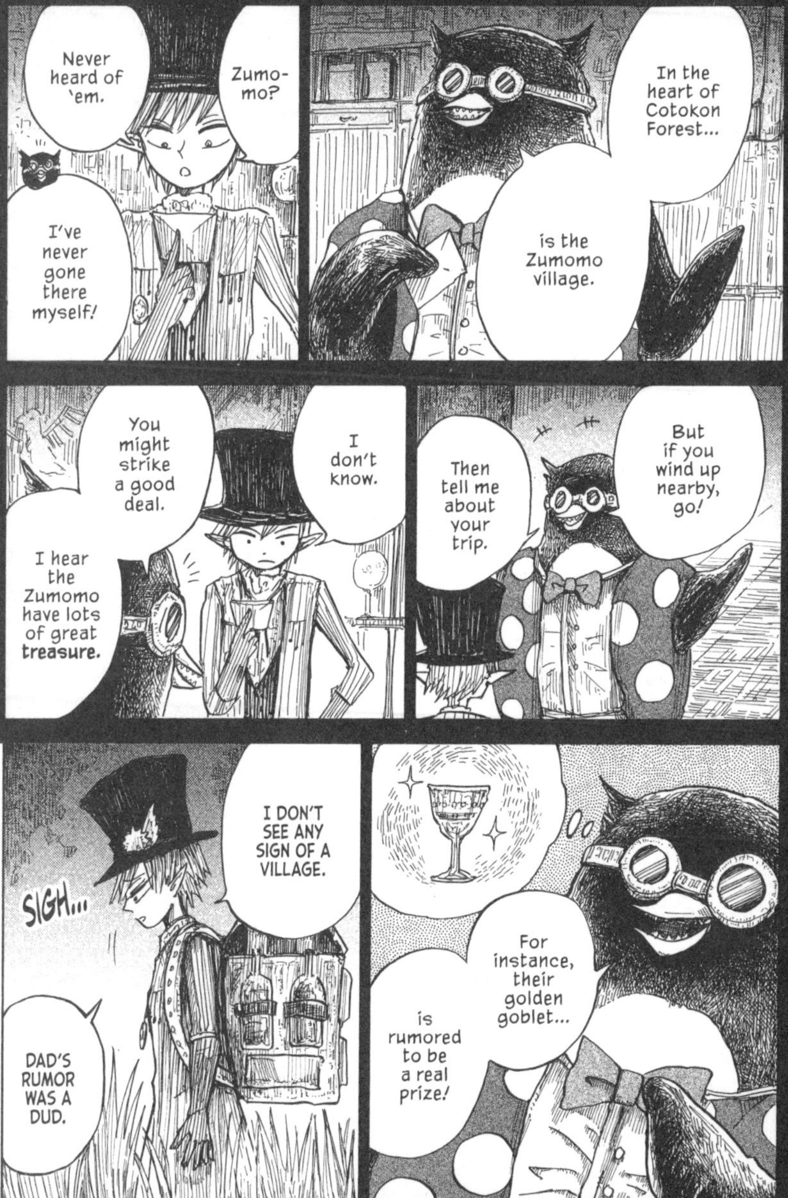

In the heart of Cotokon Forest...
is the Zumomo village.
Zumomo?
Never heard of 'em.
I've never gone there myself!
But if you wind up nearby, go!
Then tell me about your trip.
I don't know.
You might strike a good deal.
I hear the Zumomo have lots of great **treasure.**
For instance, their golden goblet...
is rumored to be a real prize!
I DON'T SEE ANY SIGN OF A VILLAGE.
SIGH...
DAD'S RUMOR WAS A DUD.

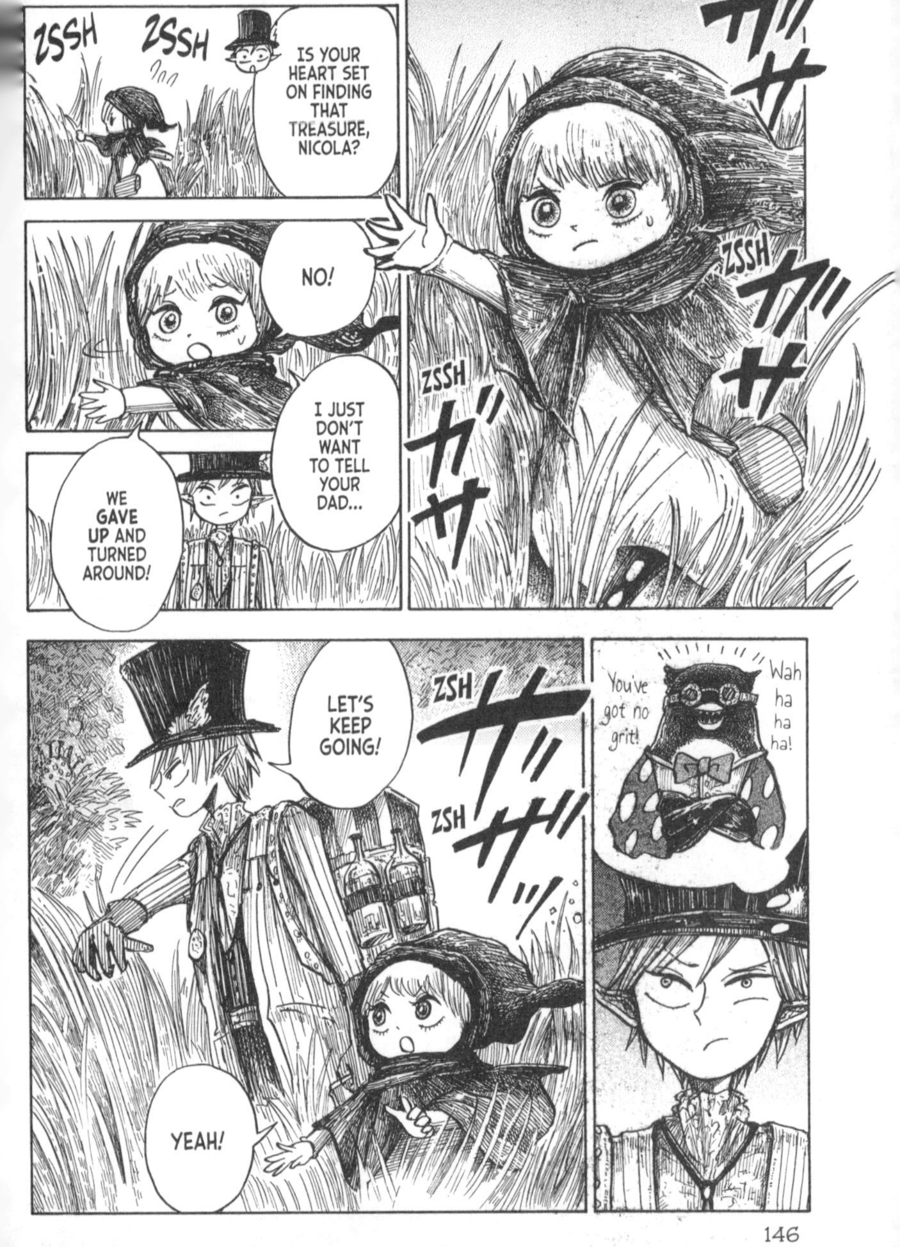
ZSSH
ガサ
ZSSH
ガサ
ZSSH
ガサ
ZSSH
ZSSH
IS YOUR HEART SET ON FINDING THAT TREASURE, NICOLA?
NO!
I JUST DON'T WANT TO TELL YOUR DAD...
WE GAVE UP AND TURNED AROUND!
Wah ha ha ha!
You've got no grit!
ZSH
ZSH
ザザッ
LET'S KEEP GOING!
YEAH!

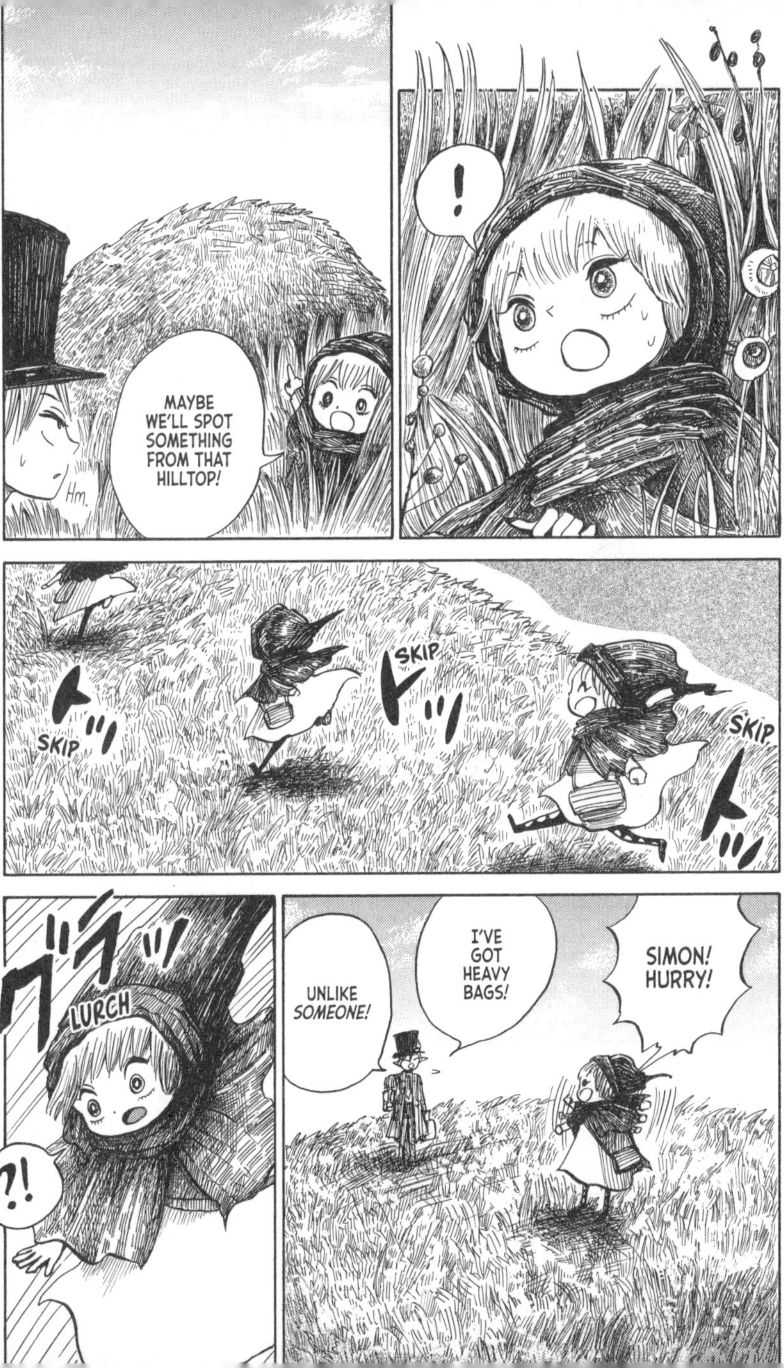
!
MAYBE WE'LL SPOT SOMETHING FROM THAT HILLTOP!
Hm.
SKIP
SKIP
SKIP
SIMON! HURRY!
I'VE GOT HEAVY BAGS!
UNLIKE SOMEONE!
LURCH
?!

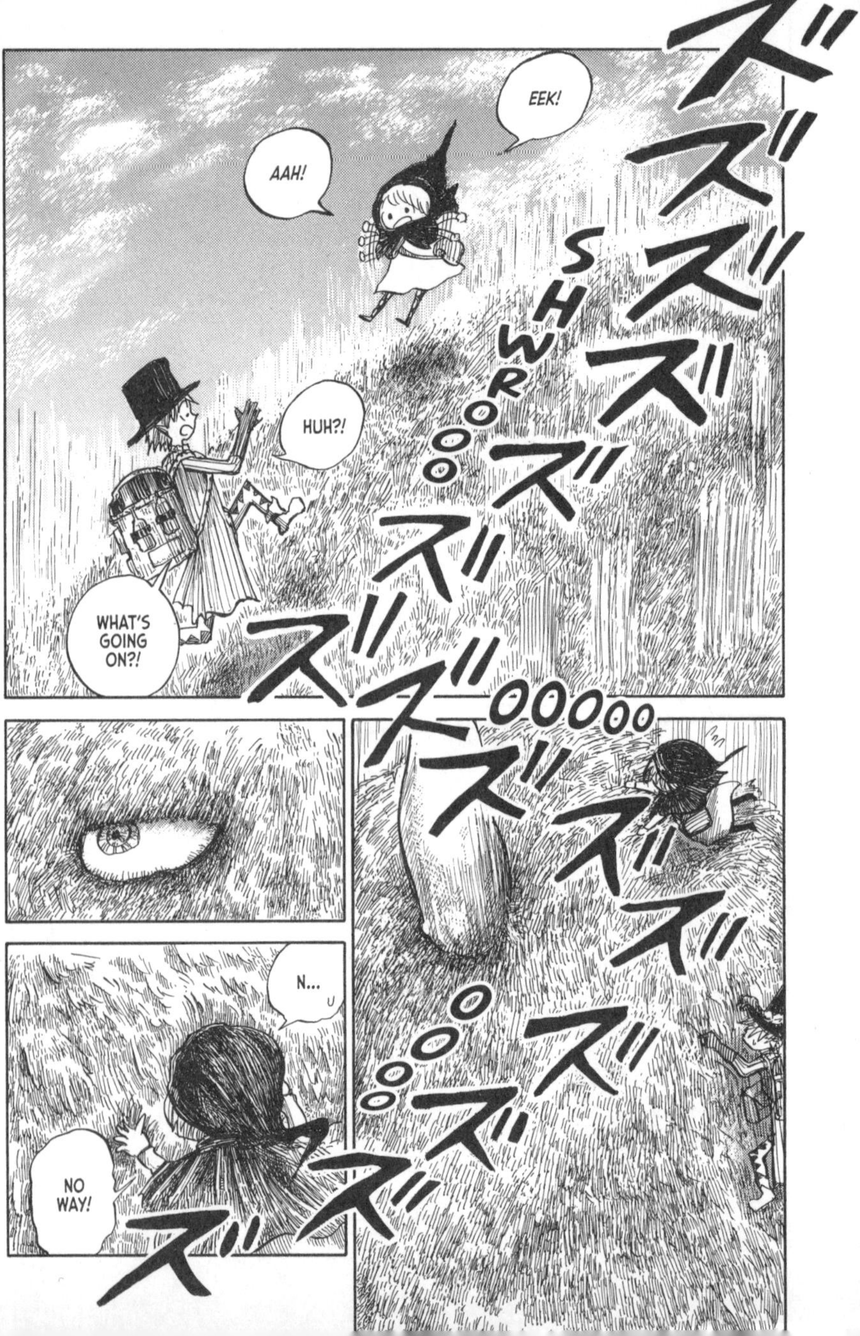
ズズズズズ
SHWROOOOO
EEK!
AAH!
HUH?!
WHAT'S GOING ON?!
N...
NO WAY!

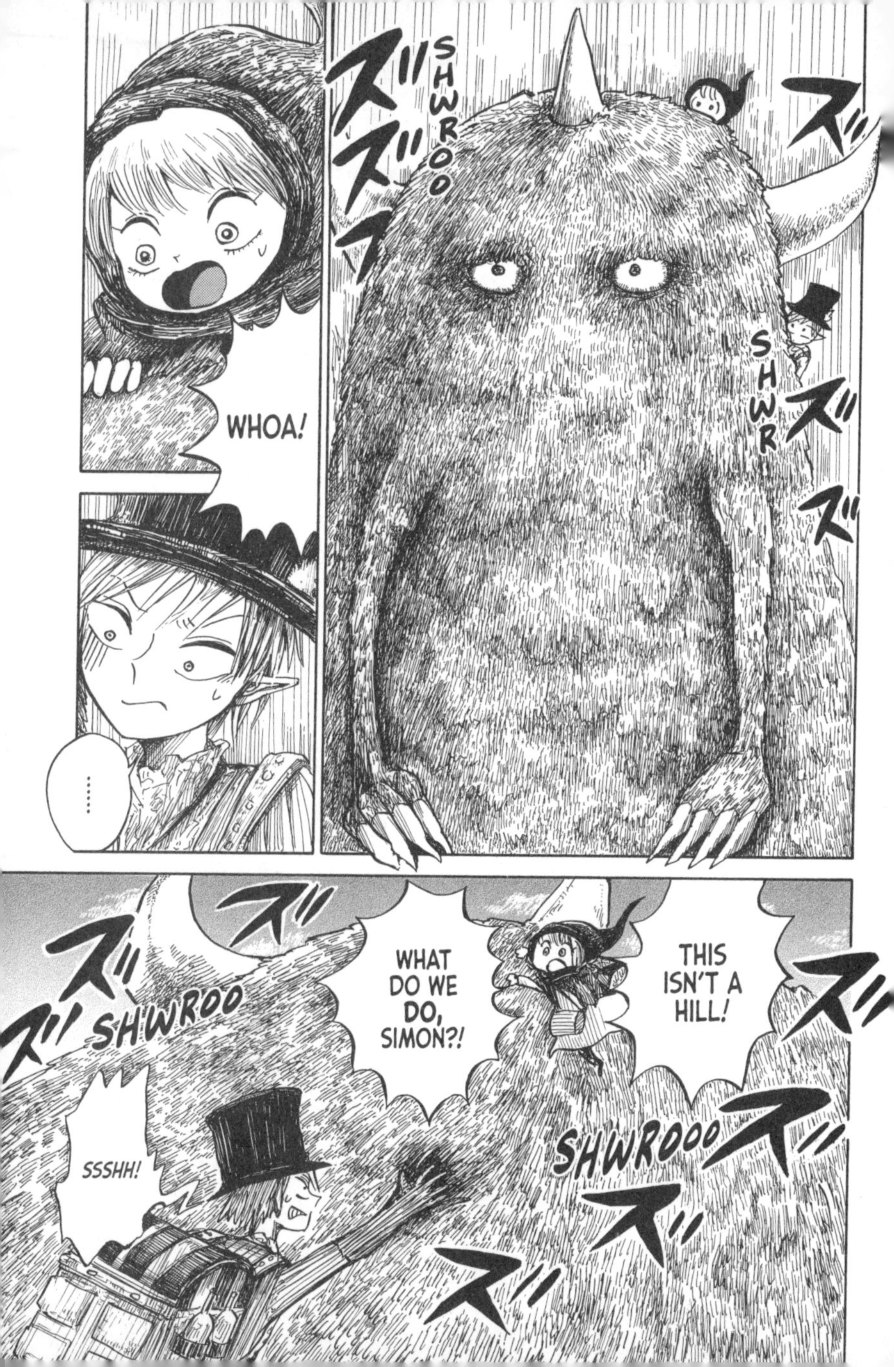
SHWROO
SHWR
WHOA!
......
THIS ISN'T A HILL!
WHAT DO WE DO, SIMON?!
SHWROO
SHWROOO
SSSHH!

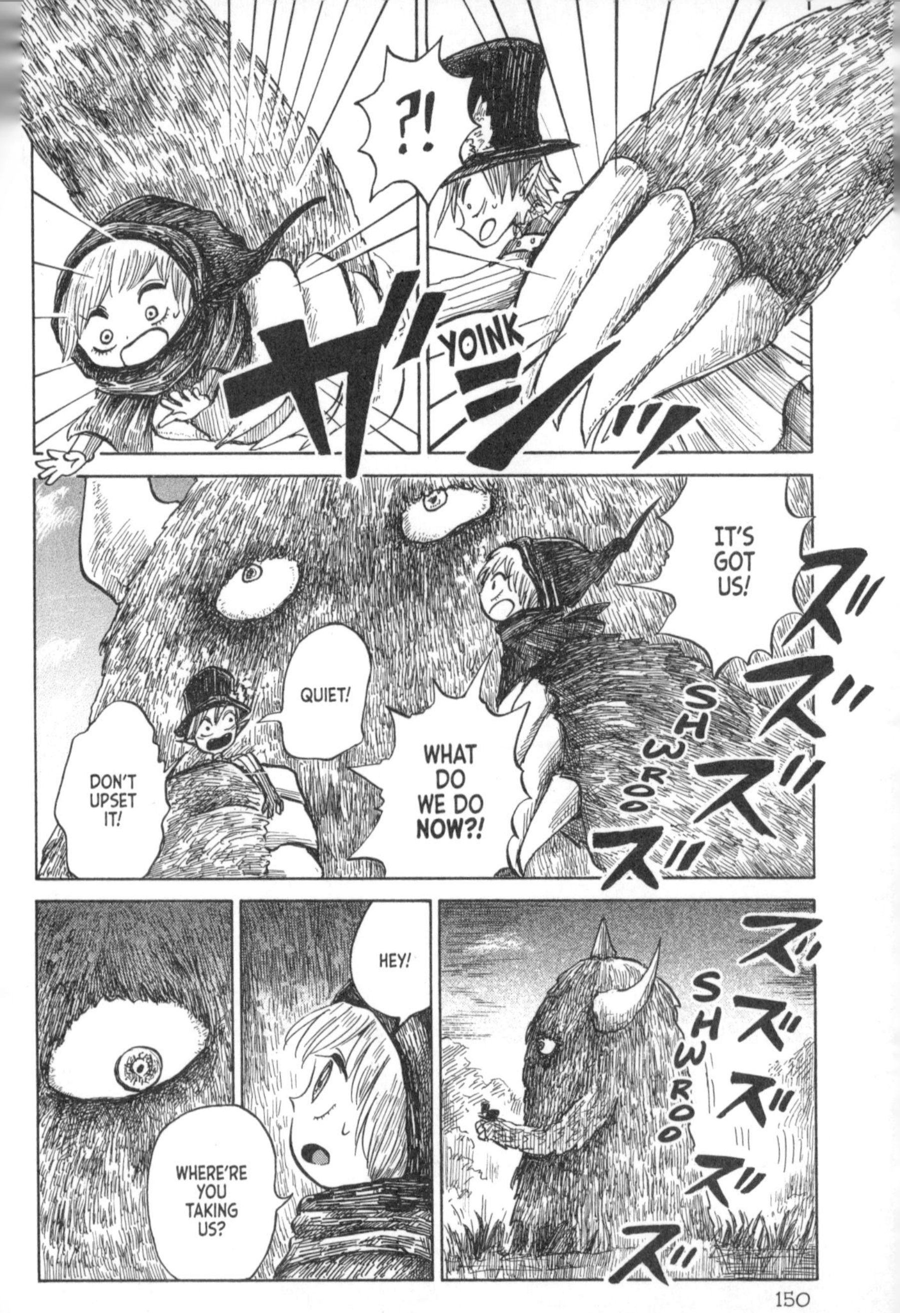
?!
YOINK
IT'S GOT US!
SHWROO
WHAT DO WE DO NOW?!
QUIET!
DON'T UPSET IT!
SHWROO
HEY!
WHERE'RE YOU TAKING US?

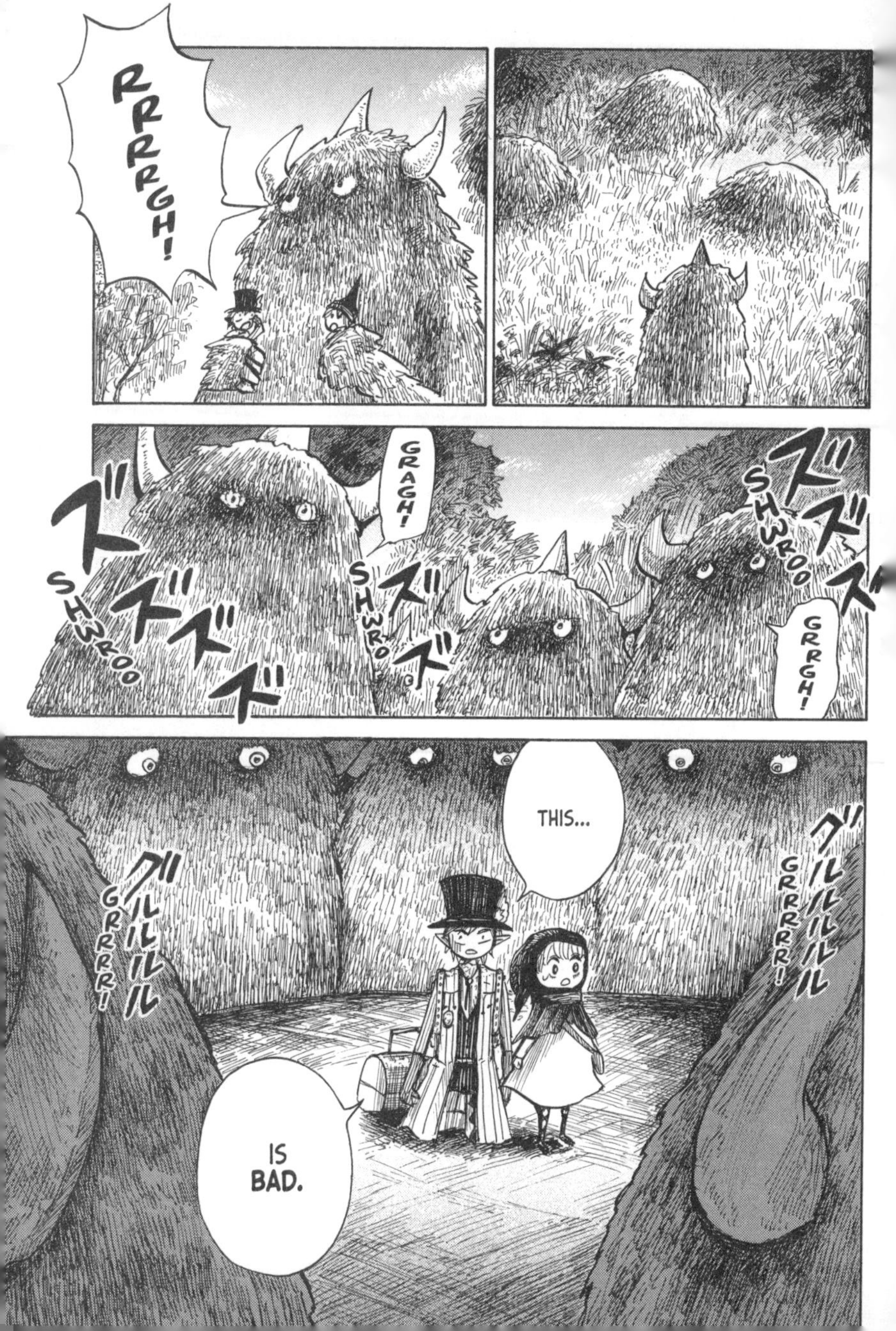
RRRRGH!
ズズズ
SHWROO
GRRGH!
GRAGH!
SHWRO
ズズ
ズズズズ
SHWROO
グルルルル
GRRRRR!
THIS...
IS BAD.
グルルルル
GRRRR!

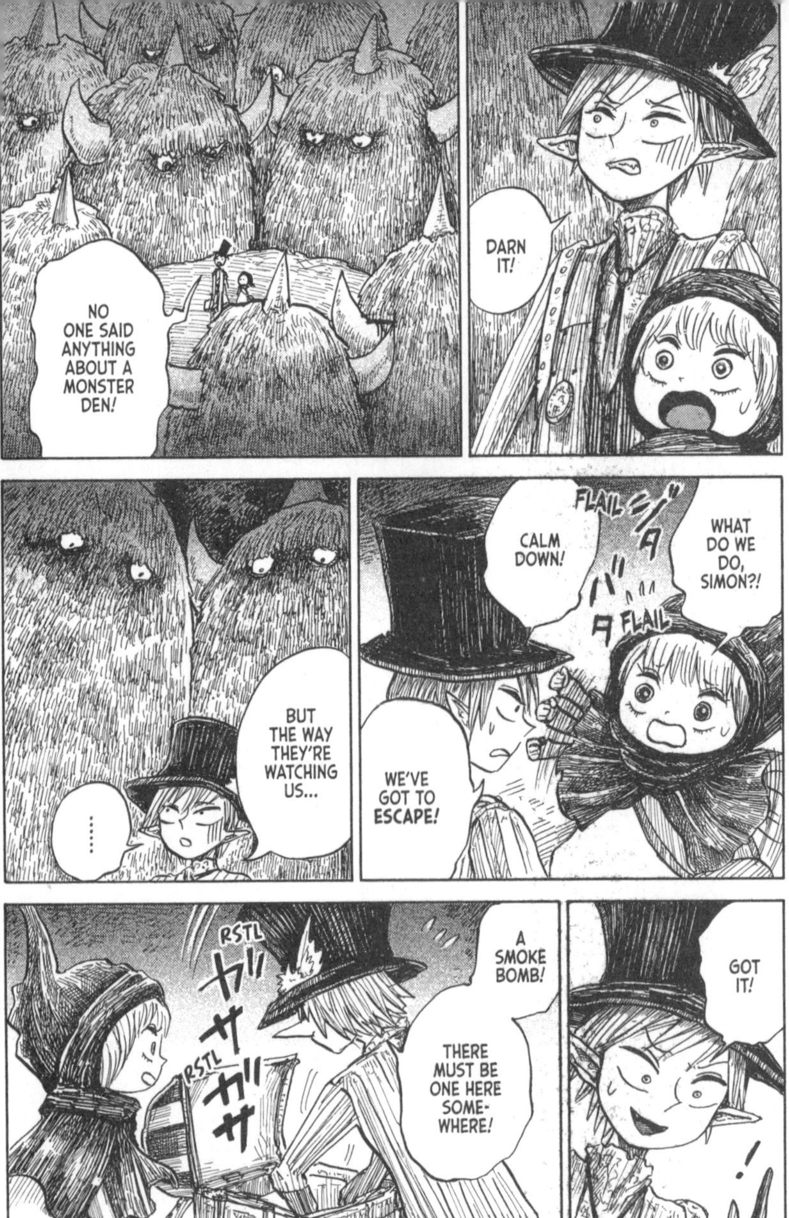
DARN IT!
NO ONE SAID ANYTHING ABOUT A MONSTER DEN!
WHAT DO WE DO, SIMON?!
FLAIL
FLAIL
CALM DOWN!
WE'VE GOT TO ESCAPE!
BUT THE WAY THEY'RE WATCHING US...
......
GOT IT!
!
A SMOKE BOMB!
THERE MUST BE ONE HERE SOME-WHERE!
RSTL
RSTL

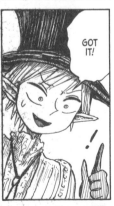

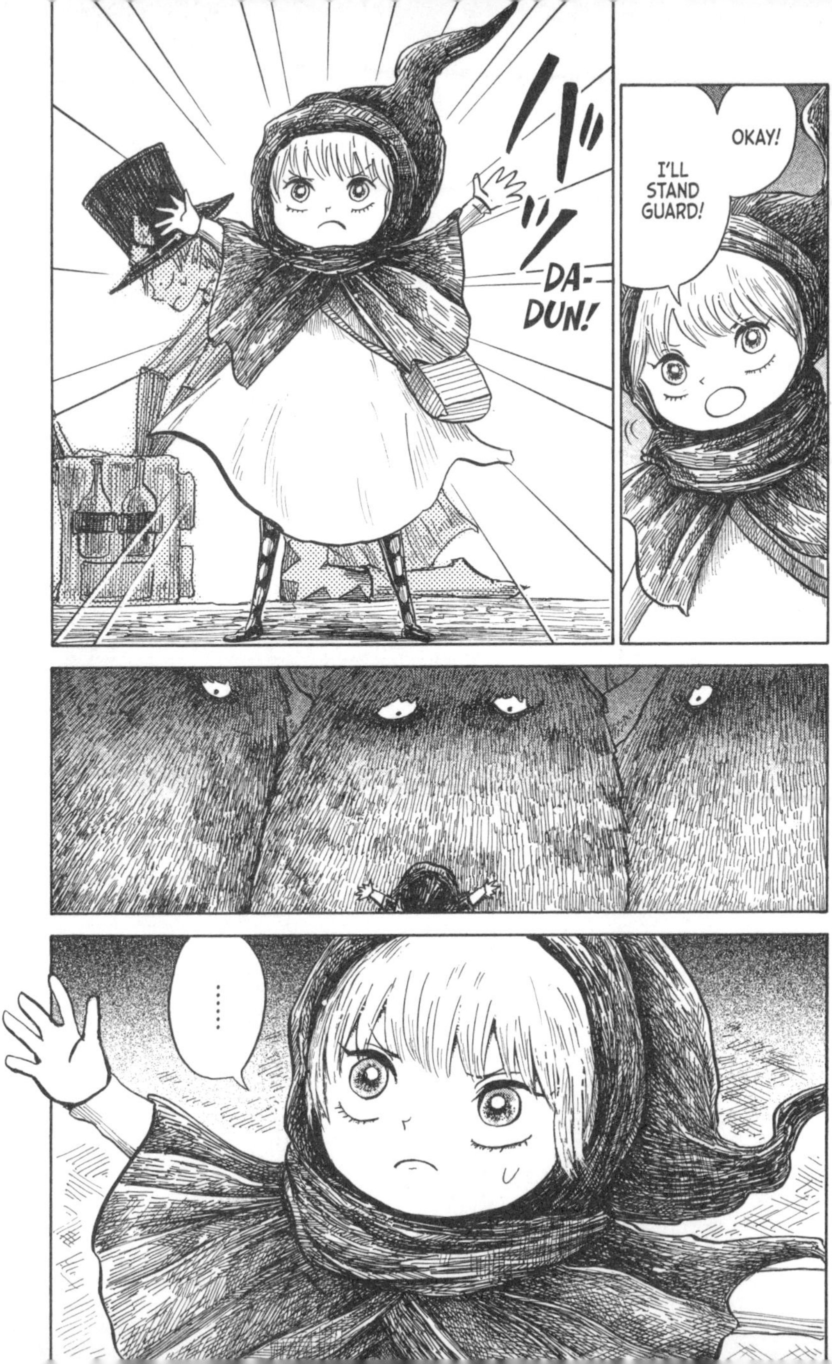
OKAY! I'LL STAND GUARD!
DA-DUN!
......

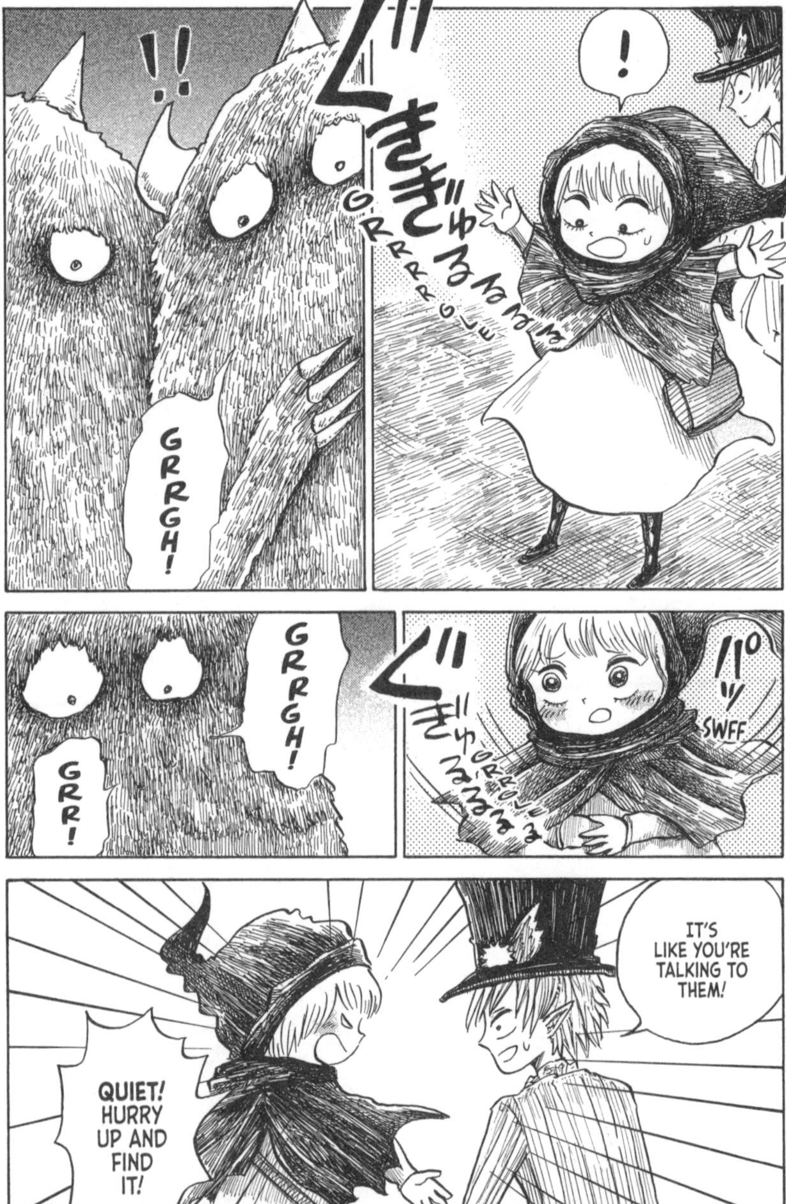
!
ぐきぎゅるるるる
GRRRRRGLE
!!
GRRGH!
ぐぎゅるるるる
GRRGLE
パッ
SWFF
GRRGH!
GRR!
IT'S LIKE YOU'RE TALKING TO THEM!
QUIET! HURRY UP AND FIND IT!

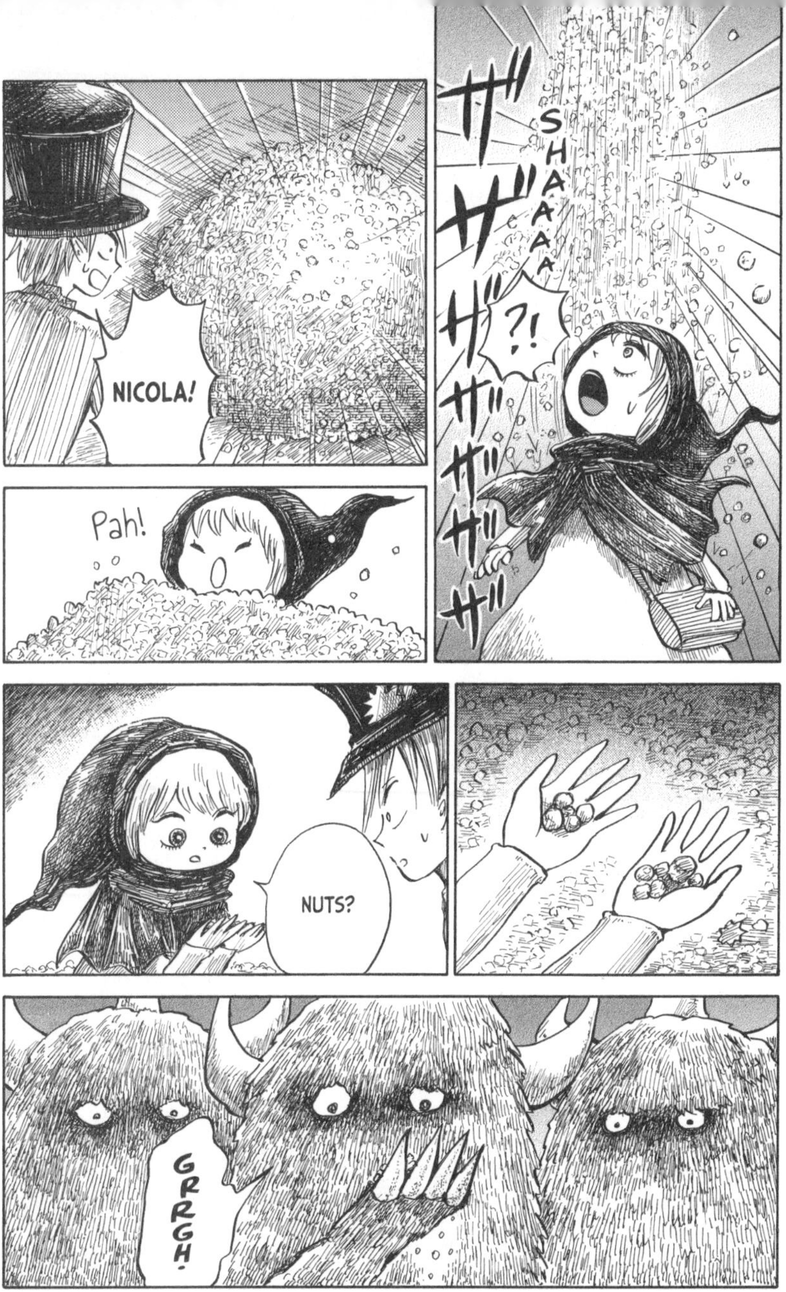
SHAAAA
?!
NICOLA!
Pah!
NUTS?
GRRGH.

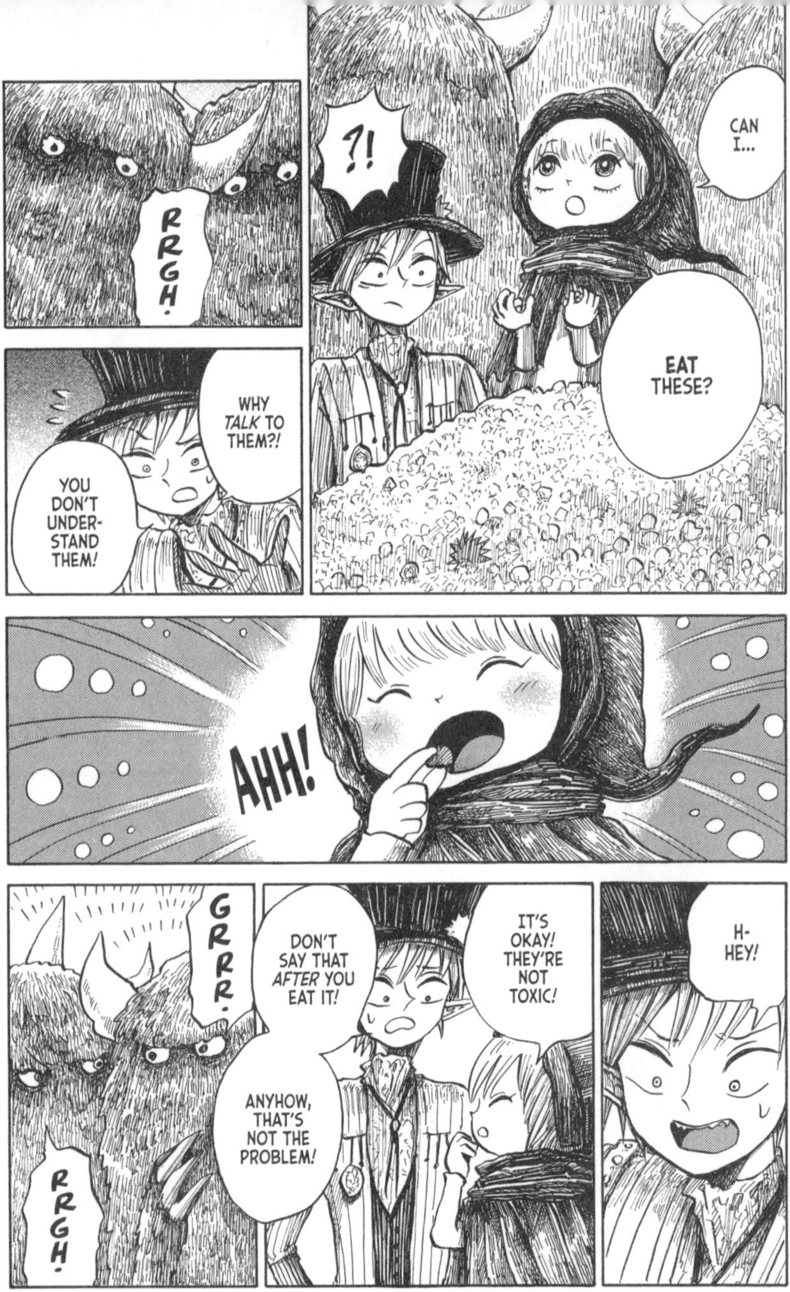
CAN I...
?!
EAT THESE?
RRGH!
WHY *TALK* TO THEM?!
YOU DON'T UNDER-STAND THEM!
AHH!
H-HEY!
IT'S OKAY! THEY'RE NOT TOXIC!
DON'T SAY THAT *AFTER* YOU EAT IT!
ANYHOW, THAT'S NOT THE PROBLEM!
GRRR.
RRGH.

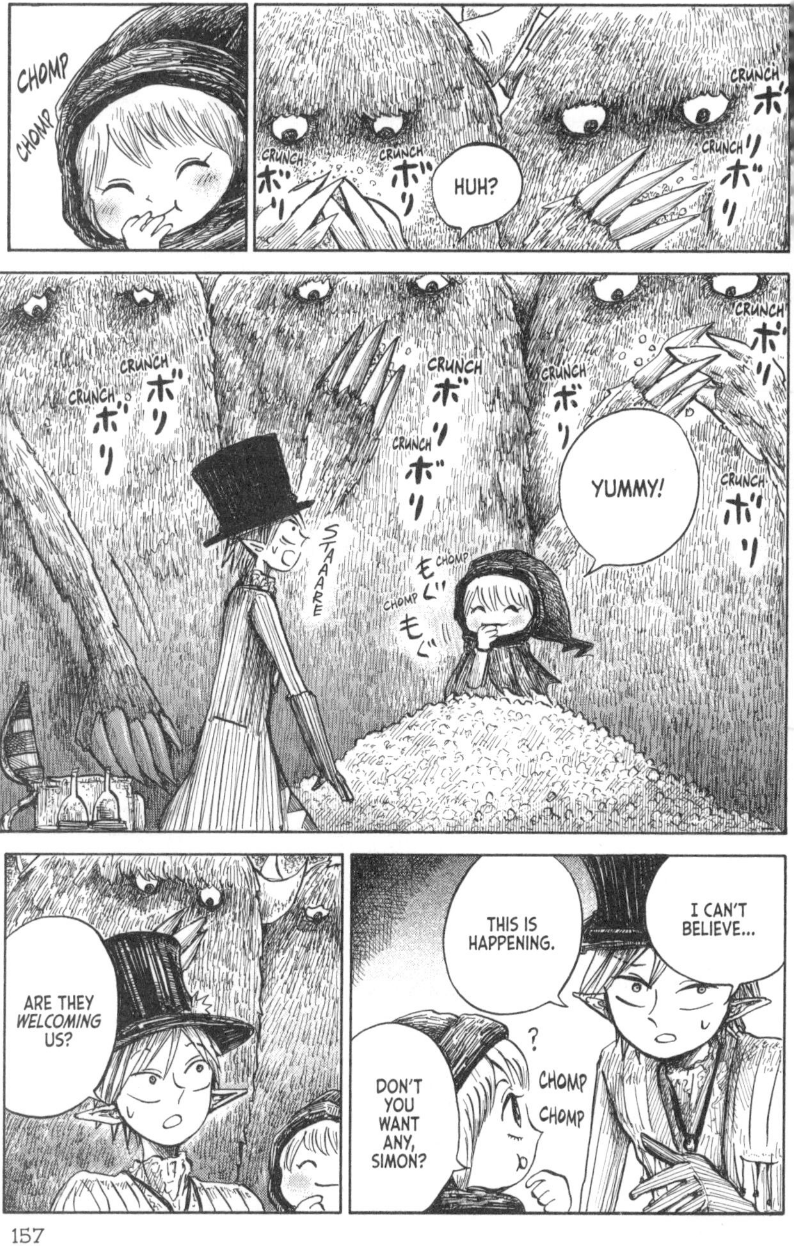
CRUNCH ボリ
CRUNCH ボリ
HUH?
CRUNCH ボリ
CRUNCH ボリ
CHOMP
CHOMP
CRUNCH ボリ
CRUNCH ボリ
YUMMY!
CRUNCH ボリ
CRUNCH ボリ
CRUNCH ボリ
CRUNCH ボリ
CRUNCH ボリ
CHOMP もぐ
CHOMP もぐ
STAAARE
I CAN'T BELIEVE...
THIS IS HAPPENING.
?
CHOMP
CHOMP
DON'T YOU WANT ANY, SIMON?
ARE THEY *WELCOMING* US?

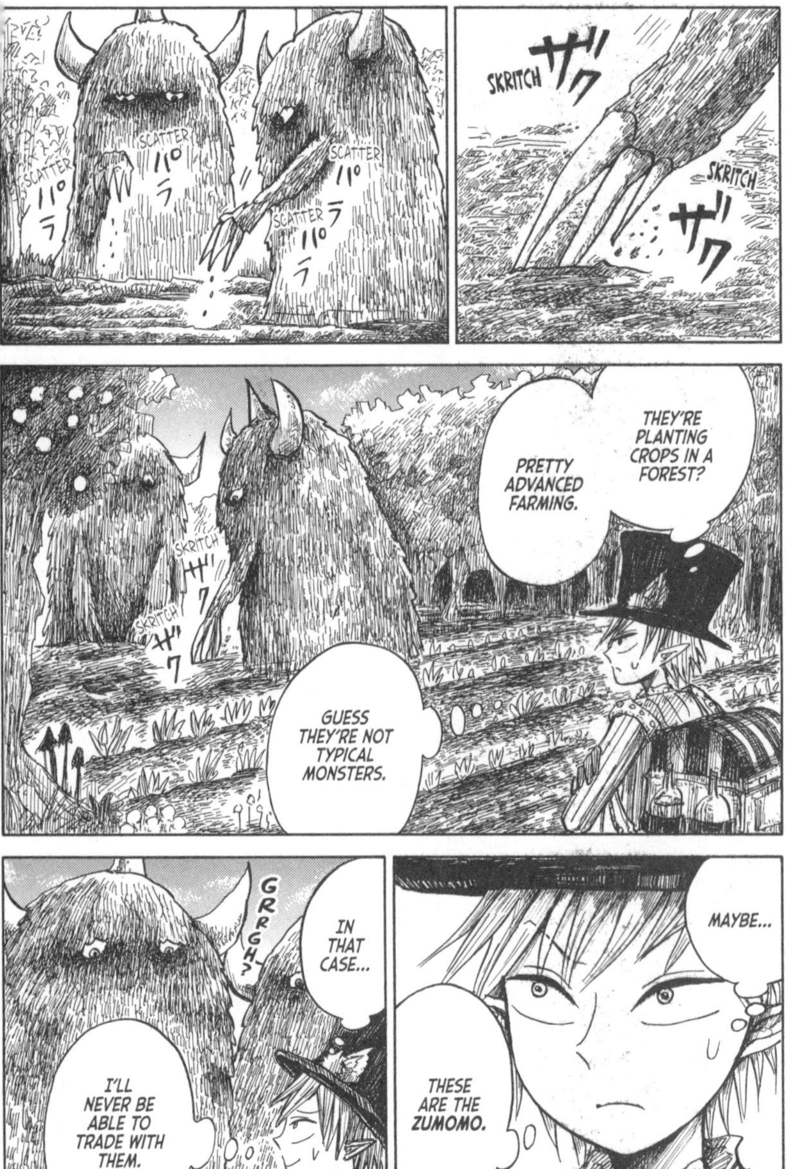
SKRITCH ザク
SKRITCH ザク
SCATTER パラ
SCATTER パラ
SCATTER パラ
SCATTER パラ
THEY'RE PLANTING CROPS IN A FOREST?
PRETTY ADVANCED FARMING.
SKRITCH ザク
SKRITCH ザク
GUESS THEY'RE NOT TYPICAL MONSTERS.
MAYBE...
THESE ARE THE ZUMOMO.
GRRGH?
IN THAT CASE...
I'LL NEVER BE ABLE TO TRADE WITH THEM.

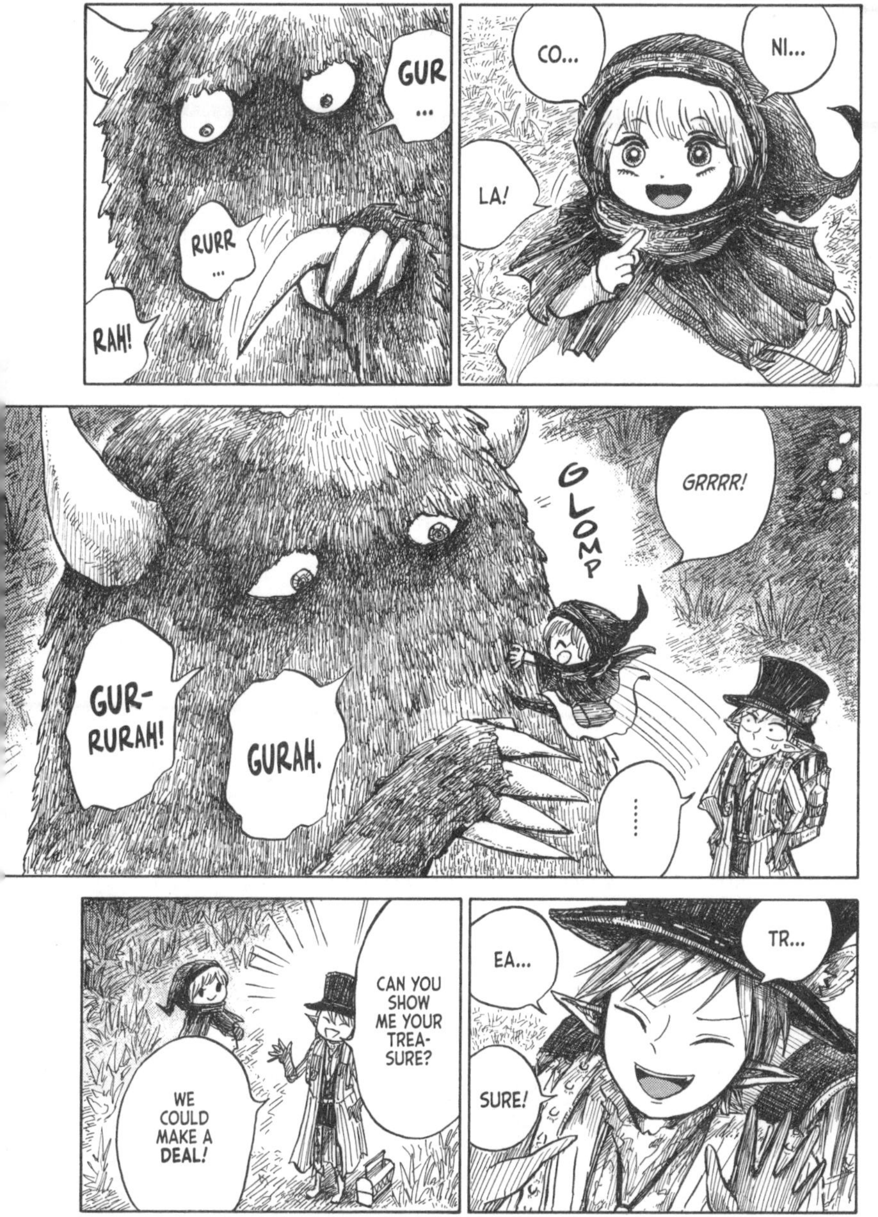
NI...
CO...
LA!
GUR...
RURR...
RAH!
GRRRR!
GLOMP
......
GURAH.
GUR-RURAH!
TR...
EA...
SURE!
CAN YOU SHOW ME YOUR TREA-SURE?
WE COULD MAKE A DEAL!

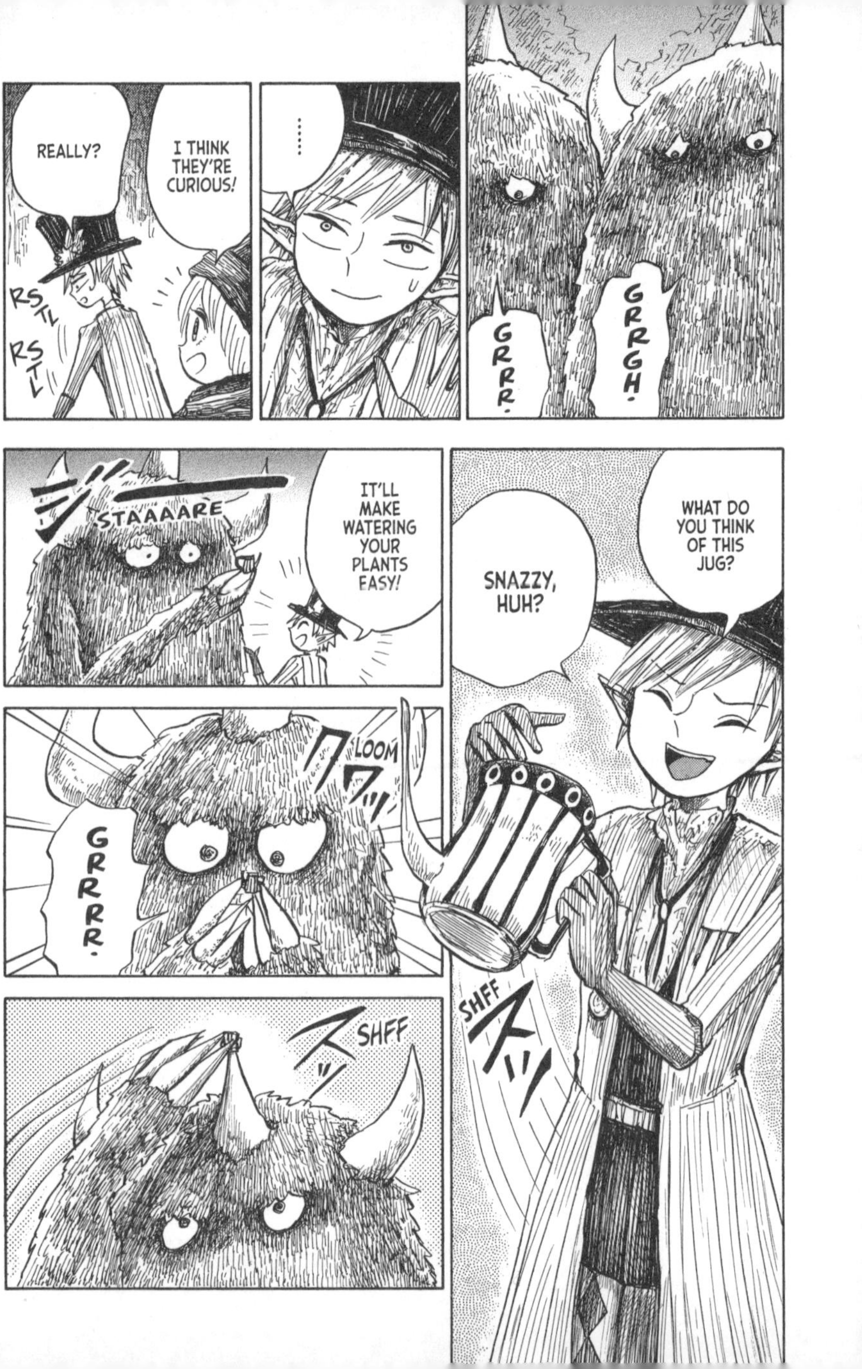
GRRGH.
GRRR.
......
I THINK THEY'RE CURIOUS!
REALLY?
RSTL
RSTL
WHAT DO YOU THINK OF THIS JUG?
SNAZZY, HUH?
SHFF
IT'LL MAKE WATERING YOUR PLANTS EASY!
STAAAARE
LOOM
GRRRR.
SHFF

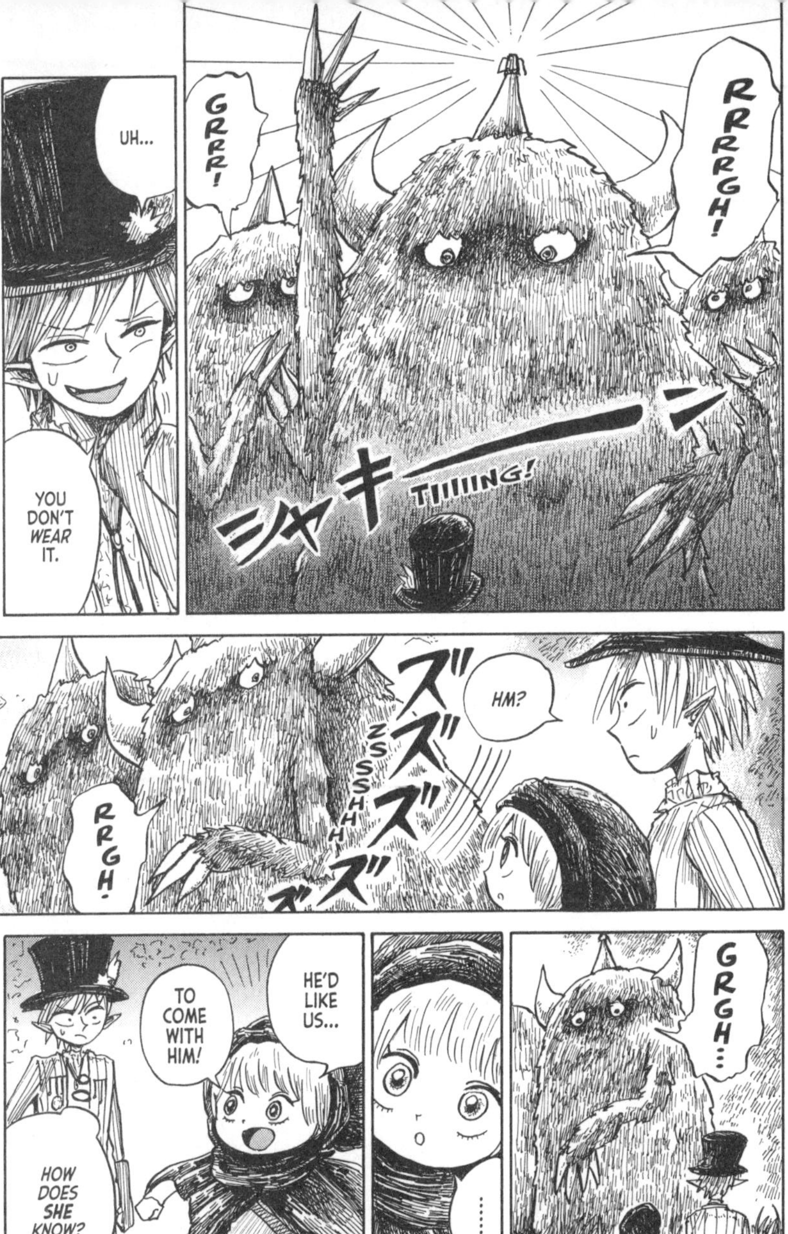
RRRRGH!
GRRR!
シャキーー
TIIIIING!
UH...
YOU DON'T WEAR IT.
HM?
ズズズズ
ZSSSHHH
RRGH!
GRGH...
......
HE'D LIKE US...
TO COME WITH HIM!
HOW DOES SHE KNOW?

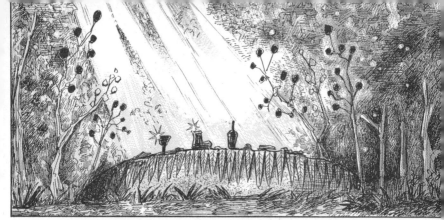

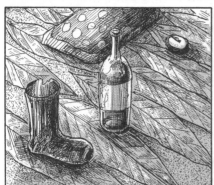

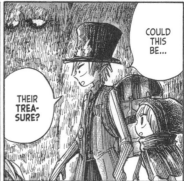

COULD THIS BE...
THEIR TREASURE?
BUT... IT'S ALL RANDOM JUNK.
DID TRAVELERS DUMP THIS STUFF?
?
GLINT
!

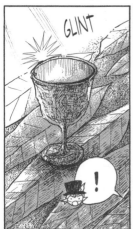

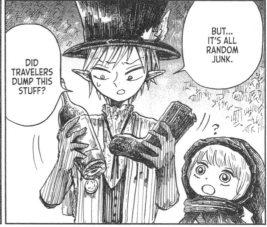

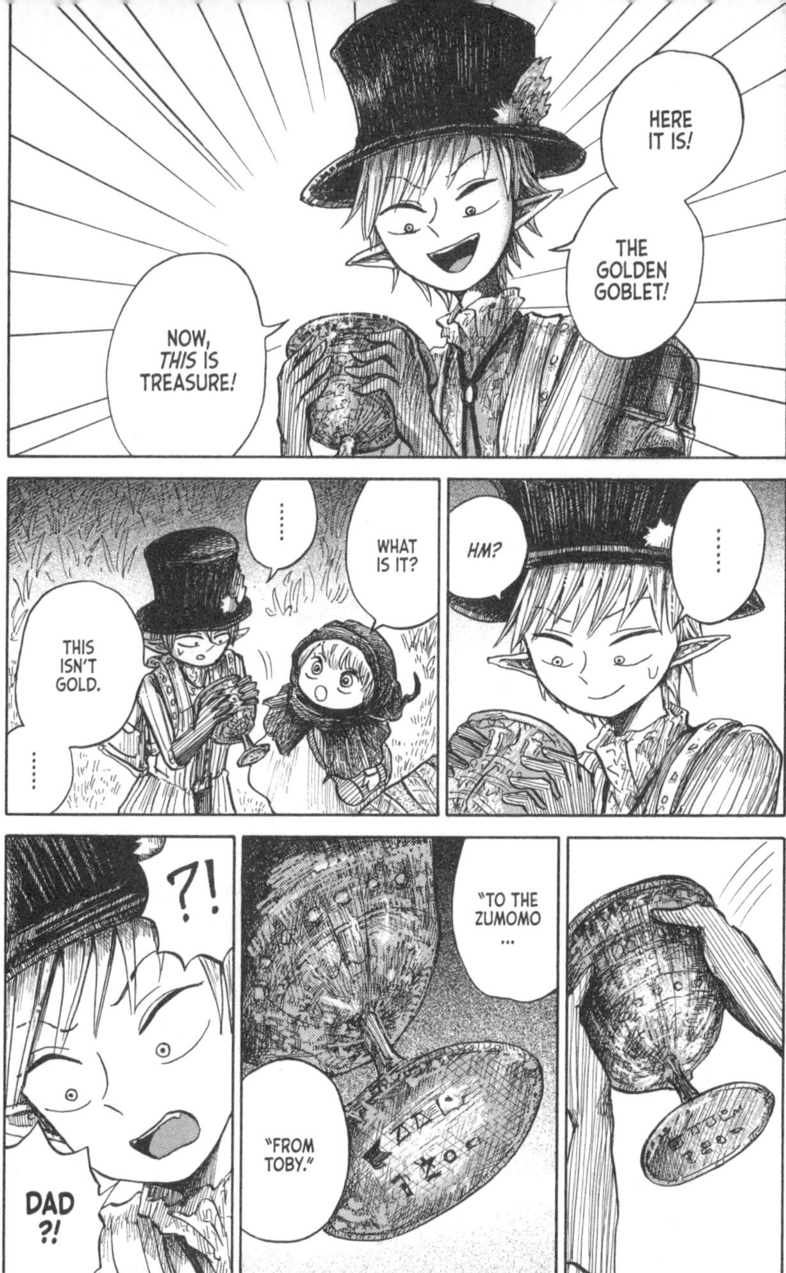

HERE IT IS!
THE GOLDEN GOBLET!
NOW, *THIS* IS TREASURE!
......
HM?
WHAT IS IT?
......
THIS ISN'T GOLD.
......
"TO THE ZUMOMO ...
"FROM TOBY."
?!
DAD ?!

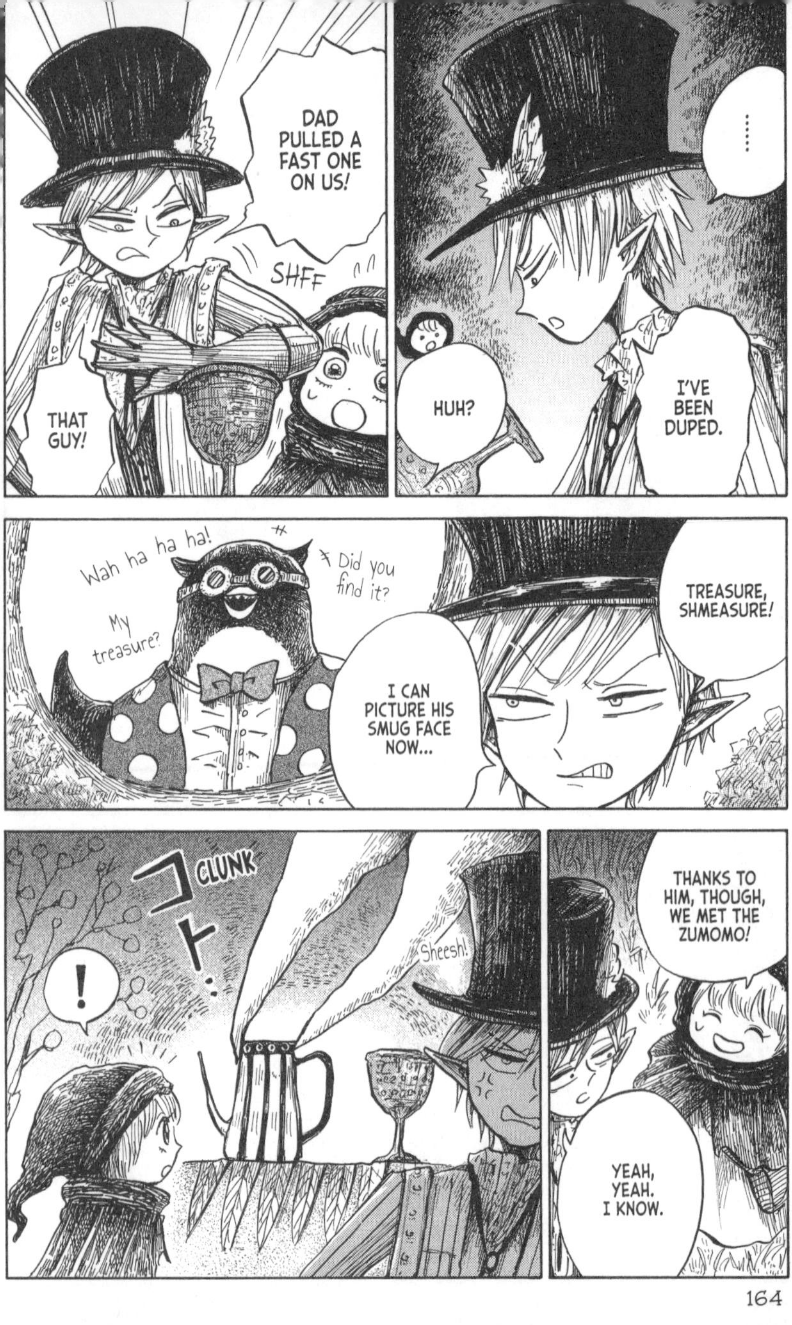
......
I'VE BEEN DUPED.
HUH?
DAD PULLED A FAST ONE ON US!
SHFF
THAT GUY!
TREASURE, SHMEASURE!
I CAN PICTURE HIS SMUG FACE NOW...
Did you find it?
Wah ha ha ha!
My treasure?
THANKS TO HIM, THOUGH, WE MET THE ZUMOMO!
YEAH, YEAH. I KNOW.
Sheesh!
CLUNK
コト
!

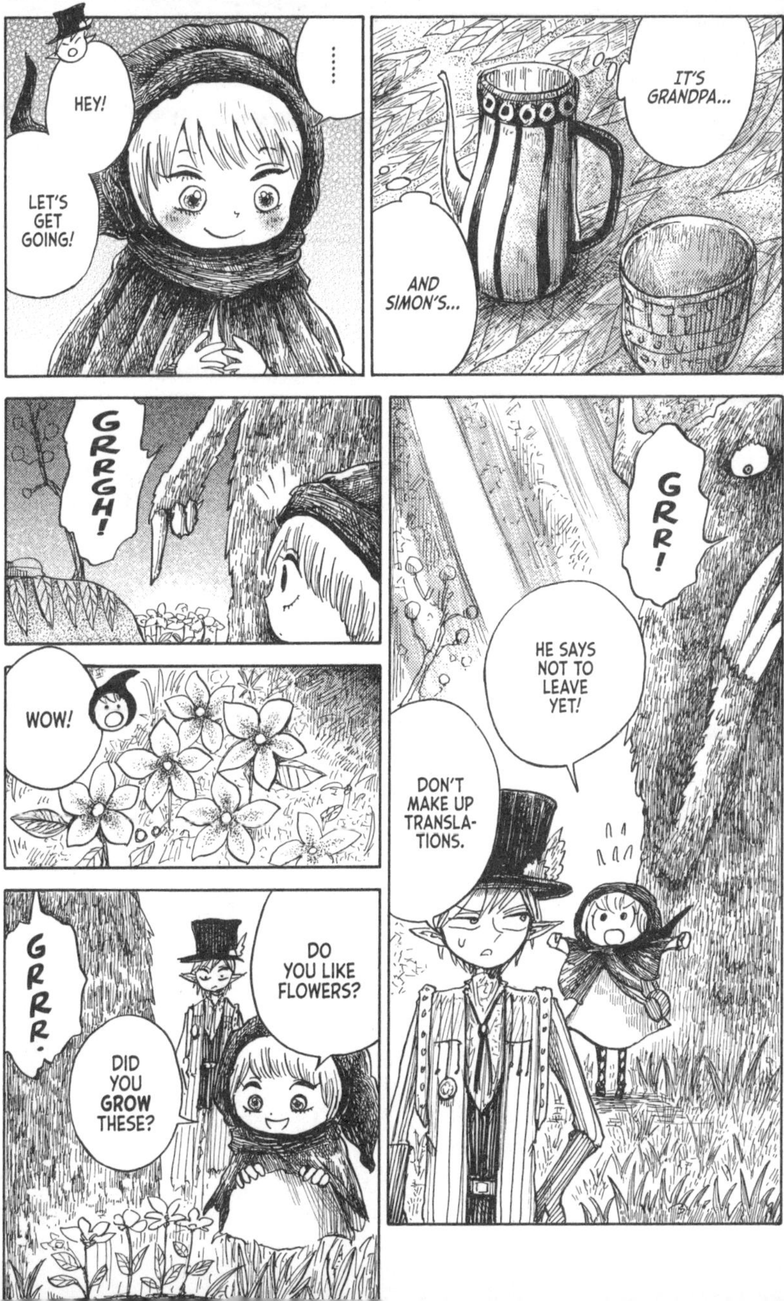
IT'S GRANDPA...
AND SIMON'S...
......
HEY!
LET'S GET GOING!
GRR!
HE SAYS NOT TO LEAVE YET!
DON'T MAKE UP TRANSLA-TIONS.
GRRGH!
WOW!
DO YOU LIKE FLOWERS?
GRRR.
DID YOU GROW THESE?

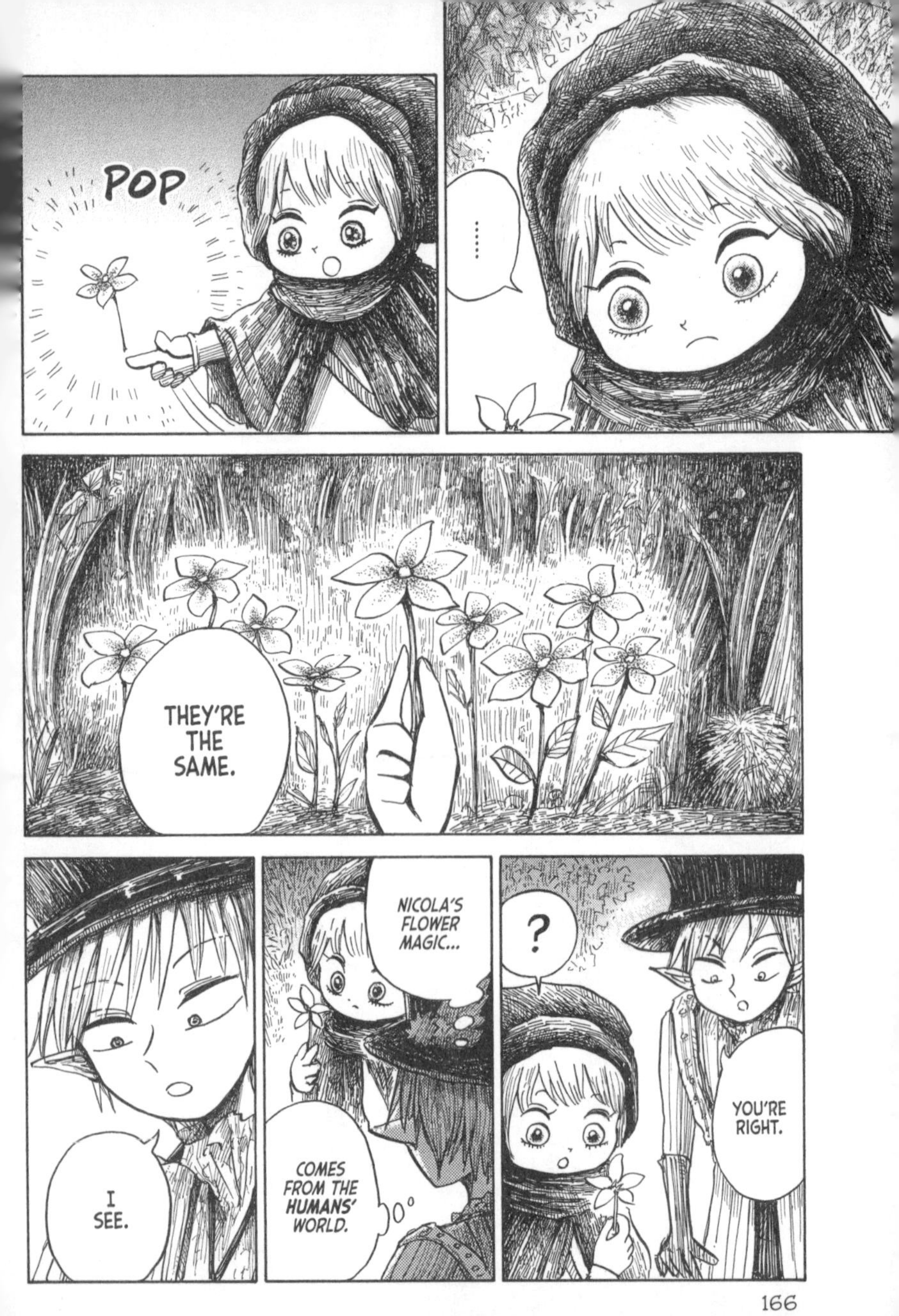
……
POP
THEY'RE THE SAME.
?
YOU'RE RIGHT.
NICOLA'S FLOWER MAGIC...
COMES FROM THE HUMANS' WORLD.
I SEE.

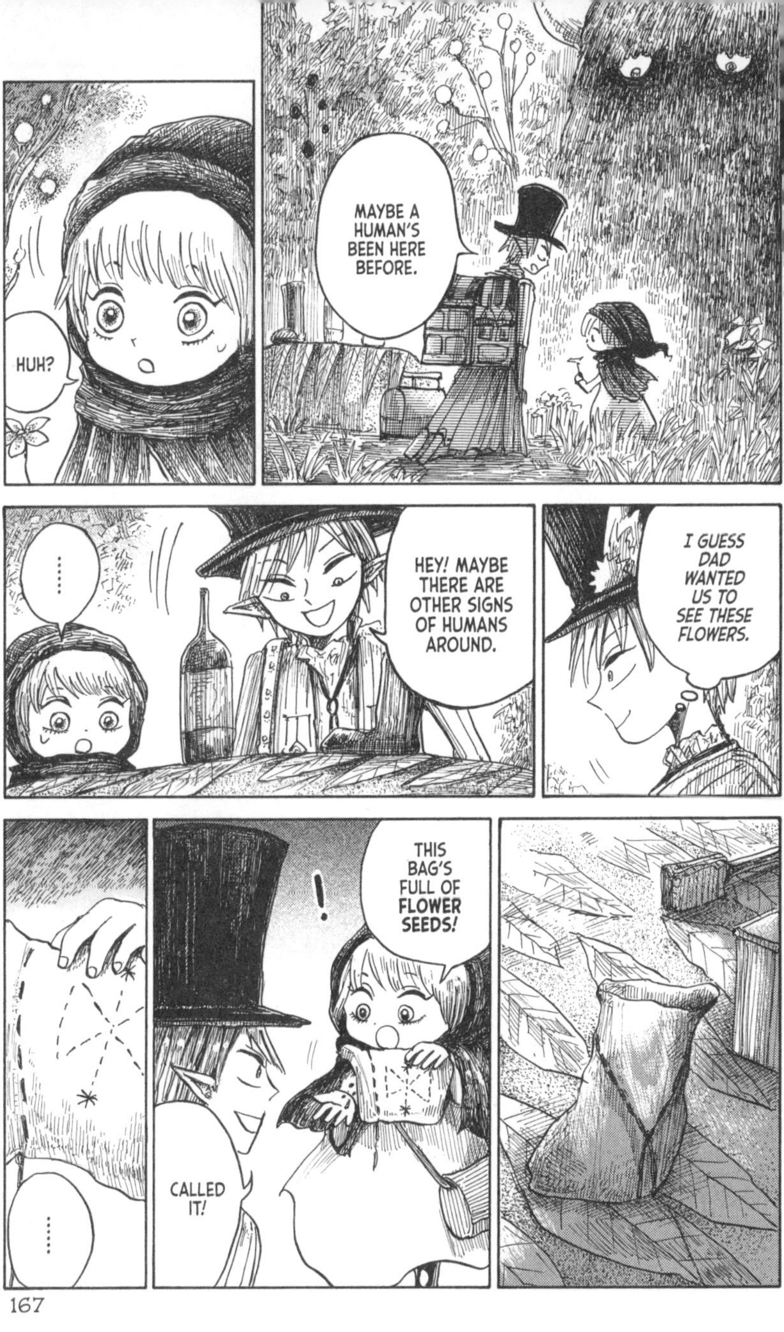
MAYBE A HUMAN'S BEEN HERE BEFORE.
HUH?
I GUESS DAD WANTED US TO SEE THESE FLOWERS.
HEY! MAYBE THERE ARE OTHER SIGNS OF HUMANS AROUND.
......
THIS BAG'S FULL OF FLOWER SEEDS!
!
CALLED IT!
......

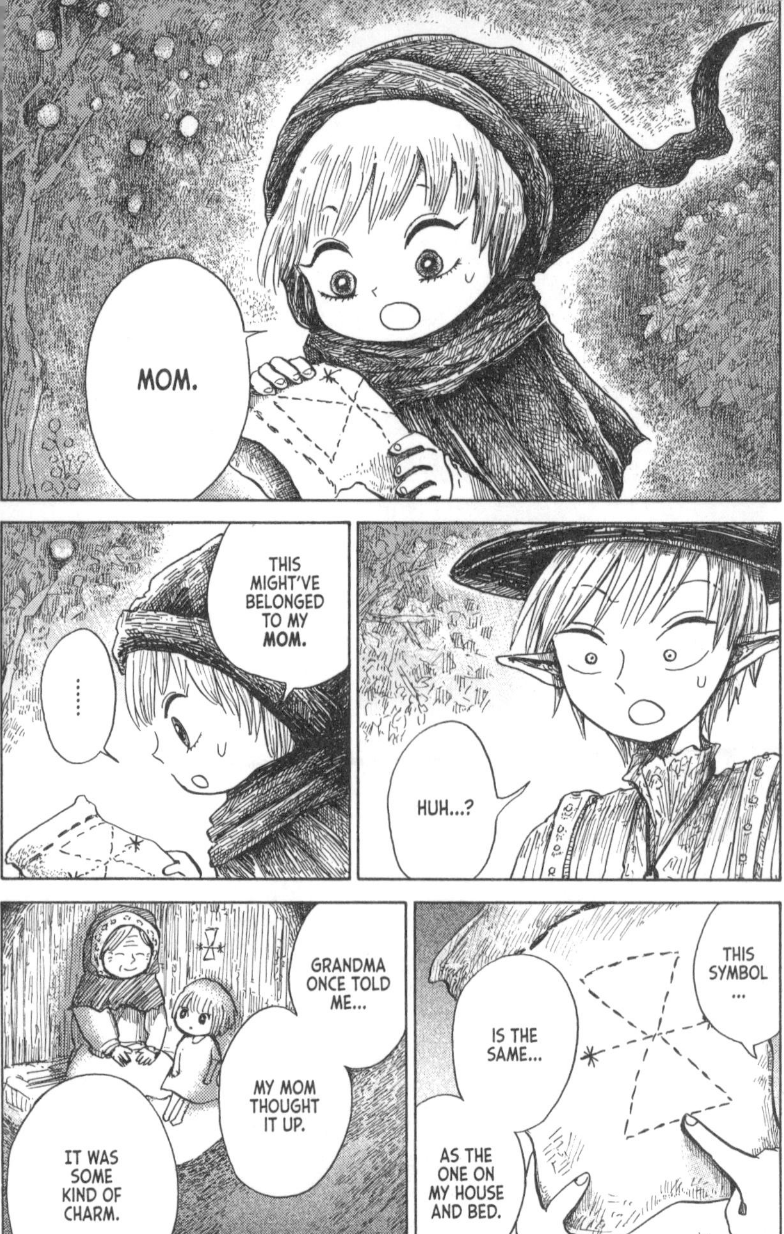

MOM.
HUH...?
THIS MIGHT'VE BELONGED TO MY MOM.
......
THIS SYMBOL...
IS THE SAME...
AS THE ONE ON MY HOUSE AND BED.
GRANDMA ONCE TOLD ME...
MY MOM THOUGHT IT UP.
IT WAS SOME KIND OF CHARM.

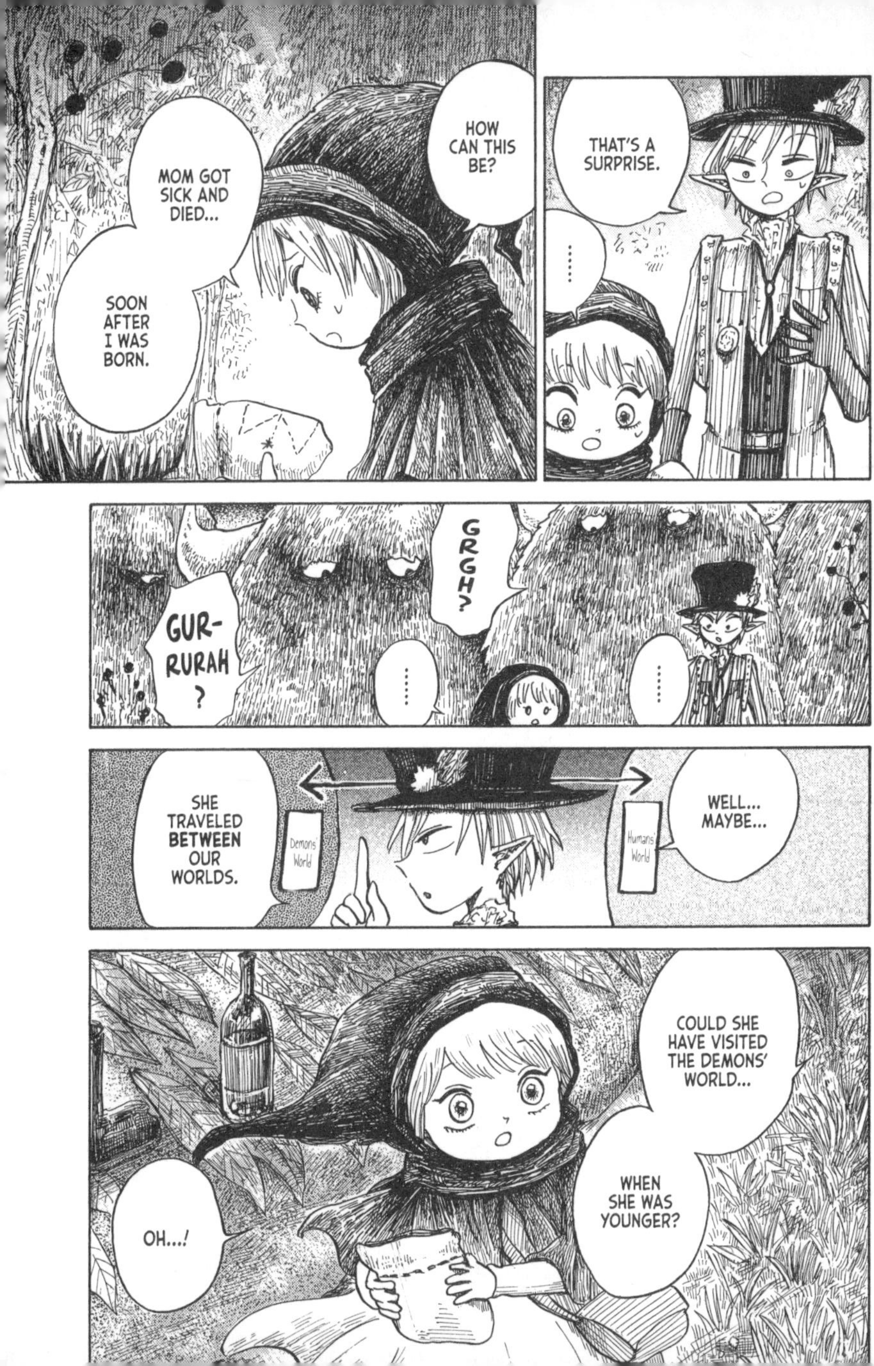
THAT'S A SURPRISE.
......
HOW CAN THIS BE?
MOM GOT SICK AND DIED...
SOON AFTER I WAS BORN.
GRGH?
......
GUR-RURAH?
......
WELL... MAYBE...
Humans' World
Demons' World
SHE TRAVELED **BETWEEN** OUR WORLDS.
COULD SHE HAVE VISITED THE DEMONS' WORLD...
WHEN SHE WAS YOUNGER?
OH...!

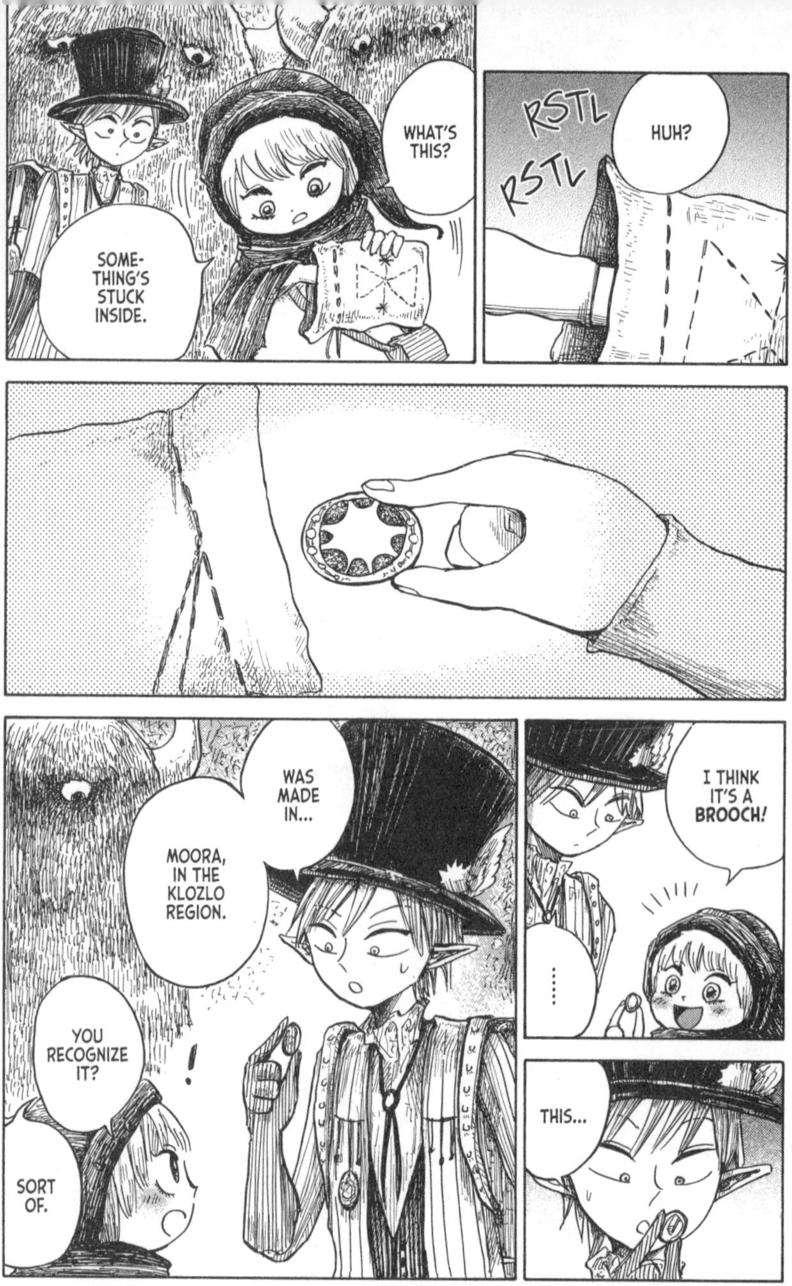
RSTL
RSTL
HUH?
WHAT'S THIS?
SOME-THING'S STUCK INSIDE.
I THINK IT'S A **BROOCH!**
......
THIS...
WAS MADE IN...
MOORA, IN THE KLOZLO REGION.
YOU RECOGNIZE IT?
!
SORT OF.

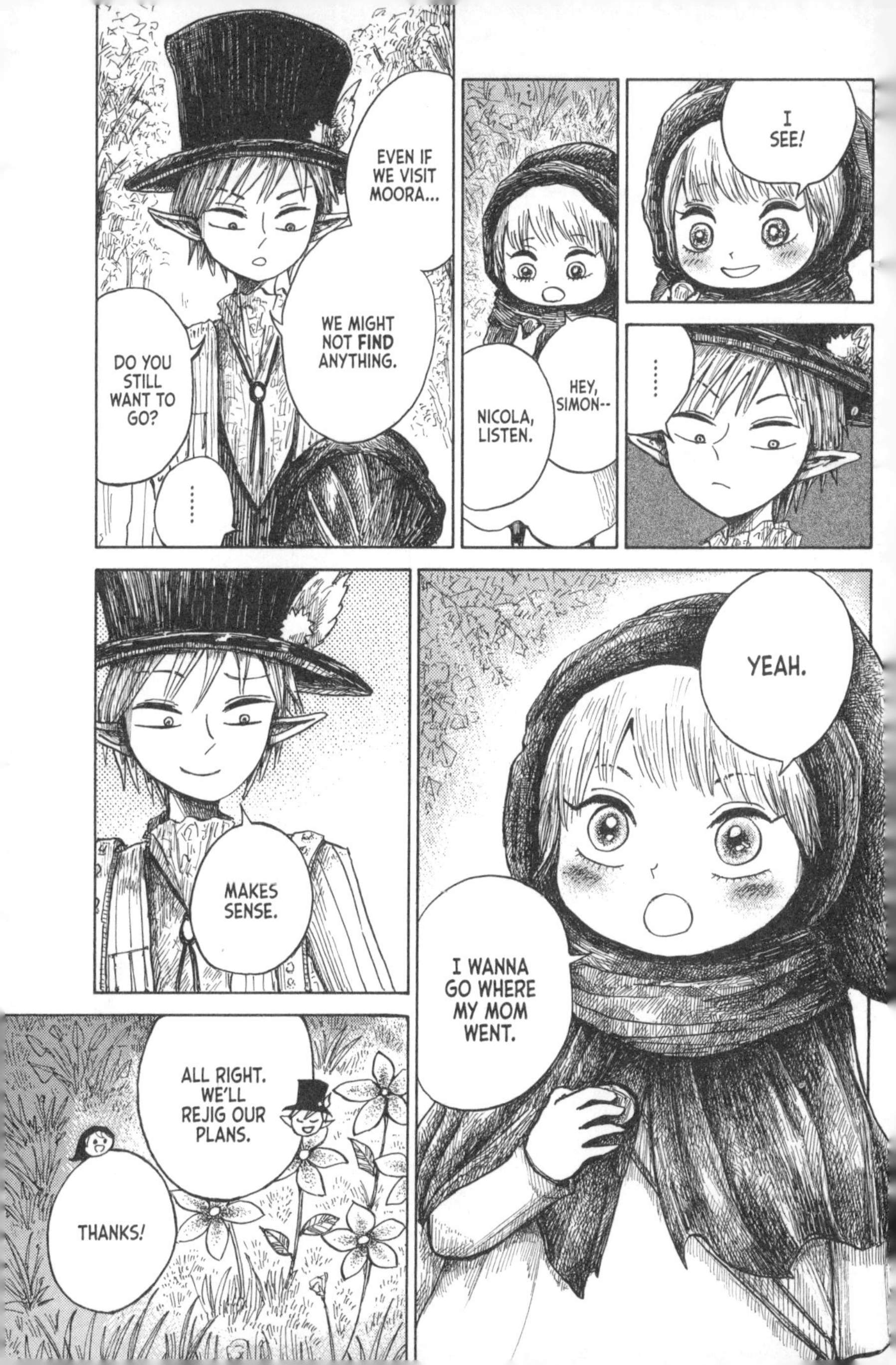
I SEE!
......
HEY, SIMON--
NICOLA, LISTEN.
EVEN IF WE VISIT MOORA...
WE MIGHT NOT FIND ANYTHING.
DO YOU STILL WANT TO GO?
......
YEAH.
I WANNA GO WHERE MY MOM WENT.
MAKES SENSE.
ALL RIGHT. WE'LL REJIG OUR PLANS.
THANKS!

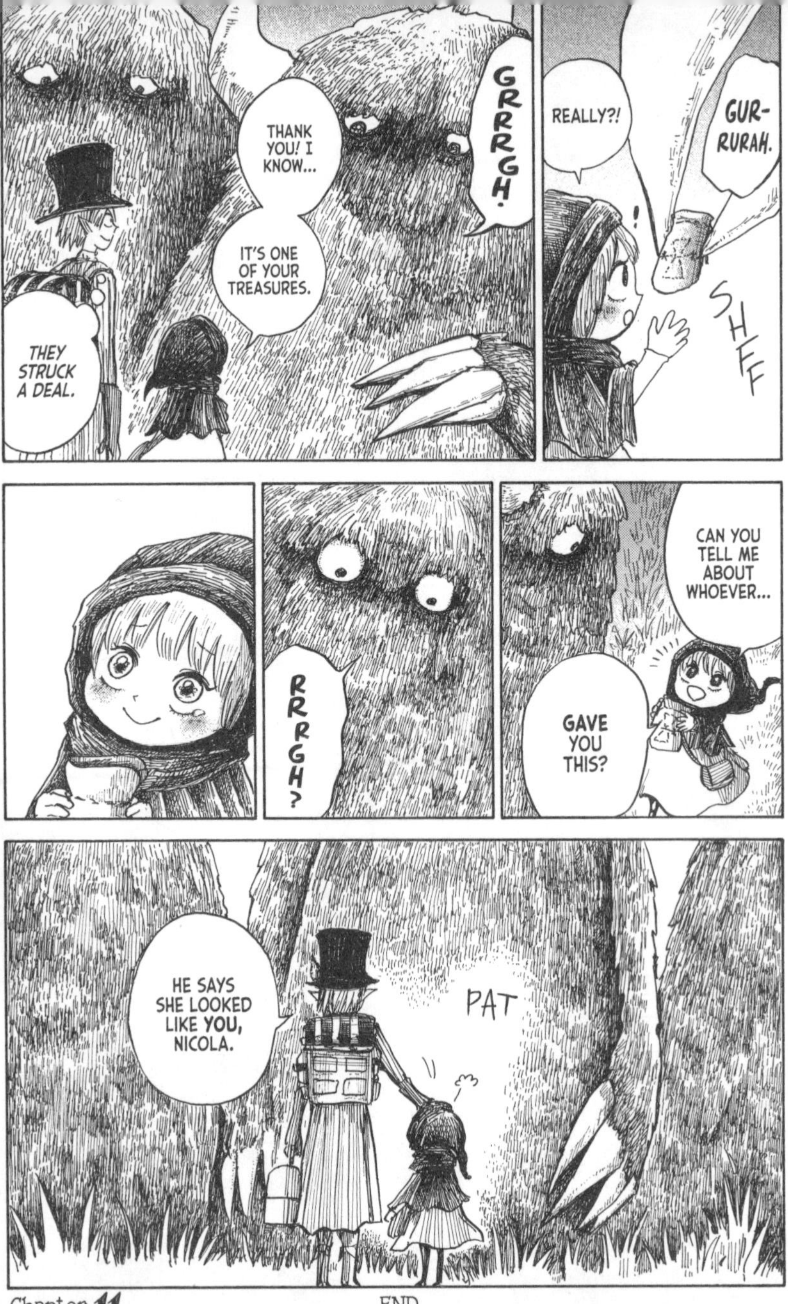
GUR-RURAH.
REALLY?!
!
SHFF
GRRRGH!
THANK YOU! I KNOW...
IT'S ONE OF YOUR TREASURES.
THEY STRUCK A DEAL.
CAN YOU TELL ME ABOUT WHOEVER...
GAVE YOU THIS?
RRRGH?
PAT
HE SAYS SHE LOOKED LIKE YOU, NICOLA.

Chapter 11 END

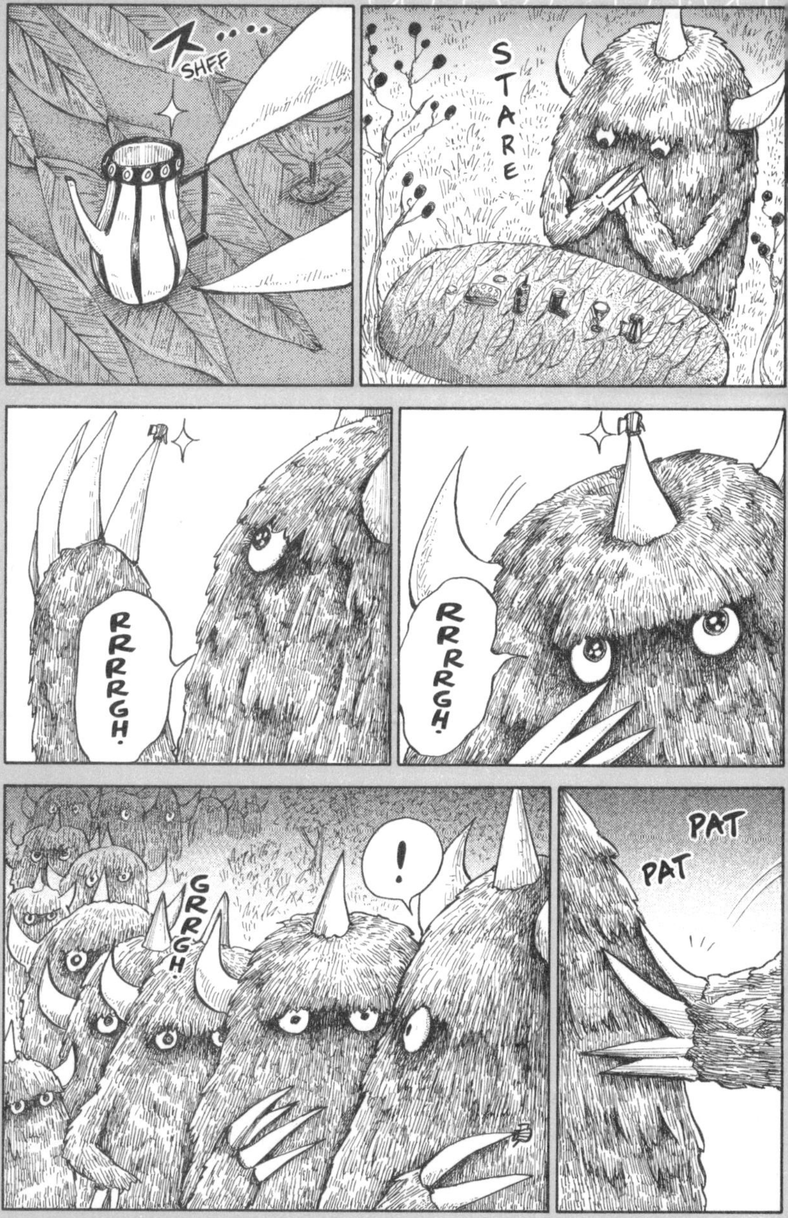
STARE
ス...
SHFF
RRRRGH!
RRRGH!
PAT
PAT
!
GRRRGH!

Nicola Traveling Around The Demons' World

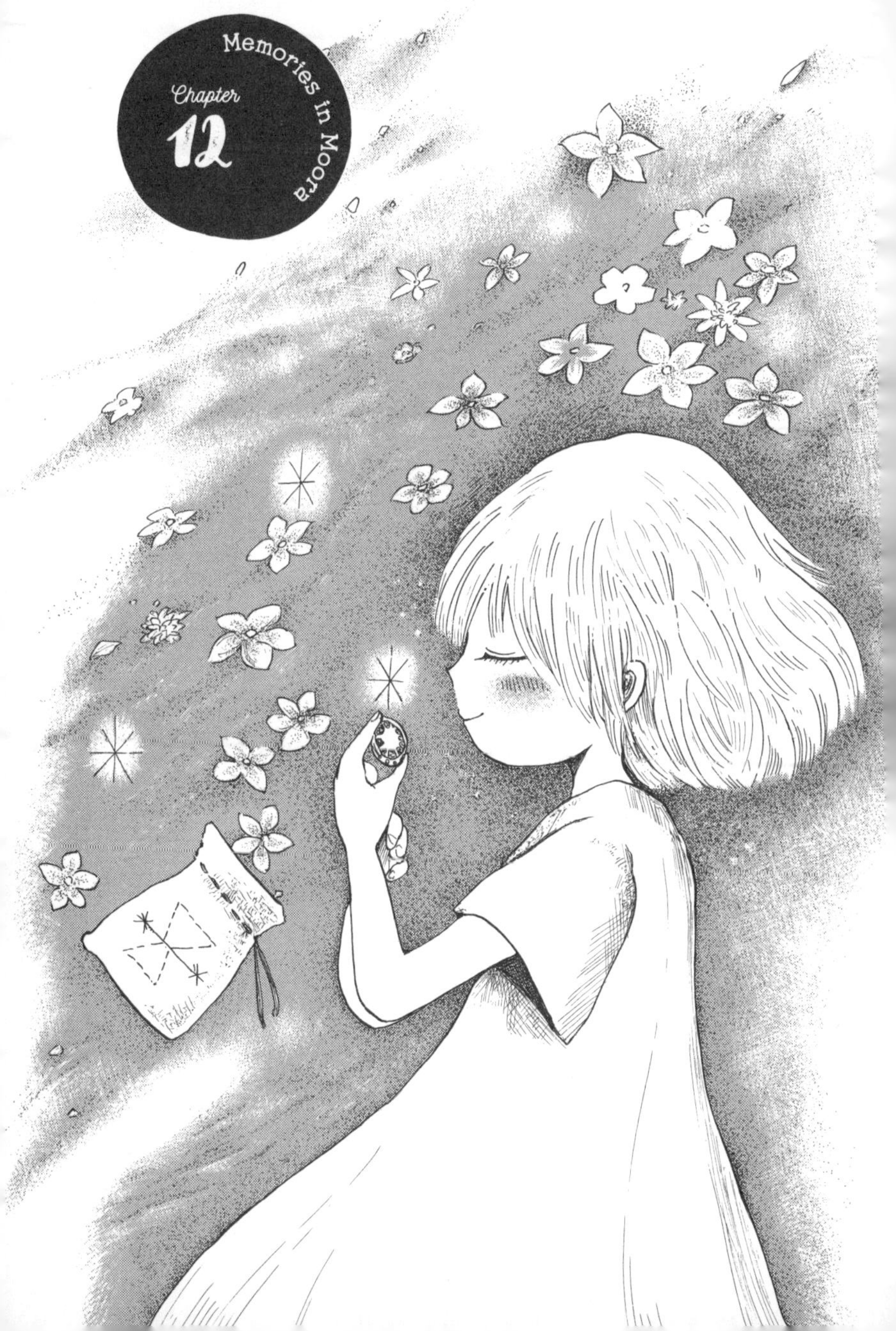
Chapter 12
Memories in Moora

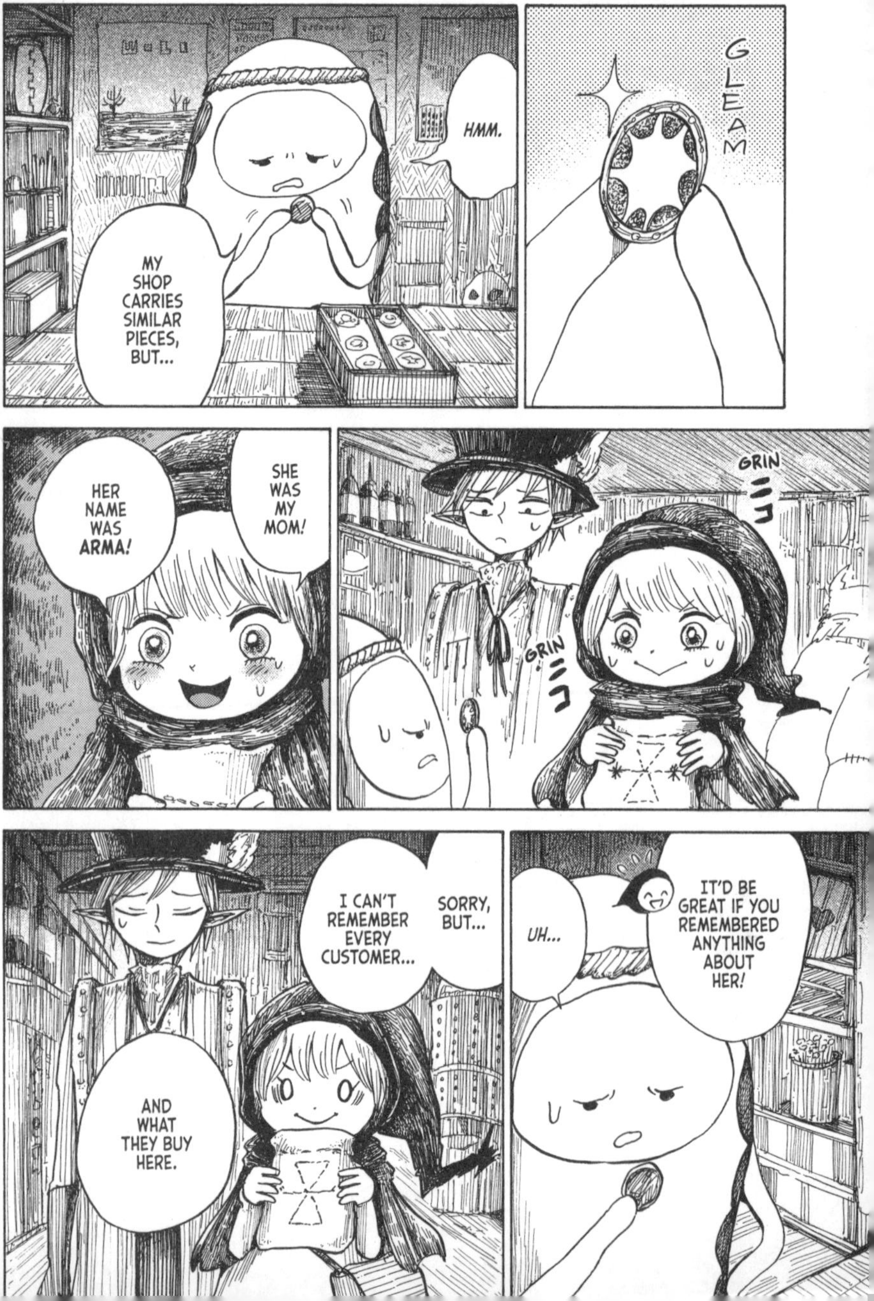

GLEAM
HMM.
MY SHOP CARRIES SIMILAR PIECES, BUT...
GRIN ニコ
GRIN ニコ
SHE WAS MY MOM!
HER NAME WAS ARMA!
IT'D BE GREAT IF YOU REMEMBERED ANYTHING ABOUT HER!
UH...
SORRY, BUT...
I CAN'T REMEMBER EVERY CUSTOMER...
AND WHAT THEY BUY HERE.

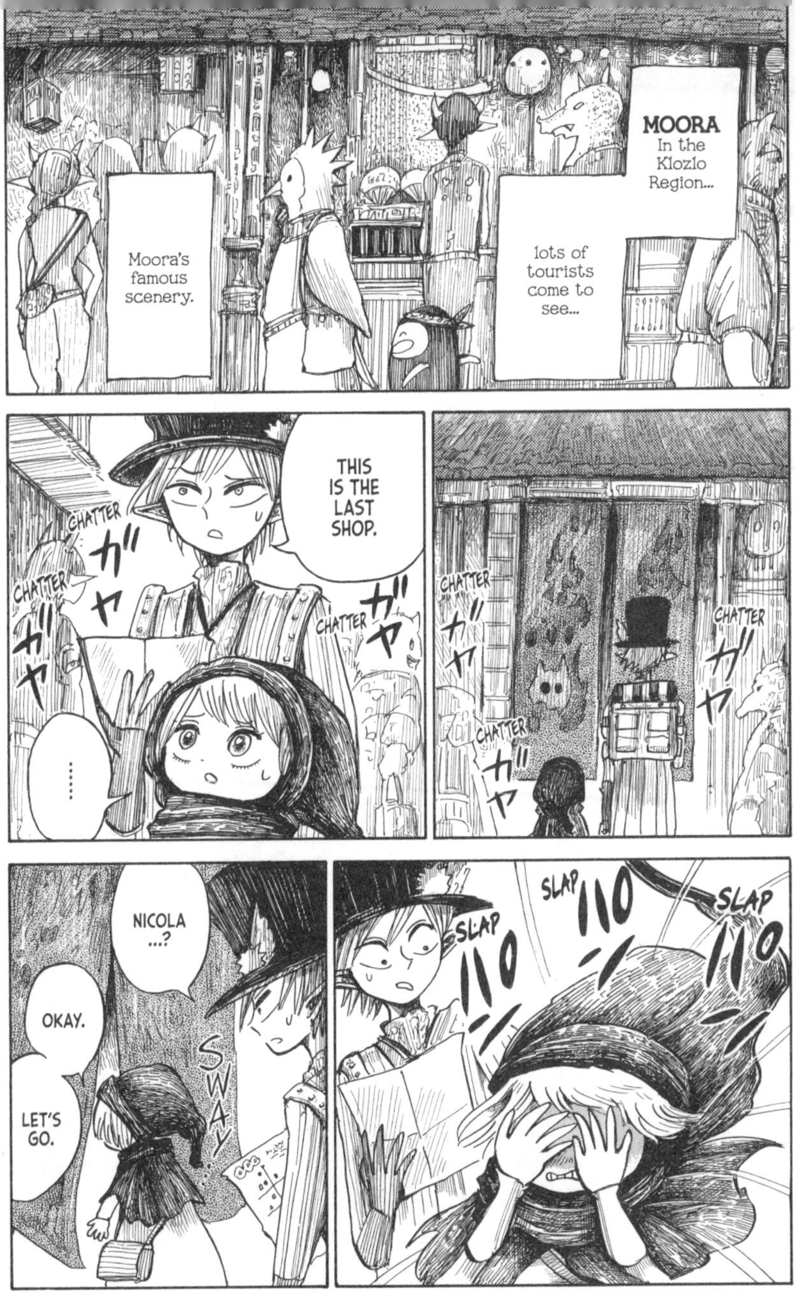
MOORA
In the Klozlo Region...
lots of tourists come to see...
Moora's famous scenery.
CHATTER ガヤ
CHATTER ガヤ
CHATTER ガヤ
CHATTER ガヤ
THIS IS THE LAST SHOP.
CHATTER ガヤ
CHATTER ガヤ
CHATTER ガヤ
......
SLAP
SLAP
SLAP
NICOLA ...?
OKAY.
LET'S GO.
SWAY

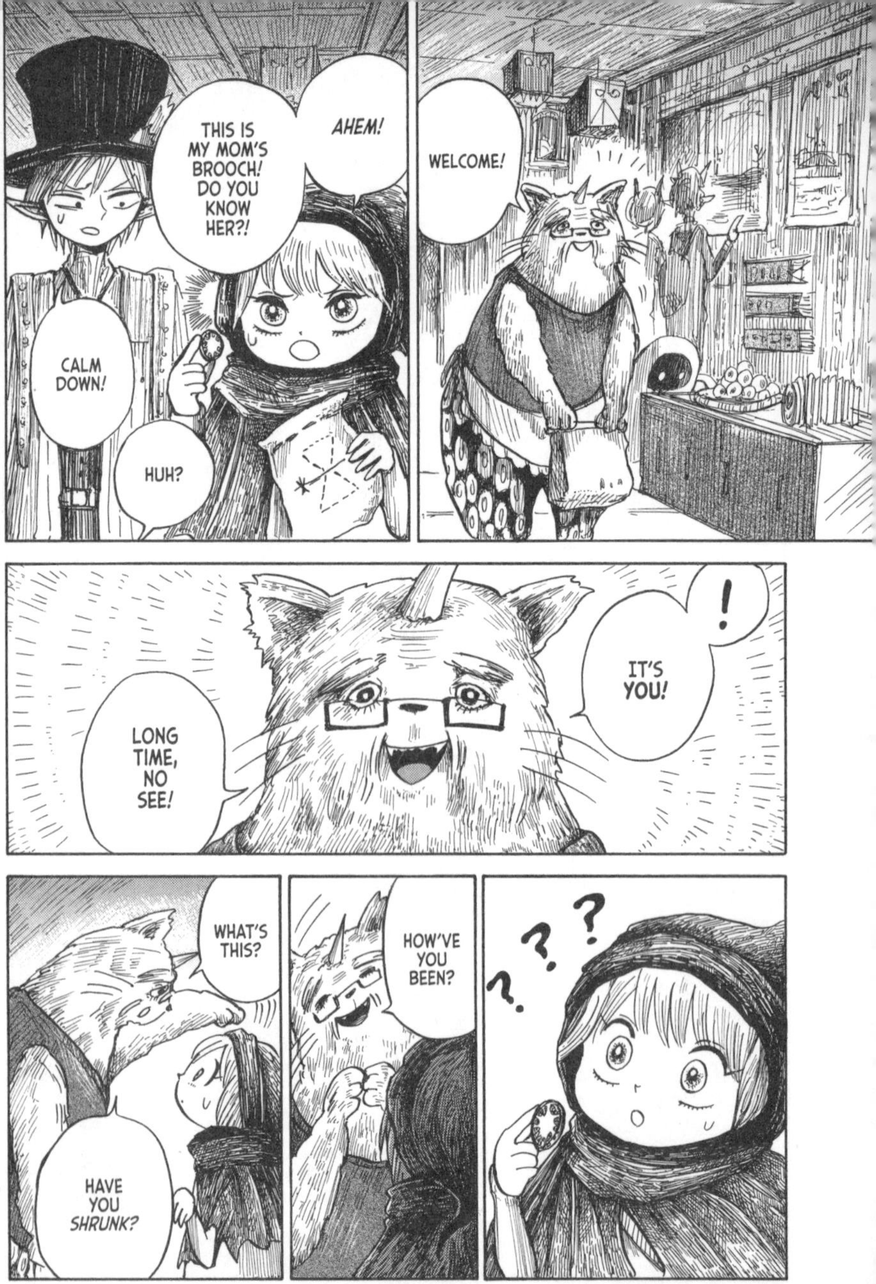
WELCOME!
AHEM!
THIS IS MY MOM'S BROOCH! DO YOU KNOW HER?!
CALM DOWN!
HUH?
!
IT'S YOU!
LONG TIME, NO SEE!
? ? ? ?
HOW'VE YOU BEEN?
WHAT'S THIS?
HAVE YOU SHRUNK?

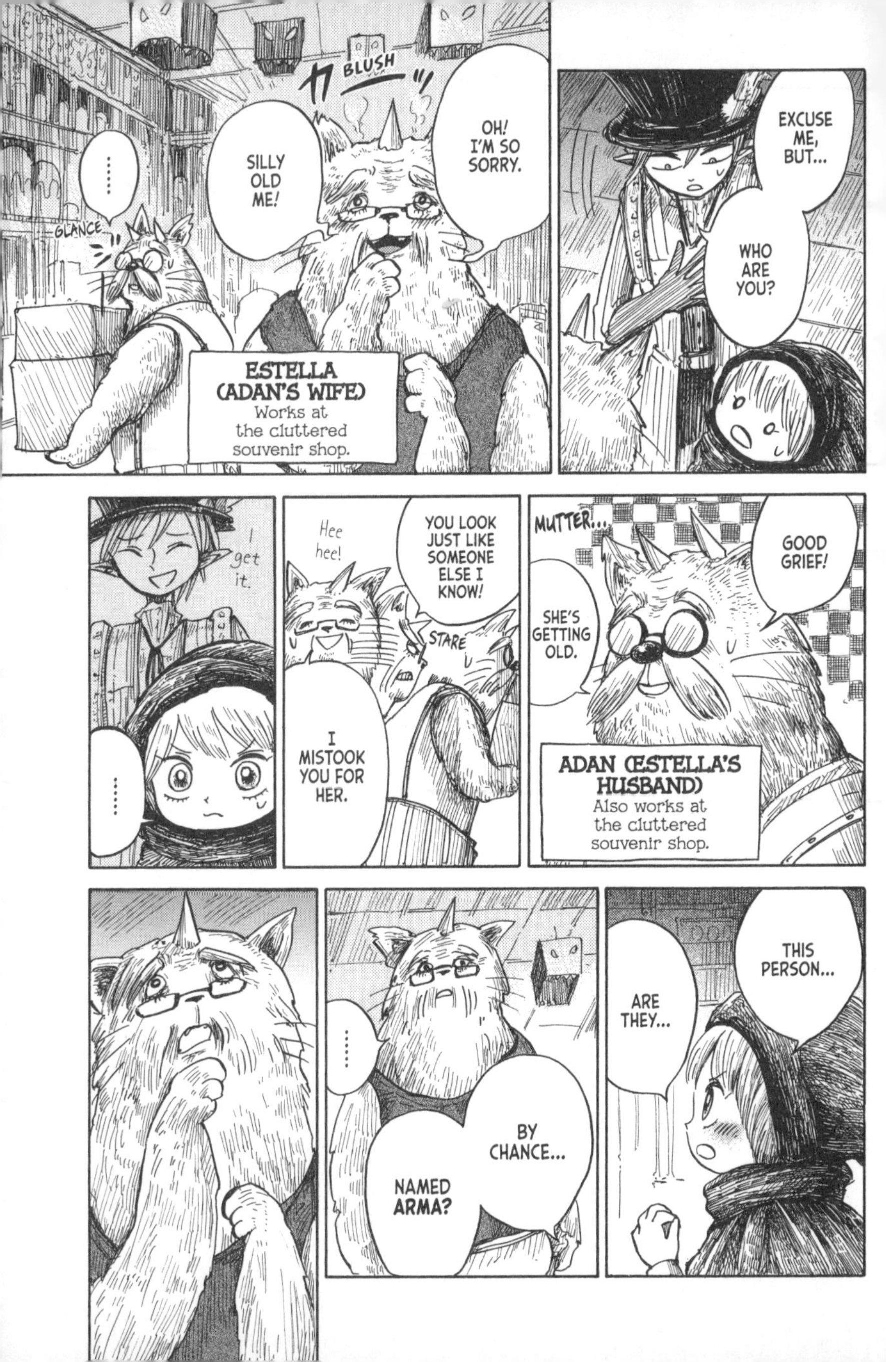
EXCUSE ME, BUT...
WHO ARE YOU?
BLUSH
OH! I'M SO SORRY.
SILLY OLD ME!
......
GLANCE
ESTELLA (ADAN'S WIFE)
Works at the cluttered souvenir shop.
GOOD GRIEF!
MUTTER...
SHE'S GETTING OLD.
ADAN (ESTELLA'S HUSBAND)
Also works at the cluttered souvenir shop.
YOU LOOK JUST LIKE SOMEONE ELSE I KNOW!
Hee hee!
STARE
I MISTOOK YOU FOR HER.
I get it.
......
THIS PERSON...
ARE THEY...
BY CHANCE...
NAMED ARMA?
......

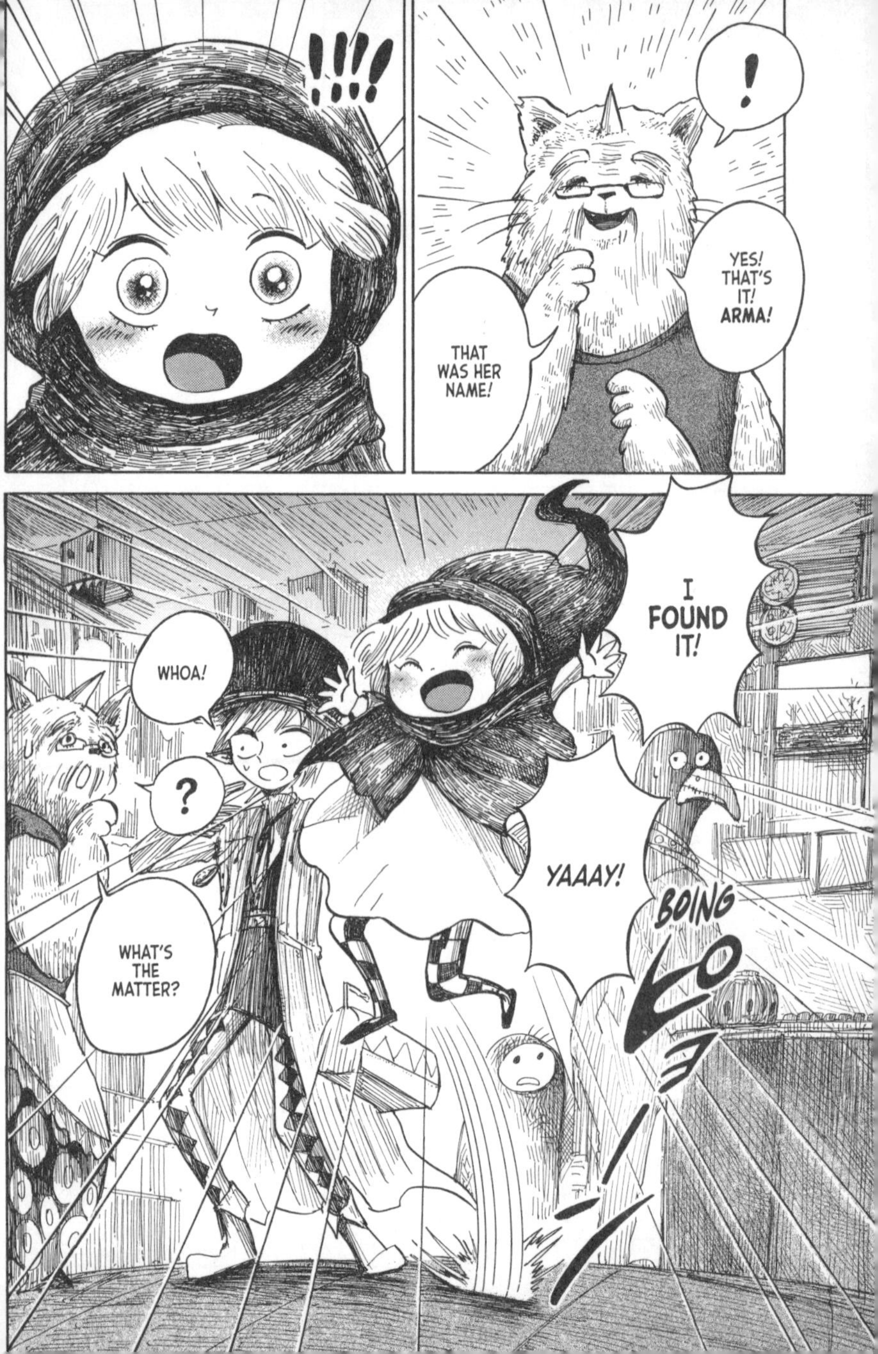
!
YES! THAT'S IT! ARMA!
THAT WAS HER NAME!
!!!!
I FOUND IT!
WHOA!
?
YAAAY!
BOING
WHAT'S THE MATTER?

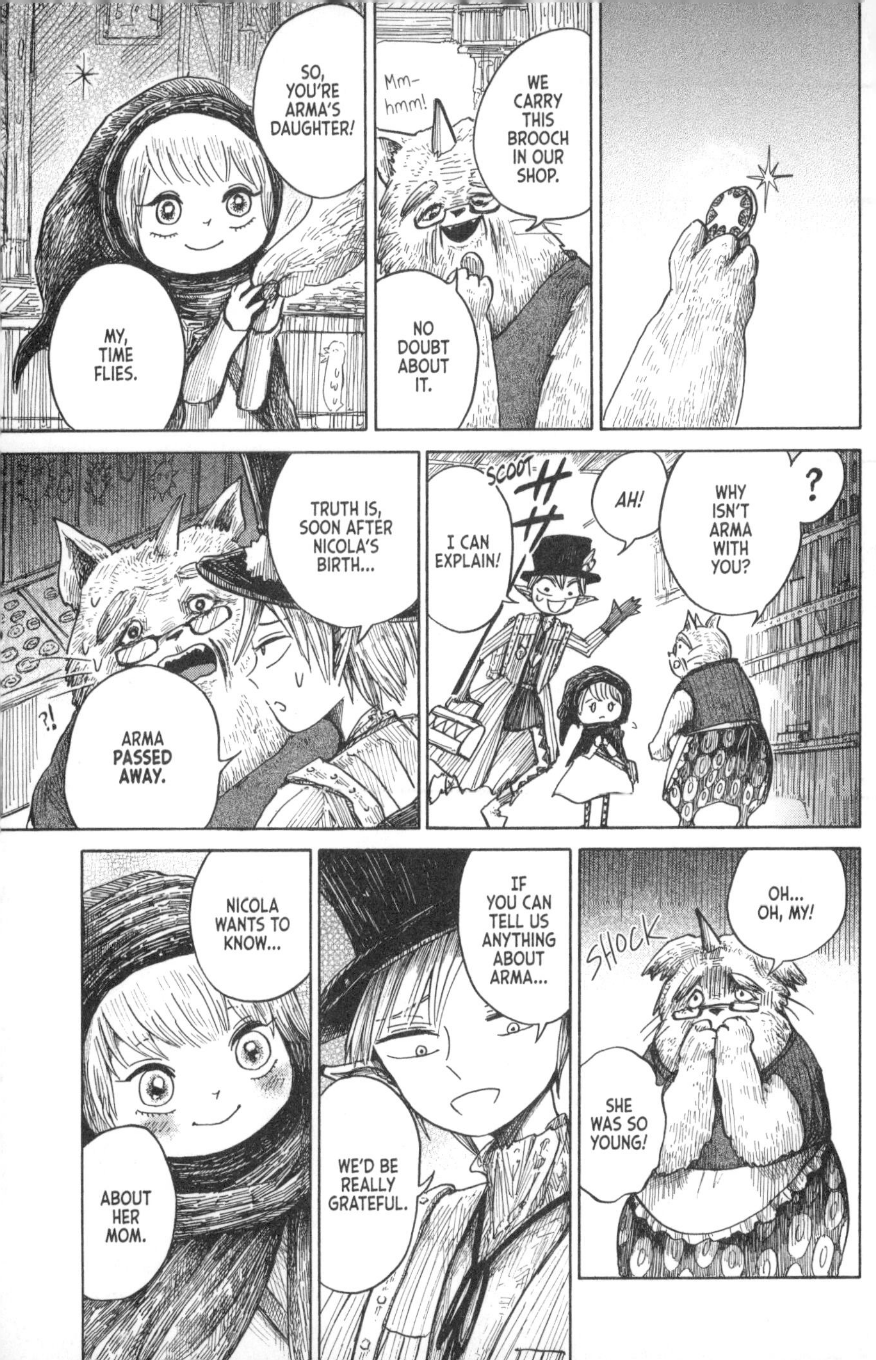
WE CARRY THIS BROOCH IN OUR SHOP.
Mm-hmm!
NO DOUBT ABOUT IT.
SO, YOU'RE ARMA'S DAUGHTER!
MY, TIME FLIES.
?
WHY ISN'T ARMA WITH YOU?
AH!
SCOOT
I CAN EXPLAIN!
TRUTH IS, SOON AFTER NICOLA'S BIRTH...
?!
ARMA PASSED AWAY.
OH... OH, MY!
SHOCK
SHE WAS SO YOUNG!
IF YOU CAN TELL US ANYTHING ABOUT ARMA...
WE'D BE REALLY GRATEFUL.
NICOLA WANTS TO KNOW...
ABOUT HER MOM.

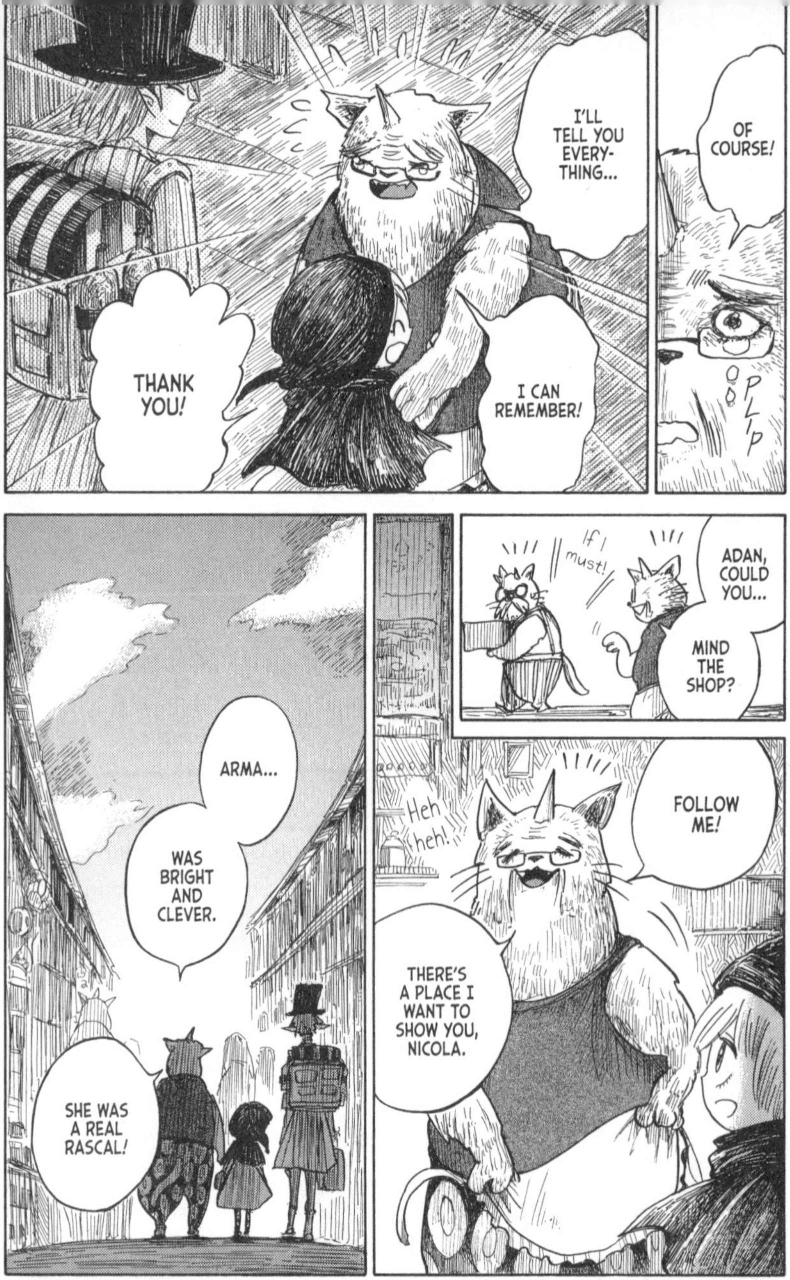
OF COURSE!
PLIP
I'LL TELL YOU EVERY-THING...
I CAN REMEMBER!
THANK YOU!
ADAN, COULD YOU...
MIND THE SHOP?
If I must!
FOLLOW ME!
Heh heh!
THERE'S A PLACE I WANT TO SHOW YOU, NICOLA.
ARMA...
WAS BRIGHT AND CLEVER.
SHE WAS A REAL RASCAL!

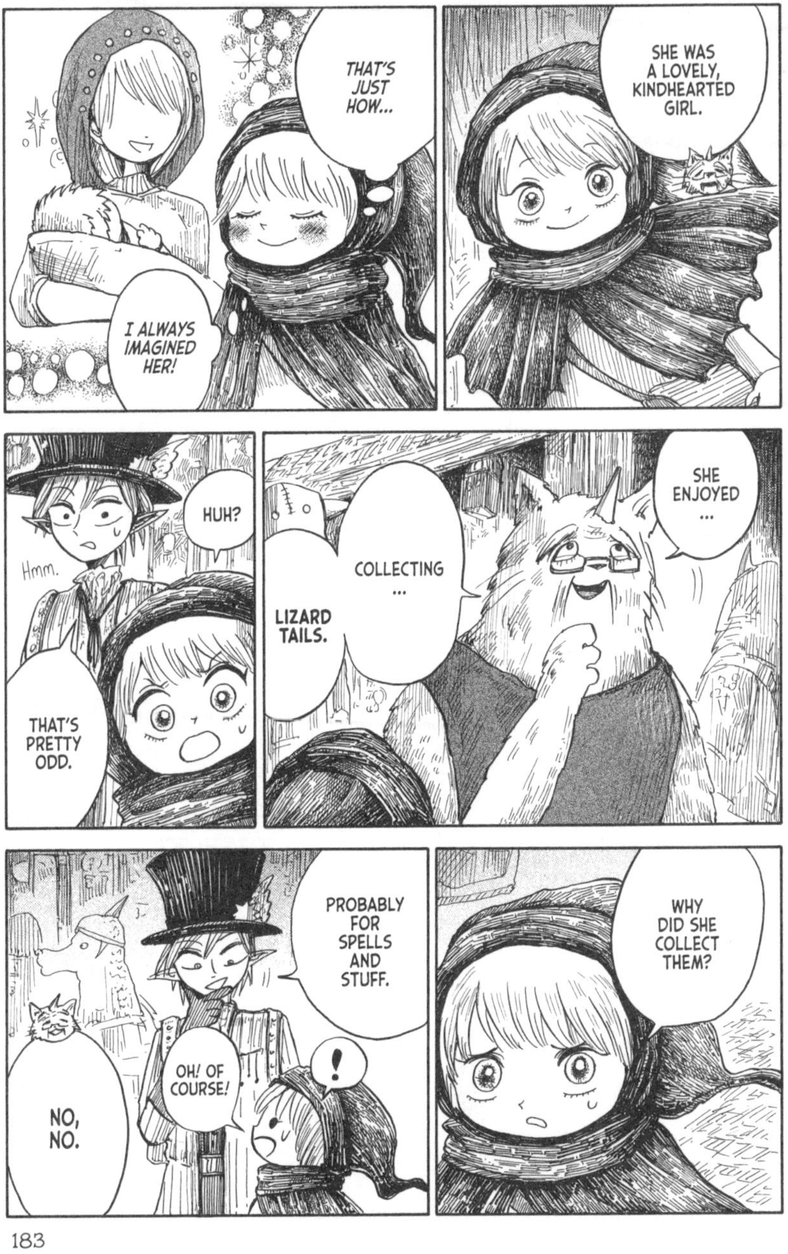
SHE WAS A LOVELY, KINDHEARTED GIRL.
THAT'S JUST HOW...
I ALWAYS IMAGINED HER!
SHE ENJOYED ...
COLLECTING ...
LIZARD TAILS.
HUH?
Hmm.
THAT'S PRETTY ODD.
WHY DID SHE COLLECT THEM?
PROBABLY FOR SPELLS AND STUFF.
!
OH! OF COURSE!
NO, NO.

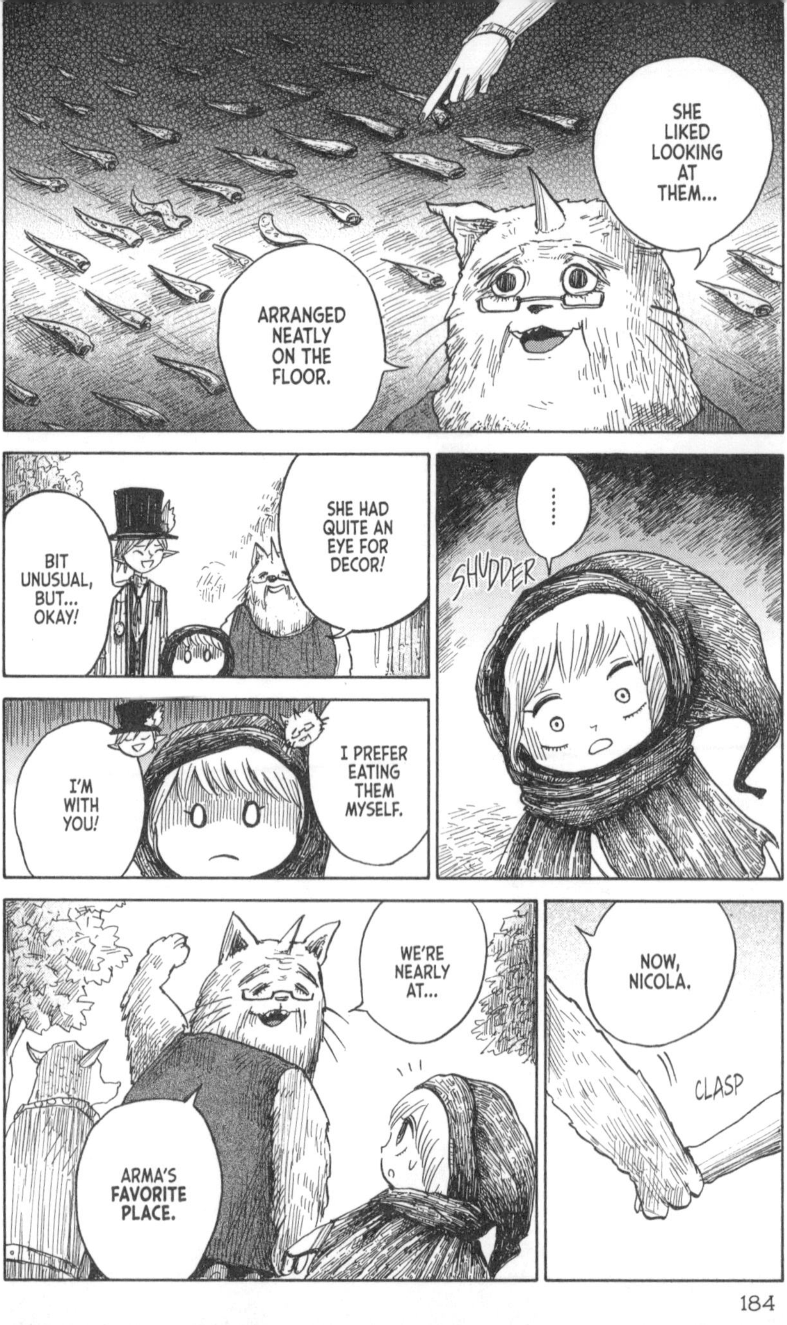
SHE LIKED LOOKING AT THEM...
ARRANGED NEATLY ON THE FLOOR.
......
SHUDDER
SHE HAD QUITE AN EYE FOR DECOR!
BIT UNUSUAL, BUT... OKAY!
I PREFER EATING THEM MYSELF.
I'M WITH YOU!
NOW, NICOLA.
CLASP
WE'RE NEARLY AT...
ARMA'S FAVORITE PLACE.

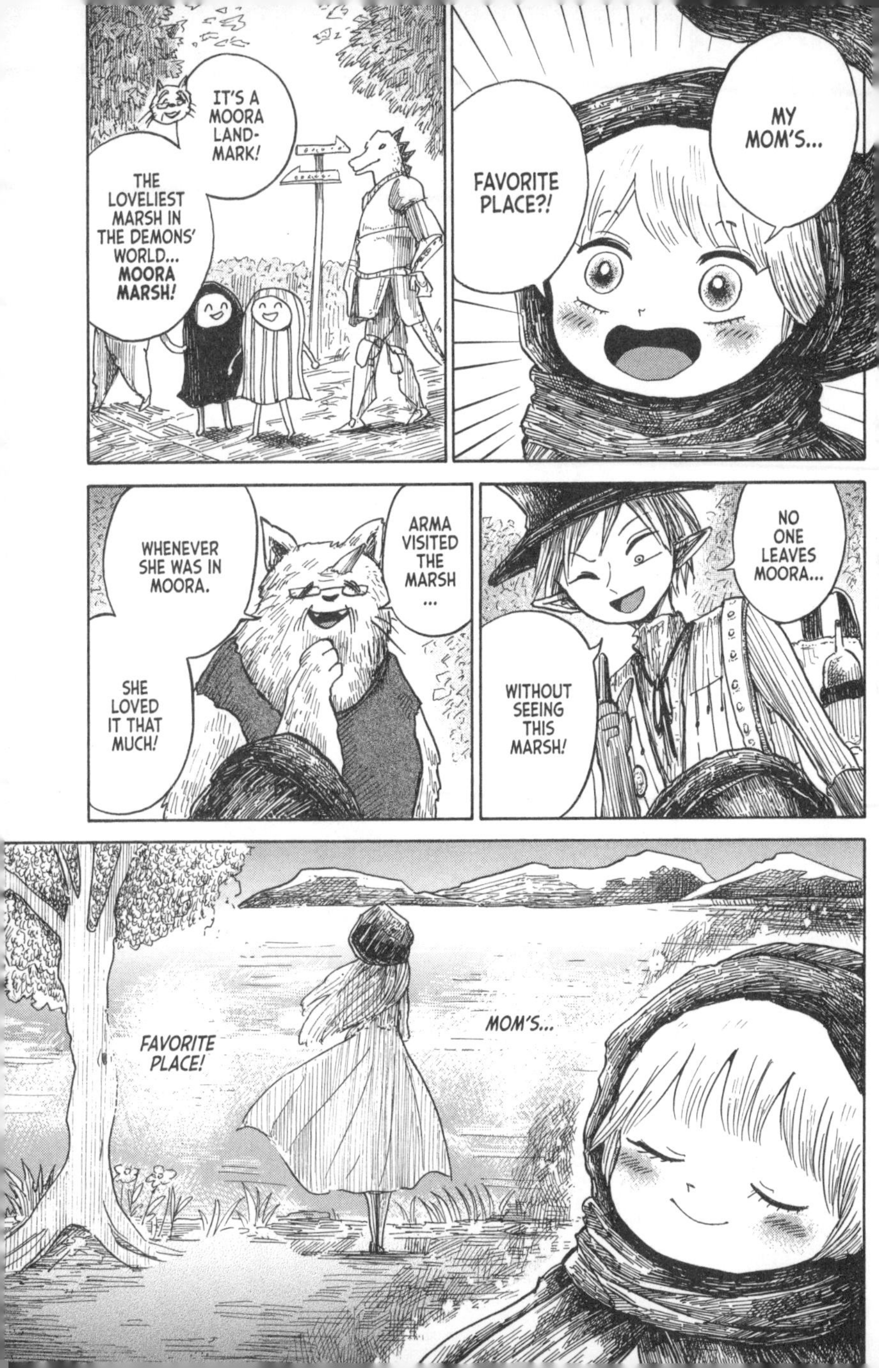
MY MOM'S...
FAVORITE PLACE?!
IT'S A MOORA LAND-MARK!
THE LOVELIEST MARSH IN THE DEMONS' WORLD... **MOORA MARSH!**
NO ONE LEAVES MOORA...
WITHOUT SEEING THIS MARSH!
ARMA VISITED THE MARSH ...
WHENEVER SHE WAS IN MOORA.
SHE LOVED IT THAT MUCH!
MOM'S...
FAVORITE PLACE!

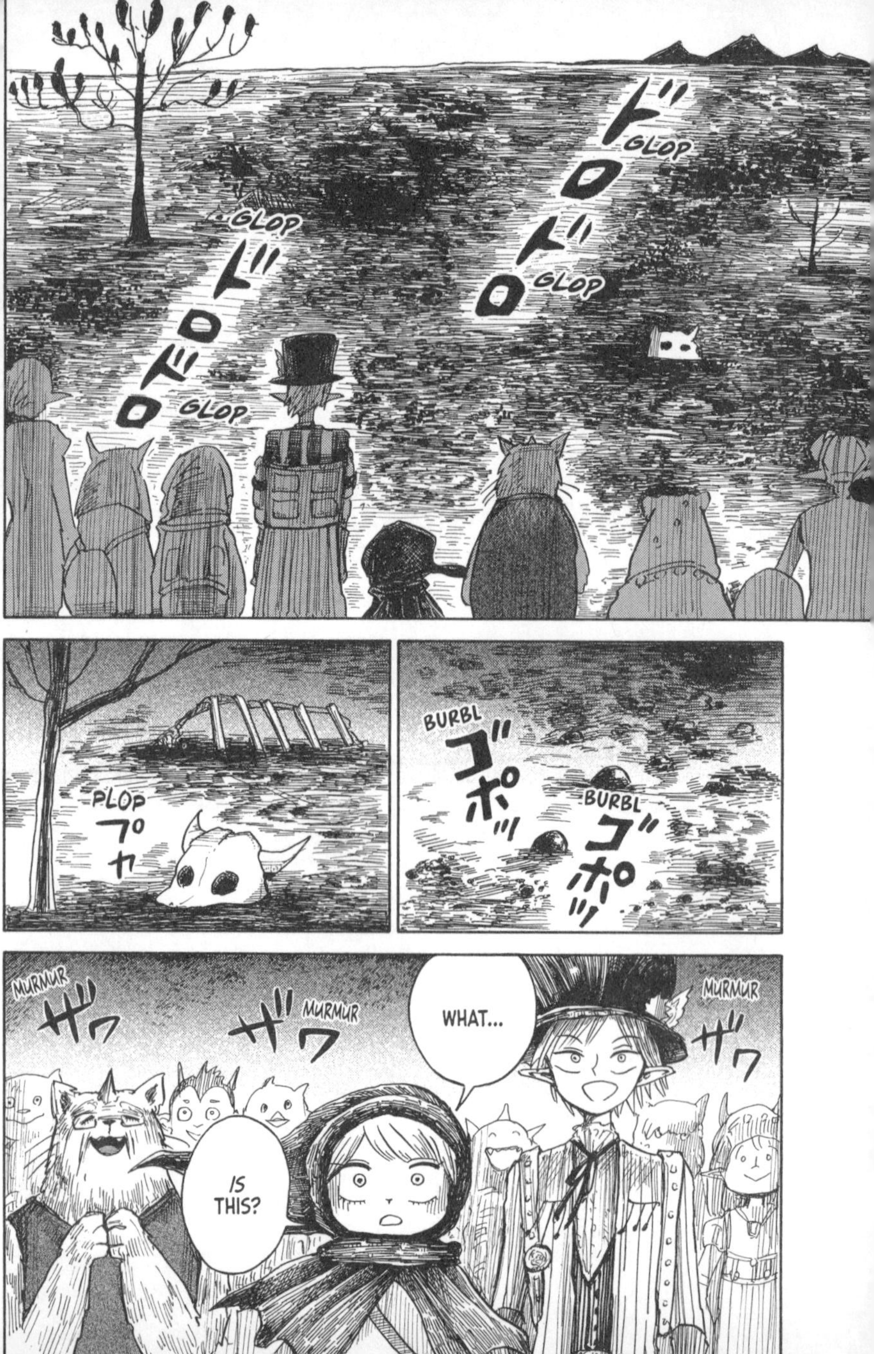

ドロドロ
GLOP
GLOP
ドロドロ
GLOP
GLOP
BURBL
ゴポッ
BURBL
ゴポッ
PLOP
プカ
MURMUR
ザワ
WHAT...
MURMUR
ザワ
MURMUR
ザワ
IS THIS?

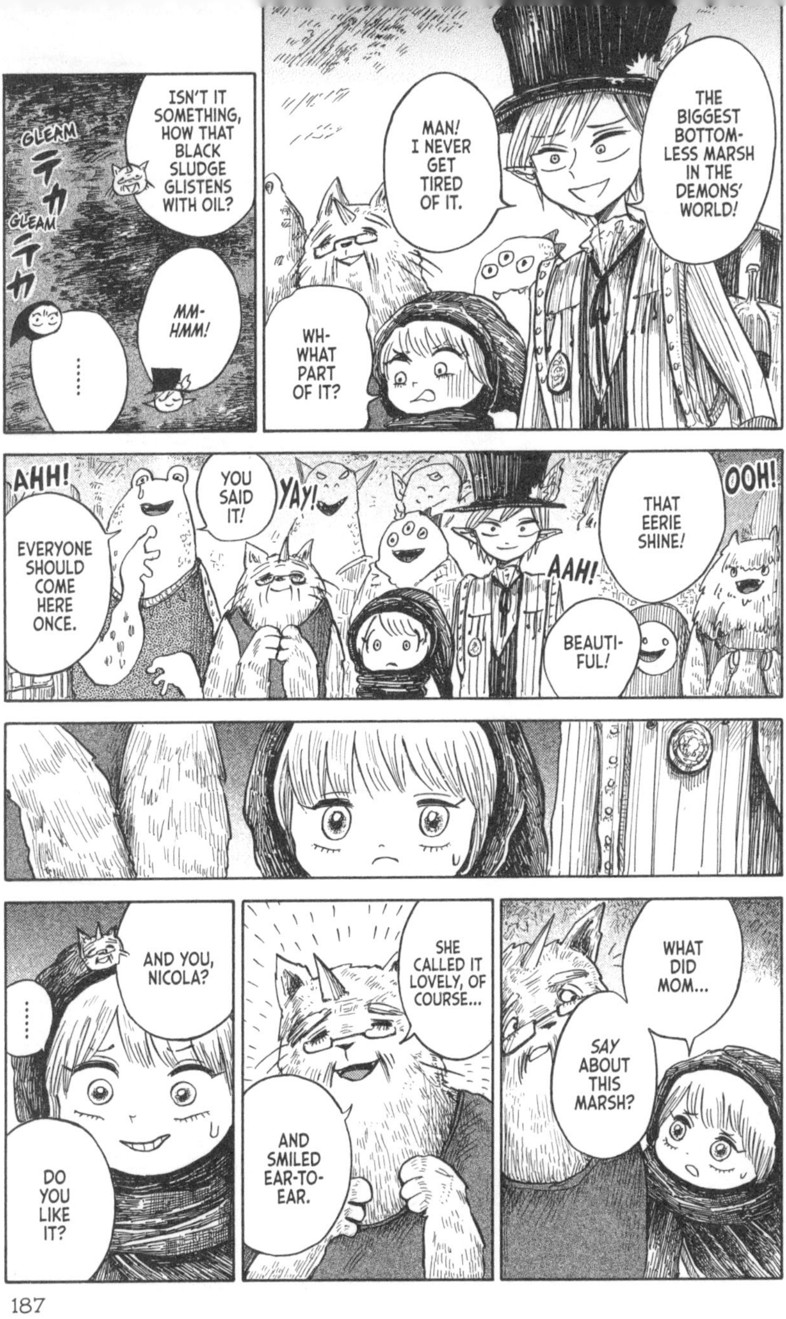
THE BIGGEST BOTTOM-LESS MARSH IN THE DEMONS' WORLD!
MAN! I NEVER GET TIRED OF IT.
WH-WHAT PART OF IT?
ISN'T IT SOMETHING, HOW THAT BLACK SLUDGE GLISTENS WITH OIL?
GLEAM テカ
GLEAM テカ
MM-HMM!
......
OOH!
THAT EERIE SHINE!
AAH!
BEAUTI-FUL!
YAY!
YOU SAID IT!
AHH!
EVERYONE SHOULD COME HERE ONCE.
WHAT DID MOM...
SAY ABOUT THIS MARSH?
SHE CALLED IT LOVELY, OF COURSE...
AND SMILED EAR-TO-EAR.
AND YOU, NICOLA?
......
DO YOU LIKE IT?

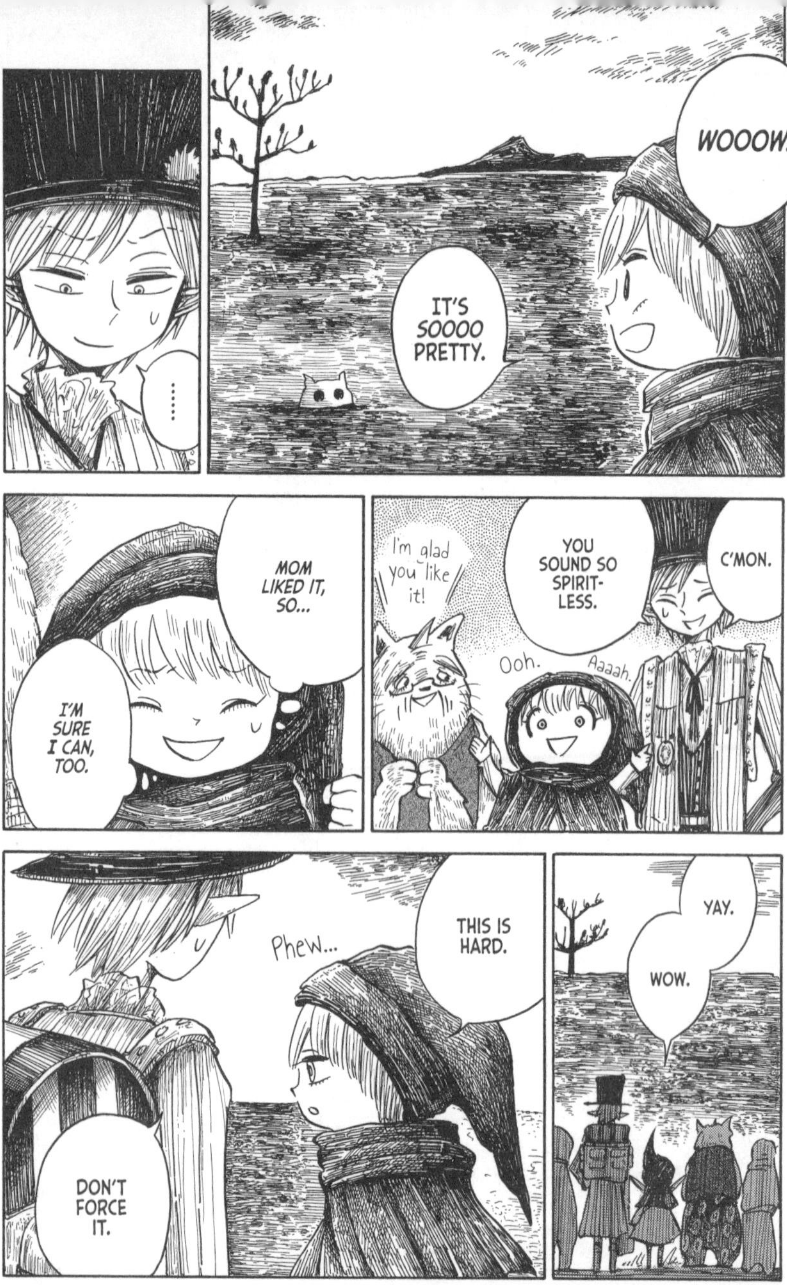
WOOOW.
IT'S SOOOO PRETTY.
......
C'MON.
YOU SOUND SO SPIRIT-LESS.
I'm glad you like it!
Aaaah.
Ooh.
MOM LIKED IT, SO...
I'M SURE I CAN, TOO.
YAY.
WOW.
THIS IS HARD.
Phew...
DON'T FORCE IT.

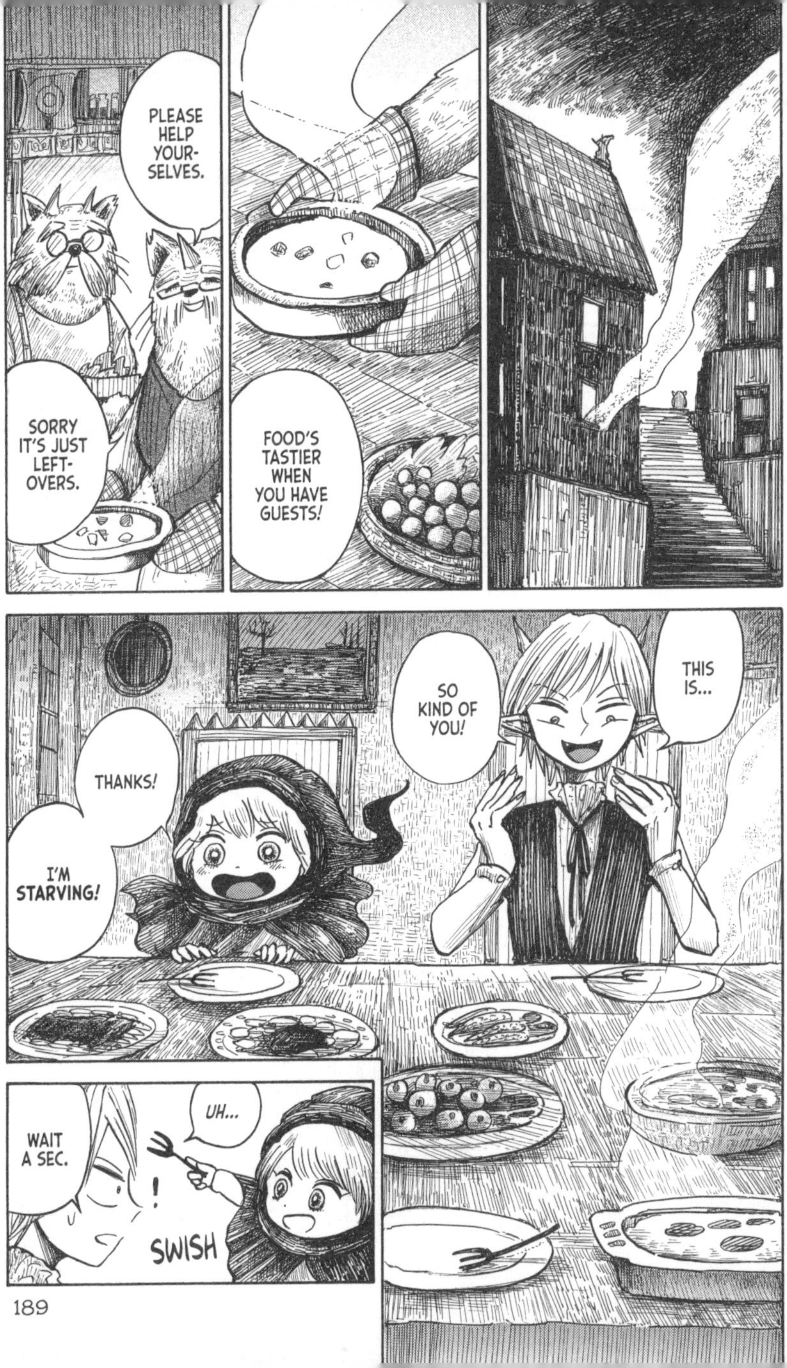
FOOD'S TASTIER WHEN YOU HAVE GUESTS!
PLEASE HELP YOUR-SELVES.
SORRY IT'S JUST LEFT-OVERS.
THIS IS...
SO KIND OF YOU!
THANKS!
I'M STARVING!
UH...
!
WAIT A SEC.
SWISH

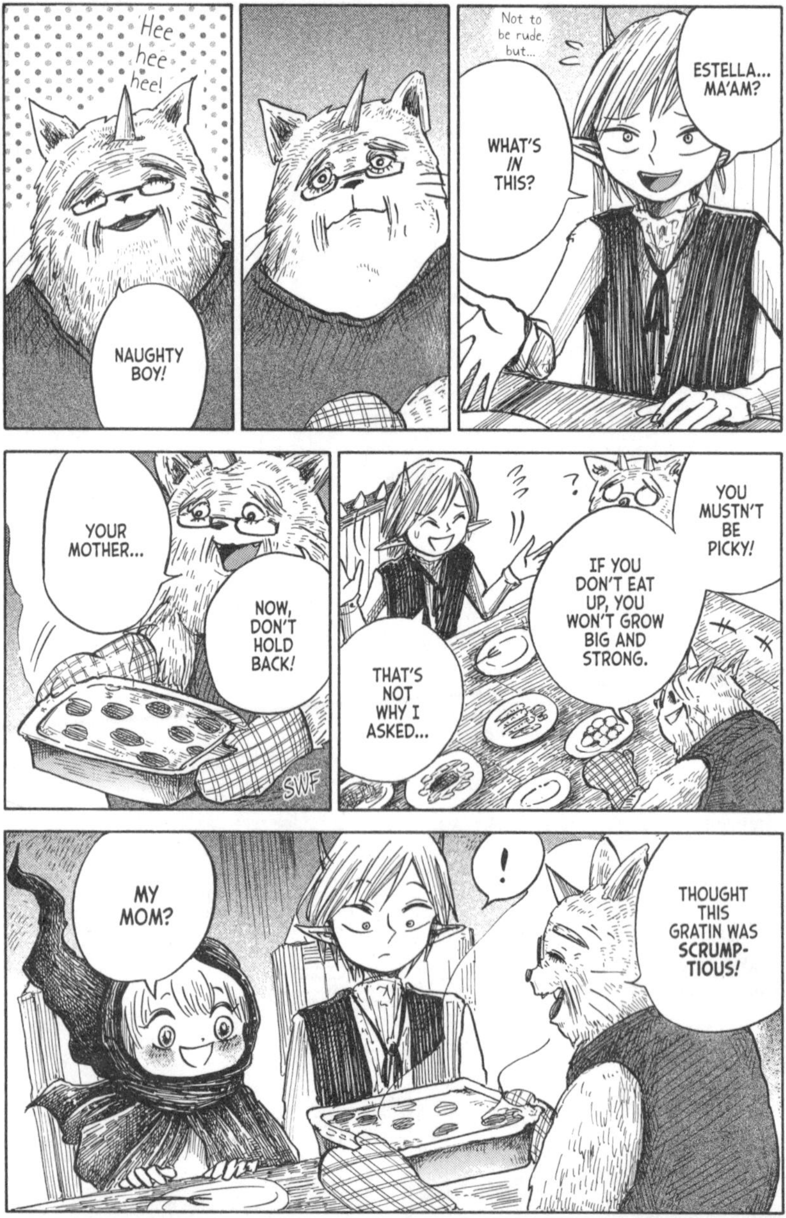
ESTELLA... MA'AM?
Not to be rude, but...
WHAT'S *IN* THIS?
Hee hee hee!
NAUGHTY BOY!
YOU MUSTN'T BE PICKY!
IF YOU DON'T EAT UP, YOU WON'T GROW BIG AND STRONG.
THAT'S NOT WHY I ASKED...
YOUR MOTHER...
NOW, DON'T HOLD BACK!
SWF
THOUGHT THIS GRATIN WAS **SCRUMPTIOUS!**
!
MY MOM?

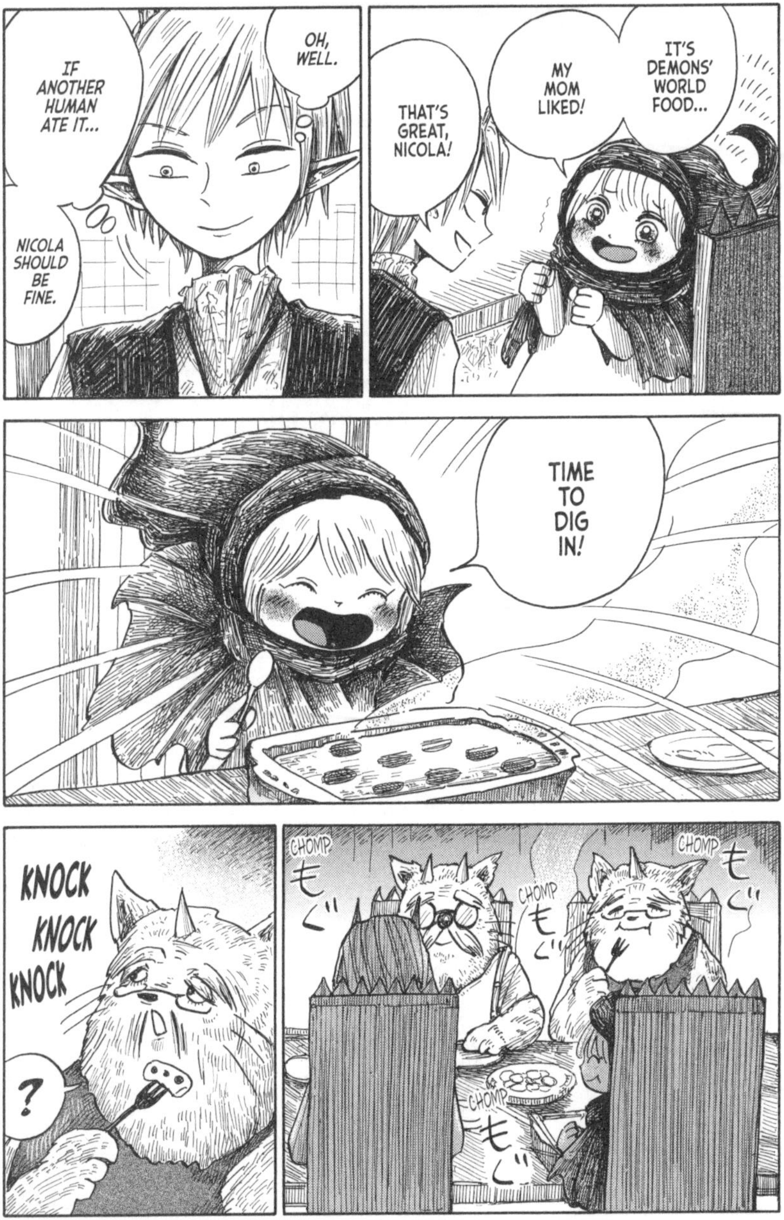
IT'S DEMONS' WORLD FOOD...
MY MOM LIKED!
THAT'S GREAT, NICOLA!
OH, WELL.
IF ANOTHER HUMAN ATE IT...
NICOLA SHOULD BE FINE.
TIME TO DIG IN!
CHOMP もぐ
CHOMP もぐ
CHOMP もぐ
CHOMP もぐ
KNOCK KNOCK KNOCK
?

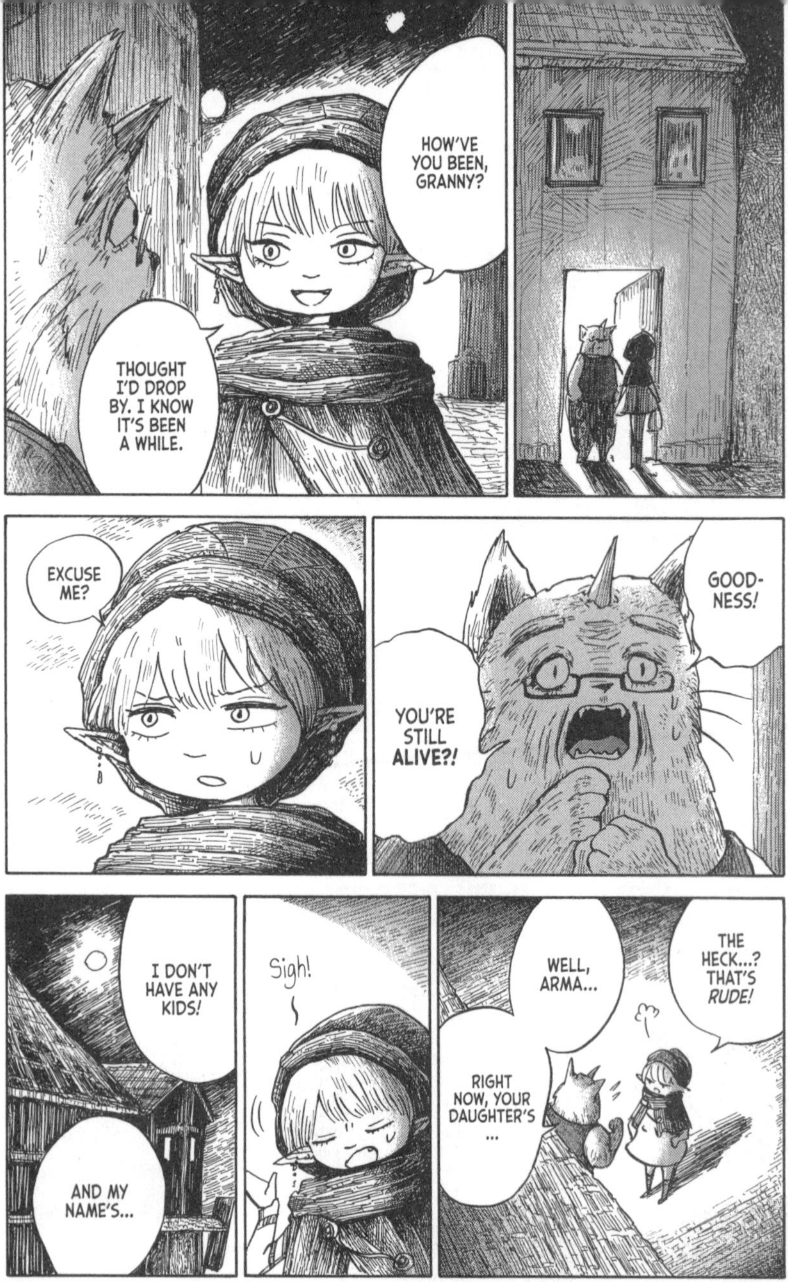
HOW'VE YOU BEEN, GRANNY?
THOUGHT I'D DROP BY. I KNOW IT'S BEEN A WHILE.
GOOD-NESS!
YOU'RE STILL **ALIVE?!**
EXCUSE ME?
THE HECK...? THAT'S *RUDE!*
WELL, ARMA...
RIGHT NOW, YOUR DAUGHTER'S ...
Sigh!
I DON'T HAVE ANY KIDS!
AND MY NAME'S...

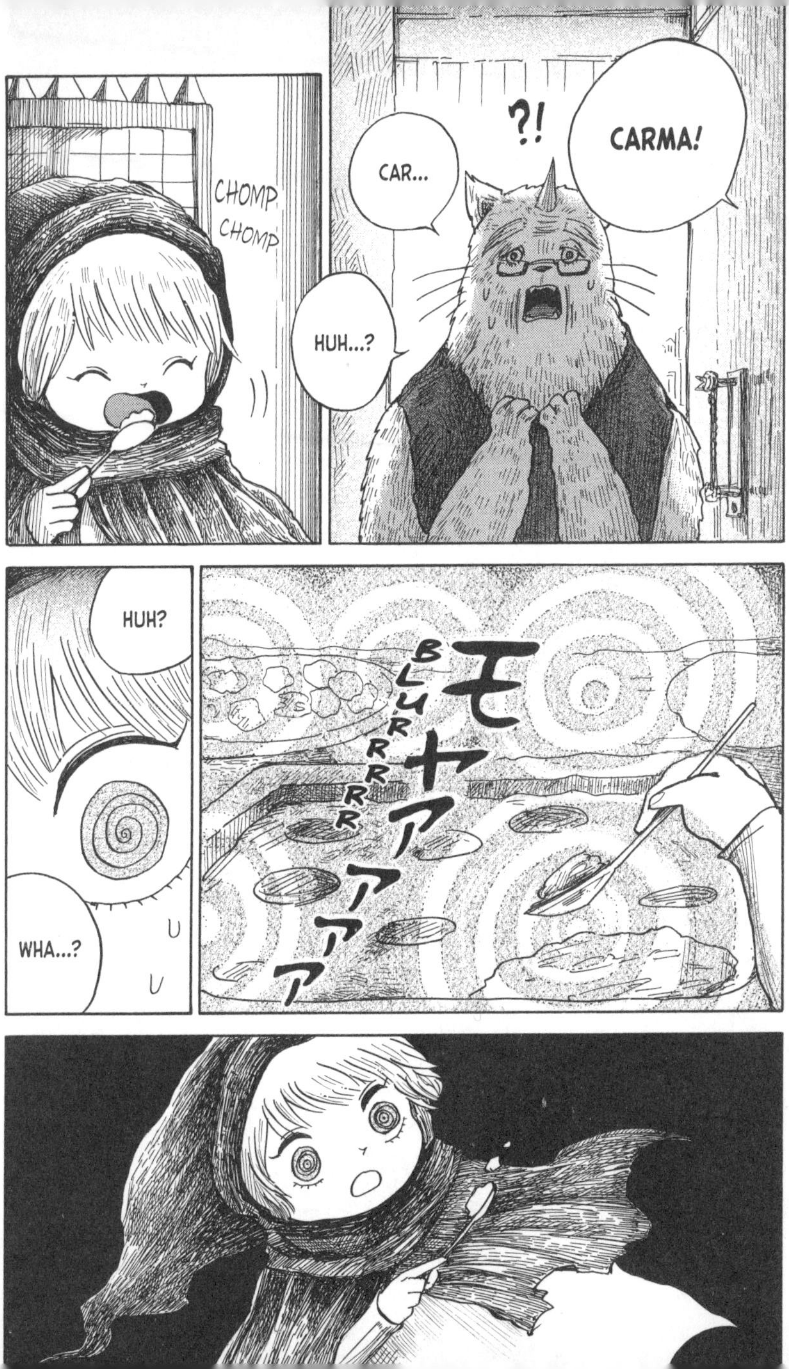
CARMA!
?!
CAR...
HUH...?
CHOMP CHOMP
モヤァァァァ
BLURRRRRR
HUH?
WHA...?

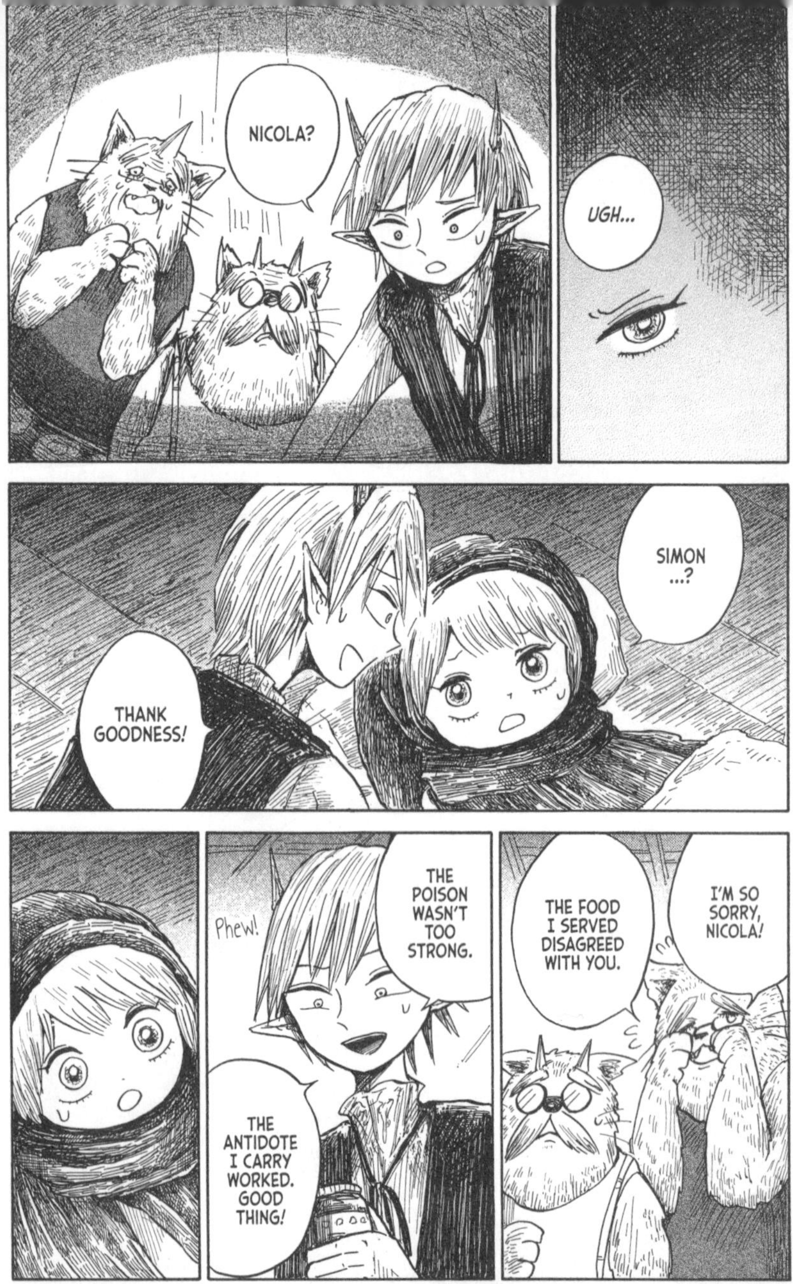
UGH...
NICOLA?
SIMON ...?
THANK GOODNESS!
I'M SO SORRY, NICOLA!
THE FOOD I SERVED DISAGREED WITH YOU.
THE POISON WASN'T TOO STRONG.
Phew!
THE ANTIDOTE I CARRY WORKED. GOOD THING!

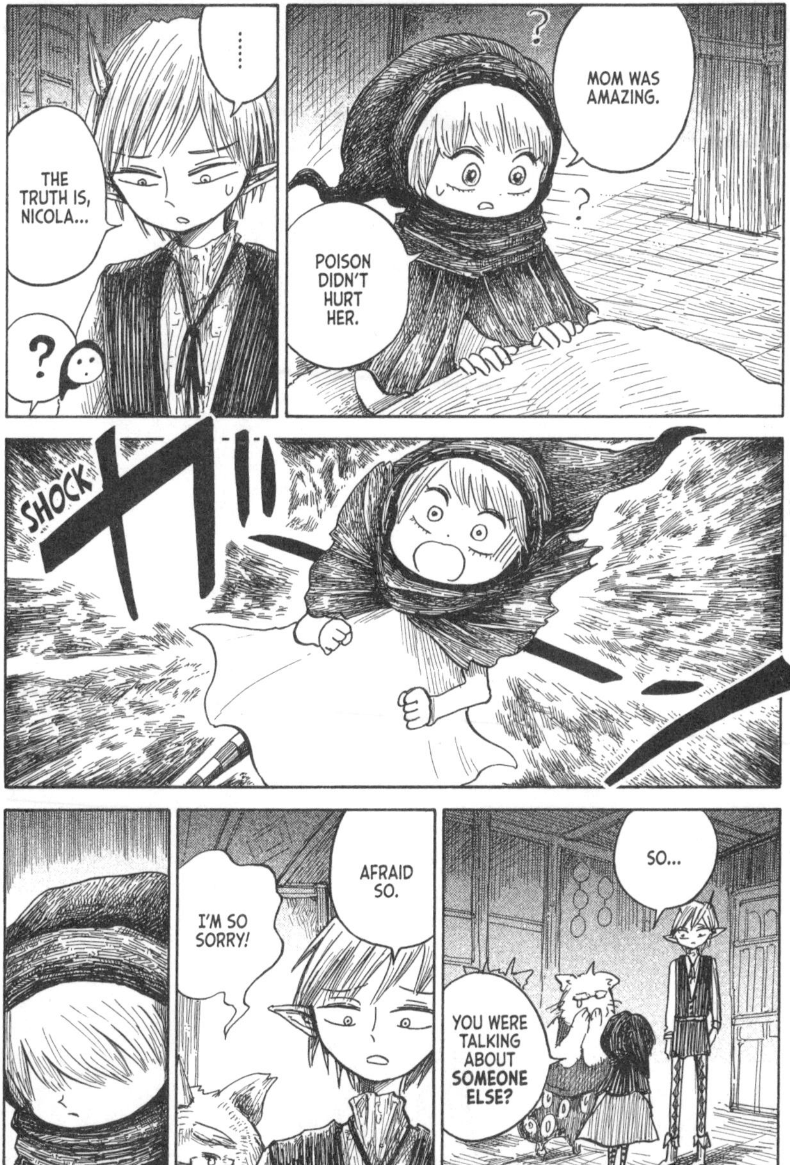
MOM WAS AMAZING.
POISON DIDN'T HURT HER.
......
THE TRUTH IS, NICOLA...
?
SHOCK
SO...
YOU WERE TALKING ABOUT SOMEONE ELSE?
AFRAID SO.
I'M SO SORRY!

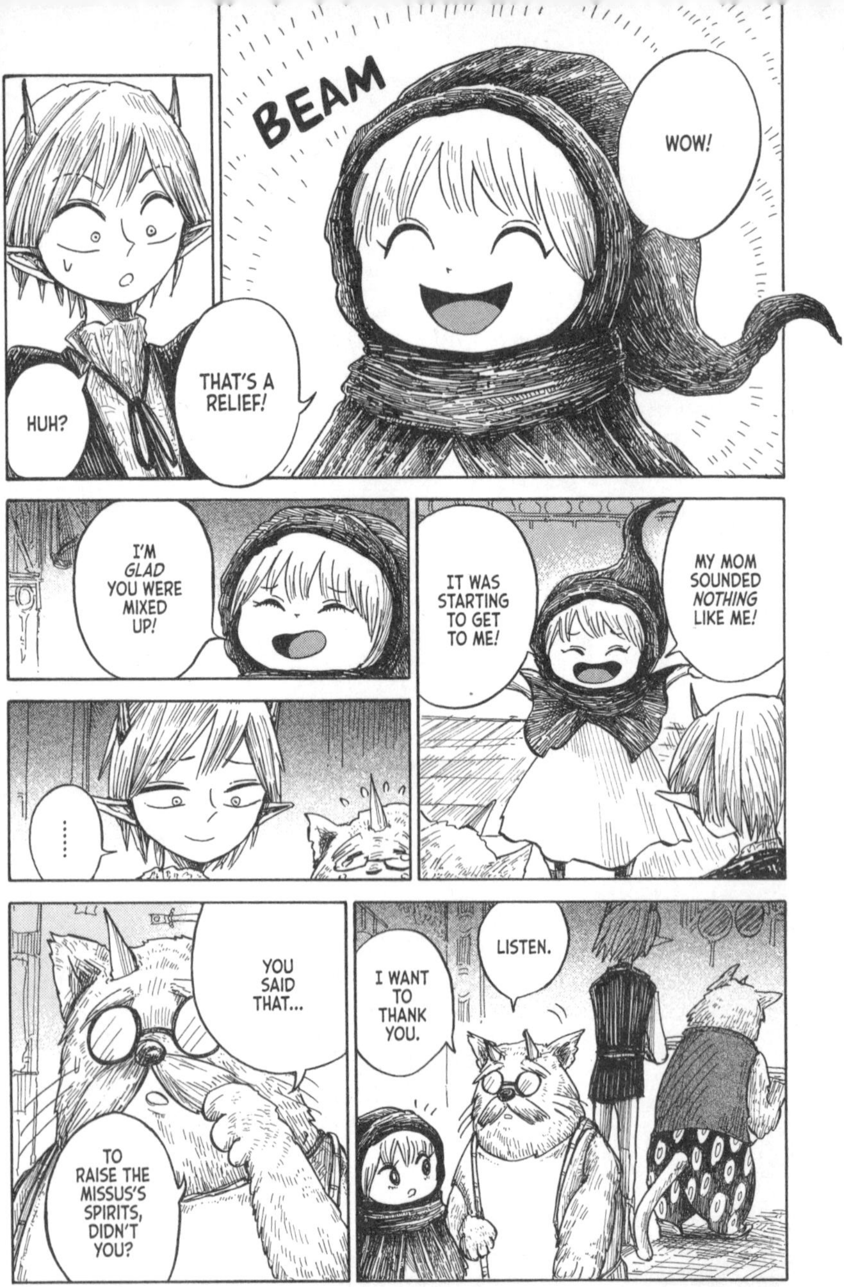
WOW!
BEAM
THAT'S A RELIEF!
HUH?
MY MOM SOUNDED *NOTHING* LIKE ME!
IT WAS STARTING TO GET TO ME!
I'M *GLAD* YOU WERE MIXED UP!
......
LISTEN.
I WANT TO THANK YOU.
YOU SAID THAT...
TO RAISE THE MISSUS'S SPIRITS, DIDN'T YOU?

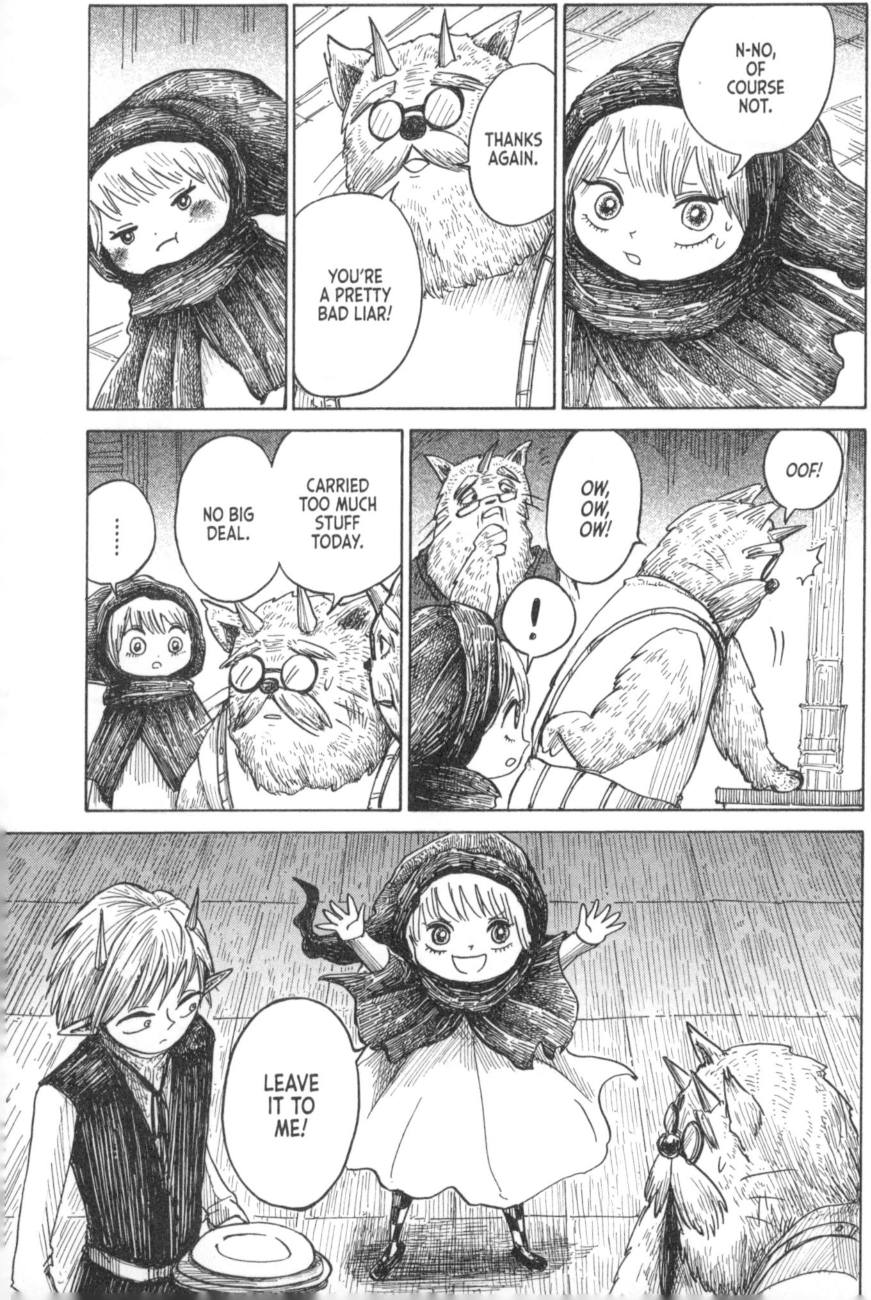

N-NO, OF COURSE NOT.
THANKS AGAIN.
YOU'RE A PRETTY BAD LIAR!
OOF!
OW, OW, OW!
!
CARRIED TOO MUCH STUFF TODAY.
NO BIG DEAL.
……
LEAVE IT TO ME!

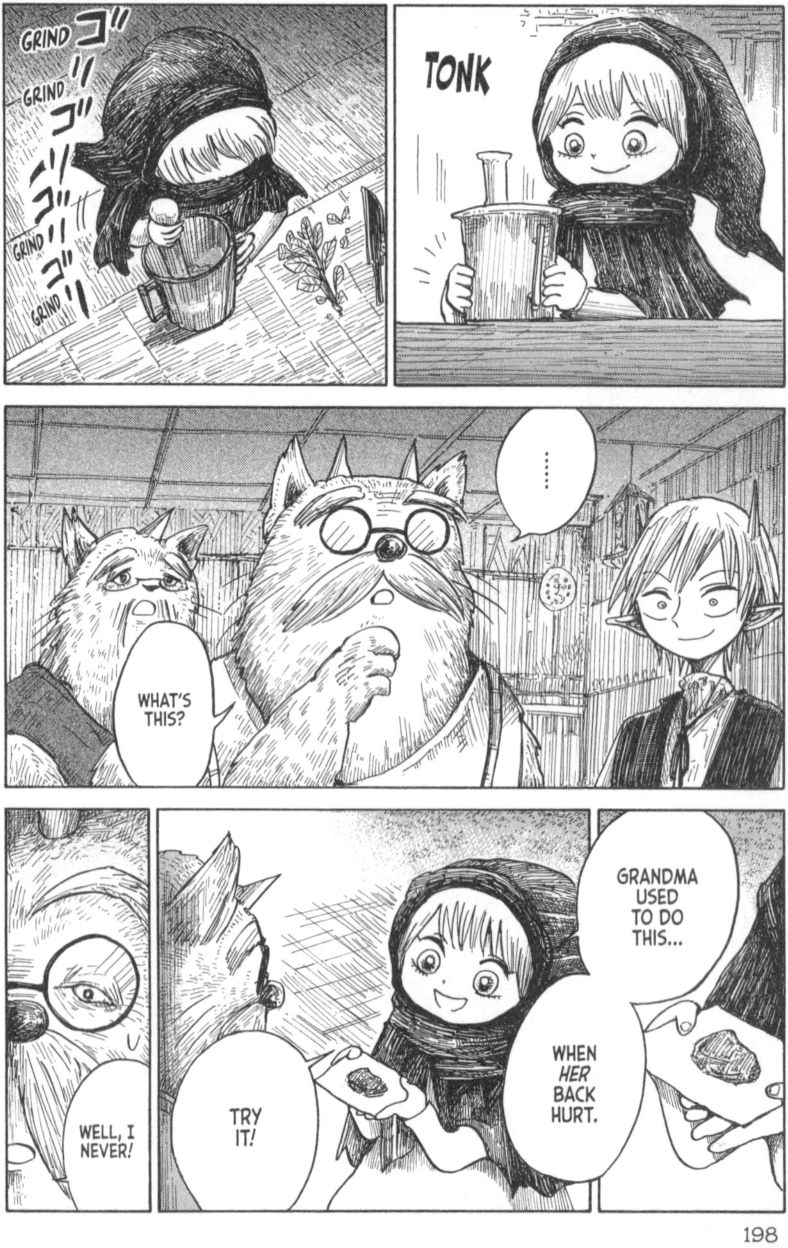
TONK
GRIND
ゴリ
GRIND
ゴリ
GRIND
ゴリ
GRIND
ゴリ
......
WHAT'S THIS?
GRANDMA USED TO DO THIS...
WHEN *HER* BACK HURT.
TRY IT!
WELL, I NEVER!

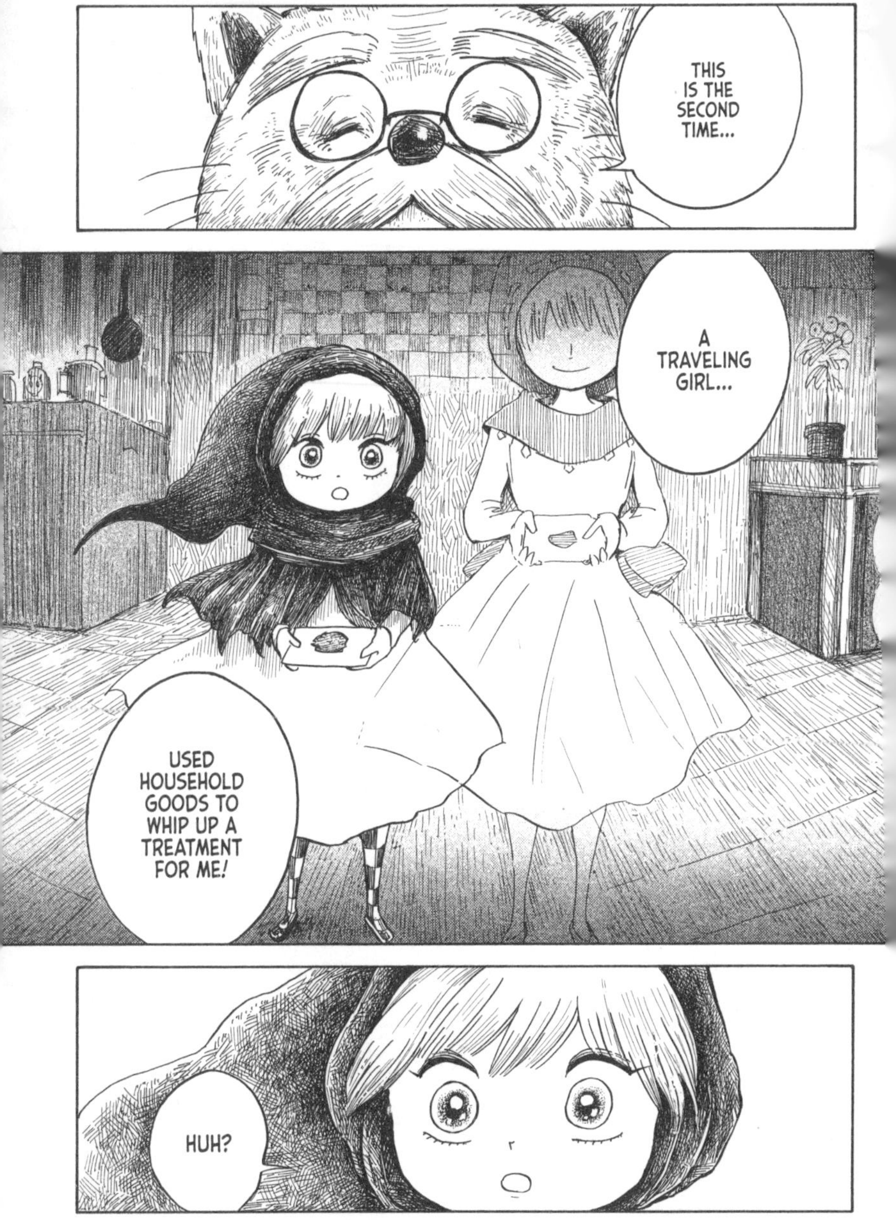
THIS IS THE SECOND TIME...
A TRAVELING GIRL...
USED HOUSEHOLD GOODS TO WHIP UP A TREATMENT FOR ME!
HUH?

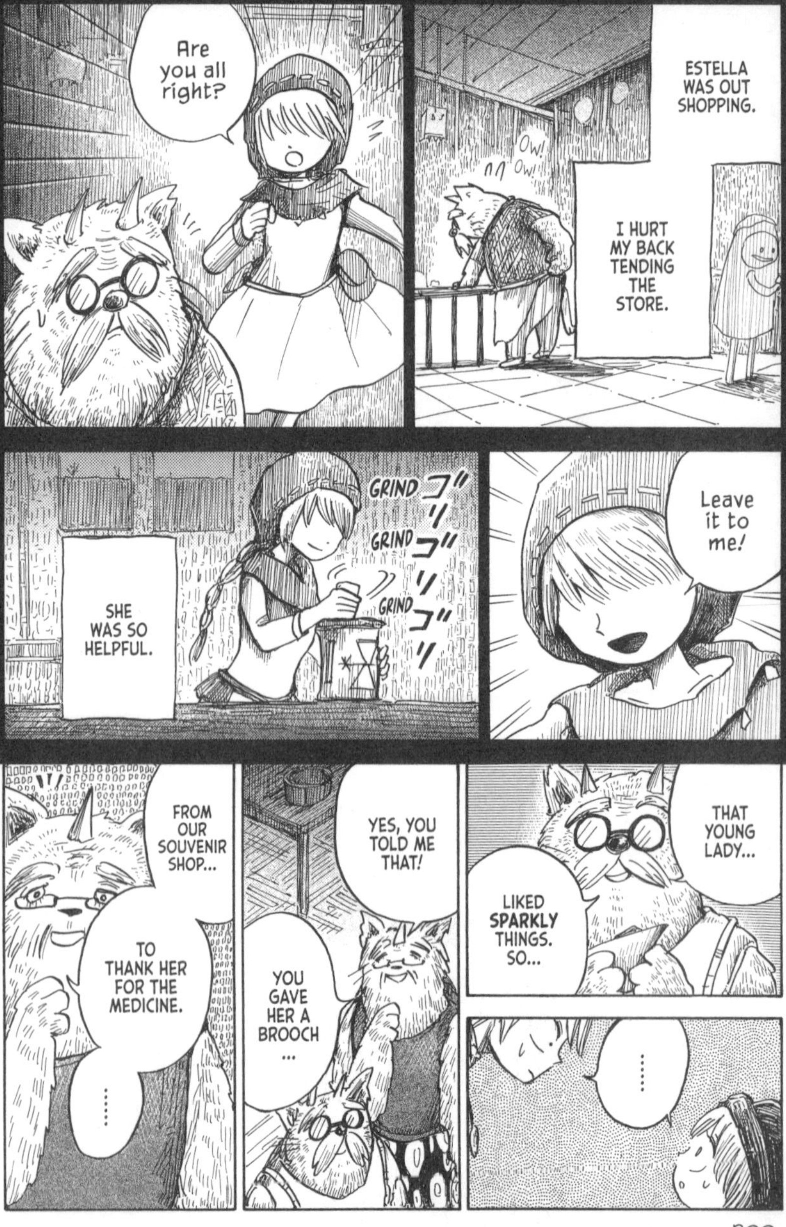
ESTELLA WAS OUT SHOPPING.
OW! OW!
I HURT MY BACK TENDING THE STORE.
Are you all right?
Leave it to me!
GRIND
GRIND
GRIND
SHE WAS SO HELPFUL.
THAT YOUNG LADY...
LIKED **SPARKLY** THINGS. SO...
......
YES, YOU TOLD ME THAT!
YOU GAVE HER A BROOCH ...
FROM OUR SOUVENIR SHOP...
TO THANK HER FOR THE MEDICINE.
......

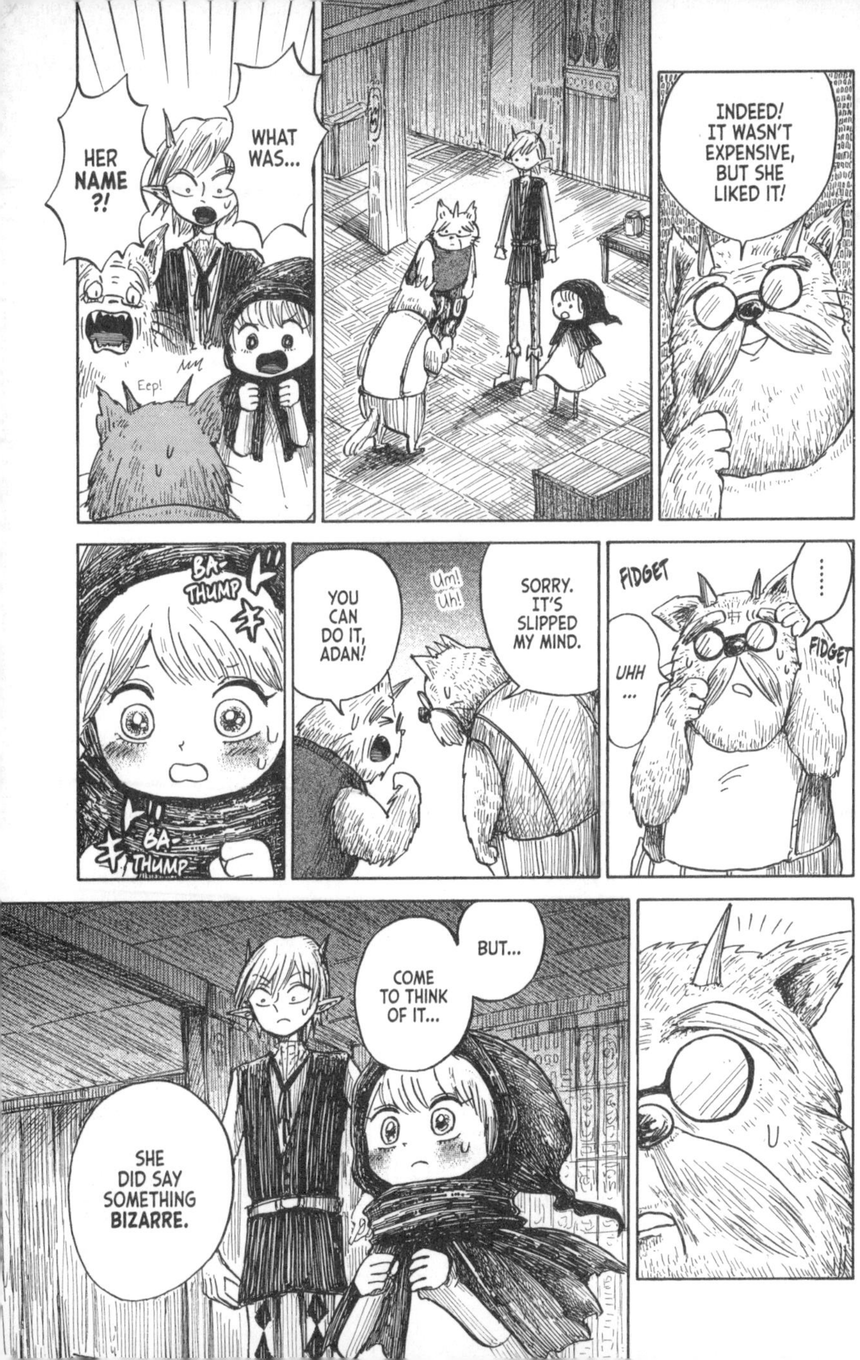
INDEED! IT WASN'T EXPENSIVE, BUT SHE LIKED IT!
WHAT WAS...
HER NAME ?!
Eep!
......
FIDGET
FIDGET
UHH ...
SORRY. IT'S SLIPPED MY MIND.
Um! Uh!
YOU CAN DO IT, ADAN!
BA-THUMP
BA-THUMP
BUT...
COME TO THINK OF IT...
SHE DID SAY SOMETHING BIZARRE.

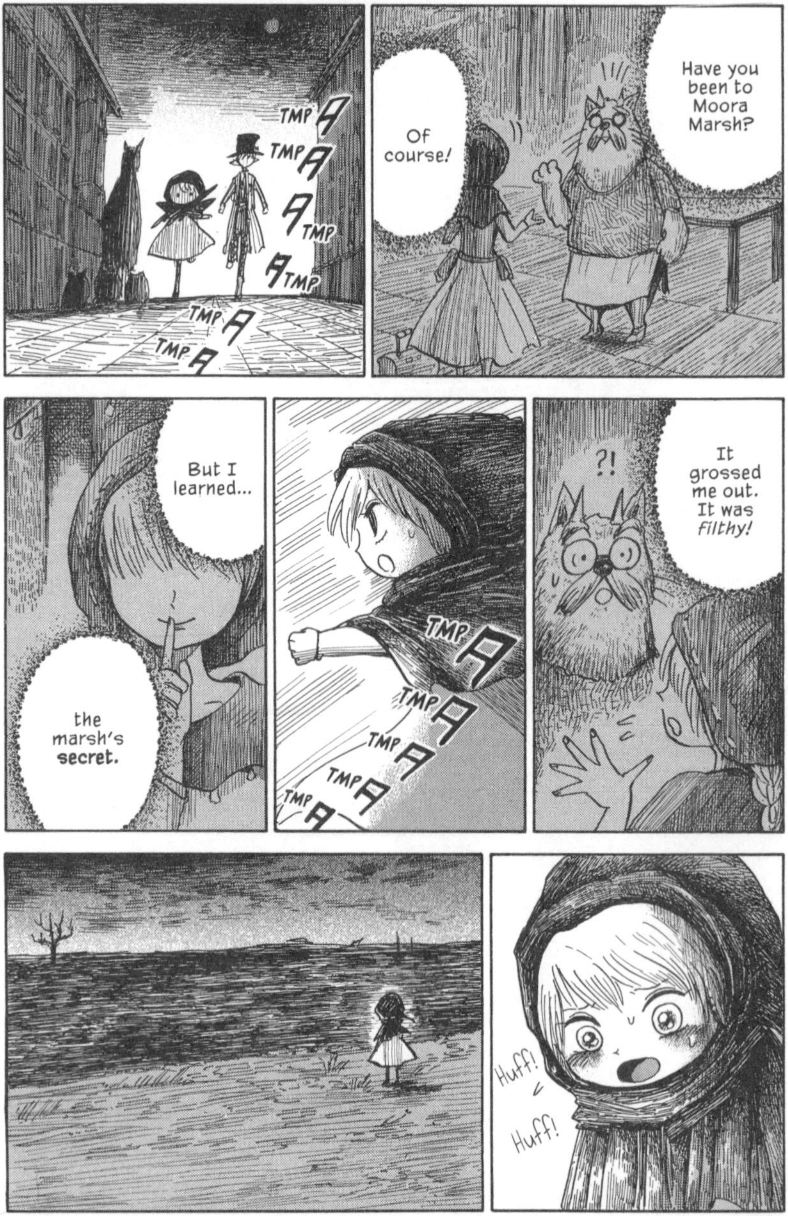
Have you been to Moora Marsh?
Of course!
TMP
TMP
TMP
TMP
TMP
TMP
It grossed me out. It was *filthy!*
?!
TMP
TMP
TMP
TMP
TMP
But I learned...
the marsh's **secret.**
Huff!
Huff!

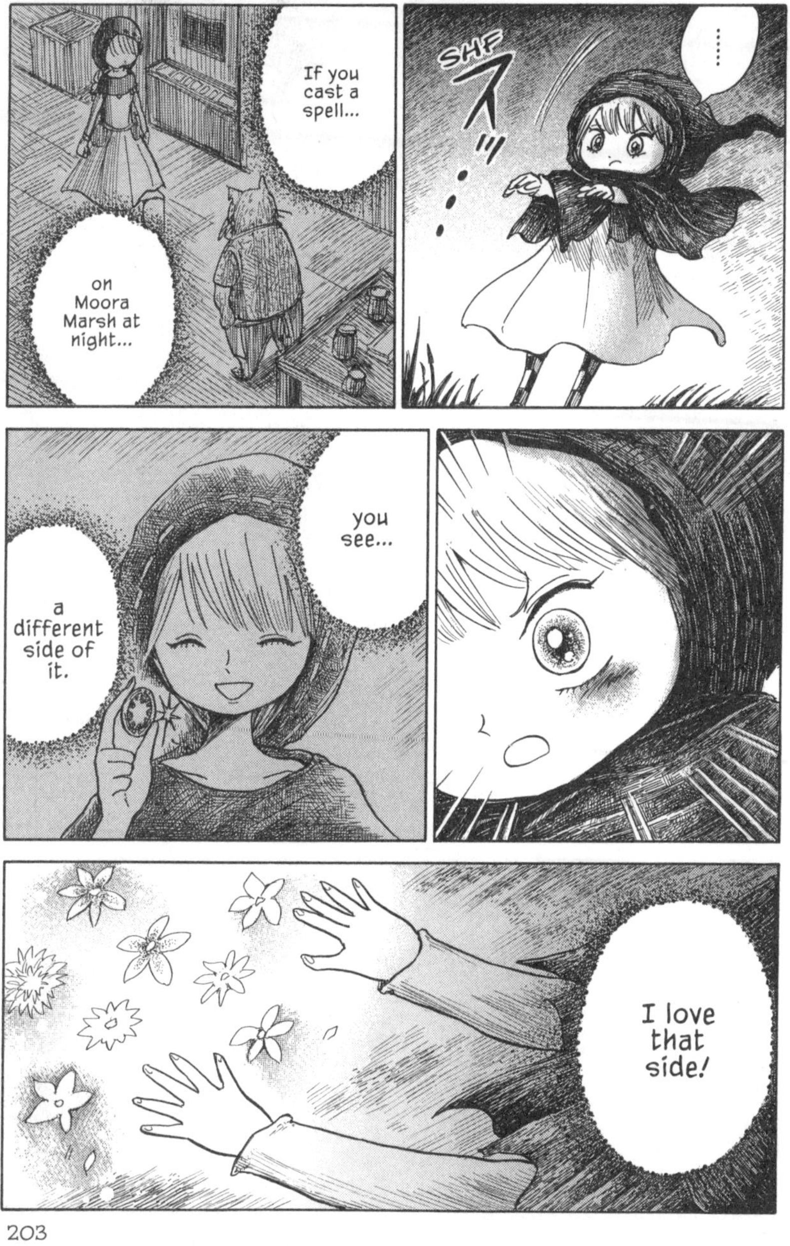
SHF
スッ
......
If you cast a spell...
on Moora Marsh at night...
you see...
a different side of it.
I love that side!

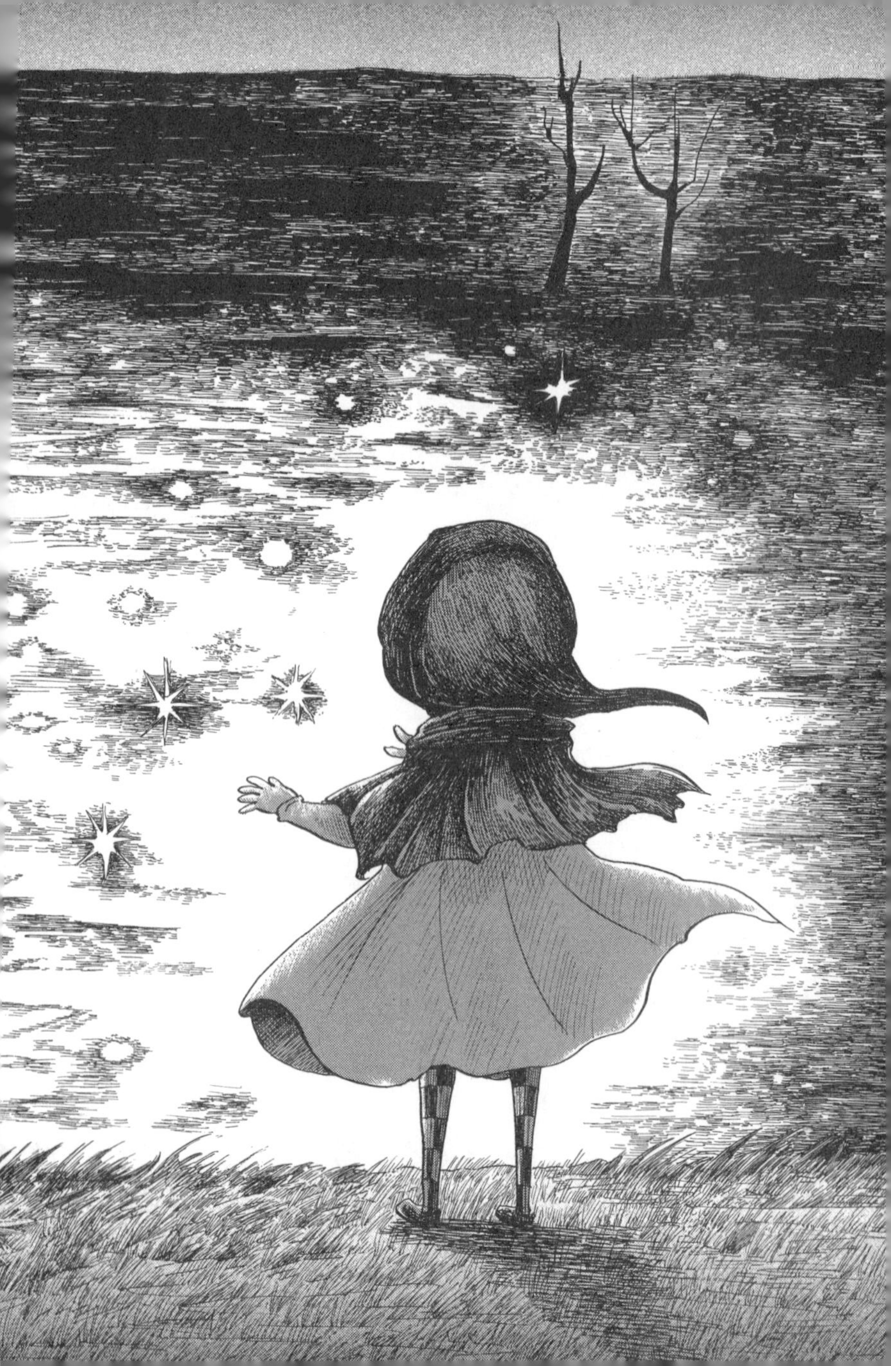

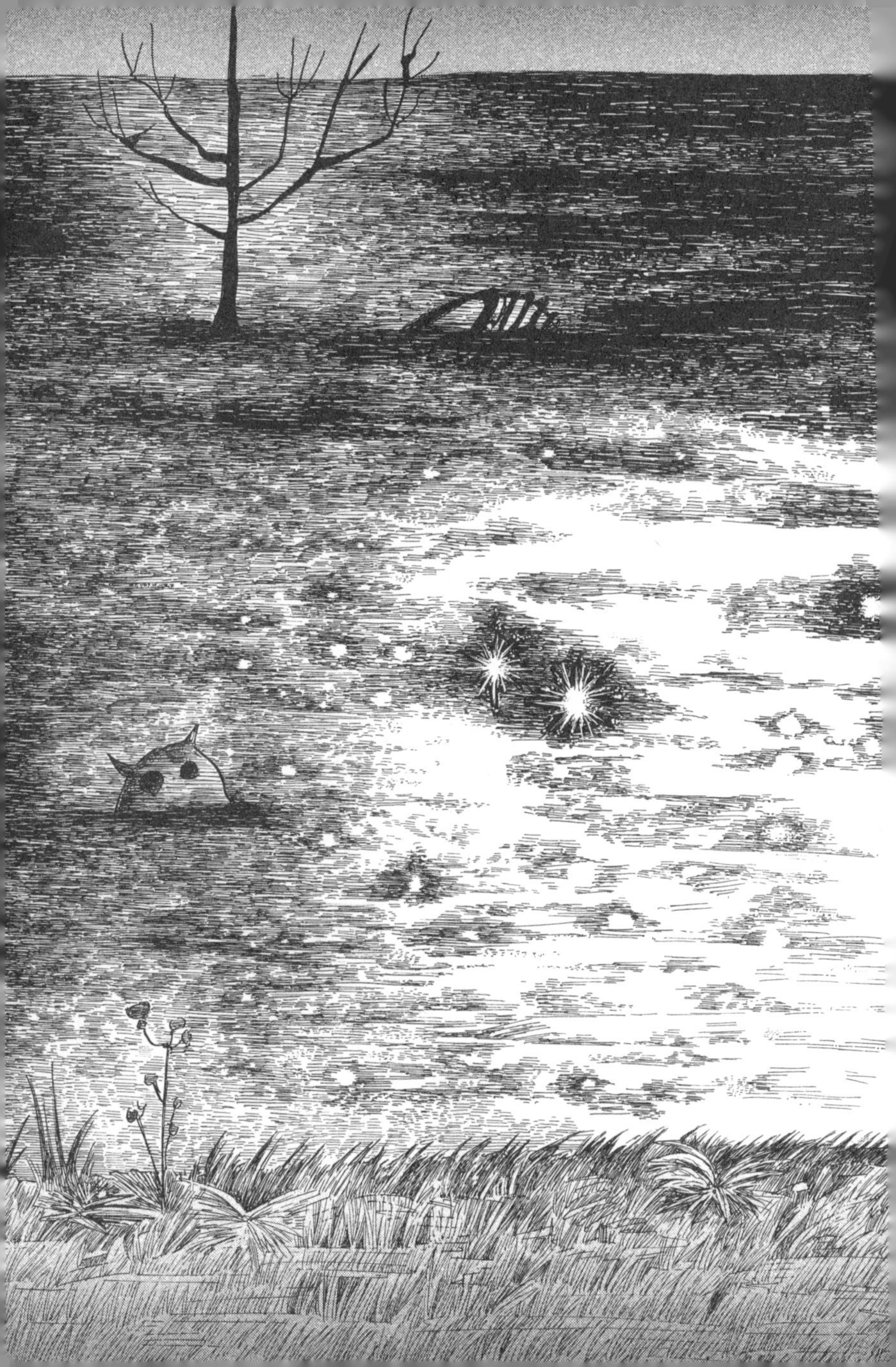

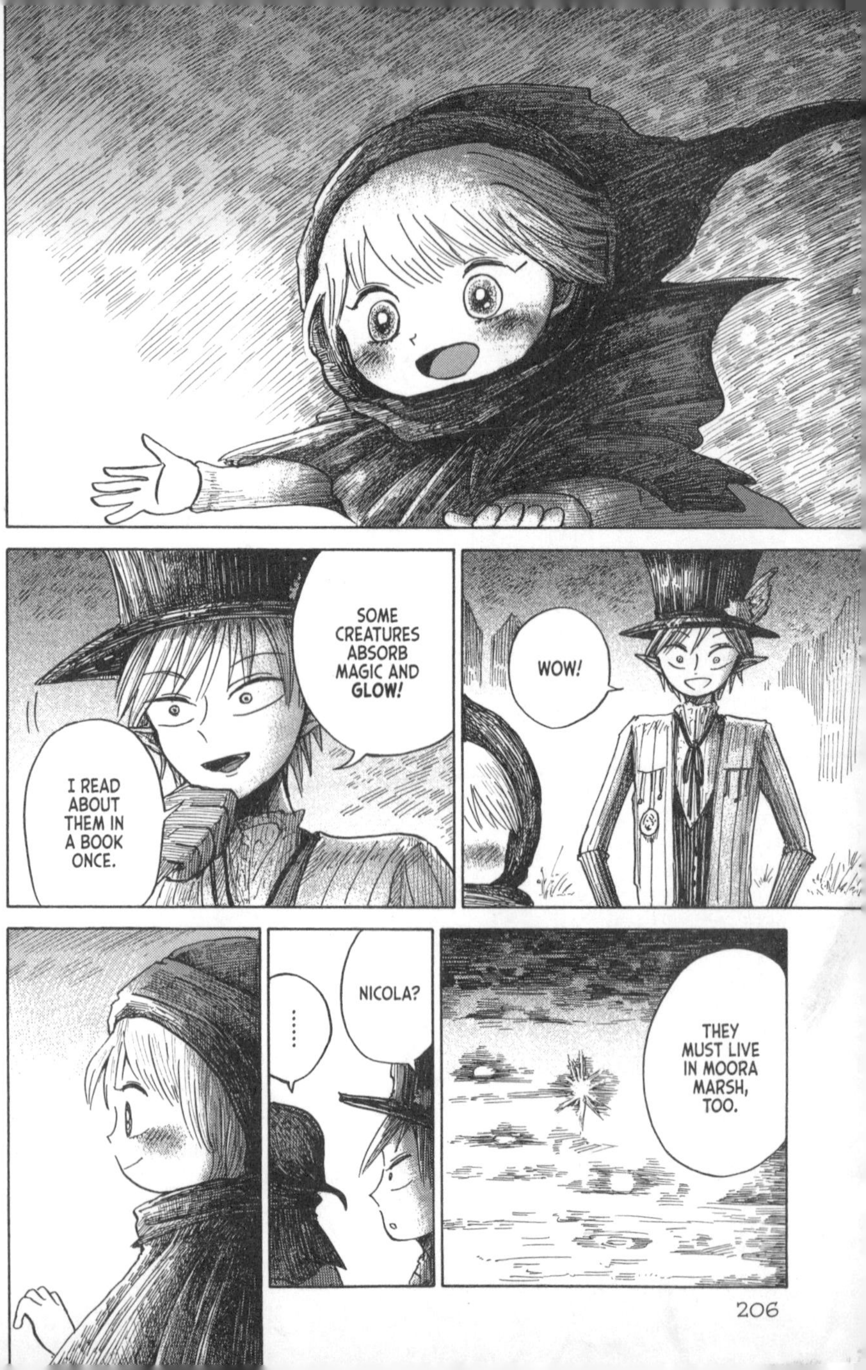
WOW!
SOME CREATURES ABSORB MAGIC AND GLOW!
I READ ABOUT THEM IN A BOOK ONCE.
THEY MUST LIVE IN MOORA MARSH, TOO.
NICOLA?
......

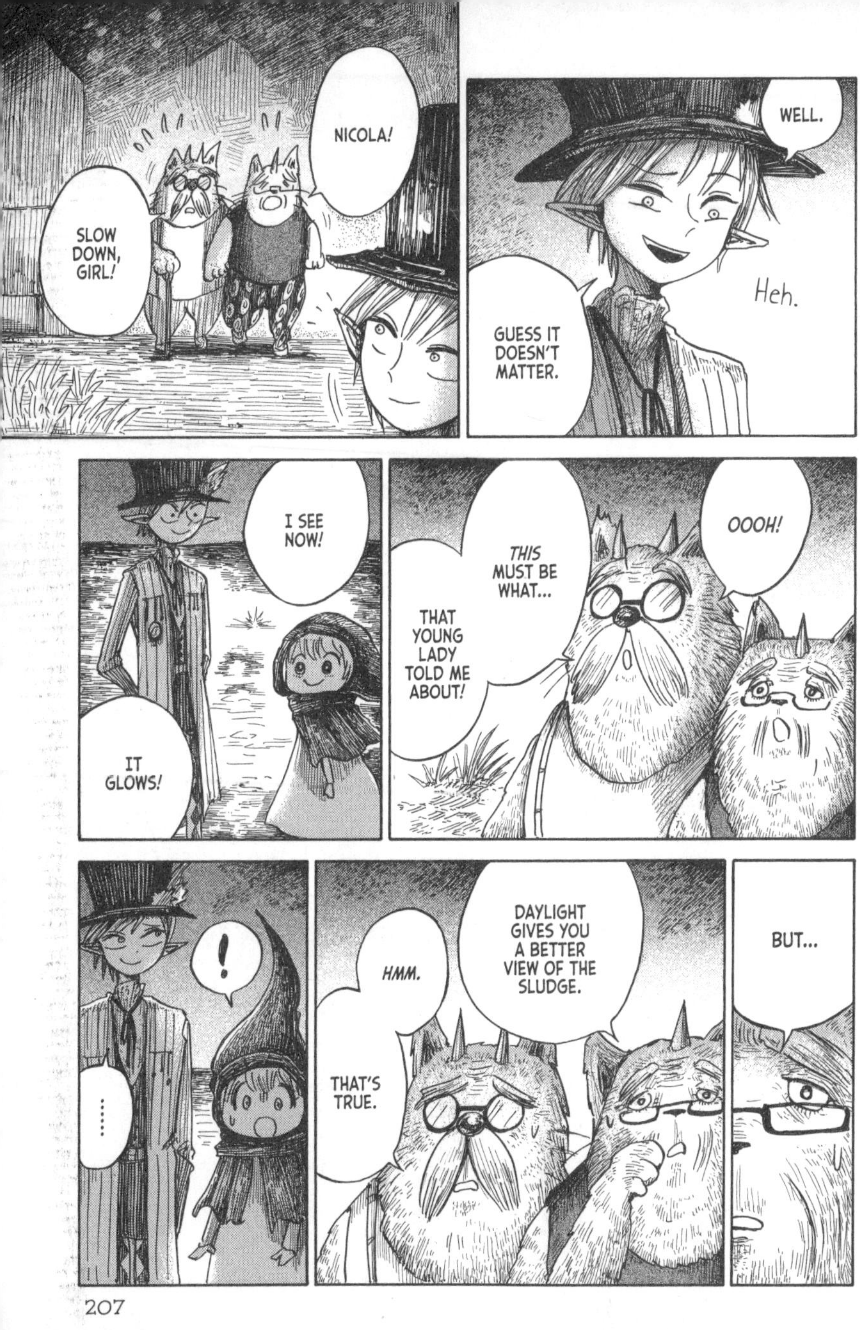
WELL.
GUESS IT DOESN'T MATTER.
Heh.
NICOLA!
SLOW DOWN, GIRL!
OOOH!
THIS MUST BE WHAT...
THAT YOUNG LADY TOLD ME ABOUT!
I SEE NOW!
IT GLOWS!
BUT...
DAYLIGHT GIVES YOU A BETTER VIEW OF THE SLUDGE.
HMM.
THAT'S TRUE.
!
......

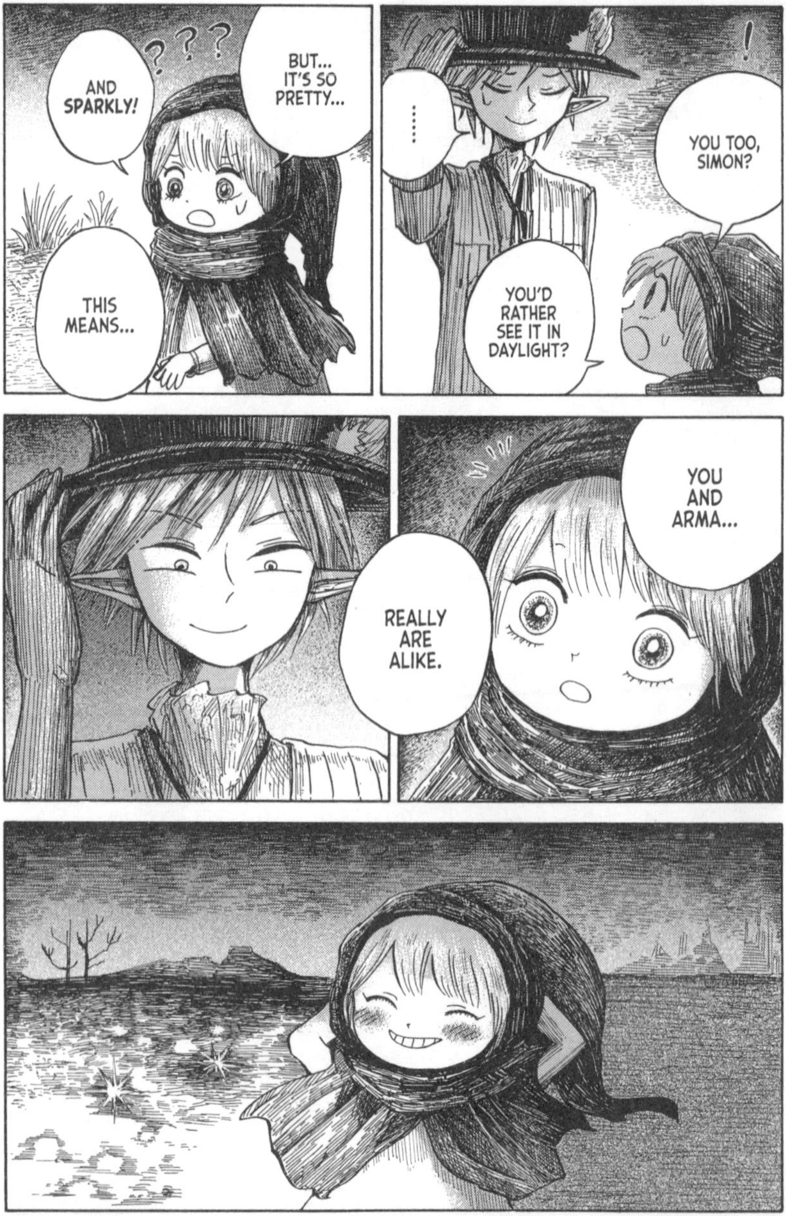
!
YOU TOO, SIMON?
......
YOU'D RATHER SEE IT IN DAYLIGHT?
BUT... IT'S SO PRETTY...
???
AND SPARKLY!
THIS MEANS...
YOU AND ARMA...
REALLY ARE ALIKE.

Chapter 12 END

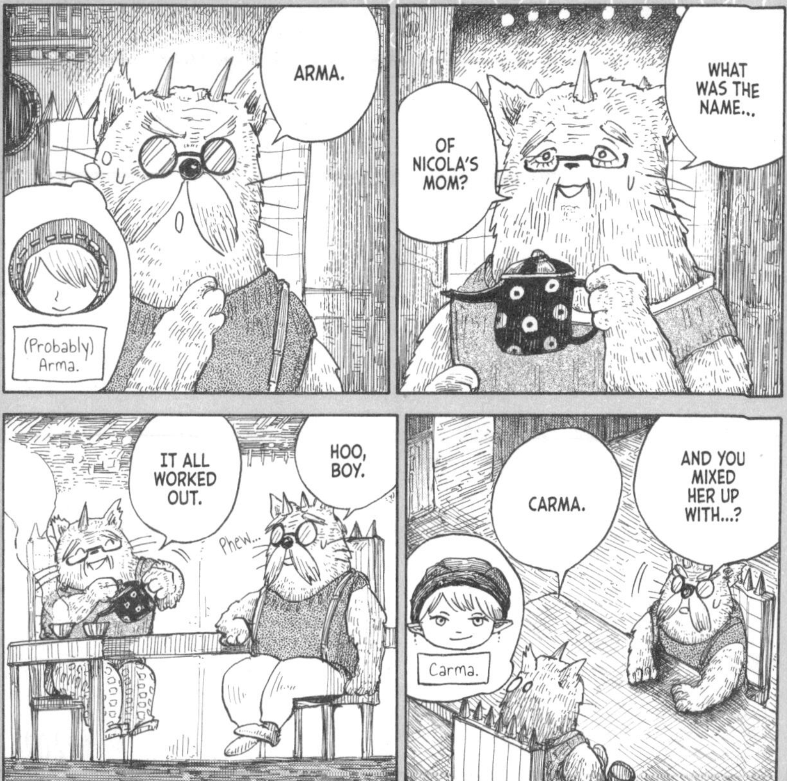
WHAT WAS THE NAME...
OF NICOLA'S MOM?
ARMA.
(Probably) Arma.
AND YOU MIXED HER UP WITH...?
CARMA.
Carma.
HOO, BOY.
IT ALL WORKED OUT.
Phew...
HMM. AND NICOLA'S FRIEND WAS...?
Nicola
......
......
Erm...

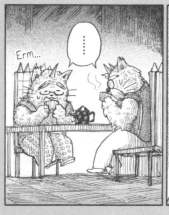

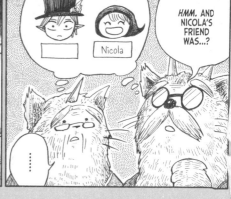

SEVEN SEAS ENTERTAINMENT PRESENTS

Nicola Traveling Around the Demons' World.

story and art by ASAYA MIYANAGA

VOLUME 2

TRANSLATION
Christine Dashiell

ADAPTATION
Rebecca Schneidereit

LETTERING
Lys Blakeslee

COVER DESIGN
KC Fabellon

PROOFREADER
Stephanie Cohen

EDITOR
Shannon Fay

PREPRESS TECHNICIAN
Rhiannon Rasmussen-Silverstein

PRODUCTION MANAGER
Lissa Pattillo

MANAGING EDITOR
Julie Davis

ASSOCIATE PUBLISHER
Adam Arnold

PUBLISHER
Jason DeAngelis

NICOLA TRAVELING AROUND THE DEMONS' WORLD VOL. 2
NICOLA NO OYURURI MAKAIKIKO VOL. 2
© Asaya Miyanaga 2019
First published in Japan in 2019 by KADOKAWA CORPORATION, Tokyo.
English translation rights reserved by Seven Seas Entertainment
under the license from KADOKAWA CORPORATION, Tokyo.

Seven Seas press and purchase enquiries can be sent to Marketing Manager
Lianne Sentar at press@gomanga.com. Information regarding the distribution
and purchase of digital editions is available from Digital Manager CK Russell
at digital@gomanga.com.

Seven Seas and the Seven Seas logo are trademarks of
Seven Seas Entertainment. All rights reserved.

ISBN: 978-1-64505-208-1

Printed in Canada

First Printing: February 2020

10 9 8 7 6 5 4 3 2 1

MAY 1 4 2021

FOLLOW US ONLINE: www.sevenseasentertainment.com

READING DIRECTIONS

This book reads from **right to left**, Japanese style.
If this is your first time reading manga, you start
reading from the top right panel on each page and
take it from there. If you get lost, just follow the
numbered diagram here. It may seem backwards at
first, but you'll get the hang of it! Have fun!!

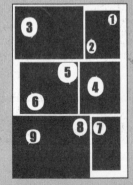